POLICYHOLDER'S REASONABLE EXPECTATIONS

Over the past two decades, protecting contractual parties' reasonable expectations has incrementally gained judicial recognition in English contract law. In contrast, however, the similar 'doctrine' of 'policyholder's reasonable expectations' has been largely rejected in English insurance law. This is injurious, firstly, to both the consumer and business policyholder's reasonable expectations of coverage of particular risks, and, secondly, to consumer policyholder's reasonable expectations of bonuses in with-profits life insurance. To remedy these problems, this book argues for an incremental but definite acceptance of the conception of policyholder's reasonable expectations in English insurance law. It firstly discusses the homogeneity between insurance law and contract law, as well as the role of (reasonable) expectations and their relevance to the emerging duty of good faith in contract law. Secondly, following a review and re-characterisation of the American insurance law 'doctrine' of reasonable expectations, the book addresses the conventional English objections to the reasonable expectations approach in insurance law. In passing, it also rethinks the approach to the protection of policyholder's reasonable expectations of bonuses in with-profits life insurance through a revisit to the (in)famous case *Equitable Life Assurance Society v Hyman* [2000] UKHL 39, particularly to its relevant business and regulatory background.

Policyholder's Reasonable Expectations

Yong Qiang Han

HART PUBLISHING
OXFORD AND PORTLAND, OREGON
2016

Hart Publishing
An imprint of Bloomsbury Publishing Plc

Hart Publishing Ltd
Kemp House
Chawley Park
Cumnor Hill
Oxford OX2 9PH
UK

Bloomsbury Publishing Plc
50 Bedford Square
London
WC1B 3DP
UK

www.hartpub.co.uk
www.bloomsbury.com

Published in North America (US and Canada) by
Hart Publishing
c/o International Specialized Book Services
920 NE 58th Avenue, Suite 300
Portland, OR 97213-3786
USA

www.isbs.com

First published 2016

British Library Cataloguing-in-Publication Data
A catalogue record for this book is available from the British Library.

ISBN: HBK: 978-1-50990-076-3
ePDF: 978-1-50990-075-6
ePub: 978-1-50990-077-0

Library of Congress Cataloging-in-Publication Data

Names: Han, Yong Qiang, author.

Title: Policyholder's reasonable expectations / Yong Qiang Han.

Description: Oxford [UK] ; Portland, Oregon : Hart Publishing, 2016. | Includes bibliographical references and index.

Identifiers: LCCN 2016028881 (print) | LCCN 2016029335 (ebook) | ISBN 9781509900763 (hardback : alk. paper) | ISBN 9781509900770 (Epub)

Subjects: LCSH: Insurance law—England. | Contracts—England. | Good faith (Law)—England | Insurance law—United States. | Contracts—United States. | Good faith (Law)—United States.

Classification: LCC KD1859 .H36 2016 (print) | LCC KD1859 (ebook) | DDC 346.42/086—dc23

LC record available at https://lccn.loc.gov/2016028881

Typeset by Compuscript Ltd, Shannon
Printed and bound in Great Britain by
Lightning Source UK Ltd

to

my parents
as well as
Li Wanglin and Yang Hanxiang

FOREWORD

MALCOLM CLARKE
PROFESSOR EMERITUS OF COMMERCIAL CONTRACT LAW
ST JOHN'S COLLEGE, UNIVERSITY OF CAMBRIDGE

The doctrine of 'reasonable expectations' is a notion still associated with the United States and courts there that disregarded unambiguous exceptions because they were, in the view of the court, unconscionable: any term which (in the view of the court) was unconscionable could be ignored because it did not correspond with the reasonable expectations of the parties. In fact something like the doctrine was to be seen in Scotland in 1896 and in England awareness (and suspicion) in the 1970s. For example "the weakness of the reasonable expectation principle is its dependence on the notion of reasonableness. Despite many judicial expeditions to find him, the reasonable man has not been reduced to captivity. In truth, as any man on the Clapham omnibus could tell us, the reasonable man does not exist" (Sir John Baker). However, Lord Steyn reminded us in 1993 that a "theme that runs through our law of contract is that the reasonable expectations of honest men must be protected".

From the perspective of 2016 Dr Yong Q Han thinks that the perception of the USA case law was mistaken but, be that as it may, his main purpose is to develop the theme of Lord Steyn for contracts of insurance, pointing to both judicial and academic support for this development; he reconsiders public policy factors behind the doctrine. In particular, given that the function of insurance is to provide policyholders with coverage, in case of conflict, it should be the 'reasonable expectations' of policyholders that should take precedence over the 'reasonable expectations' of insurers, where there is any ambiguity in the policy of insurance, which is usually drafted by insurers.

In connection with his main theme, Dr Han also considers the role of good faith not only in the law of insurance but also the wider law of contract and, importantly, premises that in certain respects the law of contract and the law of insurance contracts are homogeneous.

This book provides a stimulating and critical review of a doctrine that is far from dead.

Malcolm Clarke
July 2016

PREFACE

This is the first monograph on the judicial treatment of reasonable expectations of the policyholder or of the insured. The contrasting English judicial attitudes toward reasonable expectations in contract law and in insurance law are surprising. My interests in this issue arose at the closing stage of my PhD programme which only touched upon the interpretation of (insurance) contracts. The reasonable expectations approach thereto seemed like an issue that should merit more attention and a research output as a stand-alone book rather than a series of articles. With this in mind, soon after my viva in Aberdeen in October 2013 I put forward a research proposal for the post-doctoral fellowship at the Faculty of Law, National University of Singapore (NUS). The NUS Faculty of Law kindly offered me the post in which I mainly worked on this book project. It is unconventional for an early researcher to conduct a post-doctoral research that is not really based on the PhD programme but instead is essentially a new project that just makes his or her own academic life, at the very least, challenging. Nevertheless, it is meaningful for me to take my own challenge. Although I have no ambition to influence the positive law in the near future, I am sure this research contributes to the discussion of the issue in insurance law and also of aspects of contract law.

A word of note is that in this book 'policyholder' is the equivalent to 'an/the insured'. This is mainly for the purpose of avoiding the frequent, almost tongue-twisting effect of 'insured', 'insure' and 'insurer', or sometimes 'ensure' to appear at short intervals. 'Assured' might be an alternative, nevertheless it is slightly archaic, and it does not serve to completely avoid the tongue-twisting effect. However, the word 'policyholder' is likely to create a grammatical inconsistency due to Chapter 7, which discusses *inter alia* the actuarial principle of 'policyholders' reasonable expectations'. To clarify, though there is a big difference between two kinds, as introduced in Chapter 1, of reasonable expectations of policyholders, in this book there is no essential difference between the singular possessive (ie policyholder's) and the plural possessive (ie policyholders'). Given that the former is used more by lawyers and the latter by the actuarial profession, in this book and particularly in Chapter 7, the singular possessive is almost always used, unless the plural possessive is used in quotation. Apart from such a possible confusion, readers might find some quotations a bit long. That, however, is intended to make sure that for arguments about this controversial topic the key points of law or others' analysis of law are represented in the original with accuracy rather than in generalisation or restatement which could be prone to misinformation. Case law in the book is update to 3 March 2016, and statutory law to 17 May 2016.

Yong Qiang Han
Centre for Banking and Finance Law
Faculty of Law, National University of Singapore

ACKNOWLEDGEMENTS

Many, to whom I have been grateful, kindly gave their support to my writing of the book. In the first place, I am thankful to Scott Styles, John Paterson, and Malcolm Clarke, all of whom must have given strong support in my application for the NUS Faculty of Law post-doctoral fellowship, without which it would not have been possible for me to conduct the research. Also, the NUS Faculty of Law, and its Centre for Banking and Finance Law, have (re)appointed me to the research post, without which it would certainly be impossible for me to finish the research in good time. Many NUS Law colleagues have been helpful. Yeo Hwee-Ying insightfully advised me to think about the relationship between reasonable expectations and good faith; the advice prompted me to write Chapter 4. Other colleagues, namely Dora Neo, Hans Tjio, Kevin Tan, Andrew Simester, Michael Bridge, Stephen Girvin, James Penner, Wee Meng Sen, Ernest Lim, Alan Koh, Tan Zhongxin, Florian Gamper, Michelle Dye, and Maziar Peihani have raised helpful queries and comments on different points in my writing process.

Comments from outside NUS Law were immensely helpful too. Philip Rawlings, Miriam Goldby and Andromachi Georgosouli have offered encouragement, and also specific comments on early draft chapters presented to them in May 2015. Stephen Smith, while as Visiting Professor at NUS Law, shared with me his insights on the conception of reasonable expectations *per se*. James Creel kindly explained in long emails his own research in the relationship between expectations and intentions, which is a major theme in Chapter 3; Biplab Sikdar also gave a useful reinterpretation thereof in this regard. Tom Baker offered me the drafts of the Principles/Restatement of Liability Insurance Law, which I was not aware of then but is very useful for Chapter 5. For the same chapter, Kenneth Abraham, Jeffrey Stempel and Daniel Schwarcz have enlightened me in talks and in email exchanges. The drafts of what are now Chapters 3 and 6 were reviewed in 2015 by Malcolm Clarke, who again gave very helpful comments for which I am particularly grateful. Robert Merkin offered comments on an early draft of Chapter 6 too. Thanks are also given to the two anonymous reviewers whose comments have prompted me to sharpen my ideas. Equally important, I am particularly thankful to Hart Publishing team for the efficiency and professionalism in the whole process that culminates the publication of the book, for which the team members are Sinead Moloney, Bill Asquith, John Hort, Tom Adams and Emma Platt. I am especially grateful to Catherine Minahan for her meticulous copy-editing. All that being said, any substantive or editorial blemish rests solely with me.

Last, but not least important, heart-felt thanks are also extended to the loving family of Li Wanglin, to Tong Zhiwei, Han Changyin, Zhao Wanyi and Ge Wenjie as well, for being encouraging, supportive, and understanding. Without that, I would not have been able to write this book.

Yong Q Han
CBFL, NUS Faculty of Law

CONTENTS

TABLE OF CASES

TABLE OF STATUTES

1

Introduction

I. An Anomaly

English insurance law has been unreceptive to the notion of 'policyholder's reasonable expectations', a notion that is prominent in American insurance law. This book addresses the question of why English insurance law should instead be receptive to that notion or principle—if it could appropriately be characterised as a principle.

This, however, is certainly not mainly because English (insurance) law should be aligned with its American counterpart. Rather it is because in the first place there has been an arguably unjustifiable anomaly in this regard in English law. The anomaly is the stark contrast between general contract law and insurance law in the judicial attitude toward the notion of contractual parties' reasonable expectations. More than two decades ago, Steyn LJ, as he was then, opined that 'a theme that runs through our law of contract is that the reasonable expectations of honest men must be protected'.[1] In only two years, Lord Steyn extra-judicially professed fulfilling reasonable expectations as 'an important subject for the future development of English contract law'.[2] Similarly, Dyson LJ opined that 'an implied term is necessary in order to give effect to the reasonable expectations of the parties'.[3] As recently as six years ago, Lord Hoffmann stated extra-judicially, 'The purpose of the law of contract is to fulfil reasonable expectations and such expectations should therefore be self-fulfilling.'[4]

However, when it comes to insurance contract, judges take a markedly different approach to the concept of 'policyholder's reasonable expectations'. Whilst briefly argued for by the claimants, it was expressly rejected in the Court of Appeal in *Smit Tak Offshore Services Ltd v Youell*[5] and in *Yorkshire Water Services Ltd v Sun Alliance & London Insurance Ltd*.[6] Although soon afterwards, the

[1] *First Energy (UK) Ltd v Hungarian International Bank Ltd* [1993] 2 Lloyd's Rep 194 (CA), 196.

[2] Lord Steyn, 'Contract Law: Fulfilling the Reasonable Expectations of Reasonable Men' (1995) 9 *LQR* 433, 433.

[3] *Nash v Paragon Finance Plc* [2001] EWCA Civ 1466 [36].

[4] Lord Hoffmann, '*The Achilleas*: Custom and Practice or Foreseeability?' (2010) 14 *Edinburgh Law Review* 47, 59.

[5] *Smit Tak Offshore Services Ltd v Youell* [1992] 1 Lloyd's Rep 154 (CA).

[6] *Yorkshire Water Services Ltd v Sun Alliance & London Insurance Ltd* [1997] CLC 213 (CA), 221.

idea of (policyholder's) reasonable expectations in the context of insurance was arguably emphasised in the House of Lords in 1998 in *Cook v Financial Insurance Co Ltd*[7] and later in 2000 in the more celebrated case *Equitable Life Assurance Society v Hyman*,[8] English courts overall are far from receptive to a doctrine or a principle of 'policyholder's reasonable expectations'.[9] Most recently in May 2015 in the Supreme Court, Lord Sumption mentioned reasonable expectations of policyholders as 'a consideration which, except as background to the construction of the policy, does not have the significant place in English insurance law as it has in many jurisdictions of the United States'.[10]

The reason for this contrast is perhaps not that insurance law is so different from general contract law that judicial acceptance of the notion of reasonable expectations in contract law shall not or cannot extend to insurance law. After all, as Malcolm Clarke maintains, the presumption should always be against those who assert that insurance law is, or should be, different from general contract law.[11] Rather, the English unreceptiveness is to a large extent due to concerns that are aligned with the controversies in the United States (US) over what has been known mostly as the American insurance law 'doctrine' of reasonable expectations. The controversies and the ensuing concerns over its drawbacks migrated across the Atlantic to the United Kingdom (UK) and became well-settled there.

The contrast is similar in English legal academia. In regard to general contract law, academics for the most part recognise the notion of reasonable expectations in the general law of contract. According to John Baker, there was an evolution to a doctrine of reasonable expectations; it has two major aspects: the reasonable expectation that a serious promise will be kept and that a contract will not operate unfairly; and that the reasonable expectations unite the parties and include the attainment by fair means of the main object of their agreement.[12] According to John Adams and Roger Brownsword, reasonable expectation 'is the key to contractual obligation'.[13] However, in stark contrast, a principle or a doctrine of reasonable expectations in insurance law has been extremely under-researched. Professor Malcolm Clarke seems to be the only leading insurance law academic in the UK who has written a stand-alone piece on the topic, pointing out in 1989 that a similar doctrine was perhaps

[7] *Cook v Financial Insurance Co Ltd* [1998] 1 WLR 1765 (HL), [1998] UKHL 42.

[8] *Equitable Life Assurance Society v Hyman* [2000] 3 All ER 961, [2000] UKHL 39, [2002] 1 AC 408.

[9] See J Lowry, P Rawlings and R Merkin, *Insurance Law: Doctrines and Principles*, 3rd edn (Oxford, Hart Publishing, 2011) 269.

[10] *Zurich Insurance Plc UK Branch v International Energy Group Ltd* [2015] UKSC 33 [164].

[11] M Clarke, *Policies and Perceptions of Insurance Law in the Twenty-First Century* (Oxford, Oxford University Press, 2005) 357.

[12] JH Baker, 'From Sanctity of Contract to Reasonable Expectation?' (1979) 32 *Current Legal Problems* 17, 22, 24, 30, 33.

[13] J Adams and R Brownsword, *Key Issues in Contract* (London, Butterworths, 1995) 153–54.

operative in disguise in English insurance law.[14] He sticks to this idea, and over subsequent decades has argued for it moderately[15] in his treatises. The other substantial academic research output[16] in this regard is from John Lowry and Philip Rawlings, who are fairly pessimistic about and sceptical of the prospect of such a doctrine in English insurance law.

Given the current anomalous state of the law and relatively scant research into policyholder's reasonable expectations in English insurance law, this book seeks to address the anomaly and to advance the research in this regard.

II. Policyholder's Reasonable Expectations of Coverage and of Bonuses

Up to now in English insurance law, there have been two prominent cases in which the notion of policyholder's reasonable expectations carried weight in the judicial reasoning. Both were decided in the House of Lords, only two years apart. One is *Cook v Financial Insurance Co Ltd*,[17] decided in 1998. The other is the more celebrated (or infamous) case *Equitable Life Assurance Society v Hyman*,[18] decided in 2000. Although both concerned consumer policyholders' reasonable expectations, they were not really homogeneous. Instead they exemplified two meanings of 'policyholder's reasonable expectations'. In *Cook*, it was the policyholder's reasonable expectations of coverage (PREC) of particular risks—a medical condition in this case. This concept has been better known to and more controversial among insurance lawyers, especially in the US where it originated between the 1960s and the 1970s, and has since been the subject of judicial vacillation. The controversy and the vacillation in the US is a major reason why PREC has mostly been frowned upon, at least superficially. As has been mentioned above, in the UK, for the most part, only a few academics have briefly discussed PREC in the context of English insurance law, and it has seldom been argued, though it has received occasional mention, in the courts.

The meaning of policyholder's reasonable expectations in *Equitable Life Assurance Society v Hyman*[19] is fairly different. This case did not concern PREC

[14] M Clarke, 'The reasonable expectations of the insured—in England?' [1989] *Journal of Business Law* 389; M Clarke, 'Reasonable Expectations—Unreasonable Cost?' (1990) 16 *Managerial Finance* 25.

[15] M Clarke, J Burling and R Purves, *The Law of Insurance Contracts*, 6th edn (London, Informa, 2009) 452–53.

[16] Lowry et al, above n 9, 269.

[17] *Cook v Financial Insurance Co Ltd* [1998] 1 WLR 1765 (HL), [1998] UKHL 42.

[18] *Equitable Life Assurance Society v Hyman* [2000] 3 All ER 961, [2000] UKHL 39, [2002] 1 AC 408.

[19] Ibid.

but a policyholder's reasonable expectations of bonuses (PREB) in the context of with-profits life insurance. *Equitable Life* was not a dispute over an insurance policy's coverage of risks; rather it was over the insurer's allocation of premium investment bonuses to policyholders. Many life insurance products or contracts are designed and sold purely as a personal financial investment plan, or with many elements of such. Under these plans, as in *Equitable Life*, life insurers use policyholders' premiums to make investments, and promise to allocate bonuses or investment returns to policyholders in a certain manner, as provided for in the insurance policies. Disputes arising under such life insurance policies are often over the allocation of bonuses or benefits.

The British actuary profession has appreciated PREB since the mid-1960s, but it has perhaps remained unnoticed by most lawyers, except those few who represented the parties and/or sat in on the hearing and appeals of the celebrated *Equitable Life* case. Compared with PREC, PREB seems much less familiar to lawyers due to its actuarial technicalities, which are to be introduced when we revisit *Equitable Life* in Chapter 7.

The two types of expectations—PREB and PREC—must be distinguished from each other; otherwise, unaware of the difference, one might actually use PREB to argue for PREC, or vice versa.

III. Structure of the Book

Most of the discussions in this monograph are concerned with PREC, with only Chapter 7 being devoted to PREB. In addressing the normative question whether English law should be receptive to the notion of policyholder's reasonable expectations (especially PREC), this book combines considerable normative arguments with more analysis of relevant positive contract law rules and principles that can build up an answer to that question. Such analysis is mainly found in Chapters 2 to 5. The largely normative argument for PREC per se is in Chapter 6. As mentioned before, Chapter 7 discusses PREB. Chapter 8 draws a conclusion as an answer to the normative question to be addressed in the book.

Chapter 2 is a response to the on-going assertion that insurance (contract) law is distinctive from (general) contract law, and therefore that the notion of 'reasonable expectations', which permeates contract law, should not necessarily have a place in insurance law. It is argued that although *insurance* does operate under a distinctive, if not unique, *economic* rationale or mechanism, such distinctiveness is cancelled out by contract, an almost universal vehicle for the business of insurance, and therefore makes *insurance (contract) law* not fundamentally different from general contract law. This chapter further expands on Clarke's submission that insurance contract law is not, and should not be thought to be, different from general contract law.

Chapter 3 rediscovers the role of expectations in contract law generally. It uncovers the subsumed role of expectations in the formation of contract, and also the relevance of expectation to damages for breach of contract. This chapter also responds to doubts[20] about the notion of reasonable expectations in contract law; for that purpose it uses, among others, the distinction made by John Rawls between the 'reasonable man' and 'rational man'. Necessarily, the chapter proceeds to find out the role of reasonable expectations in contract interpretation, in particular the relation of expectations to the contextual and purposive approach to interpretation of contracts. All these lead to an argument: now that expectations are fairly relevant to contract and in contract law, why should not reasonable expectations be so too?

Chapter 4 approaches PREC from the perspective of good faith in contract law. It first discusses the relationship between good faith and reasonable expectations, arguing that the purpose of requiring good faith in contract law is to ensure that the parties' reasonable expectations can be met. In this sense, judicial support of good faith in contract law indirectly endorses the reasonable expectations approach. Although good faith in contract traditionally has limited role in contract law, very recently it has re-emerged in the common law, for example in the High Court in the UK, in the final Court of Appeal in Singapore and in the Supreme Court of Canada. Following that, the rest of Chapter 4 proceeds to expound the relevance of the insurer's duty of good faith to PREC. For this purpose it highlights the insurer's duty of good faith, which has the the purpose and the effect of protecting PREC.

Chapter 5 revisits the American insurance law 'doctrine' of reasonable expectations (DRE), which is the original American version of PREC. The key query is, since DRE/PREC has fairly diffuse versions or formulations in its application in the US, should it actually be perceived more as a principle than as a doctrine? The answer to this query depends first on the distinction between legal principles and legal doctrines (or legal rules), and, secondly, on the US judicial treatment of DRE/PREC in state courts. It is noteworthy that in 1970, Keeton put forward DRE/PREC as a principle; more noteworthy but not widely noticed is that in 1976 he stressed and applied the general distinction between legal principles and legal doctrines in his further discussion of DRE/PREC, and stated a particular standard for characterising DRE/PREC as a doctrine. Given that standard, Chapter 5 examines how each American state jurisdiction treated DRE/PREC, and shows whether, by Keeton's standard, DRE has actually been judicially (dis) applied as a doctrine or as a principle.

Chapter 6 reassesses the pessimism about or objections to a principle of PREC in English insurance law, and argues for its incremental acceptance into business

[20] C Mitchell, 'Leading a Life of its Own? The Roles of Reasonable Expectations in Contract Law' (2003) 23 *OJLS* 639. See also similarly S Smith, '"The Reasonable Expectations of the Parties": An Unhelpful Concept' (2009) 48 *Canadian Business Law Journal* 366.

insurance in addition to (already effectively) in consumer insurance. The objections are that adopting PREC into English law will cause more uncertainty and inconsistency, that American-style considerations of public policies have few roles in English contract law, and that other doctrines in (insurance) contract law suffice to protect PREC and therefore there is no need for a stand-alone PREC doctrine or principle. It is argued that concerns over uncertainty are legitimate but excessive, that concerns over inconsistency fail to appreciate that insurance law in the US is state law, that there is what can be called 'enabling public policy', which can be considered in contract law and insurance law, and that those other doctrines cannot always operate to resolve insurance coverage disputes effectively. In addition, for discussing the applicability of PREC to business insurance, this chapter considers relational contract theory in connection with insurance, the core purpose of insurance and the implication of different conceptions of insurance. For consideration of positive law, the chapter particularly examines the implications of *Smit Tak Offshore Services Ltd v Youell*,[21] which is thought to have tangentially rejected PREC in English business insurance law, as well as a few other recent commercial insurance disputes.

Chapter 7 singles out PREB as a new and distinctive meaning of 'policyholder's reasonable expectations'. Though not new to the British actuarial profession, it is perhaps new to most lawyers, and it is certainly distinctive from PREC. Its relevance is manifested through a revisit to the infamous case *Equitable Life Assurance Society v Hyman*[22] in the House of Lords, and also through an examination of the judicial approach to PREB in this case.

The conclusion in Chapter 8 is that English courts and judges should be incrementally but definitely receptive to an interpretative principle of 'policyholder's reasonable expectations'. This is not simply to copy the American insurance law principle of reasonable expectations. Instead, the English approach to PREC and PREB will continue to proceed along the contextualist interpretation of contracts, which takes relevant background into account. This is not a deviation from but an alignment with general contract law.

[21] *Smit Tak Offshore Services Ltd v Youell* [1992] 1 Lloyd's Rep 154.

[22] *Equitable Life Assurance Society v Hyman* [2000] 3 All ER 961, [2000] UKHL 39, [2002] 1 AC 408.

2

Contract Law and Insurance Law: the Homogeneity

This chapter addresses the underlying and occasionally raised argument that insurance (contract) law is *sui generis* or distinctive from (general) contract law. The argument results from confusing the features of the *economic* rationale of insurance transactions with the *legal* framework of contract law that governs them. The chapter counter-argues that whilst insurance is indeed distinctive from non-insurance transactions, the prototype of which is sales, in respect of their economic rationales, it is possible for insurance and non-insurance transactions to have a shared legal framework that governs both. To substantiate that counter-argument, this chapter revisits the common legal framework that governs insurance contract and non-insurance contracts in respect of the formation of contract, the shared legal nature of performance of contract, with focus on performance by insurers, and the common legal nature of remedies for breach of contract. It is found that in these respects insurance law still operates within the framework of general contract law. The chapter also shows that the principles of interpretation of contracts in an insurance context and in non-insurance transactions are essentially the same. In addition, it considers seeming differences between insurance law and contract law in respect of the duty of disclosure, and the meanings of 'conditions' and 'warranties'. It is discovered that regarding the former, the difference has been substantially diluted by recent insurance law reform; and that regarding the latter, the difference between insurance law and general contract law is more formalistic and apparent than substantive and real.

I. 'Special Nature' of Insurance Law, or of Insurance?

A. The *Sui Generis* Nature of Insurance Law?

In 1911, Justice Burch stated for the Kansas Supreme Court, 'The subject [of insurance] … is *sui generis*, and the rules of a legal system devised to govern the formation of ordinary contracts between man and man cannot be mechanically applied to it'.[1] Nevertheless this judicial statement was not shared by some other courts in the US. For example, in the 1920s, the New York Court of Appeals notably made opposing statements in this regard only a few years apart: 'A contract of insurance is no different from any other contract.';[2] 'What do they know of the law of insurance who only the law of contract know?'[3] Bipolar judicial statements did not discourage Franklin Schultz, then an Assistant Professor of Law at Indiana University, from elaborating on 'the special nature of insurance contract' and tentatively raising suggestions for further insurance law studies based on that perception.[4] It is also claimed that an insurance contract has never been within the classic law of contract.[5] However, it must be to Schultz's disappointment that, at least in the US, there have been almost no efforts to follow his suggestions for further study: there are voluminous books and literature on the positive rules and technicalities of insurance law, but scant attention has been paid to the assumed special nature of insurance contract or of insurance law.

Nevertheless, Schultz was not alone in believing in 'the special nature' of insurance contract and the relevant law. Professor Reuben Hasson, of Canada, made a similar assertion in his lecture at the University of Essex in 1984, with reference to English insurance law.[6] Although he pointed out some differences between *insurance law* and contract law in respect of non-disclosure, misrepresentation, agency, the policing of unfair terms and mistake, and he found the insurance industry-related social-economic reasons underlying the differences, he did not say what the special nature of *insurance contract* was exactly. Apart from Hasson, Professor John Birds (of the UK) seems to have long shared a similar perception with Schultz, believing that the contract of insurance has undoubtedly 'attracted many principles of its own to such an extent that it is perfectly proper to speak of a law of insurance'.[7]

However, Professor Malcolm Clarke does not go as far. In his enlightening book, with an impressive combination of economic, doctrinal and sociological analysis of insurance law, Professor Clarke admits that there are similarities between the common law of contract and insurance law;[8] meanwhile, he also touches upon some differences between them in the rules of causation, in some contract terminologies and in respect of the duty of disclosure.[9] However, in

[1] *Pfiester v Missouri State Life Ins Co*, 85 Kan 97, 102, II 6 Pac 245, 247 (1911).

[2] *Drilling v NY Life Ins Co*, 234 NY 234, 137 NE 314, 316 (1922) (Crane J).

[3] *Satz v Mass Bonding & Ins Co*, 243 NY 385, 153 NE 844, 846 (1926) (Pound, J).

[4] F Schultz, 'The Special Nature of Insurance Contract: A Few Suggestions for Further Study' (1950) 15 *Law and Contemporary Problems* 376.

[5] E Holmes, 'A Contextual Study of Good Faith: Good-faith Disclosure in Contract Formation' (1978) 39 *Pittsburgh Law Rev* iew 381, 393.

[6] R Hasson, 'The Special Nature of the Insurance Contract: A Comparison of the American and English Law of Insurance' (1984) 47 *MLR* 505.

[7] J Birds, *Birds' Modern Insurance Law*, 2nd edn (London, Sweet & Maxwell, 1988) 1; see also J Birds, *Birds' Modern Insurance Law*, 9th edn (London, Sweet & Maxwell, 2013) [1.0].

[8] M Clarke, Policies and Perceptions of Insurance Law in the Twenty-First Century (Oxford, Oxford University Press, 2005) 353–54.

[9] Ibid 354–56.

the end he stresses that insurance law is not, and should not be, different from general contract law.[10]

B. The Special Economic Rationale of Insurance (versus Sales)

There is indeed some truth in Schultz's perception of the special nature of insurance contract. Given that sales law is a prototype of the general contract law,[11] it is reasonable that when an insurance contract is compared with a non-insurance contract, it is often compared with a contract of sale. Schultz suggested that 'an insurance transaction is a one-sided "bargain"; if it merits the label "contract", it is in a very specialized, not an ordinary, sense'.[12] One of the starting points for Schultz's observations is that insurance is 'a unilateral, aleatory contract'[13] for the insured. This actually concerns the economic mechanism or rationale of insurance rather than its legal nature. Indeed, the economic rationale of insurance is in sharp contrast to that of non-insurance transactions, sales for example, in three key aspects. First, insurance is risk-centred, whereas non-insurance transactions are not. Although in non-insurance transactions the allocation of risk is certainly very important, yet the very purpose in a non-insurance transaction is for one party (the purchaser) to acquire property in the goods and for the other party (the seller) to receive payment of the price. Without this primary purpose in their minds, potential parties to the non-insurance transaction simply might not negotiate the allocation of risks between them. On the other hand, if one party is intent on fulfilling its purpose as aforesaid, it might carry on the transaction regardless of risk, or at its own risk.

Apart from that, the essence of a sale is the transfer of property in the subject matter, whereas insurance in itself does not involve a transfer of property. Rather, insurance facilitates the transfer of risks, which normally are not understood as property in law, though risks do have proprietary consequences. Risk is

[10] Ibid 357.

[11] 'Most contracts can be characterized as sales of commodities (using that term broadly to include goods, land and services) for a money price.' See M Einsenberg, 'The Principle of *Hadley v Baxendale*' (1992) 80 *California Law Review* 563, 565. In addition, it is recognised, in J Adams and H MacQueen, *Atiyah's Sale of Goods*, 12th edn (London, Pearson, 2010) 8, that 'there has been a noticeable tendency, first for the courts and then for Parliament, to model the common law contracts on the Sale of Goods Act and, in particular, to imply terms in these contracts very similar to those implied by the [Sale of Goods] Act. In *Young & Marten Ltd v McManus Childs Ltd* [1968] 2 All ER 1169 (HL) the House of Lords expressed strong views on the undesirability of drawing unnecessary distinctions between different classes of contract.' The paradigm status of sales law is also recognised Europe-wide. For this, it suffices to know of the European Commission proposal in October 2011 on a Common European Sales Law. The proposed sales law is expected to be the model of a uniform general contract law, because it is recognised that this proposal 'foresees a comprehensive set of uniform contract law rules'. See European Commission, *A Common European Sales Law to Facilitate Cross-Border Transactions in the Single Market* (Communication) COM (2011) 636 final [2.1].

[12] Schultz, above n 4, 377.

[13] Ibid.

the kernel of insurance: the insured intends to transfer the consequences of risk, and the insurer accepts the risk at a certain price (premium) by spreading the risk within the risk pool. In addition, insurance prices are far more risk-dependent and risk-sensitive than commodity prices, which hinge more on their utility value and demand vis-à-vis supply in the market. In relation to this, pricing a commodity might involve only basic mathematics (as in cost accounting), whereas pricing insurance products cannot be done without application of the sophisticated actuarial science.

Secondly, insurance is based on what is known as the 'law of large numbers',[14] whereas sales and most non-insurance transactions are not so based. In exchange for a premium, the insurer will pay a claim should a specified contingency arise. The insurer is able to offer such protection against financial loss by pooling the risks from a large group of similarly situated individuals or firms. Operating under the law of large numbers, an insurer can ensure that only a tiny fraction of the insured subject matter will be lost, or only a small fraction of the insured population will suffer loss in a year. If, for example, each of 100,000 individuals independently faces a 1 per cent risk in a year, on average, 1,000 will have losses. If each of the 100,000 people paid a premium of $1,000, the insurance company would have collected a total of $100 million. Leaving aside administrative costs, this is enough to pay $100,000 to anyone who had a loss. But what would happen if 1,100 people had losses? The answer, fortunately, is that such an outcome is exceptionally unlikely in a risk pool designed by insurers through actuarial methods. Insurance works through the 'magic' of the rule of large numbers. This rule ensures that when a large number of people face a low-probability event, the proportion experiencing the event will be close to the expected proportion. For instance, with a pool of 100,000 people who each face a 1 per cent risk, the law of large numbers says that 1,100 people or more will have losses only once in one thousand times.[15]

Thirdly, insurance has to operate on an aggregate basis, whereas non-insurance transactions, take sales for instance, do not have to. The aggregate nature of insurance follows naturally from the law of large numbers. The insurer must undertake transactions with sufficiently large numbers of insureds. In other words, the risk

[14] Also known as the 'laws of averages'. In terms of statistical science, it holds that 'the average of a large number of independent identically distributed random variables tends to fall close to the expected value'. Its relevance to insurance is that 'insurers have learned the wisdom of insuring the largest number of similar risks possible. A great number ensures more regular and more accurately predictable losses.' '[T]he larger the number of exposure units to which the estimate is applied, the better the chance that actual experience will approximate a good estimate of the probability [of loss].' This lies at the basis of an insurer's strategy for risk management and for solvency maintenance. See ML Smith and SA Kane, 'The Law of Large Numbers and the Strength of Insurance' in SG Gustavson and SE Harrington (eds), *Insurance, Risk Management, and Public Policy* (Boston, Kluwer, 1994) 1, fn 2.

[15] R Zeckhauser, 'Insurance' in D Henderson (ed), *The Concise Encyclopaedia of Economics*, 2nd edn (Indianapolis, Ind, Liberty Fund Inc, 2008). Also available online at www.econlib.org/library/Enc/Insurance.html.

pool must be large enough. That is why modern insurers are mostly big business entities, which have the financial competence and the insurance technologies to run an insurance business. In contrast, a seller does not have to pool its transactional resources. A sale could be merely a one-off transaction. Unless there is a chain of sales, where the same seller is both an upstream buyer in one transaction and a downstream seller in another, sales can be dispersed, in the sense that the multitude of sales could be economically independent from one another. Therefore neither the seller nor the purchaser has to be in the regular business of selling and buying.

C. One Legal Framework for Plural Types of Transactions

As is argued above, insurance does indeed have distinctive economic rationales, but that should not be over-emphasised in relation to the law of insurance contract. The distinctive economic rationales of insurance *do not necessarily* mean that it has a special or distinctive status or nature in law. At least, insurance contracts and most non-insurance contracts are subject to the same legal framework, namely, that of general contract law. It will be shown in section II. below that the rules of formation of contract, of performance and of remedies for breach of insurance contract are not distinctive from the rules in contract law.

Furthermore, it is not unusual for the law sometimes to treat subject matters that are distinctive in a particular aspect as non-distinctive in law. For example, despite the inherently different genetic structure that is definitive of gender, men and women are supposed to be equal before the law. Similarly, for a family, an adopted child and a biological child are inherently different in respect of their natural or bloodline relationship with the parents, but modern family law treats the two children as the same in regard to their legal rights and obligations within the family. More broadly, the technique of legal fiction often deems two essentially different matters as the same in law—the most obvious example is that inanimate entities such as companies, partnerships and charities are treated largely the same as natural persons in relation to their *economic* activities. These inanimate entities have no 'mind', as a natural person does, but as legal persons they are enabled by the law to enter into contracts with other entities and/or even with a natural person where there is a 'meeting of minds' between them. Inanimate entities can be also held legally liable for their torts or civil wrongs, just as natural persons are. In some circumstances, inanimate entities can even be convicted of certain crimes, although strictly they do not have the criminal 'mind' or 'intention' necessary to establish the liability of natural persons. These fictions can be said to be the pillars of the functioning of modern societies, and they are strong evidence that two things different or distinctive from each other in some respect can be, and sometimes need to be, treated similarly in law.

Schultz claimed that the insurance contract was of 'special nature', and that is indeed true as far as its *economic* rationales are concerned. It does not follow, however, that insurance contract *law* should be distinctive, because modern insurance business is always conducted through contract, as are many other non-insurance business transactions. Some types of insurance contracts, especially marine insurance policies, do have exceptional terms and conditions, such as the general average clause, the salvage clause, the excess clause, etc, and most often insurance law does give effect to those clauses. However, the way in which or the standard by which insurance law gives effect or otherwise thereto is no different from that in general contract law (with sales law being the paradigm). That is perhaps why more recently, in 2011, the European Parliament 'reiterate[d] its earlier call to include insurance contracts within the scope of the OI [ie Optional Instrument of European Contract Law]'[16] and stressed that preliminary work on European insurance contract law 'should be integrated into a body of European contract law'.[17]

The late Lord Bingham also illustrated the homogeneity of general contract law and reinsurance law. He said:

> The general contract lawyer who strays into reinsurance could well feel that he (or, of course, she) has entered a different world, one where the controversial currency of the natives is to do with fronting and retrocession, treaties and quotes shares, fac/oblig arrangements and scratching of slips. All very baffling.
>
> In reinsurance, as in other fields of law, it is of course essential to understand the terms in which business is transacted in the market place. But when that has been done … the familiar landscape of contract becomes quickly recognizable; there must be an offer and an acceptance, the terms of the contract must be interpreted, and so on. Not baffling at all.[18]

His Lordship's observation applies to insurance law as much as, if not more than, to reinsurance law. That familiar 'landscape of contract' comprises the basic rules on the formation of contract, the performance of contract and the remedies for breach of contract. As will be shown in section II. below, as regards the fundamental rules in these areas, insurance law is not distinctive from general contract law.

II. The Common Legal Framework

A. Formation of contract

Whether negotiated through intermediaries or not, insurance contracts are concluded like other contracts. An insurance contract must be a legally binding

[16] European Parliament, Policy Options for Progress towards a European Contract Law for Consumers and Businesses, Resolution of 8 June 2011, 2011/2013(INI), [25].

[17] Ibid.

[18] C Edelman and A Burns, *The Law of Reinsurance*, 2nd edn (Oxford, Oxford University Press, 2005) 'Foreword' by Lord Bingham, at v.

agreement. For there to be an agreement, there must be an offer and an acceptance. In insurance, the offer will usually be made by the proposer's (ie the prospective insured) completing a proposal form and sending it to the insurers.[19] The test of whether an agreement exists and what the terms are is objective, as is the case in general contract law. Although in practice an insurance policy is commonly used, insurance contracts do not require any special form and, except for marine contracts subject to the Marine Insurance Act 1906,[20] do not even have to be in writing, as is the case with most non-insurance contracts.

The special issue of renewal of contract arises more often in insurance, yet the rules governing renewals still fall within those of offer and acceptance under general contract law. Where an insurance policy covers only a limited period, often one year, and the parties choose to renew the cover upon the expiration of that period, it is not an extension of the period;[21] instead, in renewing the coverage the parties enter into another contract on the same or different terms. Some indemnity insurance products, such as motor insurance and buildings insurance, can be renewed if both parties agree; with this type of insurance, the insurer makes an offer in sending a notice of renewal, and the insured may accept or reject it.[22] Life insurances are often automatically renewed by continuing payment of premiums, and the insurer cannot refuse the automatic renewal.[23] This is not because the rules of offer and acceptance are different in life insurance, but because there seems to be a presumption that a life insurance contract is entire, is one contract, existing until the death of the life assured, or until a specified fixed date in the case of an endowment or term policy.[24]

Cover notes in insurance seem to be special, but they are not really so. A cover note offers provisional coverage for insurance proposers when proposal forms have been submitted but the insurer's decision to accept or reject the offer (made in the proposal forms) is pending. A cover note amounts to a provisional contract of insurance, and the normal analysis of contract formation applies.[25]

[19] *General Accident Insurance Co v Cronk* (1901) 17 TLR 233; *Rust v Abbey Life Insurance Co Ltd* [1979] 2 Lloyd's Rep 334 (CA).

[20] Under s 22 of the Marine Insurance Act 1906, a contract of marine insurance is inadmissible in evidence unless it is 'embodied in a marine policy'. However, this section has been thought to be obsolete by the Law Commission and the Scottish Law Commission, and that is also the consensus in the British insurance industry. See Law Commission and Scottish Law Commission, *Insurance Contract Law: Post-Contract Duties and Other Issues* (2nd Consultation Paper, LCCP 201/SLCDP 152, 2011) 166–67.

[21] J Lowry, P Rawlings and R Merkin, *Insurance Law: Doctrines and Principles*, 3rd edn (Oxford, Hart Publishing, 2011) 170.

[22] Ibid 170.

[23] Birds, *Birds' Modern Insurance Law*, (9th edn, Sweet & Maxwell 2013) 100.

[24] Ibid. See also *Stuart v Freeman* [1903] 1 KB 47(CA), 52–54; *Pritchard v Merchants' & Tradesmen's Mutual Life Assurance Co* (1858) 3 CBNS 622, 643 (Willes J). In the US Supreme Court, it was held that a life insurance is an entire contract of insurance for life, subject to discontinuance or forfeiture for non-payment of stipulated premiums; see *New York Life Insurance Co v Statham* 93 US 24 (1876), followed in *McMaster v New York Life Ins Co* 183 US 25 (1901).

[25] J Lowry et al, above n 21, 171–72.

Like any contract, only if there is both offer and acceptance is there a cover note. In this respect, *Taylor v Allon*[26] is a case in point, in which it was held that the cover note in question did not constitute an enforceable insurance contract, because the defendant did not accept the insurer's offer in the cover note.

'Even at Lloyd's the customary market rituals have been squeezed into the template of offer and acceptance.'[27] A Lloyd's slip, once signed by an underwriter, is a binding contract between the insurance applicant and that particular underwriter.[28]

In summary, whether concluding an original insurance contract, or in a renewal thereof, and whether in the Lloyd's market or beyond, 'insurance contract is no exception of the general rule requiring offer, acceptance, agreement, consideration and an intention to create legal relations in order to find a binding legal contract'.[29] 'In short, no difference: insurance contracts are concluded like other contracts.'[30]

B. Performance of Contract: Insurance Payment

Aleatory and Conditional Performance by Insurers

One might point out that as a matter of law, the performance of a sales contract is (or should be) certain because the transfer of the property in the subject matter is bound to happen, whereas an insurer's primary obligation to pay insurance money is aleatory because this obligation is contingent on the uncertain occurrence of eventualities. That is indeed true. But as long as an insurer must perform its payment obligation upon the occurrence of covered risks, the legal nature of its contractual performance is not essentially different from that of the performance of obligations under a non-insurance contract. Even the performance of non-insurance contractual obligations can also be conditional upon the occurrence of a certain event or action, as is insurance.

Insurance Payment in Contingency Insurance

'Performance of the contract by the insurer is mainly the provision of cover—the promise of payment in the event of a stated contingency'[31] in both indemnity insurance and contingency non-indemnity insurance. In contingency insurance (life insurance mostly), the insurer's contractual obligation is one of debt payment,

[26] *Taylor v Allon* [1966] 1 QB 304 (DC).
[27] Clarke, above n 8, 353.
[28] *Thompson v Adams* (1889) 23 QBD 361; *General Reinsurance Corp v Forsakr Fennia Patria* [1983] QB 856 (CA).
[29] Birds, *Birds' Modern Insurance Law*, above n 23, 85.
[30] Clarke, above n 8, 353.
[31] Ibid 353–54.

because it is payment of a sum liquidated and fixed at the outset of the contract. In law, the debt payment in an insurance context is not different from debt payment under other contracts: in both scenarios, the debt payment consists of paying a fixed sum of money under the terms of the contract.

Perhaps the seeming distinctiveness of an insurance payment is that it hinges on the occurrence of specified eventualities. However, the core principle of insurance payments in both indemnity insurance and contingency insurance is consistent with the operation of contingent conditions in general contract law, more specifically with that of contingent conditions precedent. It is particularly so for contingency insurance. The word 'condition' has at least two senses in contract law:[32] one is its ordinary sense, meaning an event; and the other is the more technical English terminology, meaning a term of a contract. A contract is conditional if its operation depends on an event that is not certain to occur. It is the ordinary sense of the word that is relevant here, and conditions in this sense are known as 'contingent conditions'. In this respect, Treitel describes in one of his chapters in *Chitty on Contracts*:

> Where 'condition' refers to an event, that event may be either an occurrence which neither party undertakes to bring about, or the performance by one party of his undertaking. The first possibility is illustrated by a contract by which A is to work for B, and B is to pay A £50, 'if it rains tomorrow'. Here the obligations of both parties are contingent on the happening of the specified event which may therefore be described as a contingent condition. The second possibility is illustrated by the ordinary case in which A agrees to work for B at a weekly wage payable at the end of the week. Here the contract is immediately binding on both parties, but B is not liable to pay until A has performed his promise to work. Such performance is a condition of B's liability, and, as A has promised to render it, the condition may be described as *promissory*.[33]

Treitel proceeds to describe contingent conditions precedent: 'Contingent conditions may be precedent or subsequent. A condition is precedent if it provides that the contract is not to be binding until the specified event occurs.'[34] However, this description cannot be taken as exhaustive, because a contingent condition can be determinative in a narrow sense of the performance of certain obligations under the contract and does not necessarily have to be determinative of the binding effect of contracts.

A contingent condition precedent can also provide that a particular duty under the contract does not become due unless a contingent condition is fulfilled.[35]

[32] H Beale (ed), *Chitty on Contracts*, vol I, 31st edn (London, Sweet & Maxwell, 2012) [2-151]. 'Condition' in contract law is 'a chameleon-like word which takes on its meaning from its surroundings'. See *Skips A/S Nordheim v Petrofina SA (The Varenna)* [1984] QB 599 (CA), 618.

[33] Beale (ed), above n 32, [2-151].

[34] Ibid [2-152].

[35] J Beatson et al (eds), *Anson's Law of Contract*, 29th edn (Oxford, Oxford University Press, 2010) 141.

This is so with the definition of 'condition' in the US Restatement (Second) of Contracts:

§ 224. Condition Defined

A condition is an event, not certain to occur, which must occur, unless its non-occurrence is excused, before performance under a contract becomes due.

§ 225. Effects of the Non-Occurrence of a Condition

(1) Performance of a duty subject to a condition cannot become due unless the condition occurs or its non-occurrence is excused.
(2) Unless it has been excused, the non-occurrence of a condition discharges the duty when the condition can no longer occur.
(3) Non-occurrence of a condition is not a breach by a party unless he is under a duty that the condition occurs.

In English law, the general legal effect of a contingent condition precedent is that neither party is bound to perform its contractual obligations before the occurrence of the condition, nor do they undertake that the condition will occur.[36] Apart from that, it is also recognised that whether a contingent condition precedent may have the effect of imposing some degree of obligation on the parties or one of them and, if so, what degree of obligation is imposed, depends on the true construction of the term specifying the condition.[37]

The definition and the effect of contingent conditions precedent are relevant to insurance, particularly to life insurance. In both indemnity insurance and contingency insurance, the insurer's obligation to pay insurance money is conditional upon the occurrence of the risks or eventualities covered in the insurance policy. In indemnity insurance, as a matter of law, the payment is subject to the principle of indemnity, which means that indemnity payment is available only when the covered risks lead to actual loss and the payment cannot exceed the loss. However, the indemnity principle does not apply in contingency insurance. As a result, insurance payment in contingency insurance is purely a matter of insurers' performing their payment obligations upon the fulfilment of the contingent condition precedent. Therefore it still falls within the framework of contract law.

Indemnity in Insurance and in Non-insurance Contract

The principle of indemnity lies at the heart of property insurance and liability insurance. It means that 'the assured in case of a loss is to receive a full indemnity, but is never to receive more'.[38] 'Every rule of insurance law is adopted in order to carry out this fundamental rule, and if ever any proposition is brought forward,

[36] Beale (ed), above n 31, [2-153].
[37] Ibid.
[38] *Castellain v Preston* [1881-1885] All ER 493, 495 (Brett LJ).

the effect of which is opposed to this fundamental rule, it will be found to be wrong.'[39] The insured is to be put back into the position he would have been in had the loss not occurred, less any excess and deductibles the insured has agreed to bear.[40] Indeed, the rules of reinstatement, of subrogation and contribution, and the rule against double insurance, all centre on the principle of indemnity.

Use of indemnity is not limited to insurance; it is also used in non-insurance transactions, particularly in contracts in the oil and gas industries,[41] in construction contracts[42] and occasionally in corporate acquisition agreements.[43] Indemnity in non-insurance contracts can be construed either as compensatory of losses, or as preventive of losses. The two types of indemnity were identified in *McIntosh v Dalwood (No 4)*:[44] 'an obligation to indemnify a person, in the sense of repaying to him a sum of money after he has paid it'; and 'an obligation to relieve a debtor by preventing him from having to pay his debts'. Indemnity is more frequently construed and recognised as preventive than as compensatory,[45] but the former is not the default construction of all forms of indemnity.[46] A preventive indemnity often is worded as one party shall 'defend, indemnify and hold harmless' the other party against a series of losses, liabilities, etc. The meaning of 'indemnify' in the preventive sense in a non-insurance scenario was clarified in the UKSC decision *Farstad Supply AS v Enviroco Ltd*,[47] which was an appeal from the (Scottish) Court of Session. In the UKSC, Lord Clarke delivered the leading judgment, and all five Law Lords unanimously restored the judgment by Lord Hodge in the Court of Session.

According to Lord Hodge, by agreeing to 'defend, indemnify and hold harmless' the indemnifiee from all liabilities, the indemnifier not only agreed to indemnify the indemnifiee against any loss which it might incur from such liability to another, but also renounced any right to claim damages from the indemnifiee.[48] What is more important than the decision itself is that Lord Hodge articulated the meaning of 'indemnity', an articulation was accepted by Lord Clarke as 'admirable clarity and brevity';[49] and his judgment was accepted by Lord Mance as 'lucid and compelling'.[50] Back in the Court of Session,

[39] Ibid.

[40] C Lewis, 'A Fundamental Principle of Insurance Law' [1979] *LMCLQ* 275; J Birds, 'The Measure of Indemnity in Property Insurance' (1980) 43 *MLR* 456.

[41] G Gordon, 'Risk Allocation in Oil and Gas Contracts' in G Gordon et al (eds), *Oil and Gas Law: Current Practice and Emerging Trends*, 2nd edn (Dundee, Dundee University Press 2011) [14.3].

[42] For example, *Scottish & Newcastle* plc *v GD Construction (St Albans) Ltd* [2003] EWCA Civ 16.

[43] For example, *Rust Consulting Ltd v PB Ltd* [2010] EWHC 3243 (TCC), affirmed in [2011] EWCA Civ 899.

[44] *McIntosh v Dalwood (No 4)* (1930) 30 SR (NSW) 415 (Full Court), 418 (per Street CJ).

[45] W Courtney, *Contractual Indemnities* (Oxford, Hart Publishing 2014) 19, 25.

[46] Ibid 19.

[47] *Farstad Supply AS v Enviroco Ltd* [2010] UKSC 18, [2008] CSOH 63.

[48] *Farstad Supply AS v Enviroco Ltd* [2008] CSOH 63 [26] (Lord Hodge). Here, Asco was referred to as the third party to the instant litigation, although it was a party, as the charterer, to the charterparty.

[49] *Farstad Supply AS v Enviroco Ltd* [2010] UKSC 18 [25].

[50] Ibid [49].

Lord Hodge said, 'The words "hold harmless" may in some circumstances be equated with "indemnify" but I am not persuaded that they add nothing to an obligation to indemnify.'[51] Relying on the opinion of Vice Chancellor Strine in the American (Delaware) case *Majkowski v American Imaging Management Services LLC*,[52] Lord Hodge recounted approvingly that

> he stated that the terms 'indemnify' and 'hold harmless' had a long history of joint use in Anglo-American legal practice and appeared in countless types of contracts. He stated that modern authorities confirmed that 'hold harmless' had little if any different meaning from the word 'indemnify'. However in footnote 55 of his opinion he stated that the terms 'while having similar, if not identical meanings, are typically used in subtly different contexts. In the abstract, the word indemnify generally grants rights, and the phrase 'hold harmless' generally limits liability.[53]
>
> … In (the American) *Black's Law Dictionary* (8th ed, 2004), to which Vice Chancellor Strine referred, there is the following definition: 'hold harmless, vb. To absolve (another party) from any responsibility for damage or other liability arising from the transaction; INDEMNIFY—also termed save harmless.' This definition, while suggesting a relationship with 'indemnify', supports the view that the words 'hold harmless' involve a limitation or exclusion of liability while 'indemnify' involves reimbursing another for a loss suffered. Also the Oxford English Dictionary includes in its definition of 'harmless' the meaning, 'free from liability to pay for loss or damage' especially in the phrase 'to save harmless.'[54]

It is noted by Vice Chancellor Strine in the passage quoted above, and is true indeed, that more often 'hold harmless' had little if any different meaning from 'indemnify' and that they are used jointly. Whether or not it is necessary to draw on the nuances in their meanings, it is certain that, as Lord Hodge states above, '"indemnify" involves reimbursing another for a loss suffered'.[55]

In respect of indemnity, perhaps a seeming difference between an insurance contract and a non-insurance contract is that in insurance the indemnity is unilateral (only the insurer indemnifies the insured), whereas in non-insurance contracts it might be, and frequently is, mutual (the parties indemnify each other). For example, the House of Lords recognised that in the oil and gas industry

> [i]t is … normal for the client [ie, the operator] and the contractor to assume full liability, and to give each other mutual indemnities, for claims arising out of death of or injury to their own employees and for loss or damage to their own property … regardless of any negligence or default on the part of the other party or its employees, agents or sub-contractors.[56]

[51] *Farstad Supply AS v Enviroco Ltd* [2008] CSOH 63 [24].
[52] *Majkowski v American Imaging Management Services LLC* 2006 WL 3627111 (Del Ch).
[53] *Farstad Supply AS v Enviroco Ltd* [2008] CSOH 63 [24].
[54] Ibid [25].
[55] Ibid.
[56] *Caledonia North Sea Ltd v London Bridge Engineering Ltd* 2002 SC (HL) 117, 2002 SLT 278 [81], Lord Hoffman citing TC Daintith and GDM Willoughby (eds), *Manual of United Kingdom Oil and Gas Law* (London, Sweet & Maxwell, 1984) [1-84].

There are policy reasons as well as insurance reasons underlying such practices. The policy reasons are grounded in the fact that often there are many contractors, subcontractors and sub-subcontractors in such big projects as oil and gas operations. That means that it is far from efficient to trace liabilities through layers of contracts. The indemnity is intended to

> divide the responsibility for personal injury/death among the many employers and contractors according to the identity of the injured employee rather than according to which party's fault or negligence caused the injury. In effect, each party assumes the risk of the other's negligence and agrees to be responsible for the injuries of its own employees no matter how, or by whom, caused.[57]

The insurance reason for mutual indemnity is to reduce the cost of insurance. Operators of platforms normally carry insurance cover for their own employees and property. Without indemnity, the contractors would have to carry liability insurances in respect of injuries to and/or the death of the employees of the operators and of other contractors and subcontractors, as well as damage to very expensive property. Thus the insurance cost would be high. In contrast, with indemnity between operators and contractors, each party knows that it need insure only in respect of its own property and employees.[58]

The existence of mutual indemnity does not mean it is different, as a matter of law, from unilateral indemnity in insurance. *It is only a difference in commercial practice, not a difference in law.* As long as clauses of mutual indemnity are recognised as binding in law, and they often are, mutual indemnity will be treated in law as essentially the same as unilateral indemnity, and they both mean that the indemnifier shall reimburse the other party for losses incurred to this other party. Set-off is involved in the operation of mutual indemnity, but that simply means that the two indemnities have the same nature as if they were two unilateral indemnities that can be set off against each other. It must be also noted that in non-insurance contract, one party might be willing to indemnify the other, 'regardless of any negligence or default on the part of the other party or its employees, agents or sub-contractors'.[59] This is not different from indemnity in insurance, where in principle the negligence of the insured is no bar to recovery under an insurance policy (even though a negligent act might be criminal).[60]

Law does not treat differently indemnity clauses in non-insurance contracts and in insurance contracts. By their nature, both non-insurance indemnity and

[57] *Caledonia North Sea Ltd v London Bridge Engineering Ltd* 2002 SC (HL) 117, 2002 SLT 278 [9] (Lord Bingham), affirmatively citing Judge Brown J in *Fontenot v Mesa Petroleum Co* 791 F 2d, (1986) 1216.

[58] *Caledonia North Sea Ltd v London Bridge Engineering Ltd* 2002 SC (HL) 117, 2002 SLT 278 [82] (Lord Hoffmann).

[59] *Caledonia North Sea Ltd v London Bridge Engineering L td* 2002 SC (HL) 117, 2002 SLT 278 [81], Lord Hoffman citing Daintith and Willoughby (eds), above n 56, [1-84].

[60] J Birds, B Lynch and S Milnes (eds), *MacGillivray on Insurance Law*, 12th edn (London, Sweet and Maxwell, 2012) [14-050], [26-028], [33-021].

insurance indemnity are intended by the two parties as a mechanism for risk allocation between them; they are designed for one party (the indemnifier) to put the other party back into the financial position the other party would have been in had particular losses not occurred to that other party. Non-insurance indemnity is not different in essence from indemnity in insurance, though the former can be less restrictive. They share more common features in five ways. First, like non-insurance indemnity (above), insurance indemnity can also be either preventive of loss or compensatory of loss.[61] Secondly, in both non-insurance indemnity and insurance indemnity, the person entitled to indemnity is often the other party to the contract, other than a third person. Thirdly, the loss must be caused by the other party to the contract, or by other third persons, or by pure accident. Fourthly, in regard to the conduct and the state of mind of the person to whom the loss is attributed, it can be the other party's breach of contract, or its negligence (in the sense of tort), or a third person's negligence and/or intentional act, but normally it cannot be the other party's intentional act; in other words, loss or damage incurred by the other party intentionally is often not within the scope of indemnity. Fifthly, although in principle the indemnity must be full, yet it can be subject directly or indirectly to a litany of limitations, exclusions, exceptions and deductions, as a result of which the extent of the indemnity can be less than full in both scenarios.

The wording of indemnity clauses in insurance and non-insurance settings are invariably not identical with one another, hence the specific extent of indemnity varies in different contracts, but that is the difference in commercial practice rather than in law, a difference in the extent of indemnity rather than in its legal nature. That is because, after all, the indemnity clauses themselves in insurance and in non-insurance contracts are often upheld by courts, and the approaches to construction of insurance contract and non-insurance contract are the same.[62] The extent of any indemnity is always ascertained through holistic construction of the contract, with the bottom line being that the indemnifiee is not entitled to more than is allowed. Occasionally there is mutual indemnity in non-insurance settings, whereas indemnity in insurance is always unilateral (by insurers and to the insured), but again that is a difference in commercial practice, not in law: the law indiscriminately gives homogeneous validity to mutual indemnity and to unilateral indemnity.

C. Remedies for Breach of Contract

Where insurers fail to perform their contractual obligation to pay insurance money, the law by which to enforce the contract still falls within the general law of

[61] W Courtney, *Contractual Indemnities* (Oxford, Hart Publishing, 2014) 31–32.
[62] Clarke, above n 8, 139 and 354.

contract. In English law, an action for insurance money in indemnity insurance is an action for payment of damages—though it is damages 'in an unusual sense'[63] for insurer's failure of its more unusual primary obligation to prevent losses from happening to the policyholder in question. This still does not go beyond the common law rule that an award of damages is one of the remedies in contract law. The law has just been reformed, though not directly to the said old rule of insurance law. Under section 28(1) of Enterprise Act 2016, or resultantly the added section 13A(1) of the Insurance Act 2015 with effect from 5 May 2017, 'it is an implied term of every contract of insurance that if the insured makes a claim under the contract, the insurer must pay any sums due in respect of the claim within a reasonable time.' The new law seems to indicate that insurers' primary obligation is to pay insurance money under the terms of contract, as is the case in other common law jurisdictions and under Scots law; an action for insurance money under the new law would then be an action for specific performance of the newly-prescribed primary obligation to make payments timely. The new law will thus effectively turn to specific performance as an alternative remedy in contract law. In either case, the law by which to enforce the insurance contract for the policyholder still operates within the overarching legal framework for enforcement of contracts. This is apparently more so where an action for insurance money under contingency insurance is an action for liquidated damages or an action for debt, as in any other contract that involves debt collection and payment.

Where an insured fails to pay the premium, the remedy for the insurer is that it is entitled to elect to terminate the contract, or to derogate proportionately from its obligation to pay insurance money, or even sue the insured for the premium which is overdue, though the last option may be commercially unwise for the insurer because the action will damage the insurer's customer relations. No matter how insurers exercise their rights to a remedy, those remedies apparently still reside within the framework of general contract law.

III. The Shared Principles of Interpretation of Contracts

'Insurance policies are to be construed according to principles of construction generally applicable to commercial and consumer contracts.'[64] 'The construction

[63] *Jabbour v Custody of Absentee Property for the State of Israel* [1954] WLR 139 (QB), 143 (Pearson J).

[64] Birds et al (eds), above n 60, [11-001], citing *Drinkwater v Corp of the London Ass* (1767) 2 Wils 363, 364; *Robertson v French* (1803) 4 East 130, 135 (Lord Ellenborough); *Reid v Marsden* (1803) 3 East 572, 579; *Abbott v Howard* (1832) Hayes 381, 401; *Geln v Lewis* (1853) 8 Ex 607, 617; *Smith v Accident Ins Co* (1870) LR 5 Ex 302, 307; *Hart v Standard Marine* (1889) 22 QBD 499, 501; *Jason v British Trader's Ins Co Ltd* [1969] 1 Lloyd's Rep 281, 290; *Cementation Piling & Foundations Ltd v Aegon Ins Co Ltd* [1995] 1 Lloyd's Rep 97, 101.

of words and phrases in insurance policies is generally a matter of law and is controlled by the same rules of construction as are applied to contracts generally.'[65] In this regard,

> again, in general no difference: insurance contracts are interpreted like other contracts. In particular, there is presumption that any word that has an established meaning in some other part of law is used in the same sense in the insurance contracts.[66]

Regarding interpretation of insurance contracts, Staughton LJ stated in *New Hampshire Insurance Co v MGN Ltd*:[67]

> We would reiterate the four principles … relating to the material that is relevant to the interpretation of a written contract:
>
> (1) Nothing is relevant unless it was known to, or reasonably capable of being known to, both parties at the time when the contract was made. In particular, an undisclosed intention held in pectore by one of the parties is not admissible for the purpose of interpretation.
> (2) The court looks first at the written document alone, and determines what it means from the ordinary meaning of the language used, unless some customary meaning is pleaded and proved.
> (3) However, the court may also have regard to the surrounding circumstances, now commonly referred to as the matrix, the genesis or aim, the market in which the parties are operating. But this evidence must qualify under principle (1) if it is to be admitted.
> (4) Evidence of negotiations is not admissible. This is subject to some exceptions, such as a case of rectification, or if it is said that agreement was reached in negotiations as to the meaning of a particular term, or that the contract was made by a continuous process of agreeing some terms and then turning to consider others.
>
> The boundary of what may be considered surrounding circumstances, within principle (3), is unfortunately not easy to draw. All too often a great deal of evidence is produced under that head which is of little or no help to interpretation. The present case is no exception in that respect.

This statement was made on 6 September 1996. Though made in an insurance case, Staughton LJ meant the four principles to be applicable to any written contract, insurance or not. In particular, he stressed that it was as difficult to draw the boundary of 'surrounding circumstances' in the instant insurance context as in a non-insurance context. Given the close connection among those four rules, what was true for insurance and principle (3) was equally true for insurance and the other three principles.

In less than one year, these principles reiterated by Staughton LJ were echoed in Lord Hoffmann's renowned restatement in *Investors Compensation*

[65] *Kremers-Urban Company v American Employers Insurance Co* 119 Wis 2d 722, 735; 351 NW 2d 156, 163 (Wis 1984).

[66] Clarke, above n 8, 354.

[67] *New Hampshire Insurance Co v MGN Ltd* [1996] CLC 1692, 1730; [1997] LRLR 24, 52.

Scheme Ltd v West Bromwich Building Society[68] on the principles of, and particularly the contextual and commonsense approach to, interpretation of contract. Lord Hoffmann's restatement, more widely known as principles of contract interpretation, in a non-insurance setting effectively affirmed Staughton LJ's reiteration in, but not limited to, an insurance context. It follows from the homogeneous judicial statements made respectively in insurance and non-insurance contexts that the principles of interpretation of policies in insurance law are the same as those in contract law. This observation can be supported by practitioners in insurance law. In this regard, Dr Digby Jess has more recently stressed as follows:

> The same rules of construction apply to insurance contracts (and the policy document which usually embodies the terms and conditions and limitations of that contract) as to all other contracts ... It is therefore always important to bear in mind those principles when construing the policy term, and those principles of construction have recently been restated by Lord Hoffmann.[69]

IV. Particular Differences—How Different?

A. Insurance Contract and Utmost Good Faith

One of the perceivable differences, entrenched until recent years, is said to be that an insurance contract is a contract of utmost good faith (or *uberrimae fidei*), and as a corollary insurance law requires it to be so,[70] whereas there is no general requirement of good faith at least in English contract law,[71] let alone utmost good faith. This stark contrast is believed to make insurance contracts strikingly different if not unique.

However, the very concept of 'utmost good faith' sounds problematic. The term 'utmost good faith' is a convenient expression that is not always strictly accurate.[72] 'The existence of a class of contracts called *uberrimae fidei* suggests that all other contracts should require ordinary good faith. But the use of the superlative is really only a form of hyperbole.'[73] The Court of Appeal mildly pointed out that 'it

[68] *Investors Compensation Scheme Ltd v West Bromwich Building Society* [1997] CLC 1243 (HL), 1258–59.

[69] D Jess, *The Insurance of Commercial Risks: Law and Practice* (London, Sweet & Maxwell, 2011) [2-03].

[70] Marine Insurance Act 1906, s 17.

[71] Beale (ed), above n 32, [1-039]. See also *ING Bank NV v Ros Roca SA* [2011] EWCA Civ 353 [92]; *Mid Essex Hospital Services NHS Trust v Compass Group UK and Ireland Ltd (t/a Medirest)* [2013] EWCA Civ 200 [105].

[72] M Parkington et al (eds), *MacGivallry and Parkington on Insurance Law*, 8th edn London, Sweet & Maxwell, 1988) [634], relying on *Seaton v Heath* [1899] 1 QB 782, 792 (Romer LJ).

[73] R Powell, 'Good Faith in Contracts' (1956) 9 *Current Legal Problems* 16, 25–26. Note also the opening comments in R Hasson, 'The Doctrine of *Uberrima Fides* in Insurance Law—A critical

is not necessary, even if it were possible, to go into degrees of good faith'.[74] 'The words "*uberrimae fidei*" must not … be taken too literally. One may be less than honest but one cannot be more honest than honest.'[75] 'It may be doubted whether such terms [indicating a higher degree of good faith] are judiciously chosen, and whether it is wise to introduce and encourage a comparative degree of honesty at all.'[76] 'Utmost good faith' was more 'hyperbole' than a term with a substantive meaning broader than 'good faith'. The insurance law doctrine of utmost good faith is largely the result of 'lop-sided reading'[77] of Lord Mansfield's judgment in *Carter v Boehm*,[78] which 'has been misunderstood and misapplied by English courts',[79] not only because Lord Mansfield mentioned only 'good faith' rather than 'utmost good faith', but more because 'the effect of this lop-sided reading of the judgment has been to make it appear that it is the insured's duty to supply information while the insurer's role in this process is an entirely passive one'.[80]

If we accept that insurance contract requires good faith plainly, without resort to the hyperbolic superlative 'utmost', the difference in this respect between

Evaluation' (1969) 32 *MLR* 615, 615: 'To give a legal rule a certain rubric is of course a very important way of determining the fate in the future of that particular rule. Few of us are against an "equitable" rule, for example, just as there are bound to be few supporters of a rule which is against "public policy." If we go further and translate our rule into a foreign language, its "goodness" (or "badness" as the case may be) is heavily underlined. Thus a rule requiring "uberrima fides" from a contracting party is more impressive sounding than one merely requiring the exercise of "the utmost good faith." Conversely, to say that something is "contra bonos mores" seems to be more damning than to say that the same thing is against "public policy."'

74 *CTI v Oceanus* [1984] 1 Lloyd's Rep 476, 524.

75 ADM Forte, 'Good Faith and Utmost Good Faith: Insurance and Cautionary Obligations in Scots Law' in ADM Forte (ed), *Good Faith in Contract and Property* (Oxford, Hart Publishing, 1999) 83, citing Miller JA in the South African case of *Mutual and Federal Insurance Co Ltd v Oudtshoorn Municipality* [1984] ZASCA 129. See also in the same case, Joubert JA's leading judgment: 'Moreover, there is no magic in the expression *uberrima fides*. There are no degrees of good faith. It is entirely inconceivable that there could be a little, more or most (utmost) good faith. The distinction is between good faith or bad faith. There is no room for uberrima fides as a third category of faith in our law. …*Uberrima fides* is not a juristic term with a precise connotation. It cannot be used as a yardstick with a precise legal meaning. Roberts A.J. correctly held in Iscor *Pension Fund v. Marine and Trade Insurance Co. Ltd.* 1961 (1) SA 178 (T) at p 184 that "the claim that *uberrima fides* is a necessary and inseparable concomitant of insurance is misleading". In my opinion *uberrima fides* is an alien, vague, useless expression without any particular meaning in law. As I have indicated, it cannot be used in our law for the purpose of explaining the juristic basis of the duty to disclose a material fact before the conclusion of a contract of insurance. Our law of insurance has no need for uberrima fides and the time has come to jettison it.' Also Joubert JA: 'It is obvious that both Roman-Dutch and English law of marine insurance stem from the same original sources. … The Romans were familiar with *bona fides* and *mala fides* but they never knew *uberrima fides* as another category of good faith. I have been unable to find any Roman-Dutch authority in support of the proposition that a contract of marine insurance is a contract *uberrimae fidei*. On the contrary, it is indisputably a contract *bona fides*.'

76 S Bower, *The Law Relating to Actionable Non-Disclosure*, 2nd edn (A Turner and R Sutton (eds), Butterworths, 1990) [1.02].

77 Hasson, above n 73, 616.

78 *Carter v Boehm* (1766) 3 Burr 1905.

79 Hasson, above n 73, 615.

80 Ibid 616.

insurance law and contract law is substantially diluted. This is particularly so as far as contract law in the US is concerned, because a general duty of good faith and fair dealing in performance and enforcement of contract is recognised there under the *Uniform Commercial Code* and the *Restatement (Second) of Contract Law*.[81] It is similarly so in relation to Canadian contract law, because the Supreme Court of Canada has recently recognised an organising principle of good faith and a duty of honest performance of contract.[82] The difference is even narrowed down in the context of English contract law. Though a general principle of good faith is still not part of the law, it is recognised that a duty of good faith in contract may exist by way of implication of terms in relational contracts.[83] Given that insurance contracts can also be perceived to be relational,[84] good faith in insurance contract is actually consistent with and not distinct from the new development of good faith in English contract law.

B. Pre-contractual Duty of Disclosure

Until recently there has indeed been a stark contrast between insurance law and general contract law in respect of the duty of disclosure. Before the Consumer Insurance (Disclosure and Representations) Act 2012 became effective in April 2013, the entrenched rule in English insurance law was that in the negotiation of an insurance contract, the insured should *disclose or volunteer* to the insurer any information material to the insurer, otherwise the insurer would be entitled to avoid the contract and therefore to reject the insured's claim even though the covered risks do occur. The rule is commonly believed to originate in Lord Mansfield's opinion in *Carter v Boehm*[85] 250 years ago, and was codified into section 18 of the Marine Insurance Act 1906, which was applicable to both marine insurance and non-marine insurance.[86] Nevertheless, in non-insurance general contract law, the legal status of the duty of disclosure is very different: in fact it has no place in non-insurance contract law. Although Lord Mansfield referred to good faith as 'the governing principle ... applicable to *all* contracts and dealings',[87] this principle never took root in England.[88] Rather, the rule in English contract law is that there

[81] Uniform Commercial Code, § 1-304; Restatement (Second) of Contract Law, § 205.

[82] *Bhasin v Hrynew* [2014] SCC 71, [2014] 3 SCR 495.

[83] *Yam Seng Pte Ltd v International Trade Corp Ltd* [2013] EWHC 111; *Bristol Groundschool Ltd v Intelligent Data Capture Ltd* [2014] EWHC 2145 [142].

[84] J Feinman, 'The Insurance Relationship as Relational Contract and the "Fairly Debatable" Rule for First-Party Bad Faith' (2009) 46 *San Diego Law Review* 553, 556 and note 14.

[85] *Carter v Boehm* (1766) 3 Burr 1905, 1909.

[86] This was recognised, for example in *Pan Atlantic Insurance Ltd v Pine Top Insurance Ltd* [1995] 1 AC 501, 518 (Lord Mustill).

[87] *Carter v Boehm* (1766) 3 Burr 1905, 1910.

[88] J Steyn, 'The Role of Good Faith and Fair Dealing in Contract Law: A Hair-Shirt Philosophy' [1991] *Denning Law Journal* 131, 133.

is no principle or general duty of good faith imposed by law;[89] nor does the law impose a duty of disclosure on either party in the negotiation of a contract. This has been reiterated in *Walford v Miles*[90] by the House of Lords, and more recently by the Court of Appeal in *ING Bank NV v Ros Roca SA*,[91] with a contrasting reference to insurance contract. English contract law does not recognise a general duty to perform contracts in good faith, nor does it recognised a duty to negotiate in good faith, and 'statements to the effect are legion'.[92] That is also the case in American contract law, as the late Professor Allan Farnsworth said: '[L]ike most of the common law world, including England, we Americans do not recognize a duty of good faith in negotiation in pre-contractual relations.'[93]

However, the difference is disappearing, or has been significantly diluted at least. The Consumer Insurance (Disclosure and Representations) Act 2012, section 2(1) replaced the consumer insured's duty of disclosure with a duty not to misrepresent, a duty that is common in contract law. Such a change cannot be belittled, because consumer insurance has a big market share in the British insurance industry. The Family Spending Survey for 2007 showed that UK households spent £19 billion on general insurance, representing 56 per cent of the UK insurance market, and long-term protection insurance purchased by consumers rather than employers accounted for about 60 per cent of the UK market.[94] According to statistics of the Association of British Insurers, nation-wide UK households' expenditure in 2013 on general insurance was approximately £24.5 billion, representing 70 per cent of the UK general insurance market in which the premiums income in 2013 was £24.5 billion; also in 2013, net premiums income in the UK long-term insurance market amounted to £24.5 billion.[95] Given these statistics and the change as described above and brought by the Consumer Insurance (Disclosure and Representations) Act 2012, the old duty of disclosure in insurance law no longer applies in the enormous consumer insurance market. Therefore, one can hardly insist that the duty of disclosure is still a marked, persistent and

[89] Beale (ed), above n 32, [1-039]. See also *Mid Essex Hospital Services NHS Trust v Compass Group UK and Ireland Ltd (t/a Medirest)* [2013] EWCA Civ 200 [105] (LJ Jackson).

[90] *Walford v Miles* [1992] 2 AC 128 (HL), 138 (per Lord Ackner).

[91] *ING Bank NV v Ros Roca SA* [2011] EWCA Civ 353 [92].

[92] S Whittaker and R Zimmermann, 'Good Faith in European Contract Law: Surveying the Landscape' in R Zimmermann and S Whittaker (eds), *Good Faith in European Contract Law* (Cambridge, Cambridge University Press, 2000) 39–40.

[93] A Farnsworth, 'The Concept of Good Faith in American Law', a lecture in 1993 in Italy, available at www.cisg.law.pace.edu/cisg/biblio/farnsworth3.html.

[94] D Hertzell, 'UK [Report]' in H Heiss (ed), *Insurance Contract Law between Business Law and Consumer Protection* (Zurich, Dike, 2012) 357–58. Hertzell also notes that consumer insurance accounts for the largest portion of insurance premiums in Europe.

[95] Limited UK insurance industry overview statistics are available for free in ABI website www.abi.org.uk/Insurance-and-savings/Industry-data/Free-industry-data-downloads. Particularly useful are the three sets of statistics: 'Household spending on insurance tables (xls) based on data from the ONS Living Cost and Food Survey 2013', 'Annual general insurance overview statistics 2014 (xls)', 'Annual long-term insurance overview statistics 2013 Annual Statistics (xls)'. All three sets cover the data from 2007 to 2013.

significant-as-ever distinction between insurance contract law and general contract law. Rather, what is now common, inter alia, between them is the duty not to misrepresent.

In Australia, the duty of disclosure was also significantly relaxed, as a result of the insurance law reform that culminated in the *Insurance Contract Act 1984 (Australia)* applicable to non-marine insurance.[96] There was a drastic change in respect of the duty of disclosure. The duty of disclosure was retained and has remained, but has been substantially relaxed in four respects:

1. A totally different test is adopted: the 'prudent insurer' test, following English insurance law, is effectively replaced with the 'reasonable insured' test,[97] and the constructive knowledge of the insured[98] is abolished.[99]
2. Where a person fails to answer, or gives an obviously incomplete or irrelevant answer to a question included in a proposal form about a particular matter, that would no longer amount to non-disclosure, because in that circumstance, 'the insurer shall be deemed to have waived compliance with the duty of disclosure in relation to the matter'.[100] This means that insurers can no longer be only the passive recipients of the information to be disclosed by the insured; instead, insurers shall ask questions to obtain information, and furthermore they shall ask complete and relevant questions.
3. Insurers are under a statutory duty to inform the insured clearly in writing of the general nature and effect of the duty of disclosure.[101] The duty of insurers, as required by the statutory law, to remind the insured of the consequences of non-disclosure in some way changes the active nature of the classic duty of disclosure, because the insured might feel compelled by the reminder, and essentially by the law, to disclose the material facts.
4. In motor insurance, housing insurance, sickness and accident insurance, consumer credit insurance and travel insurance,[102] the duty of disclosure is taken to have been waived by the insurer unless the insurer asks the insured 'specific' and 'relevant' questions and expressly requests the insured to disclose exceptional circumstances.[103]

[96] For marine insurance, the duty of disclosure is provided for in s 24(1) and (2) of the *Marine Insurance Act 1909 (Australia)*, which reproduce s 18(1) and (2) of the Marine Insurance Act 1906 verbatim.

[97] *Insurance Contract Act 1984 (Australia)*, s 21(1)(b).

[98] In the Marine Insurance Act 1906, s 18(1) and the *Marine Insurance Act 1909 (Australia)*, s 24(1), 'the assured is deemed to know every circumstance which, in the ordinary course of business, ought to be known by him'.

[99] *Insurance Contract Act 1984 (Australia)*, s 21(1)(a).

[100] Ibid, s 21(3).

[101] Ibid, s 22.

[102] Ibid, s 21A(1) and (9); Insurance Contracts Regulations 1999 (No. 1, Australia), reg 2B, incorporated into Contracts Regulations 1985 (SR 162, Australia), reg 2B, currently Contracts Regulations 1985 (SR 162, Australia), reg 2B, as amended by Insurance Contracts Amendment Regulation 2015 (No. 1, Australia).

[103] *Insurance Contract Act 1984 (Australia)*, s 21A(2), (3), (4).

The duty of disclosure in consumer insurance is thus effectively converted into a duty not to misrepresent: insurance consumers are only expected to answer specific and relevant questions honestly, rather than to volunteer information. This is the same as in general contract law, under which a party to a contract should not misrepresent.

That is similar to the position in the US. The US Supreme Court in *Stipcich v Metropolitan Life Insurance Co*[104] recognised that the modern practice of requiring the applicant for insurance to answer questions prepared by the insurer relaxed the traditional rule in American non-marine insurance that the insured's intentional non-disclosure of material facts would entitle the insurer to avoid the contract, since information not asked for would presumably be deemed immaterial. On the element of materiality in particular, 'more recently, numerous courts have held that unless the insurer specifically requests information, a prospective insured is under no duty to volunteer it'.[105] This means that the duty of disclosure has been gradually turned into a duty not to misrepresent upon the insurer's request for specific information. Even for marine insurance, the law of non-disclosure has occasionally been applied in federal courts, but in more cases in state courts it is not applied.[106] Therefore it remains true that in marine insurance law, the US state jurisdictions have relaxed the insured's duty of disclosure.

It can be seen that the duty of disclosure has significantly withered in insurance law. This change cannot be belittled by the fact that it will be applied only to consumer insurance. That is because, as has been described above, consumer insurance has a big market share in the British insurance industry. The bigger the consumer insurance market, the more diluted is the duty of disclosure in insurance law.

C. 'Conditions' and 'Warranties'

It is also pointed out that 'conditions' and 'warranties' are understood quite differently in insurance contracts.[107] Prima facie, that is true. Under general contract law, a condition is an essential term of a contract and is fundamental in nature; the breach of a condition entitles the innocent party to terminate the contract and sue for damages. A warranty, however, is a subsidiary promise, the breach of which entitles the innocent party only to claim damages but not to terminate the contract. In stark contrast, it is just the opposite in insurance law: a fundamental term in an insurance contract is a warranty, which is so fundamental that it 'must

[104] *Stipcich v Metropolitan Life Insurance Co* (1928) 277 US 311.

[105] R Jerry II and D Richmond, *Understanding Insurance Law*, 5th edn (New York, LexisNexis, 2012) 760.

[106] T Schoenbaun, 'The Duty of Utmost Good Faith in Marine Insurance Law: A Comparative Analysis of American and English Law' (1998) 29 *Journal of Maritime Law and Commerce* 1, 11-13.

[107] Clarke, above n 8, 354.

be exactly complied with, whether it is material to the risk or not. If it be not so complied with … the insurer is discharged from liability.'[108] A condition in an insurance contract is a subsidiary term with different meanings.

'Conditions' in insurance contracts might plainly and generally mean ordinary—perhaps subsidiary too, and if so they are more like 'warranties' in general contract law—terms of contract, or expressly mean 'conditions precedent'. They might also mean terms 'which delimit the risks covered under the policy with the effect that, while the promise made by the assured is being broken the insurer is not on risk and the cover is *temporarily suspended until the breach is remedied*'.[109] (emphasis added) That is a suspensive condition. 'Clauses of this nature are sometimes referred to as "warranties descriptive of risk" or "delimiting the risk"'.[110]

A warranty under insurance law is, in terms of general contract law, actually a promissory condition precedent to the insurers' liability. This was affirmed by Lord Goff in *The Good Luck* case:[111]

> Section 33(3) of the Act reflects what has been described, in successive editions of Chalmers, *The Marine Insurance Act* 1906, as the inveterate practice in marine insurance of using the term 'warranty' as signifying a *condition precedent*. As Lord Blackburn said in *Thomson v Weems* (1884) 9 App Cas 671, 684:
>
> > 'In policies of marine insurance I think it is settled by authority that any statement of a fact bearing upon the risk introduced into the written policy is, by whatever words and in whatever place, to be construed as a warranty, and, prima facie, at least that the compliance with that warranty is *a condition precedent to the attaching of the risk*.'
>
> Once this is appreciated, it becomes readily understandable that, if a promissory warranty is not complied with, the insurer is discharged from liability as from the date of the breach of warranty, for the simple reason that *fulfilment of the warranty is a condition precedent to the liability of the insurer*. This moreover reflects the fact that the rationale of warranties in insurance law is that the *insurer* only accepts the risk provided that the warranty is fulfilled. This is entirely understandable; and it follows that the immediate effect of a breach of a promissory warranty is to discharge the insurer from liability as from the date of the breach. *In the case of conditions precedent, the word 'condition' is being used in its classical sense in English law, under which the coming into existence of (for example) an obligation, or the duty or further duty to perform an obligation, is dependent upon the fulfilment of the specified condition.* Here, where we are concerned with a promissory warranty, ie a promissory condition precedent, contained in an existing contract of insurance, non-fulfilment of the condition does not prevent the contract from coming into existence. What it does (as section 33(3) makes plain) is to discharge the insurer from liability as from the date of the breach. Certainly, it does not have the effect of avoiding the

[108] Marine Insurance Act 1906, s 33(3).
[109] Birds et al (eds), above n 60, [10-07].
[110] *De Maurier v Bastion Ins Co* [1967] Lloyd's Rep 550, 558–59.
[111] *Bank of Nova Scotia v Hellenic Mutual War Risks Association (Bermuda) Ltd (The Good Luck)* [1992] 1 AC 233 (HL).

> contract ab initio. Nor, strictly speaking, does it have the effect of bringing the contract to an end.[112] (emphasis added)

It follows from Lord Goff's opinion, especially from the italicised parts, that as a matter of law, a warranty in insurance contract is essentially understood in terms of being a 'promissory condition precedent', a description which is used in its classical sense in English contract law.

Therefore, the purported difference between the two sets of terminologies, ie 'conditions' and 'warranties', in insurance and non-insurance contexts is more formalistic than substantive, and more apparent than real. Given the meaning of 'conditions' and 'warranties' as described above, the seeming differences in meaning under insurance law and general contract law are more nominal than essential. The nature of 'warranties' in insurance contract is quite similar to that of 'conditions' under general contract law; and 'conditions' in insurance contract could just as plainly mean 'terms' or 'warranties' in general contract law—that is, subsidiary terms, or suspensive conditions, or conditions precedent.

V. Conclusion

Whilst insurance in its economic mechanism is indeed distinctive from non-insurance transactions, the prototype of which is sales, the general law of contract governs both. From the perspective of private law, insurance transactions and non-insurance transactions are homogeneously subject to the same legal framework of contract law in respect of the formation and the performance of contract, and of the remedies for breach of contract. The principles for interpretation of contract terms are homogeneous too. The perceived particular difference in the pre-contractual duty of disclosure has been significantly diluted as a result of the insurance law reform, and the claimed difference in the meanings of 'conditions' and 'warranties' in insurance law and in contract law is more formalistic than fundamental.

The homogeneity as found between insurance law and general contract law is consistent with and complementary to Professor Clarke's observation that 'the presumption should always be against those who assert that it [insurance law] is, or should be, different [from general contract law]'.[113] The implication of this homogeneity is that in many respects insurance contract law is to be, and should be, understood from the general contract law perspective.

112 Ibid 262–63.
113 Clarke, above n 8, 357.

3

Rediscovering Expectations in Contract Law

According to Roscoe Pound,[1] reasonable expectations might be based on philosophical or metaphysical ethical considerations, or on experience, or on the presuppositions of civilised society, or on the moral sentiment of the community; some or all of them may be recognised and backed by the law, whereby they become the more reasonable. In the context of contract, this means that reasonable expectations may be protected even though they are external to a contract. However, are reasonable expectations, or expectations generally, necessarily external to contract and contract law? It does seem so, because unless put into writing in a contract, expectations are not part of the contract, and because prima facie expectations have little place in contract law doctrines.

This chapter seeks to uncover the *subsumed* role of expectations in contract law. It is firstly argued that although, as a matter of positive law, it is contractual parties' intentions that are determinative of the content of a contract, it is expectations of the performance of the contract that ensure the intention to create legal relations. This can be borne out by the observation, of Adam Smith and John Austin, as well as other classical and modern treatise writers of Anglo-American contract law, such as Anson, Pollock, Corbin, Arthur Goodhart and Hugh Collins, that expectations have a substantive role in the formation of a contract, and that the obligation of performance of the contract is founded on reasonable expectations induced by a promise. The chapter also points out that despite Perdue's famous argument on reliance damages, expectation damages and restitution damages in contract law,[2] as a matter of the positive law, what has been dominant in respect of remedies for breach of contract has been the expectation damages principle, which places expectation at the core of remedies for breach of contract and offers a yardstick for measuring the damages.

Secondly, this chapter highlights the principle of reasonable expectations in positive modern contract law, by revisiting how the reasonable expectations

[1] R Pound, *Social Control through Law* (New Haven, Ct, Yale University Press, 1942) 80.

[2] LL Fuller and WR Perdue, Jr, 'The Reliance Interest in Contract Damages' (Parts 1 & 2) (1936) 46 *Yale Law Journal* 52 and 373.

approach was incorporated into the historic Unfair Contract Terms Act 1977, how it remains in the Consumer Rights Act 2015, and how the reasonable expectations approach has been stressed by Lord Steyn and more recently by other senior English judges in commercial contract cases.

Thirdly, as a response to the doubts[3] about the notion of reasonable expectations in contract law, this chapter also argues that the notion is not just a slogan: instead it is in itself a principle of substance, not a doctrine; therefore it is not surprising that as a principle it has a number of bases or approaches, rather than a single unified approach as a doctrine usually has. Those bases or approaches do not in themselves lead to inconsistencies. The alleged inconsistencies are mainly due to a failure to distinguish the 'reasonable man' from the 'rational man' as John Rawls did.

Fourthly, this chapter considers the role of reasonable expectations in contract interpretation. For this purpose, it considers the general relationship between intentions—the orthodox focus of interpretation of contracts—and expectations from the perspective of behavioural science, as well as the particular relation of expectations to the contextual approach and the purposive approach to interpretation of contracts. All these lead to an argument: now that expectations are fairly relevant to contract and in contract law, why should not reasonable expectations be so too?

I. Expectations in Contract Formation and Damages

A. Expectations in the Formation of Contract

The standard requirements in common law for formation of a valid contract are, first, the intention to create legal relations; secondly, the 'meeting of minds' by way of exchanging promises, ie an offer and an acceptance; and, thirdly, consideration. In contrast to the general intention to create legal relations, promises in terms of offer and acceptance are specific intentions of the offeror and the offeree. The requirement of consideration apart, the orthodox analysis of the first two rules in modern contract law seems to have ignored the role of expectations in the formation of contract, and further of contractual obligations.

[3] C Mitchell, 'Leading a Life of its Own? The Roles of Reasonable Expectations in Contract Law' (2003) 23 *OJLS* 639. See also similarly S Smith, '"The Reasonable Expectations of the Parties": An Unhelpful Concept' (2009) 48 *Canadian Business Law Journal* 366.

A promise expresses a specific intention. The promise, for example an offer, upon being communicated to the promisee/offeree, raises expectations in the promisee. The expectations are of two kinds:

1. the general expectation of the offeror's performance of the promise—this is 'his expectation derived from law as he understands it'.[4] After all, the very basic (contract) law at least known to either party is that promises in contract must and should be kept; and
2. the specific expectation of benefits arising from such performance.

> [A] party estimates the desirability of the result and the probability of its achievement. And these are based, in turn, on his experience, experience which includes not only similar transactions or interactions in which he has been directly involved ...[5]

Only with these necessary expectations in mind will the offeree communicate an acceptance to the offeror. Without an expectation or assurance of the perhaps strong likelihood that the offeror will perform its promise, the offeree will simply not accept the offer; nor will it do so without an expectation or assurance of the likelihood that it will benefit from the offeror's promise which is expected to be performed.

The modern 'offer and acceptance' rule, coupled with the essential place of expectation in the midst of the formation of contract, can be illustrated as shown in Figure 1 below. In Figure 1, IO is intention in terms of an offer; IA is intention in terms of an acceptance. E1, E2 and E3 are expectations. E1 is the offeror's expectation that gives rise to the offer. It is primarily the expectation of benefits from performance of the prospective contract, and secondarily the expectation of the offeree's performance of the prospective contract if concluded. Without E1, the making of an offer is not likely at all, neither is the making of the offer to the particular offeree. E2 refers to the offeree's general expectation of performance of the offeror's promise and specific expectation of benefits from the offeror's performance. With E2, the offeree has IA or acceptance, and then communicates the acceptance to the offeror. Supposing the requirement of consideration has been satisfied, a contract is formed upon the communication of IA to the offeror. Only with E2, or the general expectation of the offeror's performance of its promise and the specific expectation of benefits from such performance, will the offeree have the incentive to accept the offer as well as the commitment to perform its own promise in terms of the acceptance. The communication of IA and the conclusion of contract also generates E3 in the mind of the offeror, which likewise is the offeror's expectation of benefits from the offeree's performance of the concluded contract.

[4] J Marshall, *Intention in Law and Society* (New York, Funk & Wagnalls, 1968) 174.
[5] Ibid.

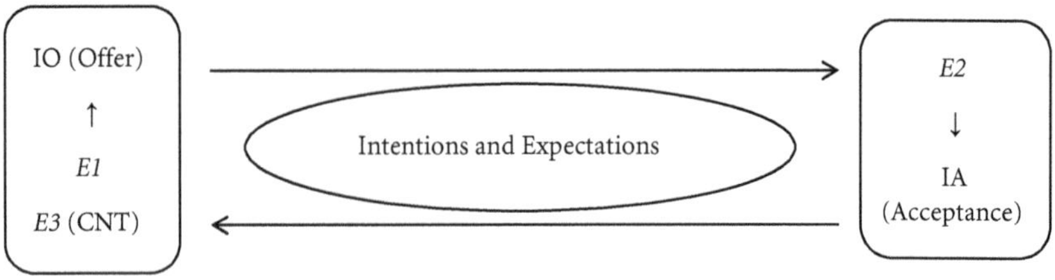

Figure 1: Offer and Acceptance and the Place of Expectation

However, among E1, E2 and E3, for the formation of a contract, E2 is most important, because E2 is the first point in the process *after* an offer is communicated, and because without E2 the offeree is unlikely to have the incentive to accept the offer, hence no intention of acceptance. Although strictly speaking E1 and E3 are not part of the contract formation process of making an offer and an acceptance—because E1 precedes the communication of the offer, and E3 arises naturally upon and after conclusion of the contract—they are both relevant to the contract in that they can be indicative of what is expected of the contract. This is particularly so for E3, because it arises upon conclusion of the contract and is likely to be grounded on the contract. E1, though somewhat speculative because it precedes the offer, is definitive of the offer. Normally for a concluded contract, E1, E2 and E3 would match one another in content.

Expectations, particularly those of the offeree, also account for the mutually binding effects of promises for a contract. An offer of course carries with it the offeror's intention to create legal relations, just as an acceptance carries with it the offeree's intention in that regard. But the offeree's willingness to bind itself by an acceptance is premised on its expectation that the offeror is highly likely to perform its promise in the future. Similarly, it is also based on the expectation that the target offeree is highly likely to be bound by a potential acceptance of its own.

Given that, in identifying the content of a contract one must look at both intentions and expectations, with weight accorded to expectations too. This is because expectations are relevant: E1 is as indispensable to initiation of an offer as E2 is to the formation of contract; and E3 on the part of the offeror is prima facie a reflection, partly at least, of the crystallisation of the intentions of the parties upon the conclusion of the contract. Therefore, to ascertain the parties' common intentions, it would not be entirely legitimate to ignore their expectations.

Considering the close relation between contractual expectations and contractual intentions in the formation of contract, it may be said, in the words of James Creel, that in this context too, 'intention is commitment with expectation'.[6]

[6] J Creel, *Intention is Commitment with Expectation—An Amendment to the Cohen-Levesque Theory of Intention* (Saarbrücken, VDM Publishing, 2007). See also J Creel, C Menzer and T Ioerger, 'Intention Is Commitment with Expectation' in DC Wilson and GCJ Sutcliffe eds, *Proceedings of the*

Although Creel put forward this proposition in the context of artificial intelligence, the proposition itself is still useful for understanding human intentions in the context of contract. This is, firstly, because discussion of artificial intelligence invariably is based partly on the understanding of the cognitive and mental processes of human beings. Secondly, it is also because, consistent with the first reason, Creel and others in that field of research wanted to define intention, for their own purposes though, in terms of beliefs, desires and choices, which are all human mental processes inherent in human conduct, including making a contract in real life. For these two reasons, Creel's discussion of intention and its relationship to expectation is relevant in a broader context. According to Creel,[7] intention is meant more strongly or weakly in different conversations and contexts, and it can be held toward actions (as in, 'I intend to go to the store') or towards states of affairs (as in, 'I intend to be rich'). In the weak sense, to intend an action means to commit oneself to the action after which some state of affairs (the justification or reason for the intended action) ensues; while to intend a state of affairs means to have commitment to an action that brings about the state of affairs. In the strong sense, to intend an action means to commit oneself to doing the action after which some state of affairs ensues, *and* to believe that one is doing the action at that moment; whereas to intend a state of affairs means to commit oneself to doing some action after which the state of affairs ensues, *and* to believe that one is doing that action right now. So, the title of Creel's thesis can be interpreted loosely as a restatement of these strong senses of the word 'intention'. The proposition that 'intention is commitment with expectation' can be interpreted as a restatement of these strong senses of the word 'intention'. It reflects the commitment coupled with the belief or expectation that the goal which is committed to is currently being brought about by the agent's action.

By Creel's definitions of 'intention', contracting certainly involves intention in the strong sense. First, the intention to create legal relations carries with it a commitment to making a contract. Secondly, in the performance of the contract, the performing party's specific intentions in the contract go with its commitment to the performance *and* with the belief that it is performing the contract at the moment. Thirdly and more importantly, prior to its performance, unless there is an anticipatory breach, both parties to the contract have a commitment to performance *and* the belief/expectation that the other party also has such a will

Twentieth International Florida Artificial Intelligence Research Society Conference (Palo Alto, California, The American Association for Artificial Intelligence Press, 2007) 50. Put forward for and in the context of artificial intelligence, the proposition stated in the titles has no direct relevance to human behaviour. However, the literal representation is very expressive of the interwoven connectedness between intention and expectation in the contracting process.

[7] Creel's e-mail correspondence (on file with me). I asked Creel to explain his thesis to me in non-technical language. He kindly e-mailed me a summary paraphrasing the core ideas in his book referred to in the preceding footnote. I owe much of this paragraph to him, and I am very grateful for his helpful summary.

or commitment or will also perform. In other words, contractual intentions are accompanied by the general expectation of the performance of contract, as well as the specific expectation of particular benefits or interests from its performance. There is no contractual intention without commitment, or without expectation of performance and of benefits. Intentions and expectations are both integral parts of the process of contracting, and both underlie and underpin the performance of contract. Therefore, in the context of contract too, intention is commitment with expectation, that is, commitment to perform and to be legally bound, with the expectation of performance and of being legally bound.

B. Expectations and the Binding Force of Contract

The relevance of expectations as illustrated and described above perhaps can explain the historical recognition by Hume, Adam Smith and Bentham[8] of the importance they attached to expectations in contractual promises. Adam Smith stated:

> Personal rights may proceed from contract. *The origin of this right is the expectation raised in him* to whom the promise was made *that the promiser will perform what he has undertaken.* Thus if one promises to give an other [sic] five pounds, this naturally creates an expectation that he will receive five pounds from him at the time promised; and here the promiser must be bound to make up to him any loss he has suffered by this expectation.[9] (emphasis added)

> *That obligation to performance which arises from contract is founded on the reasonable expectation produced by a promise*, which considerably differs from a mere declaration of intention. ... A promise is a declaration of your desire that the person for whom you promise should depend on you for the performance of it. Of consequence the promise produces an obligation, and the breach of it is an injury.[10] (emphasis added)

Similarly, John Austin stated that a promise 'binds, on account of the expectations excited in the promise. For which reason a mere pollicitation (that is, a promise made but not accepted) is not binding; for a promise not accepted could excite no expectation. So of a promise obviously made in jest. In enforcing contracts, the expectations of both parties must be looked to.',[11] By expectations in contract Austin meant 'the burden undertaken by one, and the advantage expected by the other'.[12]

[8] PS Atiyah, *The Rise and Fall of Freedom of Contract* (Oxford, Oxford University Press, 1979) 429.

[9] RL Meek, DD Raphael and PG Stein (eds), *The Glasgow Edition of the Works and Correspondence of Adam Smith*, vol 5: *Lectures on Jurisprudence* (Oxford, Oxford University Press 1978) 12; available through subscribed online library service at www.oxfordscholarlyeditions.com, published online in May 2014.

[10] Ibid 472. See also Adam Smith, at p 400: 'The foundation of contract is the reasonable expectation which the person who promises raises in the person to whom he binds himself; of which the satisfaction may be extorted by force.'

[11] J Austin, *Lectures on Jurisprudence*, 3rd edn (London, John Murray, 1869) 939–40.

[12] Ibid, 940.

Since late eighteenth century,[13] views similar to those of Adam Smith have been widely shared by some leading writers of Anglo-American contract law treatises. For example, Anson, from the second edition of his *Law of Contract* in 1882, described a promise in a contract as 'an expression of intention of one of the two parties, of expectation by the other, wherein the law requires that the intention should be carried out and the expectation fulfilled according to the terms of its expression'.[14] Anson proceeded to reiterate:

> It is not enough that the conduct of X [the promisee] was induced by the words or conduct of A [the promisor], for A cannot be made liable upon a mere statement of intention: he must have acted as though he *intended to raise an expectation* in the mind of X, and then the fact that X acted as though *influenced by his expectation* creates the liability which we term contract.[15] (emphasis added)

Likewise, from the fourth edition of his *Principles of Contracts* in 1889, Pollock described contract law as 'the endeavor of public authority ... to establish a positive sanction for the expectation of good faith which has grown up in the mutual dealings of men of average right-mindedness',[16] noting 'the modern tendency to look to "the realization of reasonable expectations" as the ground for just claims rather than an artificial equation of wills or intentions'.[17]

For Anson, every contractual promise involves an expression of common intention or expectation as to the act or forbearance to act, and the law will not allow expectations created by promises to be disappointed.[18] In subsequent editions of Anson's treatise on contract law, 'expression of common intention *or* expectation as to' has been changed into 'expression of common intention *and* of expectation as to'.[19] (emphasis added) The change seems to suggest that intention and expectation are not regarded as the same. Even if that might be somewhat elusive, and as remote as almost a century ago, there are similar and clearer points from Corbin as recently as the 1950s:

> That portion of the field of law that is classified and described as the law of contracts attempts *the realisation of reasonable expectations that have been induced by the making of a promise.* Doubtless this is not the only purpose by which men have been motivated in creating the law of contracts; but it is believed to be the main underlying purpose, and it is believed that an understanding of many of the existing rules, and a determination of their effectiveness require a lively consciousness of this underlying purpose.[20] (emphasis added)

[13] Atiyah, above n 8, 201.

[14] WR Anson, Principles of the English Law of Contract and of Agency in its Relation to Contract, 2nd edn (Oxford, Clarendon Press 1882) 4–5.

[15] Ibid 12.

[16] F Pollock, *Principles of Contracts*, 4th edn (London, Stevens & Sons, 1885) viii; also 5th edn (1889); 6th edn (1894); 7th edn (1902); 8th edn (1911); 9th edn (1921); 13th edn (1950) at 1.

[17] Pollock, above n 16, 9th edn, 1, note (a).

[18] WR Anson, Principles of the English Law of Contract and of Agency in its Relation to Contract, 6th edn (Oxford, Clarendon Press, 1891) 11.

[19] WR Anson, *Principles of the English Law of Contract* (ML Guyer (ed), Oxford, Clarendon, 1923) 18.

[20] A Corbin, *Law of Contracts*, vol 1 (St Paul, Minn, West & Co, 1950) 2.

Agreeing with Corbin, Goodhart made his point from the perspective of the historical origin of contract law:

> [T]he moral basis of the law of contract is that the promisor has by his promise created a reasonable expectation that it will be kept: it is not based on the ground that he has agreed to be bound. A failure to realise this distinction has led to confusion in some cases dealing with mistake and with impossibility of performance.
>
> ... It is of importance to remember that the law of contract found its origin in the law of tort because this emphasises the fact that *contractual liability is based on the disappointment of the promisee's reasonable expectations*. The fact that the promisor can establish that he did not intend to make the agreement on which he is being sued is therefore immaterial if he acted in such a manner as to justify the promisee's belief in the promise.[21]

Roscoe Pound also professed his preference for a principle of reasonable expectations to the will theory of contract.

> I hold no brief for the will-theory of legal transactions. On the contrary, I should argue for a theory of enforcing the realization of reasonable expectations, in order to maintain the general security, and should contend that it ... meets the requirements of the law of contracts better than the seventeenth-century doctrine of the inherent moral force of promises or the nineteenth-century doctrine of giving effect to the will. I should even contend that the Roman law of obligations is better explained on the same theory, and that nineteenth-century Romanists did violence to it when they stated it in terms of their theory of a legal transaction.[22]

However, Pound also believed that '[a]s things are in the modem world, a consistent carrying out of the will-theory would come much nearer to enforcement of realization of reasonable expectations than this hodgepodge [of various contract theories]'.[23]

Actually, there is such a widespread acceptance of a principle of reasonable expectations that it has been described as being 'traditional'.[24] As Collins has explained more recently, 'It is not the intention of the promisor but the reasonable expectation generated by the promise from the point of view of the promisee that determines the content of the contractual obligation.'[25]

The role and the relevance of the expectations of contractual parties should not just be subsumed into those of their intentions. This is because it can be seen from these observations that, in the context of contract law, intentions and

[21] A Goodhart, *English Law and the Moral Law* (London, Sweet & Maxwell, 1953) 101–02.

[22] R Pound, 'Considerations in Equity' in JH Wigmore (ed), Celebration Legal Essays: By Various Authors to Mark the Twenty-Fifth Year of Service of John H. Wigmore, As a Professor of Law in Northwestern University (Chicago, Ill, Northwestern University Press, 1919) 459. See also R Pound, Jurisprudence, vol 3 (St Paul, Minn, West & Co, 1959) 175.

[23] R Pound, 'Considerations in Equity', above n 22, 459

[24] PS Atiyah, 'Contracts, Promises and the Law of Obligations' (1978) 94 *LQR* 193, 214.

[25] H Collins, *The Law of Contract*, 4th edn (London, LexisNexis UK, 2003) 223.

expectations were not thought to be the same or identical. In the nineteenth century the expectations of contractual parties were more widely thought to be substantively relevant to the binding force of contract, and that thought persisted to some extent into the twentieth and twenty-first centuries. Contract law in and after the twentieth century gives much more weight to intentions than before, but expectations always exist and persist in contract. It is somewhat surprising that contract law has subsumed expectations into intentions: it should not be like this.

C. Expectations, Contract Liabilities and Expectation Damages

Modern contract law protects each party's expectations of the counterparty's performance of contractual obligations, primarily by an award of damages for breach of contract, and occasionally by ordering specific performance. It has been well-established since *Robinson v Harman*[26] that 'where a party sustains a loss by reason of a breach of contract, he is, so far as money can do it, to be placed in the same situation, with respect to damages, as if the contract had been performed'.[27] This is what has been known as damages for loss of expectation interest or performance interest, ie the interest of the non-breaching party if the contract had been performed as the non-breaching party had expected under the contract. This rule for the award of damages for breach of contract is invariably reaffirmed whenever an issue concerning contract damages comes before the highest appellate courts.[28] As Atiyah described:

> In modern English contract law a plaintiff is assumed to have—as a matter of course—a claim for damages for his 'loss' as a result of a breach of contract. This 'loss' is, in principle, defined by the *expectations* which the plaintiff was entitled to have as a result of the making of the contract.[29]

The orthodox view of expectation damages in modern Anglo-American contract law was not theoretically challenged until 1936, when Fuller and Perdue argued the point in their renowned article 'The Reliance Interest in Contract Damages'.[30]

[26] *Robinson v Harman* (1848) 1 Ex 850.

[27] Ibid 855 (per Parke B).

[28] To name but a few, in the House of Lords, *Ruxley Electronics & Construction Ltd v Forsyth* [1996] 1 AC 344 (HL), 355 and 365; *Attorney-General v Blake* [2001] 1 AC 268 (HL), 282; *Alfred McAlpine Construction Ltd v Panatown Ltd* [2001] 1 AC 518 (HL), 538, 562 and 580; *Farley v Skinner* [2001] UKHL 49; *Jackson v Royal Bank of Scotland plc* [2005] UKHL 3 [34]; *Golden Strait Corpn v Nippon Yusen Kubishika Kaisha (The Golden Victory)* [2007] UKHL 12 [9] and [29].

[29] Atiyah, above n 8, 143. In the same page, see also Atiyah: 'The notion that a promisee was entitled to have his expectations protected, purely and simply as such, as a result of a promise and nothing else, was not generally accepted in eighteenth-century law.' As is quoted above of Adam Smith, John Austin and Anson, the notion received significant support in the nineteenth century.

[30] LL Fuller and WR Perdue, Jr, 'The Reliance Interest in Contract Damages' (Parts 1 & 2) (1936) 46 *Yale Law Journal* 52 and 373.

In this article they saw three purposes in awarding contract damages: first, for the prevention of gain by the breaching promisor at the expense of the promisee—therefore the breaching party shall restore the benefit or gain to the promisee; secondly, for putting the non-breaching party acting in reliance on the promise back into as good a position as he was in before the promise was made; and, thirdly, for giving the promise the value of the expectation created by the promise. Correspondingly, the three kinds of interests thus protected are what Fuller and Perdue termed the restitution interest, the reliance interest and the expectation interest. Hence contract damages so awarded could be known as restitution damages, reliance damages and expectation damages.[31] Fuller and Perdue argued that the restitution interest presented the strongest case for relief, the reliance interest less and the expectation interest the least;[32] that the rationales for protection of expectation interests were not compelling;[33] and that there were ample cases showing that the contractual reliance interest 'receives a much wider (though often covert) recognition'[34] judicially, and that normatively it deserves more recognition on its own account as opposed to the orthodox protection of the expectation interest.

However, 'it has been convincingly shown that the article's conclusion is incorrect'.[35] Among the criticisms, most powerful is that of Craswell.[36] At the theoretical level, Craswell argues that Fuller and Perdue's classification of interests is not a useful starting point for their own normative analysis, because most modern scholars, including Fuller and Perdue, defend remedies only by reference to some purpose or policy they serve, but the link between interest classification and those possible theories—economic efficiency, contractualist philosophy, redistributive and/or expressive goals, distributional goals, corrective justice theory and ideological analysis—is mistaken.[37] At the level of positive law, Craswell finds that 'a large number of cases do not protect any of Fuller and Perdue's three "interests," and thus do not fit their classification'.[38] Undeniably, Fuller and Perdue's article is 'a towering classic',[39] and their analysis is of immense scholarly and academic influence, but their advocacy for reliance damages has had no discernible effect on the law, and the expectation measure continues to be the norm.[40] American courts, despite being urged by Section 90 of the *Restatement (First) of Contracts* and by Section 90 of the *Restatement (Second) of Contracts* to take a more flexible approach, have without exception used the expectation measure, almost to the

[31] Fuller and Perdue, above n 30, Part 1, 53–55.

[32] Ibid 56–57.

[33] Ibid 57–66.

[34] Fuller and Perdue, above n 30, Part 2, 418.

[35] WD Slawson, 'Why Expectation Damages for Breach of Contract Must Be the Norm: A Refutation of the Fuller and Perdue "Three Interests" Thesis' (2003) 81 *Nebraska Law Review* 839, 841.

[36] R Craswell, 'Against Fuller and Perdue' (2000) 67 *University of Chicago Law Review* 99.

[37] Ibid 107; 107–36.

[38] Ibid 137–38, with more detailed analysis at 138–53.

[39] Ibid 99.

[40] DP O'Gorman, 'Expectation Damages, the Objective Theory of Contracts, and the "Hairy Hand" Case' (2011) 99 *Kentucky Law Journal* 327, 339.

exclusion of the reliance measure and the restitution measure, for awards of damages for breaches of contract.[41] Regarding the merits of the expectation measure of damages for breach of contract, it is perceived that

> [t]he expectation measure, and only it, meets the needs of the principal institutions in a modern market economy in which contracts are used, in four critical respects. It provides a remedy for every breach. It makes contracts enforceable as soon as they are made. It compensates the injured party for what he has lost, as the institution concerned values that loss. And it provides the right incentives for decisions whether to breach. Neither of the other measures meets these institutions' needs in even one of these respects. These institutions would collapse if damages for breach of contract were limited to either of the other measures [of restitution damages and reliance damages].[42]

II. Reasonable Expectations in the Positive Law of Contract

In common law jurisdictions, protection of the reasonable expectations of the contractual parties has over the decades been enjoying judicial and/or academic support. It is observed that protection of reasonable (or legitimate) expectations is now 'part of the common rhetoric of Australian law'.[43] In respect of Anglo-Canadian contract law, the reasonable expectations approach 'is much more satisfactory than good faith as a guide to the resolution of practical problems',[44] and it has been used as a tool for contractual justice.[45] Eisenberg has noted that contract law is to a significant extent about the protection of reasonable expectations.[46] Reasonable expectation is a 'broader, open-textured standard' that can be utilised to 'expand the range of information that will describe the standard governing the contractual arrangement',[47] and protection of reasonable expectations involves a contextual approach to resolution of contract disputes,[48] which is the approach advocated by Lord Hoffmann in *Investors Compensation Scheme v West Bromwich Building Society*[49] and which has been widely accepted as an interpretative principle by the judiciary in the UK.

[41] Slawson, above n 35, 842.
[42] Ibid 862.
[43] P Finn and KJ Smith, 'The Citizen, the Government and 'Reasonable Expectations'' (1992) 66 *ALJ* 139, 140. See also J O'Donovan, *Lender Liability* (London, Sweet & Maxwell, 2005) 61, fnn 33–37, referring to a number of Australian and Canadian cases.
[44] M Bridge, 'Does Anglo-Canadian Law Need A Doctrine of Good Faith?' (1984) 9 *Canadian Business Law Journal* 385, 400.
[45] *Re Astec (BSR) plc* [1999] BCC 59.
[46] M Eisenberg, 'The Theory of Contracts' in P Benson (ed), *The Theory of Contract Law: New Essays* (Cambridge, Cambridge University Press, 2001) 246.
[47] H Collins, *Regulating Contracts* (Oxford, Oxford University Press, 1999) 146.
[48] Ibid 146–48.
[49] *Investors Compensation Scheme Ltd v West Bromwich Building Society* [1997] CLC 1243 (HL).

In the UK, due to the influence of European Union (EU) law, the reasonable expectations approach, primarily for the protection of consumers, was introduced into the Unfair Contract Terms Act 1977, whereby between contracting parties if one of them deals as consumer or on the other's written standard terms of business, as against that party, the other cannot by reference to any contract term

> claim to be entitled to render a contractual performance substantially different from that which was *reasonably expected* of him or in respect of the whole or any part of his contractual obligation, to render no performance at all, except in so far as (in any of the cases mentioned above in this subsection) the contract term satisfies the requirement of reasonableness.[50] (emphasis added)

Although as a result of the Consumer Rights Act 2015 this no longer applies to consumer contracts,[51] it still applies to standard-form contracts.

In particular, under the 1977 Act, 'the requirement of reasonableness' for a term in a consumer or standard-form contract is that 'the term shall have been a *fair and reasonable* one to be included having regard to the circumstances which were, or ought reasonably to have been, known to or in the contemplation of the parties when the contract was made'.[52] (emphasis added) Any term of a standard-form contract shall have no effect if it renders no performance, or renders performance substantially different from that which the customer reasonably expected from the contract, unless it was fair and reasonable to incorporate the term in the contract.[53]

The reasonable expectations approach was never going to be limited to consumer contracts and standard-term contracts. Steyn J (as he then was) said extra-judicially in 1991:

> The aim of any mature system of contract law must be to promote the observance of good faith and fair dealing in the conclusion and performance of contracts. The first imperative of good faith and fair dealing is that contracts ought to be upheld. But there is another theme of good faith and fair dealing: the reasonable expectations of honest men must be protected.[54]

With the benefit of hindsight, this seemed to have foreshadowed his opening statement in *First Energy (UK) Ltd v Hungarian International Bank Ltd*[55] two years

[50] Unfair Contract Terms Act 1977, s 3(2)(b).

[51] Consumer Rights Act 2015, sch 5.

[52] Unfair Contract Terms Act 1977, s 11(1). This is *not* changed by the Consumer Rights Act 2015.

[53] Unfair Contract Terms Act 1977, s 17(1)(b). Due to the Consumer Rights Act 2015, sch 5, this applies no longer to consumer contracts but still applies to customers. By UCTA 1977, s 17(2), 'customer' means a party to a standard form contract who deals on the basis of written standard terms of business of the other party to the contract, who himself deals in the course of a business.

[54] J Steyn, 'The Role of Good Faith and Fair Dealing in Contract Law: A Hair-Shirt Philosophy' [1991] *Denning Law Journal* 131, 131.

[55] *First Energy (UK) Ltd v Hungarian International Bank Ltd* [1993] 2 Lloyd's Rep 194 (CA).

later, when he was sitting as a Lord Justice in the Court of Appeal. There Steyn LJ professed:

> A theme that runs through our law of contract is that the reasonable expectations of honest men must be protected. It is not a rule or principle of law. It is the objective which has been and still is the principal moulding force of our law of contract.[56]

Similarly again in *Darlington BC v Wiltshier Northern Ltd*, 'The law of contract should give effect to the reasonable expectations of contracting parties.'[57] This is what Steyn LJ (as he was then) signalled in the twentieth century. Three years later, extra-judicially, Lord Steyn again said:

> A thread runs through our contract law that effect must be given to the reasonable expectations of honest men. Sometimes this is made explicit by judges; more often it is the implied basis of the court's decision.[58]

For Lord Steyn, the English law of contract 'draws its strength and vitality from a close adherence to the reasonable expectations of the contracting parties'.[59] Fulfilling reasonable expectations is 'an important subject for the future development of English contract law'.[60] Not surprisingly, after another three years, in the celebrated case of *Equitable Life Assurance Society v Hyman*,[61] Lord Steyn opined that implying a term into the discretion of the insurer 'is essential to give effect to the reasonable expectations of the parties'.[62] That could be seen as a preface to what he said extra-judicially two years later:

> The implication of terms fulfils an important function in promoting the reasonable expectations of parties. … [C]ourts ought not to supplement a contract by an implication unless it is perfectly obvious that it is necessary to give effect to the reasonable expectations of parties. It is, however, a myth to regard such an implied term as based on an inference of the actual intention of the parties. The reasonable expectations of the parties in an objective sense are controlling: they sometimes demand that such terms be imputed to the parties.[63]

Lord Steyn is not alone in seeing reasonable expectations as underlying the law of contract. This resonated with the observation of Sir Robin Cooke (as he then was in the Court of Appeal of New Zealand, subsequently as Lord Cooke) that 'giving effect to reasonable expectations … is a prime object of the law in almost

[56] *First Energy (UK) Ltd v Hungarian International Bank Ltd* [1993] 2 Lloyd's Rep 194 (CA), 196.
[57] *Darlington BC v Wiltshier Northern Ltd* [1995] 1 WLR 68, 76; [1994] EWCA Civ 6.
[58] J Steyn, 'Contract law: Fulfilling the Reasonable Expectations of Honest Men' (1997) 113 *LQR* 433, 433.
[59] Ibid 442.
[60] Ibid 433.
[61] *Equitable Life Assurance Society v Hyman* [2000] 3 All ER 961, [2000] UKHL 39, [2002] 1 AC 408.
[62] *Equitable Life Assurance Society v Hyman* [2002] 1 AC 408, 460G–H; see also ibid 461H–462A (per Lord Cooke).
[63] J Steyn, 'The Intractable Problem of the Interpretation of Legal Texts' (2003) 25 *Sydney Law Review* 5, 11.

all fields'.[64] (emphasis added) Similarly to Lord Steyn's approach in *Equitable Life Assurance Society v Hyman*,[65] Dyson LJ also implied a term into a loan agreement to 'give effect to the reasonable expectations of the parties'.[66] More recently, to Lord Hoffmann, 'The purpose of the law of contract is to fulfil reasonable expectations and such expectations should therefore be self-fulfilling.'[67] And according to Lady Arden:

> Now, following the decision of the House of Lords in *Investors' Compensation Scheme Ltd v West Bromwich Building Society* [1998] 1 WLR 896, courts are required to interpret documents against the background of material facts. They do this in order to ascertain the meaning which a reasonable person in the position of the parties and having the knowledge of the background which they had, or ought to have had, would give to them. Thus, in the field of interpretation of contractual documents, the courts have come to recognise, if they had not already recognised, that there is another important principle, alongside certainty and party autonomy, which underlies contract law, namely the need for the court where possible to give effect to the parties' reasonable expectations. *This is properly regarded as a principle*.[68] (emphasis added)

The reasonable expectations approach is indeed used as an operational concept in contract law. That is to say, in resolving a contract dispute, judges often try to ascertain the claimant's reasonable expectations and will take them into account when making a decision. One example is that damages for breach of contract will only compensate losses that were reasonably contemplated or expected by the parties when they made the contract. The other example is the rules of estoppel, where one party, which has induced the other party to reasonably expect benefits or interests that will accrue under the contract in question, cannot act contrary to its expectations-inducing conduct to frustrate those reasonable expectations.

III. Reasonable Expectations in Contract Law: Just a Slogan?

Contract law academics on the whole recognise, to varying degrees, the importance of the notion of the reasonable expectations of contractual parties.[69]

[64] R Cooke, 'Book Review' (1992) 108 *LQR* 334, 336.

[65] *Equitable Life Assurance Society v Hyman* [2000] 3 All ER 961, [2000] UKHL 39, [2002] 1 AC 408.

[66] *Nash v Paragon Finance Plc* [2001] EWCA Civ 1466 [36].

[67] Lord Hoffmann, '*The Achilleas*: Custom and Practice or Foreseeability?' (2010) 14 *Edinburgh Law Review* 47, 59.

[68] Lady Justice Arden, 'Coming to Terms with Good Faith' (2013) 30 *Journal of Contract Law* 199, 211–12.

[69] JH Baker, 'From Sanctity of Contract to Reasonable Expectation?' (1979) 32 *Current Legal Problems* 17, 22; J Adams and R Brownsword, *Key Issues in Contract* (London, Butterworths, 1995) 153–54. See also J Swan and B Ritter, 'Contracts and the Protection of Reasonable Expectations' in B Reiter and

However, there are also overall doubts about this notion, notably from Catherine Mitchell[70] and from Stephen Smith.[71] Mitchell argues that the notion is not always used consistently, because it has different justificatory bases, such as the institutional basis in contract law, the empirical basis in transactional experience and the normative or moral basis in considerations of fairness; and these different bases are found to have led to different understandings of reasonable expectations and have yielded different approaches and answers to what the contractual parties' reasonable expectations are. It has been argued most vividly that 'the principle [of reasonable expectations] provides a signpost that points down the right road, but it does not provide a map to the end'.[72] Using this analogy, clearly a legal principle is like a signpost, while something in the nature of a legal doctrine is like a map.

But in line with this analogy, a fundamental query could arise: why should a signpost also have the function of a map? A signpost and a map, though both used for navigational purposes, each clearly have different functions and different ways of working. Similarly, using the same analogy, can it be said to be desirable to expect a legal principle to work like a legal doctrine, even if it could so work? This brings to the fore one of the ever-present jurisprudential topics, ie the difference between legal principles and legal doctrines or rules. Principles 'are intended only as general guides for the conduct of courts and are not intended to express that universality of application to particular cases'.[73] On the other hand:

> Doctrines are sets of explicit rules of decision—the outcomes of accommodation among competing principles. Conflicts among doctrines are imperfections yet to be worked out as the operational rules of the legal system evolve. ... A principle is a generalization so broad that it does not express all the qualifications and limitations that must be expressed in an accurate statement of a rule, or a set of rules of decision that constitute at least the framework, though not the full body, of a doctrine. The qualifications and limitations arise because of the collision of underlying principles.[74]

Protection of a contractual party's reasonable expectations is a legal principle. As a principle, in itself it works broadly, and not as neatly as a doctrine. It is not to be lamented that the principle of reasonable expectations is too broad or elusive to be as practically useful as a rule. As a principle, this in itself is what it is like, or even should be like. Even if it were to be characterised as a rule,

> words like 'reasonable,' 'negligent,' 'unjust,' and 'significant' often just perform this function [of allowing a provision to operate logically as a rule and substantially as a principle].

J Swan (eds), *Studies in Contract Law* (Toronto, Butterworths, 1980) 6; WD Slawson, *Binding Promises* (Princeton, NJ, Princeton University Press, 1996) 52; BH Kuklin, 'The Plausibility of Legally Protecting Reasonable Expectations' (1997) 32 *Valparaiso Law Review* 19.

[70] Mitchell, above n 3.

[71] Smith, above n 3.

[72] Kuklin, above n 69, 33.

[73] *Restatement of Restitution* 11 (1937) (Ch 1, 'Introductory Matters', Topic 1, 'Underlying Principles', Introductory Note), as cited in R Keeton, 'Reasonable Expectations in the Second Decade' (1976) 12 *Forum* 275, 277.

[74] Keeton, above n 73, 277.

> Each of these terms makes the application of the rule which contains it depend to some extent upon principles or policies lying beyond the rule, and in this way makes that rule itself more like a principle.[75]

It has been argued[76] that *Director General of Fair Trading v First National Bank*[77] exhibited a conflict between the empirically-based approach to reasonable expectations in the House of Lords, and the normative approach in the Court of Appeal. One of the issues was whether a consumer loan contract term was unfair that allowed the creditor bank to continue to charge interest at the contract rate on a loan after a court judgment was obtained against a defaulting debtor. Under regulation 4(1) of the Unfair Terms in Consumer Contracts Regulations (SI 1994/3159), 'unfair term' means any term that, contrary to the requirement of good faith, causes a significant imbalance in the parties' rights and obligations under the contract to the detriment of the consumer. Although the Court of Appeal found the contract term in question failed the test of good faith, and hence was unfair, and the House of Lords did not find it to fail the good faith test and others, they shared a key enquiry, that is, whether the arguably unfair term in question was brought to the attention of the consumer. In the Court of Appeal, Gibson LJ opined:

> We are far from convinced that a borrower would think it fair that when he is taken to court and an order for payment by instalments has been tailored to meet what he could afford and he complied with that order, he should then be told that he has to pay further sums by way of interest. The borrower's attention is not specifically drawn to the point by the Bank at or before the conclusion of the contract nor at any later time prior to the making of the order nor in the order itself and the evidence shows that it comes as a disagreeable surprise to the borrower to find that due compliance with the order for payment by instalments, so far from eliminating the debt to the Bank, may leave him owing substantial further sums to the Bank. ... In our view the relevant term in that respect does create unfair surprise and so does not satisfy the test of good faith, it does cause a significant imbalance in the rights and obligations of the parties by allowing the Bank to obtain interest after judgment in circumstances when it would not obtain interest under the 1984 Act and the 1991 Order and no specific benefit to compensate the borrower is provided, and it operates to the detriment of that consumer who has to pay the interest.[78]

In the opinion set out above, Gibson LJ considered *a* borrower's empirical reasonable expectations regarding payment obligations under the contract term. As the Court of Appeal saw it, ordinarily a borrower would reasonably expect to make no further payment of interest after the judgment. Though the contract term in question was not in line with such an expectation, it was just found that the consumer in the instant case was not specifically reminded of the effects of the term at issue, and therefore it failed the good faith test for being unfair.

[75] R Dworkin, 'The Mode of Rules' (1967) 35 *University of Chicago Law Review* 14, 28.
[76] Mitchell, above n 3, 658.
[77] *Director General of Fair Trading v First National Bank* [2000] EWCA Civ 27, [2001] UKHL 52.
[78] *Director General of Fair Trading v First National Bank* [2000] EWCA Civ 27 [34], [35].

In the House of Lords, delivering the lead judgment, Lord Bingham said:

> It is readily understandable that a borrower may be disagreeably surprised if he finds that his contractual interest obligation continues to mount despite his duly paying the instalments ordered by the court, but it appears that the bank seeks to prevent that surprise by sending what is described in the evidence as a standard form of letter:
>
> > 'You need only pay the amount ordered by the Court under the terms of the judgment but you should be aware that under the terms of the agreement interest continues to accrue on your account.
> >
> > It is therefore in your interest to increase the instalment paid as soon as possible otherwise a much greater balance than the judgment debt may quickly build up.'
>
> On balance, I do not consider that the term can properly be said to cause a significant imbalance in the parties' rights and obligations under the contract to the detriment of the consumer in a manner or to an extent which is contrary to the requirement of good faith.[79]

Similarly, the Law Lords also considered a borrower's empirical reasonable expectations about the surprise term in the contract. As Lord Bingham saw it, ordinarily a borrower would also reasonably expect no interest payment obligation after judgment. The contract term in question was not in line with such expectation. Nevertheless, it was found that the term had been brought to the attention of the consumer in the instant case. The letter reminder conformed to the openness inherent in the requirement of good faith, openness which 'requires that the terms should be expressed fully, clearly and legibly, containing no concealed pitfalls or traps'.[80] The payment obligation 'is very clearly and unambiguously expressed in the conditions of contract'.[81] It was for this reason, among others, that the contract term did not fail the good faith test for unfair terms.

Clearly, in both the Court of Appeal and the House of Lords, the interpretation of the consumer borrower's reasonable expectations was the same: it was thought that ordinarily and empirically a borrower would not expect continuing interest payment obligations after a court judgment. It was a fact prima facie that the term in question was not aligned with such an expectation. To the learned judges, however, this did not in itself mean that the term was unfair: a term contravening reasonable expectations is not necessarily unfair, particularly if it is brought to the attention of the consumer. This is where the two courts diverged in their findings of fact. The Court of Appeal found that the term was *not* brought to the attention of the consumer, therefore it was *not* in good faith, and hence it was, among other reasons, an unfair term. In contrast, the House of Lord found that the term was actually called to the consumer's attention, hence it was not contrary to good faith, and therefore, among other reasons, it was not an unfair term. Also, since a

[79] *Director General of Fair Trading v First National Bank* [2001] UKHL 52 [20].
[80] Ibid [17] (per Lord Bingham).
[81] Ibid.

contract term contravening reasonable expectations is not necessarily unfair, there is no inherent drawback of getting '[trapped] in a circle'[82] when one maintains that fairness requires that reasonable expectations should be protected, and that there is always a reasonable expectation of fair treatment.

The foregoing discussion does not reduce the need to consider the inevitable question, 'What is "reasonable expectation"?', nor how it should or could be ascertained. Nevertheless, like many thorny questions in law, it is perhaps more practically useful to say what it is not, rather than what it is. Thus, 'reasonable expectation' is not the same as 'rational expectation', which leads on to the difference between a 'reasonable person' and a 'rational person'. Because reasonable expectations are nothing more than the expectations of a reasonable person, we can approach these queries by clarifying the meaning of a 'reasonable person'[83] and distinguishing it from that of a 'rational person'. Although it is argued that reasonable expectations may have institutional, moral and empirical bases,[84] or there are normative/moral, rational/empirical and semantic approaches thereto,[85] all claims to reasonable expectations on whichever basis or by whichever approach are intended ultimately to enhance one's own interest. This is exactly what a rational person seeks to do. The term 'rational person'

> applies to a single, unified agent (either an individual or corporate person) with the powers of judgment and deliberation in seeking ends and interests peculiarly its own. The rational applies to how these ends and interests are adopted and affirmed, as well as to how they are given priority.[86]

In contrast, according to Rawls, the concept of the 'reasonable person' embodies an idea of 'fair terms of interaction'.[87] The fairness element and the interaction element mean that reasonable expectations are not to be thought of as arbitrary expectations disregarding the interests of other parties with whom the reasonable person interacts. This is also how Rawls distinguished a reasonable person from a rational person. As Rawls put it,

> reasonable persons [are moved by a desire for] a social world in which they, as free and equal, can cooperate with others on terms all can accept. They insist that reciprocity should hold within that world so that each benefits along with others.[88]

Given the difference between 'reasonable person' and 'rational person', a claimant insisting solely on its own expectations, without regard to those of the other

[82] Mitchell, above n 3, 660.

[83] C Alvisi, 'The Reasonable Consumer under European and Italian Regulations on Unfair Business-to-Consumer Commercial Practices' in G Bongiovanni et al (eds), *Reasonableness and Law* (New York, Springer, 2009) 285.

[84] Mitchell, above n 3.

[85] Smith, above n 3.

[86] J Rawls, *Political Liberalism* (New York, Columbia University Press, 1993) 50.

[87] Ibid: '[R]reasonableness takes agents to the world of the others, where they become equals that are ready to propose or accept fair terms of interaction.'

[88] Ibid.

party, is basing its claim not on reasonable expectations but rather on rational expectations. Unaware of this distinction, one might readily take rational or purely self-interested expectations as 'reasonable' ones to argue against the principle of reasonable expectations. Reasonable expectations are not the expectations of a rational person, nor are they the expectations of the typical or the average person.[89] In a consumer context at least, for the purpose of reasonable expectations,

> [r]easonableness requires by definition an understanding of the realities of life, that is an adequate awareness of the real world arrived at by daily contact with real-life situations, and by also taking into account the individual circumstances (problems, vulnerabilities, and so on) of the person concerned.
>
> Reasonableness accordingly specifies a higher standard than that of what the market practice or trade usage is, for it must also take into account new, unusual, and marginal situations.[90]

It is noteworthy that Lord Sumption, in the UK Supreme Court, made a distinction between rationality and reasonableness:

> Rationality is not the same as reasonableness. Reasonableness is an external, objective standard applied to the outcome of a person's thoughts or intentions. … A test of rationality, by comparison, applies a minimum objective standard to the relevant person's mental processes. It imports a requirement of good faith, a requirement that there should be some logical connection between the evidence and the ostensible reasons for the decision, and (which will usually amount to the same thing) an absence of arbitrariness, of capriciousness or of reasoning so outrageous in its defiance of logic as to be perverse.[91]

However, for a number of reasons, this distinction is not really relevant to the general difference between 'reasonable expectations' and 'rational expectations'. First, the distinction made by Lord Sumption is specifically in the context of decision-making in regard to the exercise of discretion; it is not of a generality that can be applicable to expectations, and expectation is clearly very different from decision-making. Secondly, Lord Sumption's opinion is obiter,[92] so that it cannot be relied on too broadly. Thirdly, given the understanding by Rawls that rationality implies the maximisation of self-interest, it might be difficult to agree with Lord Sumption's idea that rationality imports a requirement of good faith, because rationality in terms of maximisation of self-interest is likely to involve bad faith, and often does involve it. Meanwhile, it is not difficult to see why Lord Sumption related rationality to good faith: this is because, as has just been pointed out, his Lordship's discussion of rationality and of its difference from reasonableness is in the context

[89] A Ripstein, 'Reasonable Persons in Private Law' in Bongiovanni et al (eds), above n 83, 255.
[90] Alvisi, above n 83, 292.
[91] *Hayes v Willoughby* [2013] UKSC 17 [14].
[92] *Braganza v BP Shipping Ltd* [2015] UKSC 17 [23] (per Lady Hale).

of decision-making in regard to the exercise of discretion, which by common law[93] is subject to good faith, hence the opinion that rationality (in decision-making or the exercise of discretion) requires good faith. Fourthly, it might not be so easy to agree that reasonableness applies to the outcome while rationality applies to the process. It is certain that rationality applies not only to process but also to outcome. Irrationality could be referred to as *Wednesbury* unreasonableness,[94] but the *Wednesbury* reasonableness test has two limbs, one of which focuses on the decision-making process and the other on its outcome.[95] Therefore irrationality or rationality applies to both process and outcome—this is also the majority opinion in *Braganza v BP Shipping Ltd*[96]—rather than to process only. Now that both reasonableness and rationality apply to both the process and the outcome of a person's thoughts or intentions, any perception of there being a distinction between them would perhaps be better viewed in the light suggested by Rawls.

Last but not least important, although there is no attempt here to revive the '(reasonable) expectations theory' of contract as proposed by Adam Smith, Anson and Pollock (see section I.B. above), objections[97] to that theory must be addressed, because they might also be employed for lessoning or diluting the relevance of expectations to contract. One objection is that raising an expectation is neither necessary nor sufficient for the existence of a contract. Certainly it is not sufficient. However, it has been pointed out that an offeree's expectation (ie E2—see section I.A. above), which arises from the offer communicated to him, is a necessary step towards the formation of contract—necessary in that without it, the offeree is unlikely to have any incentive to accept the offer for its own benefit. A second objection is that we do not ordinarily expect the law to make provisions for disappointment, which are rife in life, to be compensated.

> [H]ow are we to explain the decision of the House of Lords in *Addis v Gramophone Co Ltd*,[98] the effect of which in most cases is to deny compensation for the 'disappointment of mind' caused by breach of contract?[99]

This was a valid argument, but the law has changed in this regard, so that contract law now does occasionally support claims for compensation for such disappointment, albeit there is no actual financial loss involved. This was so in

[93] *Abu Dhabi National Tanker Co Ltd v Product Star Shipping Ltd ('The Product Star')* [1993] 1 Lloyd's Rep 397 (CA); *Nash v Paragon Finance Plc* [2001] EWCA Civ 1466.

[94] *Council of Civil Service Unions v Minister for the Civil Service* [1985] AC 374 (HL), 410 (per Lord Diplock); [1983] UKHL 6.

[95] *Braganza v BP Shipping Ltd* [2015] UKSC 17 [24] (per Lady Hale); Associated Provincial Pictures Houses Ltd v Wednesbury Corporation [1948] 1 KB 223, 233–34 (per Lord Green MR).

[96] *Braganza v BP Shipping Ltd* [2015] UKSC 17 [30] (per Lady Arden, agreed by Lord Kerr and Lord Hodge).

[97] B Coote, 'The Essence of Contract: Part I' (1988) 9 *Journal of Contract Law* 91, 104. But the objection that the expectations theory has circularity is not to be addressed here, because here is no attempted revival of that theory.

[98] *Addis v Gramophone Co Ltd* [1909] AC 488 (CA); *Hamlin v The Great Northern Railway Co* (1856) 1 H & N 408 (ExchD), 410–11; 156 ER 1261, 1262 (per Pollock CB).

[99] Coote, above n 97,105.

the House of Lords too, for example in *Ruxley Electronics & Construction Ltd v Forsyth*,[100] in which compensation was awarded for loss of amenity or for 'disappointed expectations', as referred to by Lord Lloyd. Similarly in *Farley v Skinner*[101] in the House of Lords. Still another potential objection is that expectations are not relevant because they are not definitive of contracts. Indeed, but, as is observed above, although expectations are merely reflective (but not definitive) of the content of promise and intention, they are the immediate source of the mutually binding force of a contract. That is why courts have generally treated expectations as the foundation of *liabilities* for breach of contract;[102] hence what is known as 'expectation damages' in contract law.

IV. Reasonable Expectations and Contract Interpretation

A. Expectations and the Contextual Approach

Since PREC concerns the interpretation of insurance contracts, it is necessary to refer to the current approach to interpretation of English contract law. The current approach was famously restated by Lord Hoffmann in *Investor Compensation Scheme v West Bromwich Building Society*:[103]

> I think I should preface my explanation of my reasons with some general remarks about the principles by which contractual documents are nowadays construed. I do not think that the fundamental change which has overtaken this branch of the law, particularly as a result of the speeches of Lord Wilberforce in *Prenn v Simmonds* [1971] 1 WLR 1381, 1384–1386 and *Reardon Smith Line Ltd v Yngvar Hansen-Tangen* [1976] 1 WLR 989, is always sufficiently appreciated. The result has been, subject to one important exception, to assimilate the way in which such documents are interpreted by judges to the common sense principles by which any serious utterance would be interpreted in ordinary life. Almost all the old intellectual baggage of 'legal' interpretation has been discarded. The principles may be summarised as follows:
>
> (1) Interpretation is the ascertainment of the meaning which the document would convey to a reasonable person having all the background knowledge which would reasonably have been available to the parties in the situation in which they were at the time of the contract.
> (2) The background was famously referred to by Lord Wilberforce as the 'matrix of fact,' but this phrase is, if anything, an understated description of what the background

[100] *Ruxley Electronics & Construction Ltd v Forsyth* [1995] UKHL 8.
[101] *Farley v Skinner* [2001] UKHL 49.
[102] Atiyah, above n 8, 201.
[103] *Investors Compensation Scheme Ltd v West Bromwich Building Society* [1997] CLC 1243 (HL), 1257–58.

may include. Subject to the requirement that it should have been reasonably available to the parties and to the exception to be mentioned next, it includes absolutely anything which would have affected the way in which the language of the document would have been understood by a reasonable man.

(3) The law excludes from the admissible background the previous negotiations of the parties and their declarations of subjective intent. They are admissible only in an action for rectification. The law makes this distinction for reasons of practical policy and, in this respect only, legal interpretation differs from the way we would interpret utterances in ordinary life. The boundaries of this exception are in some respects unclear. But this is not the occasion on which to explore them.

(4) The meaning which a document (or any other utterance) would convey to a reasonable man is not the same thing as the meaning of its words. The meaning of words is a matter of dictionaries and grammars; the meaning of the document is what the parties using those words against the relevant background would reasonably have been understood to mean. The background may not merely enable the reasonable man to choose between the possible meanings of words which are ambiguous but even (as occasionally happens in ordinary life) to conclude that the parties must, for whatever reason, have used the wrong words or syntax. (see *Mannai Investments Co Ltd v Eagle Star Life Assurance Co Ltd* [1997] 2 WLR 945).

(5) The 'rule' that words should be given their 'natural and ordinary meaning' reflects the common sense proposition that we do not easily accept that people have made linguistic mistakes, particularly in formal documents. On the other hand, if one would nevertheless conclude from the background that something must have gone wrong with the language, the law does not require judges to attribute to the parties an intention which they plainly could not have had. Lord Diplock made this point more vigorously when he said in *The Antaios Compania Neviera SA v Salen Rederierna AB* [1985] 1 AC 191, 201: '... if detailed semantic and syntactical analysis of words in a commercial contract is going to lead to a conclusion that flouts business common sense, it must be made to yield to business common sense.'

In relation to the statement that the admissible background included 'absolutely anything which would have affected the way in which the language of the document would have been understood by a reasonable man', Lord Hoffmann stressed that he 'meant anything which a reasonable man would have regarded as *relevant*'.[104] It is understood that 'this contextual method is variously described as involving reference to the "background" or "factual matrix" of the contract, or the "reasonable expectations of the parties", or the "commercial purposes" of the agreement or "business common sense"'.[105]

Contextualism is an approach to finding the intention of contractual parties. Although Lord Hoffmann did not expressly or directly refer to the reasonable expectations of the parties, he constantly referred to a reasonable person's knowledge and understanding of the transaction in question as the context for interpretation of contracts. Particularly in the second principle, he stated: 'anything'

[104] *Bank of Credit and Commerce International v Ali* [2001] UKHL 8 [39].

[105] C Mitchell, *Interpretation of Contracts* (London, Routledge Cavendish, 2007) 1.

relevant that would have affected a reasonable person's understanding of the language of the document. Lord Hoffmann also reiterated that 'there is no conceptual limit to what can be regarded as background. It is not, for example, confined to the factual background but can include … proved common assumptions which were in fact quite mistaken'.[106] Since even factually mistaken assumptions can be taken as part of the background or context for the interpretation of contracts, certainly reasonable expectations can too.

That being said, it does not follow that reasonable expectations are to define the meaning or content of contractual documents. This is because there is a difference between the background to a meaning and the meaning itself. Under Lord Hoffmann's approach, the reasonable expectations of the parties can be part of the context of or the background for interpretation. Though reasonable expectations are not definitive of the meaning of contractual documents, they are to be taken into consideration in interpreting contractual terms, and hence they may influence to varying degrees the interpretation thereof. At the minimum, reasonable expectations 'may assist in working out the intention of the parties in relation to the legal effect of the contract'.[107]

B. Expectations, Intention, Contract Purpose

Intentions and Expectations in Behavioural Science

Before discussing the relationship between intentions and expectations in the context of interpretation of contracts, it is helpful at first to explore the relationship in a non-legal or general context. In its ordinary meaning, intention 'relates to our having formulated conscious plans to perform or not perform some specified future behaviour'.[108] Intention is a chosen persistent goal, persistent in that it 'involves an agent's internal commitment to a course of events over time'.[109] Intention 'involves making a behavioral commitment to perform (or not perform) an action'.[110] Intentions 'are indications of how hard people are willing to try, of how much of an effort they are planning to exert, in order to perform the behavior'.[111]

[106] *Bank of Credit and Commerce International v Ali* [2001] UKHL 8 [39].

[107] JW Carter, *The Construction of Commercial Contracts* (Oxford, Hart Publishing, 2013) [6.27], 'the assumed expectations of the parties, gleaned from the economic and social circumstances current at the time of the contract, and enshrined in the contract institution itself, are often extremely important to the factual elements when applying contract doctrine'.

[108] PR Warshaw and FD Davis, 'Disentangling Behavioral Intentions and Behavioral Expectations' (1985) 21 *Journal of Experimental Social Psychology* 213, 214.

[109] PR Cohen and HJ Levesque, 'Intention is Choice with Commitment' (1990) 42 *Artificial Intelligence* 213, 220.

[110] Warshaw and Davis, above n 108, 215.

[111] I Ajzen, 'The Theory of Planned Behavior' (1991) 50 *Organizational Behavior and Human Decision Processes* 179, 181: 'As a general rule, the stronger the intention to engage in a behavior, the more likely should be its performance.'

Philosophers often connect intention with, or even reduce it to, some combination of belief and desire.[112] However, rational behaviour cannot be analysed merely in terms of beliefs and desires; it must involve a third mental state, ie intention.[113] Intention is related to beliefs and desires, but is not reducible thereto. It is significantly different from belief. The content of an intention is typically an action, and it is closely connected with other attitudes as well as with time and action, whereas the content of a belief is a proposition and it can be analysed in isolation.[114] Intention is also different from desire. To a social perceiver or people generally, the content of a desire might be an unlikely outcome or an action that might be indirectly affected by the desire. Intention is typically the output of reasoning, whereas desire is typically the input to reasoning; and an intention carries much more commitment than a desire.[115] From the perspective of a decision-maker, an intended action has higher perceived performability than does a desired action; intention implies a commitment, whereas desire does not; desire is usually defined from a longer-term perspective than is intention.[116]

In behavioural sciences, expectation 'is one's estimated likelihood of performing the action, whether or not a commitment has been made'.[117] Forming an expectation is a dynamic process, because the behaviours of subjects or agents could be influenced over and above their present intention by a variety of factors, such as anticipated changes in intention, non-cognitive habits, ability limitations, and possible environmental facilitators and/or constraints.[118] For example,[119] a woman presently intending to buy a house within a year may realise there is some chance she will soon be transferred to another city to work; in this case she imagines she would wait at least another year before buying; her expectation judgement could thus reflect the possible change in intention that she foresees.

Intentions and Expectations in Contract Law

Intentions and expectations are two attitudes that contribute to the parties' contractual behaviour. As a topic in law, intention features most prominently in dealing with legal liabilities, for example in criminal law, where legal liability and penal consequences are premised on criminal intent or intention. To a slightly lesser

[112] M Bratman, *Intentions, Plans and Practical Reason* (Cambridge, MA, Harvard University Press, 1987), 10.

[113] PR Cohen and HJ Levesque, 'Persistent, Intention, and Commitment', in PR Cohen et al (eds), *Intentions in Communication* (Cambridge, MA, MIT Press, 1990) 36.

[114] Cohen and Levesque, above n 109, 216–17.

[115] BF Malle and J Knotbe, 'The Distinction between Desire and Intention: A Folk Conception Analysis' in BF Malle et al (eds), *Intention and Intentionality* (Cambridge, MA, MIT Press, 2001) 51, 52, 56, 57.

[116] M Perugini and RP Bagozzi, 'The Distinction between Desires and Intentions' (2004) *European Journal of Social Psychology* 69, 72, 80–81.

[117] Warshaw and Davis, above n 108, 215.

[118] Ibid.

[119] Ibid.

extent it also features in tort law. But in regard to liabilities it features much less in contract law, where the liability for breach is generally not premised on an intention to breach the contract. However, it features substantially in interpretation of contracts, because the task of interpreting and construing a contract term is to find out the parties' intentions in relation, at least, to the contract term in question.

It seems that in a contract setting, the behavioural-science definition of intention still applies, in that an intention is both a choice and a commitment. In particular, what is known as 'interlocking commitment' is consistent with the mutually binding force of contract. Interlocking commitments are obtained when each of two agents 'will keep his intention at least as long as the other keeps it'.[120] There are two kinds of intentions or 'interlocking commitments' that feature in contract law. The first is general and overarching: it is what is usually known as 'the intention to create legal relations' as a premise for conclusion of a valid contract. Such an intention is the overarching and general commitment to be willing to be bound by the agreement between the parties. The second kind is particular: it is contractual parties' intentions manifested in specific wordings and parts of the contract. Ascertainment of the particular intention is the object of interpretation of a contract term or clause. It is understood:

> The intention of a party to a contract can also be described in terms of his expectations concerning what the other parties to the contract will do, that is, his drives, his estimation of the desirability of accomplishing certain results, and the probability that the other parties will do what he wished them to do. In a contract there is a further factor not present in the case of a testament. For a contracting party also intends to perform some act himself (except perhaps in the case of a unilateral contract). His expectations regarding his own intended acts can be analysed similarly to the analysis of his expectations of the other contracting parties. He expects of himself certain behavior as the price of achieving some purpose—receiving a purchase price, a salary, a house, a car, insurance, an education, a spouse, etc.[121]

However, understanding of expectations in the contract setting must be different to some extent from that in behavioural science. This is, first, because contract as a socio-economic behaviour is mostly mutual by nature, whereas generally the behavioural-science definition of expectations does not take into account such mutuality. Secondly, that is also because in a contract, each party's expectation is not the likelihood of a party's *own* 'performing the action', but instead is a party's *interest* in performance of the contract (ie 'performing the action') *by the counterparty.* Supposing the intention of the woman in the example above is embodied in a contract of purchase of a house, her contractual expectation is specifically the title to the house, rather than whether or when to buy the house. That being said, contractual expectation can also be understood in a general sense, which is one party's expectation of *performance* of the contract *by the counterparty.*

[120] Cohen and Levesque, above n 109, 256.
[121] Marshall, above n 4, 173.

This is not difficult to fathom, but a dispute over contract often focuses on the meaning of a particular contract clause that embodies the particular intentions of the parties.

In the contract setting, intention and expectation are interrelated. The interrelation can be seen at two levels, one general and one particular. At the general level, the intention to create legal relations is necessary for conclusion of a contract, and it corresponds to the general expectation of contract performance. It follows from such an intention that the intending party chooses to be bound by the contract and by contract law. Thus bound, the intending party is expected by the counterparty not only to perform its contractual obligations, but also to be held liable, as required by law, if there is a breach of obligations. This is the general expectation following from the intention to create legal relations, and the expectation is often mutual. In particular, expectations of specific transactional interests give rise to intention, that is the 'behavioral commitment to perform (or not perform) an action'[122]—in the contract setting it is a commitment to contract, namely, 'the intention to create legal relations' and the commitment to perform the contract. That intention, moreover, would better be put into writing or recorded in a written document, which as a manifestation and record of the general and the specific contractual intentions would in turn reinforce the expectations. What have given rise to expectations in a prospective transaction are usually social-economic needs,[123] which need not concern us here, however, because they are not taken into account in the interpretation of contracts.

It can be gathered from the above that a prospective contractual party's social-economic needs or motivations give rise to expectations of interests in contractual transactions, that expectations lead to contractual intentions, which are manifested as written contract documents, and that contract documents reinforce contractual expectations. This can be illustrated with a simplified hypothetical contract for the sale of goods. For whatever lawful needs, Buyer is seriously interested in acquiring an eighteenth-century Chinese porcelain vase. Given its affordability and likely availability, Buyer expects to get such a vase in due course. Seller, an antique dealer, is approached by Buyer. Both have the intention to create legal relations for such a deal. Buyer has the intention to buy one vase of the given type from Seller at no more than £3,000. Seller has the intention to get no less than £2,500 by selling such a vase. After negotiation, a contract is duly concluded between them, the core clause of which is that 'Within 5 working days of both parties' signing the contract, Buyer shall pay £2,800 lump sum to Seller upon delivery of the said vase'. (Surely there must be other clauses in the contract, but they are irrelevant to our consideration here.) The contract undoubtedly reinforces both Buyer's and Seller's respective expectations in the transaction. If no dispute arises, their

[122] Warshaw and Davis, above n 108, 215.
[123] Marshall, above n 4, 174.

contractual expectations may duly be met. Nevertheless, not surprisingly, disputes do sometimes arise, and the parties' expectations will be frustrated, at least initially, or before the dispute can be fully resolved. If the dispute concerns interpretation of the contract, arbitrators and judges will seek to ascertain the intentions of the contractual parties.

Ascertainment of the intentions of the parties is the nexus of contract interpretation. This had been so prior to Lord Hoffmann's above-quoted statement (see section IV.A.). As Lord Diplock stated:

> The object sought to be achieved in construing any commercial contract is to ascertain what were the mutual intentions of the parties as to the legal obligations each assumed by the contractual words in which they (or brokers acting on their behalf) chose to express them; or, perhaps more accurately, what each would have led the other reasonably to assume were the acts that he was promising to do or to refrain from doing by the words in which the promises on his part were expressed.[124]

Courts take an objective approach to ascertaining contractual intentions. As Lord Steyn stated about construction of a commercial instrument:

> The aim of the inquiry is not to probe the real intentions of the parties but to ascertain the contextual meaning of the relevant contractual language. The inquiry is objective: the question is what a reasonable person, circumstanced as the actual parties were, would have understood the parties to have meant by the use of specific language. The answer to that question is to be gathered from the text under consideration and its relevant contextual scene.[125]

It must be noted that the objective approach is 'based on the reasonable expectations of the promisor, or the promisee'.[126] It is the objective and reasonable expectations that ultimately count. '[P]erhaps more accurately', the object of construction of commercial contract is to ascertain 'what each would have led the other reasonably to assume were the acts that he was promising to do or to refrain from doing by the words in which the promises on his part were expressed.'[127] In other words, commercial contract interpretation seeks to find out what the promisee has been led—by the meaning of words, or more precisely the contract document—reasonably to expect. 'The meaning of words is a matter of dictionaries and grammars; the meaning of the document is what the parties using those words against the relevant background would reasonably have been understood to mean.'[128]

[124] *Pioneer Shipping Ltd v BTP Tioxide Ltd* [1982] AC 724 (HL), 736 (per Lord Diplock).

[125] *Sirius International Insurance v FAI* [2004] UKHL 54 [18].

[126] JM Perillo, 'The Origins of the Objective Theory of Contract Formation and Interpretation' (2000) 69 *Fordham Law Review* 427, 431.

[127] *Pioneer Shipping Ltd v BTP Tioxide Ltd* [1982] AC 724 (HL), 736 (per Lord Diplock).

[128] *Investors Compensation Scheme Ltd v West Bromwich Building Society* [1997] CLC 1243 (HL), 1258 (per Lord Hoffmann).

Contract Purpose, Intention and Expectations

The contextual approach is also thought of as a purposive approach, namely, an approach that gives effect to the commercial purpose of a contract. The purpose of a contract is interwoven with the parties' expectations:

> The form of a contractual transaction can be described as 'the practically compelling dialectics of the purpose' which has been 'produced out of the two factors of need and reward.' In this context intent is the expectation of realizing a desirable purpose by certain behaviour which is the price for achievement of that purpose.[129]

Hoffmann LJ, as he then was, stated in *Co-operative Wholesale Society Ltd v National Westminster Bank plc* that 'language is a very flexible instrument and, if it is capable of more than one construction, one chooses that which seems most likely to give effect to the commercial purpose of the agreement'.[130] This almost foreshadowed his Lordship's restatement of the principles, the fifth principle in particular (see section IV.A. above), of construction of commercial contracts.

Meanwhile, it is perhaps more accurate to say that it is the purpose of the contractual parties that must be given effect. Strictly speaking, contracts or agreements have no purpose because they are inanimate. But there are purposes underlying a contract or an agreement, and they are the purposes of the parties thereto. A contractual party's purpose is not essentially or fundamentally different from the party's expectations. After all, Lord Steyn stated extra-judicially, almost 20 years ago:

> Often there is no obvious or ordinary meaning of the language under consideration. There are competing interpretations to be considered. In choosing between alternatives a court should primarily be guided by the contextual scene in which the stipulation in question appears. And speaking generally commercially minded judges would regard *the commercial purpose of the contract as more important* than niceties of language. And, in the event of doubt, *the working assumption will be that a fair construction best matches the reasonable expectations of the parties.*[131] (emphasis added)

[129] Marshall, above n 4, 174.

[130] *Co-operative Wholesale Society Ltd v National Westminster Bank plc* [1995] 1 EGLR 97, 98. This is consistent with what Lord Diplock had declared in *Antaios Compania Naviera SA v Salen Rederierna AB* [1984] AC 191 (HL), 201: 'If detailed and syntactical analysis of words in a commercial contract is going to lead to a conclusion that flouts business common sense it must yield to business common sense.' This has been followed in *Rainy Sky v Kookmin Bank* [2011] UKSC 50 [25] by Lord Clarke, and was unanimously agreed in the UKSC: '[T]he exercise of construction is essentially one unitary exercise in which the court must consider the language used and ascertain what a reasonable person, that is a person who has all the background knowledge which would reasonably have been available to the parties in the situation in which they were at the time of the contract, would have understood the parties to have meant. In doing so, the court must have regard to all the relevant surrounding circumstances. If there are two possible constructions, the court is entitled to prefer the construction which is consistent with business common sense and to reject the other.'

[131] Lord Steyn, 'Contract Law: Fulfilling the Reasonable Expectations of Honest Men' [1997] 113 *LQR* 433, 441.

This has more recently been cited by Justices with approval in the UK Supreme Court.[132] For the Supreme Court, a commercially-purposive construction of business contracts is consistent with the reasonable expectations of the commercial parties. Prior to the Supreme Court, in the eyes of Lord Steyn, the commercial construction was also consistent with the intention of the parties. A couple of years after aligning commercial construction with reasonable expectations, Lord Steyn, in *Society of Lloyd's v Robinson*,[133] disapproved of Lloyd's reliance on the literalist approach to interpretation of an underwriting agreement employed by Saville J in *Napier v Kershaw*.[134] Lord Steyn favoured the commercial purpose construction, stating that

> in the process of interpreting the meaning of the language of a commercial document the court ought generally to favour a commercially sensible construction. The reason for this approach is that *a commercial construction is likely to give effect to the intention of the parties*. Words ought therefore to be interpreted in the way in which a reasonable commercial person would construe them. And the reasonable commercial person can safely be assumed to be unimpressed with technical interpretations and undue emphasis on niceties of language.[135]

Given that contractual party's expectations are relevant to contractual intentions, and that the purposive and the contextual approaches to interpretation of commercial contracts are consistent in English law with both the reasonable expectations and the intentions of parties thereto, it follows that the contextualist and intentionalist approaches to construction of commercial contracts are orientated toward protection of the reasonable expectations of the contractual parties.

V. Conclusion

Expectations in general and reasonable expectations in particular actually have a more relevant, though not controlling, place in contract law than they are thought to have. The role of expectations has long, and perhaps too long, been subsumed in contractual intentions, with the result that contemporary contract lawyers pay little attention to the role of expectations in formation of contract, or to the relevance of expectations to performance of contract in the way that some leading contract lawyers in the nineteenth century did. However, the concept of 'expectations damage', or the principle that damages for breach of contract are awardable for losses of reasonably expected benefits or interests, has remained orthodox. This is

[132] *Rainy Sky v Kookmin Bank* [2011] UKSC 50 [25] (per Lord Clarke, unanimously agreed).
[133] *Society of Lloyd's v Robinson* [1999] Lloyd's Rep IR 329 (HL), 333–34.
[134] *Napier v Kershaw* [1993] 1 All ER 385.
[135] *Society of Lloyd's v Robinson* [1999] Lloyd's Rep IR 329 (HL), 333–34.

an unusual anomaly: contemporary contract law on one hand does not recognise the role of expectations in contract formation and performance; but on the other hand it rightly continues to regard (frustration of) reasonably expected interests as the foundation of liability for breach of contract. This seems inconsistent.

This is not to say that with the role of expectations having been rediscovered, we shall over time replace contractual intentions with expectations in the interpretation of contracts. Rather, it needs to be recognised that intentions and expectations are interrelated in contract. An intention is both a choice and a commitment, and a choice of one's own, coupled with a commitment to others, inevitably creates others' expectations of fulfilment of the commitment. In particular, what is known as 'interlocking commitment' in behavioural science is consistent with the mutually binding force of contract. Interlocking commitments are obtained when each of two agents 'will keep his intention at least as long as the other keeps it'.[136] A prospective contractual party's social-economic needs or motivations give rise to expectations of interests in contractual transactions, and expectations lead to contractual intentions manifested as contract documents, which in turn reinforce contractual expectations. Ascertainment of the intentions of the parties is indeed the nexus of contract interpretation. To that, courts take an objective approach, which is 'based on the reasonable expectations of the promisor, or the promisee'.[137] It is the objective and reasonable expectations that ultimately count. What is objective and reasonable is to be established contextually. So the objective approach to interpretation of contracts leads naturally and logically to a contextual approach. However, expectations are part of the context. Contractual intentions, purposes and the contextual approach ultimately are not isolated from expectations. Since expectations are actually fairly relevant in contract law, why not reasonable expectations?

[136] Cohen and Levesque, above n 109, 256.

[137] Perillo, above n 126, 431.

4

Relating Good Faith to Reasonable Expectations

Over the past few years, there has emerged a renewed judicial interest in good faith in English contract law. Accompanying this is judicial recognition of the special relationship between good faith and reasonable expectations, such as that in 2013 by Leggat J in *Yam Seng Pte Ltd v International Trade Corporation Ltd.*[1] Speaking extra-judicially in a lecture given to the Singapore Academy of Law on 26 April 2013, Lady Arden said that she would (and actually did) 'apply the principle of giving effect to the reasonable expectations of the parties to the debate on good faith clauses'.[2] To some extent, this echoes the observation[3] that an argument before an English judge framed in terms of good faith in contract might be dismissed as abstract and vague, but one couched in terms of reasonable expectations might be more likely to find favour.

In such a context, this chapter discusses the relationship between good faith and reasonable expectation in contract law. First, it shows how good faith is relevant to reasonable expectations, arguing that protection of reasonable expectations is the aim of contract law while good faith is a means to that end. Secondly, by sketching the development of good faith in contract law in common law jurisdictions, particularly in the UK and in Canada most recently, it shows how contract-law good faith exists and operates to protect reasonable expectations. Thirdly, given that insurance contract prototypically requires good faith, it also highlights how insurance law requires good faith on the part of insurers to make sure that a policyholder's reasonable expectations will not be frustrated.

[1] *Yam Seng Pte Ltd v International Trade Corporation Ltd* [2013] EWHC 111 (QB) [145].

[2] Lady Justice Arden, 'Coming to Terms with Good Faith' (2013) 30 *Journal of Contract Law* 199, 212.

[3] S Styles, 'Good Faith: A Principled Matter' in ADM Forte (ed), *Good Faith in Contract and Property Law* (Oxford, Hart Publishing, 1999) 157, 168.

I. The Relevance of Good Faith to Reasonable Expectations

Good faith is understood to be closely connected with reasonable expectations. In the US, the language of reasonable expectations is manifest in the *Restatement (Second) of Contracts*. The first entry of the Official Comment on its Section 205—providing that 'Every contract imposes upon each party a duty of good faith and fair dealing in its performance and its enforcement.'—explains: 'Good faith performance or enforcement of a contract emphasizes faithfulness to an agreed common purpose and consistency with the justified expectations of the other party'.[4] In relation to the Uniform Commercial Code provision (ie its Article 2) on good faith in contract law, it is observed that good faith performance as used by the courts serves to 'effectuate the intentions of the parties, or protect their reasonable expectations'.[5]

Beyond the US, a similar observation in the UK is that 'there is not a world of difference between the objective requirement of good faith and the reasonable expectations of the parties',[6] that 'in essence, good faith and reasonable expectations amount to the same thing',[7] and that an argument before an English judge framed in terms of good faith in contract might be dismissed as 'abstract and vague', but one made 'on the basis of "reasonable expectations" or the "legitimate expectations of persons in that particular line of business"' is likely to receive 'a much warmer [judicial] reception.'[8] Likewise, Professor Michael Bridge has argued that Anglo-Canadian contract law 'has evolved sufficiently towards the protection of justified expectations by undermining the mystique of the written word, especially where it is located in standard forms',[9] observing that although the reasonable expectations approach 'is in danger of being obscured by the resort to an excessively diffuse standard of good faith', it 'is much more satisfactory than good faith as a guide to the resolution of practical problems'.[10] In the UK, prominent judges have, both extra-judicially and judicially, perceived the connection between good faith and reasonable expectations to be close. Steyn LJ (as he was then) saw a normative relation between good faith and reasonable expectations:

> The aim of any mature system of contract law must be to promote the observance of good faith and fair dealing in the conclusion and performance of contracts. The first

[4] ALI, *Restatement of the Law Second: Contracts* 2d, vol 2 (St Paul, Minn ALI Publishers, 1981) 100.
[5] SJ Burton, 'Good Faith Performance of a Contract within Article 2 of the Uniform Commercial Code' (1981) 67 *Iowa Law Review* 1, 3.
[6] Lord Steyn, 'Contract Law: Fulfilling the Reasonable Expectations of Honest Men' (1997) 113 *LQR* 433, 439.
[7] S Styles, 'Good Faith: A Principled Matter' in Forte (ed), above n 3, 157, 168.
[8] Ibid.
[9] M Bridge, 'Does Anglo-Canadian Law Need A Doctrine of Good Faith?' (1984) 9 *Canadian Business Law Journal* 385, 426.
[10] Ibid 400.

> imperative of good faith and fair dealing is that contracts ought to be upheld. But there is another theme of good faith and fair dealing: the reasonable expectations of honest men must be protected.[11]

For Steyn LJ, it amounted to the good faith of one party to have reasonable expectations, just as it amounted to good faith for the other party to honour those expectations. Some years later, inclined toward the reasonable expectations approach as an alternative to a principle of good faith, and aware of the entrenched objection in English law to such a principle, Lord Steyn saw the two as functionally the same. He stated:

> I have no heroic suggestion for the introduction of a general duty of good faith in our contract law. It is not necessary. As long as our courts always respect the reasonable expectations of parties our contract law can satisfactorily be left to develop in accordance with its own pragmatic tradition. … After all, there is not a world of difference between the objective requirement of good faith and the reasonable expectations of the parties.[12]

More recently, Lady Arden, arguing extra-judicially for good faith in contract law, connected good faith with reasonable expectations more closely. Having found 'giving effect to the parties' reasonable expectations' as another important principle for interpretation of contracts, Lady Arden said:

> I would apply the principle of giving effect to the reasonable expectations of the parties to the debate on good faith clauses in the following way. If the parties have agreed that contractual obligations should be performed in good faith, the court should, so far as it can, give effect to that agreement and, by doing so, to the parties' reasonable expectations.[13]

The close relationship between good faith and reasonable expectations has also been recognised judicially. In the High Court, Leggat J opined, in *Yam Seng Pte Ltd v International Trade Corporation Ltd*,[14] that 'recognising an implied duty of good faith in the performance of contracts … is consonant with the theme identified by Lord Steyn as running through our law of contract that reasonable expectations must be protected'. This was not disputed in the Court of Appeal six weeks later in *Mid Essex Hospital Services NHS Trust v Compass Group UK and Ireland Ltd*,[15] which dealt with both an express contractual duty of good faith and an arguably implied duty of good faith in the performance of the contract.

Moreover, the Court of Appeal has similarly recognised that close relationship for over a decade since *Nash v Paragon Finance Plc*.[16] This case concerned interest

[11] J Steyn, 'The Role of Good Faith and Fair Dealing in Contract Law: A Hair-Shirt Philosophy' [1991] *Denning Law Journal* 131, 131.

[12] Lord Steyn, above n 6, 439.

[13] Lady Justice Arden, 'Coming to Terms with Good Faith' (2013) 30 *Journal of Contract Law* 199, 212.

[14] *Yam Seng Pte Ltd v International Trade Corporation Ltd* [2013] EWHC 111 (QB) [145].

[15] *Mid Essex Hospital Services NHS Trust v Compass Group UK and Ireland Ltd* [2013] EWCA Civ 200. The Court of Appeal expressed 'no element of disapproval' of the judgment of Leggat J. See also Spearman J in *Bristol Groundschool Ltd v Intelligent Data Capture Ltd* [2014] EWHC 2145 (Ch) [196].

[16] *Nash v Paragon Finance Plc* [2001] EWCA Civ 1466.

rates set by a finance company under a 'variable interest clause', which gave the company discretion to change rates on notice to borrowers. One issue arising was whether that clause was subject to an implied term constraining the discretion and, if so, how. The finance company contended against such an implication, asserting that the discretion was unfettered. The lead judgment of Dyson LJ relied heavily on *Gan Insurance Co v Tai Ping Insurance Co*[17] and *Abu Dhabi National Tanker Co Ltd v Product Star Shipping Ltd ('The Product Star')*,[18] both of which affirmed a contractual obligation of good faith in exercising discretion in the performance of contract. It was opined in *The Product Star* that contractual discretion must 'be exercised honestly and in good faith'.[19] Following this, Dyson LJ said in his lead judgment in *Nash v Paragon Finance Plc*:[20]

> I would hold that there were terms to be implied in both agreements that the rates of interest would not be set dishonestly, for an improper purpose, capriciously or arbitrarily. I have no doubt that such an implied term is necessary in order to give effect to the reasonable expectations of the parties. I am equally in no doubt that such an implied term is one of which it could be said that 'it goes without saying'.

Clearly in this case the good faith term was implied out of necessity under the then effective 'officious bystander' test[21] for implication of terms into a contract.

Although English lawyers have been very reluctant to recognise a principle of good faith in contract law, '[i]f arguments of principle do not appeal as motivating factors [for recognising so], utilitarian ones must'.[22] In view of the foregoing judicial and extra-judicial observations indicative of the relationship between good faith and reasonable expectations, the utilitarian argument may be that good faith is an approach to practical protection of reasonable expectations. In other words,

17 *Gan Insurance Co v Tai Ping Insurance Co* [2001] EWCA Civ 1047. This was a reinsurance dispute. I have reservations about using this case as an authority or a leading case for finding good faith, as Arden LJ argues and Dyson LJ did, in (non-insurance) contract law. That is because, unlike in many other contracts, a principle of good faith has been well recognised and required in insurance contract law, and it has also been recognised to be binding on insurers (or reinsurers in the context of reinsurance). It does not necessarily apply to non-insurance contracts.

18 *Abu Dhabi National Tanker Co Ltd v Product Star Shipping Ltd ('The Product Star')* [1993] 1 Lloyd's Rep 397 (CA).

19 Ibid 404 (per Leggat LJ).

20 *Nash v Paragon Finance Plc* [2001] EWCA Civ 1466 [36].

21 *Shirlaw v Southern Foundries* (1926) Ltd [1939] 2 KB 206, 227 (per MacKinnon LJ). Arguably this is no longer relevant since *Attorney General of Belize v Belize Telecom Ltd* [2009] UKPC 10 [25] per Lord Hoffmann. Particularly, in *Marks and Spencer plc v BNP Paribas Securities Services Trust Company (Jersey) Ltd* [2015] UKSC 72 [24] per Lord Neuberger delivering the lead judgment: 'if one approaches the issue by reference to the officious bystander, it is "vital to formulate the question to be posed by [him] with the utmost care", to quote from Lewison, The Interpretation of Contracts 5th ed (2011), para 6.09.' That being said, it must be noted that Lord Neuberger in para. [23] has meanwhile reiterated Lord Steyn's statement in *Equitable Life Assurance Society v Hyman* [2002] 1 AC 408, 459 that a term will be implied if it is 'essential to give effect to the reasonable expectations of the parties' as sustaining the general test of necessity for implication of terms. Lord Steyn's approach is to be discussed in length in Chapter 7.

22 ADM Forte, 'Good Faith and Utmost Good Faith: Insurance and Cautionary Obligations in Scots Law' in Forte (ed), above n 3, 101.

good faith is a means, though perhaps not the only one, to protect reasonable expectations, which is the end or purpose. That is why for Steyn LJ, 'as long as'[23] reasonable expectations (ie the end) can be honoured, he is content that English contract law does not have a principle of good faith (ie the means). While Lady Arden, by applying the principle of giving effect to the reasonable expectations of the parties to the debate on good faith clauses in contract, seems to use the end to justify the means—and this is not necessarily problematic—she does so by stating that courts should endeavour to give effect to the parties' agreement that contractual obligations should be performed in good faith, and consequently to their reasonable expectations.[24] Still, she sees reasonable expectations as the purpose of or the end of contractual agreement on performance in good faith. The means-and-end relationship between good faith and reasonable expectations is more apparent in implying a term of good faith in *Nash v Paragon Finance Plc*,[25] as referred to above.

It is noteworthy that in a broad sense of what is expected in a contract, the concept of 'reasonable expectations' actually is broader than that of good faith, in that, undoubtedly, contracting parties reasonably assume or expect good faith or honesty, at least from each other. The fact that commerce takes place against a background expectation of honesty was recognised by the House of Lords: 'Parties entering into a commercial contract ... will assume the honesty and good faith of the other; absent such an assumption they would not deal.'[26] 'Parties contract with one another in the expectation of honest dealing.'[27] '[I]t goes without saying that underlying the contractual arrangements of the parties there will be a common assumption that the persons involved will behave honestly.'[28] More recently, in 2013, this was further considered and reiterated in the High Court:

> A paradigm example of a general norm which underlies almost all contractual relationships is an expectation of honesty. That expectation is essential to commerce, which depends critically on trust. Yet it is seldom, if ever, made the subject of an express contractual obligation. Indeed if a party in negotiating the terms of a contract were to seek to include a provision which expressly required the other party to act honestly, the very fact of doing so might well damage the parties' relationship by the lack of trust which this would signify.[29]

But the relevance of this broad expectation to good faith cannot be overstated. That is not just because it is perhaps too broad to be very useful, but more importantly because honesty is only one of the (perhaps many) aspects of good faith. Honesty

[23] Lord Steyn, above n 6, 439.
[24] Lady Justice Arden, above n 13, 212, and the text associated with n 13.
[25] *Nash v Paragon Finance Plc* [2001] EWCA Civ 1466.
[26] *HIH Casualty and General Insurance Ltd v Chase Manhattan Bank* [2003] UKHL 6 [15] (per Lord Bingham).
[27] Ibid [68] (per Lord Hoffmann citing and affirming Rix LJ).
[28] Ibid (per Lord Hoffmann).
[29] *Yam Seng Pte Ltd v International Trade Corporation Ltd* [2013] EWHC 111 (QB) [135] (per Leggat J).

is necessary, but not sufficient, for good faith. 'Put the other way round, not all bad faith conduct would necessarily be described as dishonest.'[30]

It must be clarified that in the context of contract law, the means-and-end relationship between good faith and reasonable expectations applies only to objective good faith and objective reasonable expectations. Objective good faith means the conduct of fair dealing, or a norm of conduct that requires one party to take into account the interest of another party.[31] Subjective good faith refers to a state of mind characterised generally by 'honesty in fact', or the party's honestly believing it is acting in good faith. A typical example of subjective good faith is a bona fide purchaser in property law: 'It is, however, objective good faith which is chiefly relevant to contract law.'[32] Expectations might be subjective, but reasonable expectations are not really so, because the reasonableness qualifier is 'an objective norm of behaviour'[33] and is 'to be objectively ascertained, having regard to the nature and purpose of what is being done, to the circumstances of the case and to any relevant usages and practice'.[34] The submission that good faith and reasonableness are separate concepts because good faith refers to a subjective state of mind whereas reasonableness is objective[35] arises from a confusion of subjective good faith, which is more relevant to property law, with objective good faith, which is, as said above, more relevant to contract law.

II. Good Faith in the Common Law of Contract

Now that good faith is a means to reasonable expectations as the end, the more roles good faith has in contract law, the more judicial movement there is, though indirect and inconspicuous, towards protection of reasonable expectations.

A. Good Faith in English Contract Law

This section is concerned with the duty of good faith in contract performance generally, rather than with the more established duty of good faith specifically in

[30] Ibid [138] (per Leggat J).

[31] MW Hesslelink, 'The Concept of Good Faith' in AS Hartkamp et al (eds), *Toward a European Civil Code* (Leiden, Kluwer Law International, 2004) 471. For objective good faith as fair dealing, see also Forte, above n 22.

[32] H MacQueen, 'Good Faith in Scottish Law of Contract: An Undisclosed Principle?' in Forte (ed), above n 3, 7. MacQueen's statement applies not only to Scots contract law, but also to English contract law.

[33] R Hooley, 'Controlling Contractual Discretion' (2013) 72 *CLJ* 65, 74.

[34] Article I-1:104, in C Von Bar and E Clive (eds), Principles, Definitions and Model Rules of European Private Law, Draft Common Frame of Reference (DFCF) (Oxford, Oxford University Press, 2010).

[35] Hooley, above n 33, 74.

the exercise of discretion in the performance of contract, which has been discussed in section I. above in connection with cases such as *Abu Dhabi National Tanker Company Ltd v Product Star Shipping Ltd ('The Product Star')*,[36] *Gan Insurance Co Ltd v Tai Ping Insurance Co Ltd*[37] and *Nash v Paragon Finance Plc.*[38] In this regard, it is now more settled than ever that *at least* 'in some situations where a contracting party is given a discretion, the Court will more readily imply an obligation that the discretion should not be exercised in bad faith or in an arbitrary or capricious manner'.[39] The UK Supreme Court further affirmed in 2014 that 'in the absence of very clear language to the contrary, a contractual discretion must be exercised in good faith and not arbitrarily or capriciously'.[40]

For an insurance lawyer, however, when it comes to a general duty of good faith in English contract law, the inevitable starting point in common law is undoubtedly *Carter v Boehm*.[41] This is not, however, just because it is thought to be the case definitive of the principle of *uberrima fides* (also *uberrimae fidei* as genitive) or utmost good faith in the common law of insurance, but also because in this case Lord Mansfield stated that good faith was '[t]he governing principle … applicable to all contracts and dealings'.[42] This cannot be taken as authority, though, because whilst this particular opinion was shared in the eighteenth and nineteenth centuries by Lord Kenyon[43] and Lord St Leonards,[44] a principle or a general duty of good faith failed to be accepted generally in English contract law. That is because from the late 1870s, the notion of good faith as a governing principle was overridden by the development of law reflecting a *laissez-faire* economy and favouring autonomy in contract.[45] As a result, *caveat emptor* gradually prevailed, and contract law tipped the scales against general standards of fairness in favour of predictability.[46] Incrementalism was favoured over high principle, and this was fatal to a paternalistic general doctrine of good faith.[47] Consequently, good faith became a

[36] *Abu Dhabi National Tanker Co Ltd v Product Star Shipping Ltd* ('The Product Star') [1993] 1 Lloyd's Rep 397 (CA), 404 (Leggatt LJ).

[37] *Gan Insurance Co Ltd v Tai Ping Insurance Co Ltd* [2001] EWCA Civ 1047.

[38] *Nash v Paragon Finance Plc* [2001] EWCA Civ 1466.

[39] *Greenclose Ltd v National Westminster Bank plc* [2014] EWHC 1156 (Ch) [150] (per Andrew J).

[40] *British Telecommunications Plc v Telefónica O2 UK Ltd* [2014] UKSC 42 [37] (per Lord Sutton).

[41] *Carter v Boehm* (1766) 3 Burr 1905.

[42] *Carter v Boehm* (1766) 3 Burr 1905, 1910.

[43] *Mellish v Motteux* (1792) 170 ER 113, 113–14. In 'contracts of all kinds, it is of the highest importance that courts of law should compel the observance of honesty and good faith'.

[44] *Lumley v Wagner* [1852] EWHC (Ch) J 96, (1852) 42 ER 687, 693: 'Wherever this court has not proper jurisdiction to enforce specific performance, it operates to bind men's consciences … to a true and literal performance of their agreements … The exercise of this jurisdiction has, I believe, had a wholesome tendency towards the maintenance of that good faith which exists in this country to a much greater degree perhaps than in any other …'.

[45] R Harrison, *Good Faith in Sales* (London, Sweet & Maxwell, 1997) 7.

[46] HK Lücke, 'Good Faith and Contractual Performance' in P Finn (ed), *Essays on Contract* (Sydney, Law Book Co., 1987), 157.

[47] PS Atiyah, *The Rise and Fall of the Freedom of Contract* (Oxford, Oxford University Press, 1979) 168.

matter of mere marginal interest in England,[48] particularly in commercial law. It was persistently not recognised as part of the English law of commercial contract, or commercial law more broadly. Although Lord Diplock said in the early 1970s that he preferred 'to deal with each appeal by considering first the transaction between the buyer and the seller in the light of common sense and good faith in businesses',[49] this was not followed. In the late 1980s, Bingham LJ, as he was then, stated that a principle of good faith was not part of English contract law; what he said, as reproduced below, has been familiar to English lawyers ever since:

> In many civil law systems, and perhaps in most legal systems outside the common law world, the law of obligations recognises and enforces an overriding principle that in making and carrying out contracts parties should act in good faith. This does not simply mean that they should not deceive each other, a principle which any legal system must recognise; its effect is perhaps most aptly conveyed by such metaphorical colloquialisms as 'playing fair', 'coming clean' or 'putting one's cards face upwards on the table'. It is in essence a principle of fair and open dealing. In such a forum it might, I think, be held on the facts of this case that the plaintiffs were under a duty in all fairness to draw the defendants' attention specifically to the high price payable if the transparencies were not returned in time and, when the 14 days had expired, to point out to the defendants the high cost of continued failure to return them.
>
> English law has, characteristically, committed itself to no such overriding principle but has developed piecemeal solutions in response to demonstrated problems of unfairness. Many examples could be given. Thus equity has intervened to strike down unconscionable bargains. Parliament has stepped in to regulate the imposition of exemption clauses and the form of certain hire purchase agreements.[50]

Apparently there are moral elements in the principle of good faith, but it seems that English contract law tolerates 'a certain moral insensitivity in the interest of economic efficiency'.[51] So English law does not recognise a general duty of good faith in the performance of contracts, nor a duty to negotiate in that manner,[52] and statements to that effect are legion.[53] More recently the Court of Appeal has reiterated that 'there is no general doctrine of "good faith" in English contract

[48] R Brownsword, N Hird and G Howells, 'Good Faith in Contract: Concept and Context' in R Brownsword, N Hird and G Howells (eds), *Good Faith in Contract* (Aldershot, Ashgate, 1999) 2.

[49] *Ashington Piggeries Ltd v Christopher Hill Ltd* [1972] AC 411, 502.

[50] *Interfoto Picture Library Ltd v Stiletto Visual Programmes Ltd* [1989] QB 433 (CA), 439.

[51] B Nicholas, 'The Pre-contractual Obligation to Disclose Information, English Report' in D Harris and D Tallon (eds), *Contract Law Today: Anglo-French Comparisons* (Oxford, Oxford University Press, 1991) 187.

[52] *Walford v Miles* [1992] 2 AC 128 (HL), 138. Lord Ackner stated: 'However, the concept of a duty to carry on negotiations in good faith is inherently repugnant to the adversarial position of the parties when involved in negotiations. Each party to the negotiations is entitled to pursue his (or her) own interest, so long as he avoids making misrepresentations. … A duty to negotiate in good faith is as unworkable in practice as it is inherently inconsistent with the position of a negotiating party.'

[53] S Whittaker and R Zimmermann, 'Good Faith in European Contract Law: Surveying the Landscape' in R Zimmermann and S Whittaker (eds.), *Good Faith in European Contract Law* (Cambridge, Cambridge University Press, 2000) 39–40.

law',[54] although there seems to be, as will be noted below, an incremental movement towards a law of good faith in the performance of contract.

Two significant changes occurred in 1993 in relation to good faith in English contract law. One change, in commercial contract law, arose from *Abu Dhabi National Tanker Co v Product Star Shipping Ltd ('The Product Star')*.[55] In this case, a charterer (ie Abu Dhabi National Tanker Co) by terms of contract conferred on the ship-owner (Product Star Shipping Ltd) and the master of the ship a discretionary power to determine whether or not a port to which the charterer ordered the vessel was dangerous, and to proceed to that port for trading or avoid it accordingly. The charterer contended that the ship avoided ports it could have reached for loading and/or the discharge of cargo. The ship-owner not only contested this claim, but also cross-claimed. On the surface, the discretion was unfettered, but that was the question over which the dispute arose. It was held in the Court of Appeal that the discretion should be restrained. Leggat LJ stated 'that not only must the [contractual] discretion be exercised honestly and in good faith, but, having regard to the provisions of the contract by which it is conferred, it must not be exercised arbitrarily, capriciously or unreasonably'.[56] This was followed a few years later in *Ludgate Insurance Co v Citibank NA*[57] and *Gan Insurance Co v Tai Ping Insurance Co*,[58] as well as in *Nash v Paragon Finance Plc*,[59] all involving involving the exercise of discretion in the performance of commercial contracts.

The other significant change in 1993 was the promulgation of the European Community Council Directive on Unfair Terms in Consumer Contracts,[60] which was to be implemented in the UK through the Unfair Terms in Consumer Contracts Regulations 1994 (SI 1994/3159). The Directive was promulgated so as to facilitate the establishment of the internal market and to provide consumers in the internal market with unified protection from unfair terms in contracts. It was recognised in the Directive that 'it is the responsibility of the Member States to ensure that contracts concluded with consumers do not contain unfair terms';[61] and regarding 'unfair terms', Article 3(1) of the Directive provided:

> A contractual term which has not been individually negotiated shall be regarded as unfair if, contrary to the requirement of good faith, it causes a significant imbalance in the parties' rights and obligations arising under the contract, to the detriment of the consumer.

[54] *Mid Essex Hospital Services NHS Trust v Compass Group UK & Ireland Ltd (t/a Medirest)* [2013] EWCA Civ 200 [105] (per Jackson LJ).

[55] *Abu Dhabi National Tanker Co v Product Star Shipping Ltd ('The Product Star')* [1993] 1 Lloyd's Rep 397 (CA).

[56] Ibid 404.

[57] *Ludgate Insurance Co Ltd v Citibank NA* [1998] Lloyd's Rep IR 221, 239-40.

[58] *Gan Insurance Co v Tai Ping Insurance Co* [2001] EWCA Civ 1047.

[59] *Nash v Paragon Finance Plc* [2001] EWCA Civ 1466.

[60] Council Directive 93/13/EEC [1993] OJ L95/29.

[61] Council Directive 93/13/EEC, the fourth 'Whereas clause' in the recital is also recognised in the sixteenth 'Whereas clause' as follows: '[T]he assessment, according to the general criteria chosen, of the unfair character of terms, ... must be supplemented by a means of making an overall evaluation of the different interests involved; ... this constitutes the requirement of good faith; ... in making an

This, amongst other provisions, was implemented by the UK Government in regulation 4(1) of the Unfair Terms in Consumer Contracts Regulations 1994. The House of Lords had an opportunity in 2001 to comment on regulation 4(1):

> The requirement of good faith in this context is one of fair and open dealing. Openness requires that the terms should be expressed fully, clearly and legibly, containing no concealed pitfalls or traps. Appropriate prominence should be given to terms which might operate disadvantageously to the customer. Fair dealing requires that a supplier should not, whether deliberately or unconsciously, take advantage of the consumer's necessity, indigence, lack of experience, unfamiliarity with the subject matter of the contract, weak bargaining position or any other factor listed in or analogous to those listed in Schedule 2 of the regulations. Good faith in this context is not an artificial or technical concept; nor, since Lord Mansfield was its champion, is it a concept wholly unfamiliar to British lawyers. It looks to good standards of commercial morality and practice. Regulation 4(1) lays down a composite test, covering both the making and the substance of the contract, and must be applied bearing clearly in mind the objective which the regulations are designed to promote.[62]

After being operative for almost five years, and for the purpose of being more aligned with the language of the Directive, the 1994 Regulations were replaced by the Unfair Terms in Consumer Contracts Regulations 1999 (SI 1999/2083), regulation 5(1) of which was the same as Article 3(1) of the Directive.[63] Under regulation 8(1), if a term in a contract concluded with a consumer by a seller or supplier was unfair, the term 'shall not be binding on the consumer'. The same provisions were enacted in the Consumer Rights Act 2015, which repealed the 1999 Regulations, with the same rules applicable to consumer notices as to consumer contract terms.[64]

It is perhaps not surprising that not long after the 1999 Regulations became the catalyst for renewing academic interest in good faith—the prospect of a principle of good faith in English general contract law was still met with lasting suspicion[65]—the House of Lords in January 2001 generally recognised, in

assessment of good faith, particular regard shall be had to the strength of the bargaining positions of the parties, whether the consumer had an inducement to agree to the term and whether the goods or services were sold or supplied to the special order of the consumer; … the requirement of good faith may be satisfied by the seller or supplier where he deals fairly and equitably with the other party whose legitimate interests he has to take into account.'

[62] citation t/c. *Director General of Fair Trading v First National Bank* [2002] 1 AC 481; [2001] UKHL 52 [17] (Lord Bingham).

[63] Council Directive 93/13/EEC, [1993] OJ L95/29.

[64] Consumer Rights Act 2015, s 62.

[65] *Yam Seng Pte Ltd v International Trade Corporation Ltd* [2013] EWHC 111 (QB) [123] (per Leggat J): 'Three main reasons have been given for what Professor McKendrick has called the "traditional English hostility" towards a doctrine of good faith: see McKendrick, *Contract Law* (9th Ed) pp 221–2. The first is the one referred to by Bingham LJ …: that the preferred method of English law is to proceed incrementally by fashioning particular solutions in response to particular problems rather than by enforcing broad overarching principles. A second reason is that English law is said to embody an ethos of individualism, whereby the parties are free to pursue their own self-interest not only in negotiating but also in performing contracts provided they do not act in breach of a term of the

Manifest Shipping v Uni-Polaris Insurance Co ('The Star Sea'):[66] 'Having a contractual obligation of good faith in the performance of the contract presents no conceptual difficulty in itself. Such an obligation can arise from an implied or inferred contractual term.' This, however, could not readily be extended to contract law generally, or to non-insurance contract broadly. That is because *The Star Sea* was an insurance case, for which the concept of good faith is prototypical. However, in October of the same year (2001), the Court of Appeal in *Nash v Paragon Finance Plc*[67] implied a duty of good faith in the exercising of contractual discretion. In less than a decade, Rix LJ stated, in the lead opinion in *Socimer International Bank Ltd v Standard Bank London Ltd*:[68]

> [T]he requirements of good faith and rationality are a sufficient protection. ... [A]buse caused by self-interest ... is precisely what implicit good faith deals with. Commercial contracts assume such good faith, which is why express language requiring it is so rare.

To date, the most significant judicial development of good faith in English contract law occurred as recently as 2013 in *Yam Seng Pte Ltd v International Trade Corporation Ltd*.[69] It is significant, first, for the reason that it concerns good faith in the performance of commercial contracts generally, rather than merely discretion in the performance or in particular kinds of contract (such as insurance), which typically requires good faith. Secondly, it was opined that the English refusal to recognise any general obligation of good faith in contract law 'would appear to be swimming against the tide'.[70] Thirdly, it was stated that 'there seems ... to be no difficulty, following the established methodology of English law for the implication of terms in fact, in implying such a duty in any ordinary commercial contract based on the presumed intention of the parties'.[71] Fourthly, for the first time, in *Yam Seng* the theory of 'relational contract' was recognised in an English court in connection with discussion of good faith in contract law.[72]

Yam Seng might be a new beacon for implying a duty of good faith in the performance of contract. Leggat J has to date made the most in-depth judicial exposition of good faith in English contract law. Apart from briefly summarising the traditional English hostility toward the concept of good faith, the learned Judge looked at how a contractual duty of good faith had been established in contract law in the US, Canada, Australia and Scotland, and how it has been advocated in

contract. The third main reason given is a fear that recognising a general requirement of good faith in the performance of contracts would create too much uncertainty. There is concern that the content of the obligation would be vague and subjective and that its adoption would undermine the goal of contractual certainty to which English law has always attached great weight.'

66 *Manifest Shipping v Uni-Polaris Insurance Co ('The Star Sea')* [2001] UKHL 1 [50] (per Lord Hobhouse).

67 *Nash v Paragon Finance Plc* [2001] EWCA Civ 1466.

68 *Socimer International Bank Ltd v Standard Bank London Ltd* [2008] EWCA Civ 116 [116].

69 *Yam Seng Pte Ltd v International Trade Corporation Ltd* [2013] EWHC 111 (QB).

70 Ibid [124] (per Leggat J).

71 Ibid [131] (per Leggat J).

72 Ibid [142].

New Zealand.[73] More importantly, Leggat J explained how and why implying such a duty in any ordinary commercial contract was actually not incongruent with English contract law, based on the presumed intention of the parties and through the contextual approach to construction of contract terms. Meanwhile, referring to a string of English cases (some of which have been discussed in section I. above), he found good faith to comprise:

1. honesty, as expected more implicitly than expressly by one contractual party of the other; or likewise
2. expected observance of accepted commercial standards; and
3. fidelity to one's bargain, which could again be reduced to a matter of contextual and objective interpretation of contract.[74]

Understood that way, for Leggat J 'there is nothing novel or foreign to English law in recognising an implied duty of good faith in the performance of contracts. … Moreover such a concept is … already reflected in several lines of authority that are well established'.[75] Lastly but not least importantly, having repudiated[76] the reasons for the English reluctance toward good faith in contract law, Leggat J concluded that 'the traditional English hostility towards a doctrine of good faith in the performance of contracts, to the extent that it still persists, is misplaced'.[77]

Leggat J's analysis in *Yam Seng* remains part of the law and was soon applied in *Bristol Groundschool Limited v Intelligent Data Capture Limited*.[78] However, it 'is not to be regarded as laying down any general principle applicable to all commercial contracts'[79]—because as Leggatt J expressly recognised, the content of the duty of good faith 'is heavily dependent on the context'.[80] In connection with and one month in the wake of *Yam Seng*, the Court of Appeal stressed that

> there is no general doctrine of 'good faith' in English contract law, although a duty of good faith is implied by law as an incident of certain categories of contract … If the parties wish to impose such a duty they must do so expressly.[81]

That being said, though not definitive of good faith in English contract law,[82] *Yam Seng* represents a remarkable step towards that.

[73] Ibid [125]–[130].
[74] Ibid [137]–[139].
[75] Ibid [145].
[76] Ibid [147]–[152].
[77] Ibid [153].
[78] *Bristol Groundschool Ltd v Intelligent Data Capture Ltd* [2014] EWHC 2145 (Ch).
[79] *Greenclose Ltd v National Westminster Bank plc* [2014] EWHC 1156 (Ch) [150] (per Andrew J), cited approvingly in *Myers v Kestrel Acquisitions Ltd* [2015] EWHC 916 (Ch) [40] (Blackburne J).
[80] *Yam Seng Pte Ltd v International Trade Corporation Ltd* [2013] EWHC 111 (QB) [147].
[81] *Mid Essex Hospital Services NHS Trust v Compass Group UK and Ireland Ltd (t/a Medirest)* [2013] EWCA Civ 200 [105] (per Jackson LJ).
[82] It is noteworthy that in *British Telecommunications Plc v Telefónica O2 UK Ltd* [2014] UKSC 42, the Justices seemed to be cautious in not even mentioning *Yam Seng* when concluding (at [82]) that 'in the absence of very clear language to the contrary, a contractual discretion must be exercised in good faith and not arbitrarily or capriciously'. For this purpose, not surprisingly, they cited *Abu Dhabi*

Perhaps what is really more noteworthy in *Yam Seng* is that the concept or theory of relational contract, put forward by the late Ian Macneil and discussed among legal scholars as well as business scholars for more than four decades, was judicially recognised for the first time in English law and good faith was applied thereto. More discussion of the theory of relational contract is to follow in Chapter 6 of this book. For our purposes here, it is noteworthy that Leggatt J observed:

> [M]any contracts … involve a longer term relationship between the parties [to] which they make a substantial commitment. Such 'relational' contracts, as they are sometimes called, may require a high degree of communication, cooperation and predictable performance based on mutual trust and confidence and involve expectations of loyalty which are not legislated for in the express terms of the contract but are implicit in the parties' understanding and necessary to give business efficacy to the arrangements. Examples of such relational contracts might include some joint venture agreements, franchise agreements and long term distributorship agreements.[83]

This was cited approvingly in *Bristol Groundschool Ltd v Intelligent Data Capture Ltd*,[84] which characterised the contract in question as relational and also implied into it a duty of good faith. In more general terms, it is pointed out that 'English law has, to its advantage, developed a nuanced conception of good faith in performance [of contracts] by using its chosen mechanism of implied terms'.[85]

B. Good Faith in Contract Law of Other Common Law Jurisdictions

Australia

Whilst '[t]he question whether a standard of good faith should be applied generally to contracts has not been resolved'[86] in the High Court of Australia, Australian courts at state level, and occasionally at federal intermediate level, have given good faith a more overt role in resolving contractual disputes over the past 20 years. The watershed case was *Renard Constructions (ME) Pty Ltd v Minister for Public Works*,[87] where the issue was whether the Minister (the Principal) had acted

National Tanker Co Ltd v Product Star Shipping Ltd ('The Product Star') [1993] 1 Lloyd's Rep 397 (CA), *Gan Insurance Co Ltd v Tai Ping Insurance Co Ltd* [2001] EWCA Civ 1047 and *Nash v Paragon Finance Plc* [2001] EWCA Civ 1466.

[83] *Yam Seng Pte Ltd v International Trade Corporation Ltd* [2013] EWHC 111 (QB) [142].

[84] *Bristol Groundschool Ltd v Intelligent Data Capture Ltd* [2014] EWHC 2145 (Ch).

[85] H Collins, 'Implied Terms: The Foundation in Good Faith and Fair Dealing' (2014) 67 *CLP* 297, 330.

[86] *Commonwealth Bank of Australia v Barker* (A1-2014) [2014] HCA 32 [107] (per Justice Kiefel), referring to *Royal Botanic Gardens and Domain Trust v South Sydney City Council* [2002] HCA 5 [40], [156].

[87] *Renard Constructions (ME) Pty Ltd v Minister for Public Works* (1992) 26 NSWLR 234.

reasonably and in good faith when it cancelled the construction contract during the final weeks of the construction works, even though Renard had shown, as required in the contract, that it was willing and able to complete the construction on time. Priestley JA said, 'The kind of reasonableness I have been discussing seems to me to have much in common with the notions of good faith.'[88] He went into detail about the development of an implied duty of good faith in performance of contracts under Australian law, and considered:

> Although this implication has not yet been accepted to the same extent in Australia as part of judge-made Australian contract law, there are many indications that the time may be fast approaching when the idea, long recognised as implicit in many of the orthodox techniques of solving contractual disputes, will gain explicit recognition in the same way as it has in Europe and in the United States.[89]

The 'many indications' included the Australian experience of judicial control over the operation of general rescission clauses for prevention of their use 'for improper and extraneous purposes',[90] and the numerous Australian statutory provisions[91] requiring parties to a contract to act reasonably and fairly in a variety of circumstances. For Priestley JA, 'in ordinary English usage there has been constant association between the words fair and reasonable. Similarly there is a close association of ideas between the terms unreasonableness, lack of good faith and unconscionability'.[92] In particular, Priestley JA saw that legislative interference with freedom of contract had the result

> that people generally, including judges and other lawyers, from all strands of the community, have grown used to the courts applying standards of fairness to contract which are wholly consistent with the existence in all contracts of a duty upon the parties of good faith and fair dealing in its performance. In my view this is in these days the expected standard, and anything less is contrary to prevailing community expectations.[93]

Renard Constructions is perceived as 'the watershed case' that 'paved the way for the emergence of a good faith doctrine'.[94] The doctrine became settled in New South Wales when the New South Wales Court of Appeal considered itself bound by *Renard Constructions* in *Hughes Bros Pty Ltd v Trustees of the Roman*

[88] Ibid 263.

[89] Ibid 263–64.

[90] *Godfrey Constructions Pty Ltd v Kanagra Park Pty Ltd* (1972) 128 CLR 529, 548; *Pierce Bell Sales Pty Ltd v Frazer* (1973) 130 CLR 575, 587 (Barwick CJ). Cited among others by Priestley JA.

[91] For example (referred to by Priestley JA), the Money-Lenders and Infants Loan Act 1905, the Hire Purchase Agreement Acts of 1941 and 1960, the Industrial Arbitration Act 1940, s 88F, the Contracts Review Act 1980, the Credit Act 1984 and the Trade Practices Act 1974 (Cth), s 51A.

[92] *Renard Constructions (ME) Pty Ltd v Minister for Public Works* (1992) 26 NSWLR 234, 265.

[93] Ibid 268.

[94] M Warren AC, 'Good Faith: Where We Are at?' [2010] *Melbourne University Law Review* 344, 345.

Catholic Church for the Archdiocese of Sydney.[95] It was further concluded and reaffirmed in *Alcatel Australia Limited v Scarcella*:[96]

> The decisions in *Renard Constructions* and *Hughes Bros* mean that in New South Wales a duty of good faith, both in performing obligations and exercising rights, may by implication be imposed upon parties as part of a contract. There is no reason why such a duty should not be implied as part of this lease.

The duty of good faith in contract was also similarly found in New South Wales in *Burger King Corp v Hungry Jack's Pty Ltd*,[97] *Overlook Management BV v Foxtel Management Pty Ltd*,[98] *Vodafone Pacific Ltd v Mobile Innovations Ltd*;[99] in Victoria in *Esso Australia Resources Pty Ltd v Southern Pacific Petroleum*;[100] and in the Federal Court of Australia in *Hughes Aircraft Systems International v Air Services Australia*,[101] for example. Admittedly, overall the Australian law of good faith in contract lacks coherence,[102] and it has not been recognised yet in the High Court of Australia. However, this is not necessarily because the concept of good faith is itself too problematic to be accepted, but mainly because till now there has been no judicial opportunity for the High Court of Australia to position itself on this. After all, in *Royal Botanic Gardens and Domain Trust v South Sydney Council*[103] the High Court of Australia identified the debate about implied good faith terms as important, but simply thought the instant case was not an appropriate judicial opportunity to examine the issue closely.[104] With this in mind, the observation that a duty of good faith can be found to exist in Australian contract law is largely valid. In this respect, particularly noteworthy is that, more recently, Flick J, in the Federal Court of Australia in *NA Retail Solutions Pty Limited v St George Bank Ltd*,[105] suggested that more and more Australian courts are proceeding on an assumption that a duty of good faith, or a duty to act reasonably, may be implied as an incident of a commercial contract, noting an 'increasing acceptance ... that if terms of good faith and reasonableness are to be implied, they are implied as a matter of law'.[106]

[95] *Hughes Bros Pty Ltd v Trustees of the Roman Catholic Church for the Archdiocese of Sydney* (1993) 31 NSWLR 91.
[96] *Alcatel Australia Limited v Scarcella* (1998) 44 NSWLR 349, 369 (per Sheller JA).
[97] *Burger King Corp v Hungry Jack's Pty Ltd* (2001) 69 NSWLR 558, [2001] NSWCA 187.
[98] *Overlook Management BV v Foxtel Management Pty Ltd* [2002] NSWSC 16.
[99] *Vodafone Pacific Ltd v Mobile Innovations Ltd* [2004] NSWCA 15.
[100] *Esso Australia Resources Pty Ltd v Southern Pacific Petroleum* [2005] VCSA 228.
[101] *Hughes Aircraft Systems International v Air Services Australia* (1997) 76 FCR 151.
[102] JW Carter, 'Good Faith in Contract: Why Australian Law is Incoherent?', *Sydney Law School Legal Studies Research Paper* No 14/38, 2014.
[103] *Royal Botanic Gardens and Domain Trust v South Sydney Council* [2002] HCA 5.
[104] Ibid [40].
[105] *NA Retail Solutions Pty Limited v St George Bank Ltd* [2010] FCA 259.
[106] Ibid [21] (per Flick J).

Canada and the USA

In the US, a post-contractual duty of good faith was established in the *Uniform Commercial Code* (UCC). Its immediate intellectual source was attributable to Professor Karl Llewellyn, Chief Reporter for the UCC, who was greatly inspired by the *Treu and Glauben* provision of the German Civil Code. Meanwhile it also aligned, at least to some extent, with positive law: courts in the US had already recognised in 1930s a general duty of good faith, for example in *Kirke La Shelle Co v Armstrong Co*[107] and in *Wigand v Bachmann-Betchtel Brewing Co.*[108] However, the general duty of good faith in the UCC applies only to 'performance and enforcement', after a contract has already been concluded. The most relevant provisions are UCC Section 1-304 on 'obligations of good faith' ('Every contract or duty within [the UCC] imposes an obligation of good faith in its performance and enforcement.') and UCC Section 1-201(20) on the definition of good faith ('"Good faith," except as otherwise provided in Section 5,[109] means honesty in fact and the observance of reasonable commercial standards of fair dealing.'). This general duty of post-contractual good faith applies only to commercial contracts in all 50 states where the UCC has been enacted. The ambit of the applicability of the post-contract good faith duty was expanded as a result of the reiteration in the *Restatement (Second) of Contract Law*, Section 205 that 'Every contract imposes upon each party a duty of good faith and fair dealing in its performance and enforcement.' This and the Restatement apply to both commercial contracts and consumer contracts.

In Canada, until very recently, like English contract law, the common law of contract was reluctant to adopt a general duty or general principle of good faith. However, in November 2014, the Supreme Court of Canada took an unequivocal turn toward a principle of good faith in contract law in *Bhasin v Hrynew.*[110] Justice Cromwell, writing for the Court, surveyed the current state of the law in Canada and in common law jurisdictions, and pointed the way forward. In his opinion, 'considerations of good faith are apparent in doctrines that expressly consider the fairness of contractual bargains, such as unconscionability',[111] and 'good faith also plays a role in the law of implied terms, particularly with respect to terms implied by law',[112] and also in contract interpretation;[113] in addition, 'the concept of "good faith" is used in hundreds of statutes across Canada'.[114] From his survey and review

[107] *Kirke La Shelle Co v Armstrong Co* 263 NY 79 (1933).
[108] *Wigand v Bachmann-Betchtel Brewing Co* 222 NY 272 (1918) 277: '[E]very contract implies good faith and fair dealing between the parties to it.'
[109] Section 5-102(7): '"Good faith" means honesty in fact in the conduct or transaction concerned.'
[110] *Bhasin v Hrynew* 2014 SCC 71, [2014] 3 SCR 495.
[111] Ibid [43].
[112] Ibid [44].
[113] Ibid [45].
[114] Ibid [46].

of the recent legal developments in this regard in the UK and in Australia, Justice Cromwell pointed out two steps towards good faith in contract law:

> The first step is to recognize that there is an organizing principle of good faith that underlies and manifests itself in various more specific doctrines governing contractual performance. That organizing principle is simply that parties generally must perform their contractual duties honestly and reasonably and not capriciously or arbitrarily. As the Court has recognized, an organizing principle states in general terms a requirement of justice from which more specific legal doctrines may be derived.[115]

The second step is to recognise, normatively, that 'there is a general duty of honesty in contractual performance. This means simply that parties must not lie or otherwise knowingly mislead each other about matters directly linked to the performance of the contract'.[116] The two steps are related: '[t]he requirement to act honestly is one of the most widely recognized aspects of the organizing principle of good faith'.[117] The particular implications of the broad organising principle of good faith for specific cases 'are determined by resorting to the body of doctrine that has developed which gives effect to aspects of that principle in particular types of situations and relationships', and the general duty of honest performance of contract is 'a manifestation of the general organizing principle of good faith'.[118] Following from the judicial reasoning as such and the facts, it was found that in this case, the defendant—actually its precursor—breached its duty to perform the agreement honestly, specifically the non-renewal clause of the contract concerned.

This decision of the Supreme Court of Canada is by far perhaps the fullest judicial survey of good faith in the common law of contract, and certainly represents the most express and most 'heart-felt' embracing of the good faith principle. This is a move that must be welcomed. Nevertheless, the judicial cautiousness in this case from the Supreme Court of Canada is not inconspicuous. Good faith is characterised as an 'organizing principle', which 'is not a free-standing rule, but rather a standard that underpins and is manifested in more specific legal doctrines and may be given different weight in different situations'.[119] In particular, the organising principle 'is a standard that helps to understand and develop the law in a coherent and principled way'.[120] This is not essentially different from, and even seems somewhat weaker than, good faith as an 'interpretative' principle

[115] Ibid [63], [64], note in [65]: 'This general principle has strong conceptual differences from the much higher obligations of a fiduciary. Unlike fiduciary duties, good faith performance does not engage duties of loyalty to the other contracting party or a duty to put the interests of the other contracting party first.'

[116] Ibid [73], note in [73]: 'This does not impose a duty of loyalty or of disclosure or require a party to forego advantages flowing from the contract; it is a simple requirement not to lie or mislead the other party about one's contractual performance.'

[117] Ibid [73].

[118] Ibid [93].

[119] Ibid [64].

[120] Ibid.

or guide;[121] weaker because an interpretative principle can be used to interpret documents such as a contract for a particular end, whereas an organising principle might serve primarily to organise existing piecemeal doctrines and occasionally newly established rules, as in this Supreme Court of Canada case, under the umbrella of good faith. This case has established a new general duty of honest performance of contracts, and has this duty as an aspect and a manifestation of the organising principle of good faith.

It is predictable that other doctrines and duties might be judicially developed under the umbrella organising principle of good faith if appropriate cases arise in the future. 'The requirement to act honestly is *one of* the most widely recognized aspects of the organizing principle of good faith.'[122] Therefore, honest performance is not all that good faith requires, and it is not to be understood otherwise. In recognising the general duty of honest performance of contract, the Supreme Court of Canada certainly was not just retreating to what was known as 'honest in fact', ie honesty, in the initial drafting of the UCC south of the border, though it did not leap forward to include fair dealing as good faith in the instant case. However, under the organising principle of good faith there is likely to be another judicial opportunity for recognising good faith in the sense of fair dealing, though the opportunity will not arise soon.

Singapore

The role of good faith in Singapore commercial law is also noteworthy, particularly after the Singapore International Commercial Court was launched in January 2015 'to enhance its status as a leading forum for legal services and commercial dispute resolution'.[123] In Singapore there have been two notable judicial developments of the law of good faith in a commercial context. One occurred in *Ng Giap Hon v Westcomb Securities Pte Ltd*,[124] in which one of the main issues was whether a duty of good faith should be implied in law into the agency agreement concerned. In the Singaporean Court of Appeal (actually the final court), Andrew Phang JA held that it would not be advisable to apply the duty or doctrine of good faith in the practical sphere before its theoretical foundations and its structure were settled in common law jurisdictions, because

> implying a 'term implied in law' into a contract not only involves broader policy considerations, but also establishes a precedent for the future. … This would, in and of itself, require that caution should be exercised on the part of the court.[125]

[121] For example, in Art 7(1), of the Convention on Contracts for the International Sale of Goods (Vienna, 1980), that in 'the interpretation of this Convention, regard is to be had to its international character and to the need to promote uniformity in its application and the observance of good faith in international trade'.

[122] *Bhasin v Hrynew* 2014 SCC 71, [2014] 3 SCR 495 [73].

[123] Report of the Singapore International Commercial Court Committee [4(a)] (Nov 2013).

[124] *Ng Giap Hon v Westcomb Securities Pte Ltd* [2009] SGCA 19.

[125] Ibid [46].

Andrew Phang JA also mentioned in passing that, for similar reasons, to incorporate a duty of good faith under 'terms implied in fact' would '*not* be a very persuasive argument'.[126] That being said, he also said:

> Nevertheless, what *is* clear in the context of an analysis based on the category of 'terms implied in *fact*' is that, whilst the *concept* of good faith (or, more likely, the elements thereof) might be present, the focus of the court would, as already stated earlier in the present paragraph, be on the *particular factual matrix* before it.[127]

Not inconspicuously, the Singaporean Court of Appeal in *Ng Giap Hon* was prepared to leave open the possibility that such a duty could be implied by way of the *narrower* category of 'terms implied in *fact*'.[128] Although Andrew Phang JA refused to imply a term or duty of good faith in law in *Ng Giap Hon*, and also refused to imply on the facts of the case a term to the effect of good faith or in favour of the claimant, in the closing remarks his Honour notably reiterated:

> Returning to the more general issue at hand, we would hasten to add that, where the relevant factual matrix justifies it, the court might nevertheless be prepared to imply either a 'term implied in fact' or a 'term implied in law' in favour of the agent ... Where an *express* term (which does not lack any ambiguity) exists, that would of course be the ideal solution.[129] (emphasis added)

There indeed arose in the same court a case in which there was an express term of good faith in a contract: *HSBC Institutional Trust Services (Singapore) Ltd v Toshin Development Singapore Pte Ltd*.[130] It focused on good faith in negotiations under rent review exercises between parties to a commercial lease agreement, in which a clause provided that the parties 'shall in good faith endeavour to agree on the prevailing market rental value' of the premises concerned. It is well known that a duty of good faith in negotiation of contracts was forthrightly denied in *Walford v Miles*.[131] But rightly in the opinion of the Justices of Appeal, 'that case does *not* have the effect of invalidating an express term in a contract which employs the language of good faith', because 'a valid distinction can be drawn between the pre-contractual negotiations in *Walford* and the "negotiations" between the Parties under the Rent Review Exercise in the present case'.[132] More importantly, the

[126] Ibid [61].

[127] Ibid [61].

[128] *The One Suites Pte Ltd v Pacific Motor Credit (Pte) Ltd* [2015] SGCA 21 [44] (Andrew Phang JA).

[129] *Ng Giap Hon v Westcomb Securities Pte Ltd* [2009] SGCA 19 [99].

[130] *HSBC Institutional Trust Services (Singapore) Ltd v Toshin Development Singapore Pte Ltd* [2012] SGCA 48.

[131] *Walford v Miles* [1992] 2 AC 128 (HL); see above n 52.

[132] *HSBC Institutional Trust Services (Singapore) Ltd v Toshin Development Singapore Pte Ltd* [2012] SGCA 48 [37]. In particular, 'Unlike parties who are merely in pre-contractual negotiations [as in *Walford v Miles*], the Parties are not free to simply walk away from the negotiating table for no rhyme or reason. By virtue of entering into the Lease Agreement, the Parties have committed themselves to a rent review exercise for the purposes of determining the new rent for each new rental term after the first rental term: the new rent will eventually have to be determined during one of the three stages provided for under the Rent Review Mechanism. ... In a *Walford*-type situation, the parties have much greater latitude as there is no overarching contractual framework binding them.' In contrast, in the present

Justices of Appeal held the express 'good faith clause' in an agreement to be valid because, inter alia, such clauses are 'not contrary to public policy' and instead 'are in the public interest as they promote the consensual disposition of any potential disputes' and

> are consistent with [the Asian contracting practice of incorporating such clauses, and also with] our cultural value of promoting consensus whenever possible. Clearly, it is in the wider public interest in Singapore as well to promote such an approach towards resolving differences.[133]

Although in this case the dispute and the decision were prima facie concerned with good faith in negotiations, they have implications for good faith in the performance of a contract. This is because of the particular nature of the clause in the context of the factual matrix, on which basis the Justices of Appeal rightly distinguished it from *Walford v Miles*.[134] In the Singaporean case, the 'negotiation/agree in good faith' clause was part of the Lease Agreement in question, and the negotiation on rent review was actually an essential part of the *performance* of this Lease Agreement. In this sense, the agreed contractual duty of 'negotiation' in good faith in this case can also be perceived as a duty of good-faith performance of the contract. Apart from this, it is also noteworthy that in summarising more generally, Rajah JA stated:

> At its core, the concept of good faith encompasses the threshold subjective requirement of acting honestly, as well as the objective requirement of *observing accepted commercial standards of fair dealing in the performance of the identified obligations.* This encompasses a duty to act fairly, having regard to the legitimate interests of the other party. It is important that the courts, as upholders of bargains, give practical effect to agreements entered into by commercial persons, rather than be quick in finding abstract difficulties [such as uncertainty].[135]

Last but not least important in this respect is that the concept of good faith is not a stranger to Singaporean law. At the very least, it has been a statutory requirement in the Land Titles (Strata) Act, by which an application for the collective sale of parcels of land by a majority of subsidiary proprietors who have made a conditional sale and purchase agreement shall not be approved if the Singaporean High Court or the Strata Titles Board, as the case may be, 'is satisfied that the transaction is not in good faith'.[136] Complementing the statutory standards of good faith

case there had already been an overarching binding Lease Agreement of which the 'negotiate/agree in good faith' clause was part.

[133] *HSBC Institutional Trust Services (Singapore) Ltd v Toshin Development Singapore Pte Ltd* [2012] SGCA 48 [37].

[134] *Walford v Miles* [1992] 2 AC 128 (HL).

[135] *HSBC Institutional Trust Services (Singapore) Ltd v Toshin Development Singapore Pte Ltd* [2012] SGCA 48 [45].

[136] Land Titles (Strata) Act, s 84A(9)(*a*)(i), see also s 84D(7)(*a*)(i), s 84E(9)(*a*)(i) and s 84FA(9)(*a*)(i).

in context, the Singaporean Court of Appeal further clarified that good faith in the Land Titles (Strata) Act, section 84A(9)(*a*)(i)(A)

> is not merely confined to whether the sale price is fair or not, but also how the price is arrived at. The collective sale agreement is governed by the common law. Its formation, validity, expiry and renewal are subject to the common law.[137]

This means that good faith is not merely required of decision per se in the lease agreement, but also of the decision-making process. Therefore, as far as the Land Titles (Strata) Act is concerned, it would at least be surprising if one were completely to deny that a law of good faith has existed in some contractual transactions at least for decades in Singapore. Although good faith in section 84A of the Act relates only to sales of or transactions in land and real property, its meaning admittedly draws on the notion of good faith in common law. In relation to the transaction price, it connotes fairness. More than that, it is relevant to the life of a contract or transaction—'its formation, validity, expiry and renewal'—in this context.

New Zealand and Hong Kong

Although in New Zealand and Hong Kong a principle or a general duty of good faith is not expressly recognised—which is not surprising, thanks to their alignment with the English law—yet given the recent development of the law of good faith in contract in other common law jurisdictions, as outlined above, it is likely that these jurisdictions will give more consideration to it when an opportunity or case arises. Meanwhile, good faith has not been expressly rejected by the supreme courts in the two jurisdictions. The New Zealand Supreme Court accepted that the issue of contractual good faith in New Zealand was a matter of general importance capable of qualifying for a grant of leave to appeal.[138] Also in that Court, it was stated by Justice Thomas, though obiter:

> Notwithstanding its widespread acceptance in most common law and civil jurisdictions in the world and growing judicial support, the courts have not yet incorporated the doctrine of good faith into our law. There is a widespread belief that existing doctrines or judicial devices already encompass a requirement of good faith. It would, it is said, add nothing to the existing tools and principles of the common law, such as estoppel and implied terms. This case serves to demonstrate that this belief is misplaced.[139]

[137] *Ng Eng Ghee v Mamata Kapildev Dave* [2009] SGCA 14 [131] (Rajah JA (delivering the judgment of the Court). Under the Land Titles (Strata) Act, s 84A(9)(*a*)(i)(A), one of the factors for considering whether the transaction is in good faith or not is 'the sale price for the lots and the common property in the strata title plan'.

[138] *Prime Commercial Ltd v Wool Board Disestablishment Company Ltd* [2007] NZSC 9 [2] (decision of 7 March 2007).

[139] *Wholesale Distributors Ltd v Gibbons Holdings Ltd* [2007] NZSC 37 [149] (decision of 30 May 2007).

Justice Thomas had persistently given judicial support, though not widely accepted, to good faith in contract law. In early 1990s, sitting in the New Zealand High Court, he stated in *Livingstone v Roskilly*,[140] 'I would not exclude from our common law the concept that, in general, the parties to a contract must act in good faith in making and carrying out the contract.' A decade later, sitting in the Court of Appeal, he stated, though dissenting, in *Bobux Marketing Ltd v Raynor Marketing Ltd*,[141] that 'the concept of good faith is the latent premise of much of the law of contract relating to the performance of contractual obligations'. Drawing on Lücke[142] and Fried,[143] he perceived good faith as 'closely associated with notions of fairness, honesty and reasonableness which are already well recognised in the law',[144] and also as 'loyalty to a promise'[145] and as 'a standard, rather than a rule', and stated that it 'does not require the abandonment of self-interest'.[146] Although courts and other judges in New Zealand have not accepted Justice Thomas's enthusiasm for good faith in contract law, his perception of it has long been in line with what turns out to the mainstream accepted understanding thereof. The reason why it has not received judicial recognition in New Zealand is perhaps more because of judicial loyalty to the then common contract law tradition of reluctance or even objection to good faith.

In Hong Kong, uncritical of Lord Ackner's approach in *Walford v Miles*,[147] the Hong Kong Court of Appeal, in *Hyundai Engineering and Construction Co Ltd v Vigour Ltd*,[148] aligned itself with the English rule that there is no duty to negotiate in good faith, though the Court of First Instance in the same case had constructed a persuasively-reasoned analysis to the opposite effect.[149] Apart from that, it seems to be accepted as a given in Hong Kong contract law that there is no general duty of good faith, nor a duty of good faith in the performance of contracts. The Hong Kong Court of Appeal, in *Skibsfinansiering v Wheelock Marden & Co Ltd*,[150] approvingly cited Bingham LJ's statement[151] that English law did not commit itself to an overriding duty of good faith in contract. The *Wheelock* decision was upheld in the Hong Kong Court of Final Appeal.[152]

However, now that in common law there seems to be an obvious judicial movement in England, Canada and Singapore towards good faith, and a stable if not

140 *Livingstone v Roskilly* [1992] 3 NZLR 230, 237.

141 *Bobux Marketing Ltd v Raynor Marketing Ltd* [2002] 1 NZLR 506 [40].

142 HK Lücke, 'Good Faith and Contractual Performance' in P Finn (ed), *Essays on Contract* (Sydney, Law Book Co, 1987).

143 C Fried, *Contract as Promise* (Cambridge, MA, Harvard University Press, 1981) 85.

144 *Bobux Marketing Ltd v Raynor Marketing Ltd* [2002] 1 NZLR 506 [41], citing Lücke at 161.

145 Ibid [41].

146 Ibid.

147 *Walford v Miles* [1992] 2 AC 128 (HL).

148 *Hyundai Engineering and Construction Co Ltd v Vigour Ltd* [2005] HKCU 258.

149 *Hyundai Engineering and Construction Co Ltd v Vigour Ltd* [2004] 2 HKC 505.

150 *Skibsfinansiering v Wheelock Marden & Co Ltd* [1998] 3 HKC 153.

151 *Interfoto Picture Library Ltd v Stiletto Visual Programmes Ltd* [1989] QB 433 (CA).

152 *Skibsfinansiering v Wheelock Marden & Co Ltd* [2000] 1 HKC 511.

strong similar development in Australia and in the US, it is likely that as long as an appropriate case arises, courts in New Zealand and/or Hong Kong will start to reconsider their reluctance to recognise a duty of good faith in contract law. The dictum and dissention of Thomas J will perhaps have its appeal in the future.

Summary

It can be seen from the common law jurisdictions noted above that although good faith is not well settled in contract law, it is beginning to gain ground incrementally, particularly in Anglo-Canadian and Singaporean contract law. It seems to have remained entrenched and stable in the US, though less so in Australia. It is not part of contract law in New Zealand or Hong Kong. However, it seems quite likely, given the recent development of good faith in English, Canadian and Singaporean contract law, that that will be a stimulus to the establishment of a law of good faith in New Zealand and Hong Kong, and perhaps it will become less unsettled in Australia too.

These developments in the recent past have huge implications for a principle of reasonable expectations. This is because, as has been argued in section I. above, good faith is (only) a means to an end, which is to honour or protect the reasonable expectations of the parties. The 'construction of a contract on the basis of honesty, loyalty to promise and reasonable regard for the other party's interests', namely construction in line with good faith, 'is, in the end, about vindication of reasonable expectations'.[153] Given that, it is not surprising that Leggatt J opined that 'the basis of the duty of good faith is the presumed intention of the parties and meaning of their contract', 'which is ascertained by attributing to them the purposes and values which reasonable people in their situation would have had'[154]—in other words, the reasonable expectations of the parties. Equally not surprising is that it has recently been stressed in the Supreme Court of Canada that recognising good faith as an organising principle and recognising a duty of honesty in the performance of contracts, 'accords with the reasonable expectations of commercial parties'.[155]

III. Insurer's Duty of Good Faith

Now that good faith in contract law generally is for the purpose of protecting the reasonable expectations of the parties, it is even more so in insurance contract law. This is because, almost without exception, an insurance contract is typically a

[153] R Ashton, 'Keeping the Faith—Good Faith in Insurance and the Emergence of General Contractual Good Faith' (2011) 22 *Insurance Law Journal* 81, 95.

[154] *Yam Seng Pte Ltd v International Trade Corporation Ltd* [2013] EWHC 111 (QB) [148], [144].

[155] *Bhasin v Hrynew* 2014 SCC 71, [2014] 3 SCR 495.

contract of good faith. Good faith in insurance conventionally binds policyholders (or insurance applicants), but it is binding on insurers too. Its binding force on insurers has implications for policyholders: an insurer's duty of good faith is for the purpose of protecting policyholder's reasonable expectations.

A. Mutuality of the Duty of Good Faith in Insurance Law

Although the duty of good faith in insurance law is supposed to be binding on both parties to an insurance contract, the judicial and academic discussion of insurance good faith has long focused on policyholders (the insured). The term '(utmost) good faith' in insurance law has been associated most often with a policyholder's pre-contractual duty of disclosure of material facts, and also with a policyholder's duty not to make fraudulent claims. There has been an ocean of case law and academic literature on the former, as well as considerable court decisions and academic discussion on the latter. In contrast, there has been much less academic or judicial discussion of the insurer's duty of good faith.

That is not because the law does not require good faith from insurers. Rather, it has been established by Lord Mansfield, and has become entrenched, that the duty of good faith is mutual—'Good faith forbids *either* party by concealing what he privately knows, to draw the other into a bargain, from his ignorance of that fact, and his believing the contrary.'[156] (emphasis added) The mutuality of good faith was confirmed a century later in *Britton v Royal Insurance Company*,[157] and was reaffirmed more frequently in the twentieth century: 'Contracts of insurance are contracts in which *uberrima fides* is required, not only from the assured, but also from the company assuring.'[158] 'A contract of insurance was one of the utmost good faith on *both* sides.'[159] (emphasis added) For Steyn J (as he then was), 'it is established beyond doubt that the *uberrima fides* principle, as it is sometimes called, imposes reciprocal duties on the insured and the insurer'.[160] More recently, over the past three decades, the mutuality of the duty of good faith has been further confirmed by the Court of Appeal[161] and by the

[156] *Carter v Boehm* (1766) 3 Burr 1905, 1910.

[157] *Britton v Royal Insurance Company* (1866) 4 F & F 905, 909.

[158] *Re Bradley and Essex and Suffolk Accident Indemnity Society* [1912] 1 KB 415 (CA), 430 (per Farwell LJ).

[159] *Leen v Hall* (1923) 16 Lloyd's L Rep 100 (KB), 103 (per Avory J).

[160] *Banque Keyser Ullman SA v Skandia (UK) Insurance Co Ltd* [1987] 1 Lloyd's Rep 69 (QBD Comm), 93. See also *Bank of Nova Scotia v Hellenic Mutual War Risks Association (Bermuda) Ltd ('The Good Luck')* [1988] 1 Lloyd's Rep 514 (QBD), 546–47 (per Hobhouse J); *Sharp v Sphere Drake Insurance plc ('The Moonacre')* [1992] 2 Lloyd's Rep 501 (QBD Comm), 520 (per Mr Colman QC).

[161] *Container Transport International Inc v Oceanus Mutual Underwriting Association (Bermuda) Ltd* [1984] 1 Lloyd's Rep 476 (CA), 525 (per Stephenson, LJ); *Banque Keyser Ullman SA v Skandia (UK) Insurance Co Ltd* [1990] 1 QB 665 (HL), 700 (per Slade LJ); *Bank of Nova Scotia v Hellenic Mutual War Risks Association (Bermuda) Ltd ('The Good Luck')* [1989] 2 Lloyd's Rep 238 (CA), 264 (per May LJ); *Diggens v Sun Alliance & London Insurance plc*, [1994] CLC 1146 (CA); *St Paul Fire &*

House of Lords.[162] In this regard, on the Australian *Insurance Act 1984*, section 13 of which imposes a duty of good faith on each party to an insurance contract, it has been stated more recently, in *CGU Insurance Ltd v AMP Financial Planning Pty Ltd*:[163]

> The language of section 13, including the statement of the general principle [of utmost good faith] as a legal obligation separate from the implication of a provision into the contract ... had the effect of introducing a larger and reciprocal obligation between the insurer and the insured in the place of what had, for all practical purposes, previously had been a one-way street.

In the UK, the mutuality of good faith in common law remains unaffected by the recent insurance law reform by Parliament. Although under the Insurance Act 2015, section 14(3)(a), the provision in the Marine Insurance Act 1906, section 17, to the effect that 'if the utmost good faith be not observed by either party, the contract may be avoided by the other party' is deleted, this amendment is only intended to abolish avoidance of contract as a harsh remedy for an insured's breach of duty of fair presentation of risks under the Insurance Act 2015, rather than to negate the mutual duty of good faith or its binding force on insurers. In other words, the reform is intended to do away not with the duty of good faith or its mutuality, but just the draconian all-or-nothing consequence of the duty of good faith.

B. Insurer's Pre-contractual Good Faith: Disclosure

Insurer's Duty to Disclose Material Circumstances

Insurers are also bound by the pre-contractual duty of good faith, more specifically by the duty of disclosure.[164] That the duty of voluntary disclosure on the part of a consumer policyholder is abolished—and converted into a duty not to misrepresent upon insurer's enquiry—in consumer insurance does not exempt insurers from such a duty, and certainly not in business insurance; this is because the insured's 'duty of fair presentation',[165] as newly provided for in the

Marine Insurance Co (UK) Ltd v McConnell Dowell Contractors Ltd [1995] 2 Lloyd's Rep 116 (CA), 124 (per Evans LJ); *Société Anonyme d'Intermédiaires Luxembourgeois v Farex Gie* [1995] LRLR 116 (CA), 157 (per Saville LJ); *HIH Casualty and General Insurance Ltd v Chase Manhattan Bank* [2001] EWCA Civ 1250 [67] (per Rix LJ); *Drake Insurance plc v Provident Insurance plc* [2003] EWCA Civ 1834 [83] (per Rix LJ).

162 *Banque Keyser Ullman SA v Skandia (UK) Insurance Co Ltd* [1990] 2 All ER 947 (HL), 960 (per Lord Jauncey); *Pan Atlantic Insurance Co Ltd v Pine Top Insurance Co Ltd* [1994] 2 Lloyd's Rep 427 (HL), 456 (per Lord Loyd).

163 *CGU Insurance Ltd v AMP Financial Planning Pty Ltd* [2007] HCA 36, [2007] HCA 36 [127] (per Justice Kirby).

164 *Banque Keyser Ullman SA v Skandia (UK) Insurance Co Ltd* [1990] 2 All ER 947 (HL).

165 Insurance Act 2015, s 3(1) and (2).

Insurance Act 2015, still comprises the duty of disclosure[166] and the duty of non-misrepresentation.[167] Given the mutuality of good faith in insurance, an insurer too has a duty of disclosure and truthful representation toward itspolicyholders. In regard to an insurer's duty of disclosure, Slade LJ stated in the Court of Appeal that

> the duty falling upon the insurer must at least extend to disclosing all facts known to him which are material either to the nature of the risk sought to be covered or *the recoverability of a claim* under the policy which a prudent insured would *take into account in deciding* whether or not to place the risk for which he seeks cover with that insurer.[168] (emphasis added)

However, the House of Lords in this case was divided on the test of materiality for disclosure by an insurer. Although the foregoing opinion was affirmed by Lord Bridge,[169] Lord Jauncey found a somewhat different test of materiality: the duty would be limited only to 'facts which would influence a prudent insurer in deciding whether to accept the risk and, if so, upon what terms, and [influence] a prudent insured in entering into the contract on the terms proposed by the insurer'.[170] (emphasis added) But in just a few years, this was partly overruled in the House of Lords in *Pan Atlantic Insurance Co Ltd v Pine Top Insurance Co Ltd*,[171] where the majority confirmed part of the materiality test, which was that the circumstances in question for disclosure would have been taken into account by a prudent insurer in assessing the risks, rather than would have decisively influenced the insurer's decision in whether (and/or on what terms) to underwrite the risks.

The two cases effectively mean that 'the recoverability of a claim' is relevant, as found by Lord Jauncey and referred to in *Banque Keyser Ullman SA v Skandia (UK) Insurance Co Ltd*[172] above, which in relation to the materiality test for *disclosure by insurers* was not overruled in *Pan Atlantic* in the House of Lords. In other words, arguably, the materiality test for disclosure by insurers is still the 'decisive test', though for disclosure by policyholders it is what can be called the 'mere influence test'. Although it is suggested, very logically, that given the mutuality of the duty of disclosure, 'it is preferable that the test of materiality is the same, *mutatis mutandis*, for the insurer as it is for the assured',[173] this cannot be taken too literally. That is because what the insured and the insurer respectively consider in the course of negotiation are not quite the same, though the premium rate is a

[166] Insurance Act 2015, s 3(3)(a), (b), (4).

[167] Insurance Act 2015, s 3(3)(c).

[168] *Banque Keyser Ullman SA v Skandia (UK) Insurance Co Ltd* [1990] 1 QB 665 (CA), 772.

[169] *Banque Keyser Ullman SA v Skandia (UK) Insurance Co Ltd* [1991] 2 AC 249 (HL), 268.

[170] Ibid, 281. This test of materiality is said to be applied in *Aldrich v Norwich Union Life Insurance Co Ltd* [2000] Lloyd's Rep IR 1. See PM Eggers, P Foss and S Picken, *Good Faith and Insurance Contracts*, 3rd edn (London, LLP, 2010) [12.15].

[171] *Pan Atlantic Insurance Co Ltd v Pine Top Insurance Co Ltd* [1994] 2 Lloyd's Rep 427 (HL), [1994] 3 All ER 581 (HL), 531.

[172] *Banque Keyser Ullman SA v Skandia (UK) Insurance Co Ltd* [1991] 2 AC 249 (HL), 268, 281.

[173] Eggers et al, above n 170, [12.14].

common concern. Just like acceptability of particular (kinds of) risks is a paramount and ultimate concern for insurers, so is the recoverability of a claim for the insured. In this regard their considerations are symmetrical. Given this, it might be more reasonable to say that in line with the mutuality of the duty of disclosure, now that the insured is required to disclose a circumstance material to the acceptability of particular risks, so the insurer shall disclose a circumstance material to the recoverability of particular claims.

For the reasons given above, in relation to the insurer's duty of disclosure, the better test of materiality is the one stated by Slade LJ. Simply put, an insurer has the duty to disclose circumstances that are material to the nature of the risks to be assessed and material to the recoverability of claims under the policy. Circumstances or facts material to the recoverability of claims are relevant to the insurer's policyholder's reasonable expectations of coverage (PREC). It is suggested that the following classes of facts might be material for an assured, so that the insurer must disclose them, namely, facts concerning:[174]

1. the risk of loss under the policy, or the status or safety of the subject matter insured;[175]
2. the effect of the insurance and benefits available thereunder;[176]
3. the authorisation or constitution of the insurer permitting the insurer to issue the product which is to be taken by the assured and to pay claims;[177]
4. the existence of fraud in connection with the risk;[178]
5. foreign illegality which might have an impact on the risk or the policy;
6. the financial impact of the policy as regards premiums,[179] provided it is material to the risk;
7. any defence that might be raised by the insurer under the proposed policy.[180]

Pre-contractual non-disclosure and/or misrepresentation by insurers may give rise to PREC or induce the policyholder to have reasonable expectations of coverage. Apparently that is because the policyholder proposes insurance for the purpose of having coverage for certain risks, or in the expectation that a claim in relation thereto is recoverable. In this regard and in relation to type 1 facts referred to above, reinsurance is a good example. Reinsurance used to be thought of as liability insurance. However, the established law today is that reinsurance is not

[174] Ibid [12.16].

[175] See, eg, *Carter v Boehm* (1766) 3 Burr 1905; *Duffell v Wilson* (1808) 1 Camp 401; 170 ER 999. Cf *Aldrich v Norwich Union Life Insurance Co Ltd* [2000] Lloyd's Rep IR 1.

[176] See, eg, *British Workman's & General Insurance Co v Cunliffe* (1902) 18 TLR 425, 502; *Tofts v Pearl Life Assurance Company Limited* [1915] 1 KB 189; *Hughes v Liverpool Victoria Legal Friendly Society* [1916] 2 KB 482.

[177] See, eg, *Pontifex v Bignold* (1841) 3 Man & G 63; 133 ER 1058.

[178] Cf *Banque Keyser Ullman SA v Skandia (UK) Insurance Co Ltd* [1991] 2 AC 249 (HL).

[179] Cf *Mutual Reserve Life Insurance Co v Foster* (1904) 20 TLR 715; *Cross v Mutual Reserve Life Insurance Co* (1904) 21 TLR 15; *Merino v Mutual Reserve Life Insurance Co* (1904) 21 TLR 167; *Molloy v Mutual Reserve Life Insurance Co* (1906) 22 TLR 525.

[180] *Banque Keyser Ullman SA v Skandia (UK) Insurance Co Ltd* [1991] 2 AC 249 (HL).

insurance of 'the primary insurer's potential liability or disbursement' but 'double cover': it is 'an independent contract between reinsured and reinsurer in which the subject-matter of the insurance is the same as that of the primary insurance, that is to say, the risk to the ship or goods or whatever might be insured'.[181] A claimant under a reinsurance contract shall prove the loss suffered by the primary policyholders rather than its payment to them.[182] Another example in relation to 'the status or safety of the subject matter insured', as in number 1 above, is where the insured, not knowing that the risk has occurred, proposes insurance to an insurer which does know of the occurrence of the risk.[183] More interested in the premium, the insurer does not disclose the occurrence to the insured and accepts the risk, but subsequently refuses to pay the insured's claim on other grounds, such as breach of warranty.

Insurer's Duty to Remind Policyholders of Non-coverage

It can be doubted that the duty of good faith requires the insurer '*only* to inform the assured of material facts'.[184] (emphasis added) An insurer's duty of good faith certainly goes beyond that. As early as 100 years ago, Farwell LJ stated:

> I think it is the duty of all insuring companies to state in clear and plain terms, as conditions precedent, those provisions only which are such, not to wrap them up in a number of clauses which are not conditions precedent at all; and I think further that *it is their duty to call attention to such conditions in their form of proposal* so as to make sure that the insurers understand their liabilities.[185] (emphasis added)

Although his first reference to 'duty' is not to be understood in a legal or doctrinal sense,[186] the second reference thereto, as emphasised above, certainly could be a legal doctrine. It was a dissenting opinion in insurance law then, but it came to prominence several decades later. It was recognised by Lord Denning MR and Megaw LJJ in *Thornton v Shoe Lane Parking Ltd*[187] that one contractual party had a duty to bring exemptions and exclusions to the notice/attention of the other party. That was confirmed and reiterated by Dillon LJ in *Interfoto Picture Library Ltd v Stiletto Visual Programmes Ltd*, who said, 'if one condition in a set of printed conditions is particularly onerous or unusual, the party seeking to enforce it must

[181] *Charter Reinsurance Co Ltd v Fagan* [1997] AC 313 (HL), 392 and 387; *WASA International Insurance Co v Lexington Insurance Co* [2009] UKHL 40, [2010] 1 AC 180, [2009] 2 Lloyd's Rep 508.

[182] M Clarke, *Law of Liability Insurance* (London, Informa, 2013) [3.2.1].

[183] This is retrospective insurance. It is legal in marine insurance as 'lost or not lost' coverage. See Marine Insurance Act 1906, Sch 1, construction rule 1.

[184] Eggers et al, above n 170, [12.37].

[185] *Re Bradley and Essex and Suffolk Accident Indemnity Society* [1912] 1 KB 415 (CA), 433 (per Farell LJ).

[186] Meanwhile it is noteworthy that Coulson LJ also opined in *English v Western* [1940] 2 KB 156 (CA) 165 that it was the 'duty' of insurers to make clear their desired meaning in a contract by using unambiguous language.

[187] *Thornton v Shoe Lane Parking Ltd* [1970] EWCA Civ 2.

show that that particular condition was fairly brought to the attention of the other party'.[188]

This naturally has implications for insurance contracts. Although exemptions and exclusions in an insurance contract, unlike the warranties therein, hardly 'impose any extra burden upon the claimant'[189] and therefore are not onerous, they are certainty 'unusual' given the general purpose of an insurance contract: to the public, to potential policyholders and to an actual policyholder, the purpose of an insurance contract is normally to provide insurance coverage—that is the norm, and it is an exception to exclude coverage and/or to exempt the insurer from its normally expected payment obligation. Such an exception is unusual because it contravenes the perceived purpose of the insurance contract. Since exemptions and exclusions in an insurance contract are unusual, under the *Interfoto* rule, insurers have the duty to call such clauses to the attention of policyholders.[190] This is a part of an insurer's duty of good faith.

Duty to Explain the Terms and Conditions?

Unlike some insurance law in Continental jurisdictions,[191] good faith in English insurance law does not require the insurer to explain the terms of the policy.[192] The rationale seems to be that a duty, not strictly in a doctrinal sense, for insurers to make their terms and conditions clear in an insurance contract, makes a duty of explanation unnecessary. As was stressed in the Court of Appeal:

> [I]t is their [ie insurers'] duty to make the policy accord with and not exceed the proposal, and to express both in clear and unambiguous terms, lest (as Fletcher Moulton LJ, quoting Lord St Leonards, says in *Joel v Law Union and Crown Insurance Co*) provisions should be introduced into policies which 'unless they are fully explained to the parties, will lead a vast number of persons to suppose that they have made a provision for their families by an insurance on their lives, and by payment of perhaps a very considerable portion of their income, when in point of fact, from the very commencement, the policy was not worth the paper upon which it was written.'[193]

[188] *Interfoto Picture Library Ltd v Stiletto Visual Programmes Ltd* [1989] QB 433 (CA), 439, Bingham LJ concurring: '[T]he more outlandish the clause the greater the notice which the other party, if he is to be bound, must in all fairness be given.'

[189] *O'Brien v MGN Ltd* [2001] EWCA Civ 1279 [21], per Hale LJ, who also commented at [23]: 'In any event, the words "onerous or unusual" are not terms of art. They are simply one way of putting the general proposition that reasonable steps must be taken to draw the particular term in question to the notice of those who are to be bound by it and that more is required in relation to certain terms than to others depending on their effect.'

[190] But see M Clarke, *The Law of Insurance Contracts* (London, Informa 2009) [15-5B2] fn6: 'A duty not to conceal adverse terms is one thing, he [Mustill LJ] thought, and well-established in law, but a duty to highlight and explain conditions in such a situation is something else.' Referring to *Smit Tak Offshore Services Ltd v Youell* [1992] 1 Lloyd's Rep 154 (CA), 159, and *Yorkshire Water Services Ltd v Sun Alliance & London Insurance Ltd* [1997] CLC 213 (CA).

[191] For example, the Chinese Insurance Act (as amended in 2009), s 17.

[192] Eggers et al, above n 170, [12.37].

[193] *Re Bradley and Essex and Suffolk Accident Indemnity Society* [1912] 1 KB 415 (CA), 430 (per Farwell LJ).

This certainly does not indicate that an insurer has the duty to explain the insurance terms to its policyholders. What follows is that an insurer's duty to make terms of insurance policies clear and unambiguous is expected to ensure that the policyholder's expectations of coverage are not frustrated, even with those terms being unexplained by insurers. Although Farwell LJ also stressed that '[i]t is especially incumbent on insurance companies to make clear, both in their proposal forms and in their policies, the conditions which are precedent to their liability to pay'[194]—and this was cited approvingly in the Court of Appeal in *Pilkington UK Ltd v CGU Insurance Plc*[195]—this does not mean that insurers have a duty to explain the conditions. To 'make clear' is not the same as 'to explain'; making terms and conditions clear in insurance documents, including proposal forms and policies, is different from explaining them outside these documents. The former would more likely entail further defining and qualifying the terms, and what is defined and qualified in the documents is an integral part of the policy terms and conditions. The latter, that is explanation of the terms, is external to, and hence not a part of, the insurance policy. As long as insurers' duty to make insurance terms and conditions clear works effectively, there is no need to impose on them a further duty to explain.

The other reason why there is not and should not be a duty for insurers to explain, is that such a duty has inherent practical difficulties that give rise to potential legal complications. In what way is the insurer or its agent expected to make an *effective* explanation? To what extent, or how far, should the explanation go, and what is the measurement for that? For these considerations, insurers would presumably prefer to explain in writing and in detail, but that is not likely to be effective—policyholders tend not to read much of the insurance contract *per se*, and it is doubtful that they would read the detail of any written explanatory leaflets with which they might be bombarded. There might also be arguments over whether or to what extent the explanation should be incorporated into the contract in question.

C. Insurer's Post-contractual Good Faith: Claims Handling

The development of the concept of good faith as a post-contract duty of the insurer has been described as 'embryonic',[196] and the law in this respect is not

[194] Ibid 433 (per Farwell LJ).

[195] *Pilkington UK Ltd v CGU Insurance Plc* [2004] EWCA Civ 23.

[196] R Merkin, 'Reforming Insurance Law: Is There a Case for Reverse Transportation?' *Report for the English and Scottish Law Commissions* (London and Edinburgh, The Law Commission and Scottish Law Commission, 2008) 12.

well settled. However, as a regulatory measure, the Insurance Conduct of Business Sourcebook (ICOBS), Rule 8 requires that an insurer must:

1. handle claims promptly and fairly;
2. provide reasonable guidance to help a policyholder make a claim, and appropriate information on its progress;
3. not unreasonably reject a claim (including by terminating or avoiding a policy); and
4. settle claims promptly once settlement terms are agreed.[197]

Although this is not strictly law, it has some legal basis in common law.

Duty to Handle Claims Promptly and Fairly

The consequences of an insurer's failure to handle a policyholder's claim promptly and fairly are best illustrated in *Sprung v Royal Insurance (UK) Ltd*.[198] In this lamentable case, after the insurer's initial rejection of the policyholder's claim, there was a lengthy delay of payment by the insurer, which caused substantial consequential loss; this, however, could not be compensated under the law then. This was due to one rule in English insurance law and another rule in English general contract law. The rule in English insurance law was that 'a contract of indemnity gives rise to an action for unliquidated damages, arising from the failure of the indemnifier to prevent the indemnified person from suffering damage, for example, by having to pay a third party.'[199] The rule in English general contract law is that no damages could be awarded for late payment of damages.[200] As a corollary to these two rules, there can be no compensatory damages for belated insurance payment.

Following from that lesson and other grounds, the Law Commission and the Scottish Law Commission, in their joint report presented to the Government in July 2014 with the initial draft bill, recommended an implied term about insurers' payment of 'sums due'. The phrase 'sums due' implies that there must be a valid claim for which sums are recognised to be due, and it encompasses sums which are 'due' either by virtue of an agreement between the parties or because they have been determined by a court to be payable by the insurer.

Although the recommended clause was even not accepted by the Government into the bill submitted to Parliament, and hence not enacted in 2015, the Law Commission and the Scottish Law Commission continued their efforts to reform the law in this respect. The recommendations were incorporated in the Enterprise

[197] Financial Conduct Authority Handbook ICOBS 8.1.

[198] *Sprung v Royal Insurance (UK) Ltd* [1999] 1 Lloyd's Rep IR 111 (CA).

[199] *Firma C-Trade SA v Newcastle Protection and Indemnity Association (The Fanti)*; *Socony Mobil Oil Co Inc v West of England Ship-owners Mutual Insurance Association* (London) Ltd (The Padre Island) [1991] 2 AC 1, 35-36 (per Lord Goff).

[200] *President of India v Lips Maritime Corporation* [1988] AC 395 (HL), 425.

Bill, which received Royal Assent on 4 May 2016. Part V, comprising sections 28, 29 and 30, of the Enterprise Act 2016 addresses late payment of insurance claims. The most essential provision, as in section 28(1) which meanwhile incorporates the reformed rule as section 13A of the Insurance Act 2015, is as follows:[201]

13A Implied term about payment

(1) It is an implied term of every contract of insurance that if the insured makes a claim under the contract, the insurer must pay any sums due in respect of the claim within a reasonable time.
(2) A reasonable time includes a reasonable time to investigate and assess the claim.
(3) What is reasonable will depend on all the relevant circumstances, but the following are examples of things which may need to be taken into account—
 (a) the type of insurance,
 (b) the size and complexity of the claim,
 (c) compliance with any relevant statutory or regulatory rules or guidance,
 (d) factors outside the insurer's control.
(4) If the insurer shows that there were reasonable grounds for disputing the claim (whether as to the amount of any sum payable, or as to whether anything at all is payable)—
 (a) the insurer does not breach the term implied by subsection (1) merely by failing to pay the claim (or the affected part of it) while the dispute is continuing, but
 (b) the conduct of the insurer in handling the claim may be a relevant factor in deciding whether that term was breached and, if so, when.
(5) Remedies (for example, damages) available for breach of the term implied by subsection (1) are in addition to and distinct from—
 (a) any right to enforce payment of the sums due, and
 (b) any right to interest on those sums (whether under the contract, under another enactment, at the court's discretion or otherwise).

In addition to the statutory reform, current case law has held that on receiving a claim, an insurer is expected to make enquiries before attempting avoidance of the policy,[202] not to act arbitrarily and not to take into account wholly extraneous circumstances.[203] This entails honesty and fair dealing, which are 'the hallmarks of good faith'.[204] With the Enterprise Act 2016 sections 28, 29 and 30 to be effective as of 5 May 2017, the requirement of procedural reasonableness and fairness will be in place. This is consistent with 'an emerging principle of good faith in the way in which insurers handle claims.'[205]

[201] Insurance Contract Law: Business Disclosure; Warranties; Insurers' Remedies for Fraudulent Claims; and Late Payment (Cm 8898; SG/2014/131) (Law Com No 353/ ScotLaw Com No 238) 357–58.

[202] *Drake Insurance plc v Provident Insurance plc* [2003] EWCA Civ 1834 [177] (per Rix LJ).

[203] *Gan Insurance Co v Tai Ping Insurance Co* [2001] EWCA Civ 1047 [68], [76], followed in *Eagle Star Insurance Co Ltd v Cresswell* [2004] EWCA Civ 602.

[204] Eggers et al, above n 170, [12.36].

[205] A Naidoo and D Oughton, 'The confused post-formation duty of good faith in insurance law: from refinement to fragmentation to elimination' [2005] Journal of Business Law 346, 364.

Duty to Provide Guidance?

The duty of good faith 'must be tailored in light of the expectations and moral and professional standards of the industry concerned, even though such practices and models are not matters of law'.[206] In line with this, the ICOBS Rules are relevant. Rule 8.1 of ICOBS requires insurers to 'provide reasonable guidance to help a policyholder make a claim and appropriate information on its progress'. Though it is understandable that information on the progress of claims-handling must be provided to policyholder claimants, it is not clear what kind of 'guidance' should be provided. Are insurers expected to provide substantive guidance on the legal or contractual ground of the claim, or mainly procedural guidance on how the policyholder should file a claim?

The more reasonable interpretation would be that insurers are expected to provide procedural rather than substantive guidance about making insurance claims. The guidance does not need to be on substantive grounds for making claims, because the relationship between insurers and policyholders, albeit subject to good faith, is not fiduciary.[207] Actually, good faith

> has strong conceptual differences from the much higher obligations of a fiduciary. Unlike fiduciary duties, good faith performance does not engage duties of loyalty to the other contracting party or a duty to put the interests of the other contracting party first.[208]

A duty of good faith obliges an insurer to handle insurance claims fairly, but that does not oblige the insurer to do so proactively to subordinate its own interests to that of policyholder claimants as if it were a fiduciary or trustee. This is particularly so in business insurance. Therefore, it should suffice if the insurer reasonably takes into account the claimants' interest and provides them with procedural guidance, as well as with information on the progress of the claims-handling process.

Duty not to Abuse Avoidance or Termination of Contract

One aspect of an insurer's post-contractual duty of good faith concerns its right to avoid the insurance contract. It was acknowledged in *Pan Atlantic Insurance v Pine Top Insurance*[209] that the insurer's duty of good faith was not limited to disclosure and might extend to a wrongful avoidance at the post-formation stage. It was also opined that 'the doctrine of good faith should be capable of limiting the insurer's right to avoid in circumstances where that remedy, which has been described in recent years as draconian, would operate unfairly'.[210] This is particularly so with

[206] Ibid [3.19].

[207] Clarke, above n 182, [9.2.1], referring to *Plaza Fibreglass Manufacturing Ltd v Cardinal Insurance Co* (1994) 115 DLR 4th 37 (CA Ontario).

[208] *Bhasin v Hrynew* 2014 SCC 71 [65]; [2014] 3 SCR 495.

[209] *Pan Atlantic Insurance Co Ltd v Pine Top Insurance Co Ltd* [1994] 2 Lloyd's Rep 427 (HL), [1994] 3 All ER 581 (HL) 623 (per Lord Lloyd).

[210] *Drake Insurance plc v Provident Insurance plc* [2003] EWCA Civ 1834 [87] (per Rix LJ).

what is known as 'the danger of "underwriting at claims stage" whereby the insurer agrees to the risk, however inadequately presented, and asks questions only if a claim arises'.[211] If the insurer discovers even only minor non-disclosure or misrepresentation by the policyholder, it may refuse all claims. In line with the statement above by Rix LJ, the Consumer Insurance (Disclosure and Representations) Act 2012 and the Insurance Act 2015 have substantially limited the insurer's right of avoidance.[212]

Duty in Relation to Defence and Settlement

'English insurance law premises that normally the third-party claim is defended by the person, the insured, against whom the claim was brought',[213] and 'it is also commonly provided that the insurer shall be *entitled* to defend the action and settle the claim against the insured'.[214] Although defence for the liability policyholder is a right rather than a duty, the liability insurer has the duty to exercise the right in good faith, as it is a discretionary right under a contract.[215] The effect of insurance contract terms and conditions that entitle insurers to have control of all or any proceedings against the insured/policyholder is—as stated in *Groom v Crocker*[216]—'to give to the insurers the right to decide upon the proper tactics to pursue in the conduct of the action, provided that they do so in what they bona fide consider to the common interest of themselves and their assured'. To illustrate, it was held in this case that the insurer in question was not entitled to do what it actually did, ie to have admitted negligence on behalf of its policyholder, only for some advantage outside the litigation with which the policyholder was not concerned.

In the 1970s, referring approvingly to the insurer's duty of good faith and fair dealing in American insurance law, the High Court of Australia stated that insurer's duty of good faith must 'control the actions of an insurer who has taken over its insured's defence'.[217] More recently, the same court recognised:

> In particular, we accept that utmost good faith may require an insurer to act with due regard to the legitimate interests of an insured, as well as to its own interests [referring

[211] LC/SLC Joint Consultation Paper 3, [4.3]. It has been found that 'Section 18 [of the Marine Insurance Act 1906] generates a large number of disputes. In 2010, almost a third (31%) of Airmic members said that insurers had raised non-disclosure issues against them in the last five years. Of these, only around half reported that the claim had been resolved satisfactorily. There was also a high level of litigation: 5% of all Airmic members in the survey had been involved in litigation on the issue of non-disclosure in the last five years' See LC/SLC Joint Consultation Paper 3 (Summary) [S.31], [S.32].

[212] Consumer Insurance (Disclosure and Representations) Act 2012, Sch 1; Insurance Act 2015, Sch 1.

[213] Clarke, above n 182, [9.1].

[214] Ibid [9.2].

[215] *Abu Dhabi National Tanker Co Ltd v Product Star Shipping Ltd ('The Product Star')* [1993] 1 Lloyd's Rep 397 (CA); *Gan Insurance Co v Tai Ping Insurance Co* [2001] EWCA Civ 1047; *Nash v Paragon Finance Plc* [2001] EWCA Civ 1466.

[216] *Groom v Crocker* [1939] 1 KB 194, 203 (per Sir Wilfrid Green MR).

[217] *Distillery v Ajax* [1975] HCA 3 [54] (per Menzies J).

> to *Distillery v Ajax* [1975] HCA 3] … Conversely, an insurer's statutory obligation to act with utmost good faith may require an insurer to act, consistently with commercial standards of decency and fairness, with due regard to the interests of the insured. Such an obligation may well affect the conduct of an insurer in making a timely response to a claim for indemnity.[218]

A duty of good faith 'will apply equally to the insurer's exercise of its power of granting or withholding consent to the making of admissions etc even if it elects not to take over the defence'.[219] Further,

> [an insurer's] power of restraining settlement by the insured must be exercised in good faith having regard to the interests of the insured as well as to its own interests and in the exercise of its power to withhold consent the insurer must not have regard to considerations extraneous to the policy of indemnity.[220]

This was reiterated in *Gan Insurance v Tai Ping Insurance*,[221] where it was held that the reinsurer's contractual right of approving the insured's settlement with a third party

> is a right to be exercised in good faith after consideration of and on the basis of the facts giving rise to the particular claim, and not with reference to considerations wholly extraneous to the subject-matter of the particular reinsurance or arbitrarily.[222]

Similarly, in *Eagle Star Insurance Co Ltd v Cresswell*,[223] a claims control clause stated that reinsurers 'shall control the negotiations and settlements of any claims under this Policy'. The Court of Appeal held that the clause gave the reinsurers discretion to take control of any negotiation or settlement, but the discretion was bound by mutual good faith in insurance. Rix LJ said:

> [I]f, while exercising or refusing to exercise control, the reinsurers act in bad faith, capriciously or arbitrarily, then there is the implied term found by Mance LJ and Latham LJ in *Tai Ping* to protect the reinsured … But this protection may not depend only on a term to be implied 'for business efficacy', but may be inherent as a matter of law in the very essence of the reinsurers' mutual obligation of good faith.[224]

In the US, similar to the lead opinion in *Gan Insurance v Tai Ping Insurance*,[225] it was held, for example, in Illinois that the duty of good faith and fair dealing implied into every contract 'requires a party vested with contractual discretion to exercise that discretion reasonably and not arbitrarily, capriciously, or in a manner

[218] *CGU Insurance Ltd v AMP Financial Planning Pty Ltd* [2007] HCA 36 [15] (per Gleeson CJ and Crennan J).
[219] *Distillery v Ajax* [1975] HCA 3 [54] (per Menzies J).
[220] Ibid [42] (per Menzies J).
[221] *Gan Insurance Co v Tai Ping Insurance Co* [2001] EWCA Civ 1047.
[222] Ibid [76], and see also [54] and [67].
[223] *Eagle Star Insurance Co Ltd v Cresswell* [2004] EWCA Civ 602.
[224] Ibid [54].
[225] *Gan Insurance Co v Tai Ping Insurance Co* [2001] EWCA Civ 1047.

inconsistent with the reasonable expectations of the parties'.[226] Further quoting a federal court opinion in *Craft v Economy Fire and Casualty Company*[227] that the insurer's duty of good faith and fair dealing

> is based on the reasonable expectations of the insured and the unequal bargaining positions of the contractants ... After all, the insured is the one who pays the premiums ... and the 'reasonable expectation' that he will be dealt with fairly and in good faith by his insurer is still present,[228]

the Supreme Court of Tennessee thought the position taken by the court in *Craft* 'more nearly conforms with an insured's expectations'.[229]

IV. Conclusion

Good faith in contract law is more than a moral requirement. It serves a utilitarian and practical purpose, ie the realisation or protection of the reasonable expectations of the parties. This can be seen from judicial recognition of a growing but qualified doctrine of good faith in the performance of contract in common law jurisdictions, particularly recently in England and in Canada. For example, in the High Court (of England and Wales), 'recognising an implied duty of good faith in the performance of contracts ... is consonant with the theme identified by Lord Steyn as running through our law of contract that reasonable expectations must be protected'.[230] In the Supreme Court of Canada, it has been pointed out that lack of a generalised and independent doctrine of good faith 'produces results that are not consistent with the reasonable expectations of commercial parties',[231] and further that recognising an 'organizing principle of good faith' plus 'a common law duty to act honestly in the performance of contractual obligations' will 'put in place a duty that is just, that accords with the reasonable expectations of commercial parties'.[232] Such development of contract-law good faith has huge implications for contract law in general, and for insurance contract law in particular. An emerging, though qualified, judicial recognition of good faith in contract (performance) means that courts are beginning to take an overarching and principled approach, along with the piecemeal conventional approach, to protecting reasonable expectations.

[226] *Teachers Insurance & Annuity Association of America v La Salle National Bank*, 295 Ill App 3d 61, 73; 691 NE 2d 881, 890 (1998), quoting *Northern Trust Co v VIII South Michigan Associates*, 276 Ill App 3d 355, 367, 212 Ill Dec750, 657 NE 2d 1095 (1995).

[227] *Craft v Economy Fire and Casualty Co* 572 F 2d 565 (7th Cir1978).

[228] Ibid 569.

[229] *MFA Mutual Insurance Company v Flint*, 574 SW 2d 718, 722 (1978).

[230] *Yam Seng Pte Ltd v International Trade Corporation Ltd* [2013] EWHC 111 (QB) [145] (per Leggat J).

[231] *Bhasin v Hrynew* 2014 SCC 71, [2014] 3 SCR 495 [32] (per Justice Cromwell).

[232] Ibid [33], [34] (per Justice Cromwell).

In other words, courts are taking reasonable expectations more seriously, though still indirectly.

For insurance contract, the implication is greater. This is because insurance contract prototypically requires good faith, not only of policyholders but also of insurers. The law of good faith in insurance conventionally emphasises a policyholder's duty of good faith in terms of disclosure and representation of material information, with far less attention paid to the insurer's duty of good faith. Given that, highlighting insurers' duty of good faith, as is done in this chapter and provided for in the Australian *Insurance Act 1984*, sections 13, 14, 35, 37 and 22, which all deal with the insurer's pre-contractual obligation essentially to look after the interests of policyholders,[233] will serve to show that insurance contract law has had an indirect, principled but insufficient mechanism to ensure that the policyholder's reasonable expectations can be honoured. As far as this is concerned, the notion of 'policyholder's reasonable expectations' is not and should not be alarming at all, or prone to scepticism. Indeed, it prospered in the US from the 1960s—hence the American insurance law 'doctrine' of reasonable expectations—to the early 1990s, and still exhibits much life there, where it is understood that 'although the doctrine of reasonable expectations does not require pre-contractual disclosure by insurers, it creates an obvious incentive for full and detailed disclosure'.[234] This also shows the real connectedness between reasonable expectations and the insurer's good faith.

[233] S Traves, 'Utmost Good Faith, Reliance upon and Notification of Terms: The Obligations of Insurers and the Rights of Insureds' (2012) 23 *Insurance Law Journal* 1, 4.

[234] M Davies, 'Insurer's Pre-contractual Disclosure Obligations: The Position in the United States' (2012) 23 *Insurance Law Journal* 70, 76.

5

Revisiting the Doctrine of Reasonable Expectations in American Insurance Law

The purpose of this chapter is to revisit what has generally been known as 'the doctrine of reasonable expectations'[1] (DRE) in its current state in American insurance law. From its name, it is clear that DRE is essentially the US version of policyholder's reasonable expectations of coverage (PREC), Hence, for ease of reference in this chapter, 'DRE' is used interchangeably with 'PREC'. As a re-examination of and revisit to the law, this chapter is more descriptive of than normative about DRE/PREC in the US, though it does far more than merely describing. In spite of that, rediscovering and revisiting the American DRE is essential here. This is, firstly, because since the *Connecticut Insurance Law Journal* symposium papers in 1998 on DRE,[2] there has been only sporadic discussion of it in American insurance law academia.[3] This necessitates a revisit. Secondly and more importantly, it is because much of English insurance lawyers' reluctance to embrace PREC is substantially based on or aligned with the controversies over the American DRE. Therefore, in order to see whether such reluctance is sound and justifiable, it certainly is necessary to evaluate the status of DRE in American state courts.

[1] RS Jerry II and DS Richmond, *Understanding Insurance Law*, 5th edn (Albany, NY, LexisNexis, 2012) [25D]; JW Stempel, *Principles of Insurance Law*, 4th edn (Albany, NY, LexisNexis, 2012) [2.09]. See also in particular all articles in (1998) 5 *Connecticut Insurance Law Journal*, where most authors, except Kenneth Abraham, classed the reasonable expectations approach in insurance law as a 'doctrine'.

[2] (1998) 5 Connecticut Insurance Law Journal 1–473.

[3] PN Swisher, 'A Realistic Consensus Approach to the Insurance Law Doctrine of Reasonable Expectations' (2000) 35 *Tort and Insurance Law Journal* 729; DJ Seno, 'The Doctrine of Reasonable Expectations in Insurance Law: What to Expect in Wisconsin' (2002) 85 *Marquette Law Review* 859; D Schwarcz, 'A Products Liability Theory for the Judicial Regulation of Insurance Policies' (2007) 48 *William & Mary Law Review* 1389, 1426–35; T Plotkin, 'Case Note: A Congregation of Vapours: *Clendenin Brothers, Inc. v. United States Fire Insurance Company*, Welding Rod Litigation, the Total Pollution Exclusion, the Futility of the Judicial Search for Ambiguity in Commercial General Liability Insurance Contracts, and the Reasonable Expectations of the Insured' (2007) 13 *Connecticut Insurance Law Journal* 364; S Randall, 'Freedom of Contract in Insurance' (2008) 14 *Connecticut Insurance Law Journal* 107, 111–18; AJ Park, 'What to Reasonably Expect in the Coming Years from the Reasonable Expectations of the Insured Doctrine' (2012) 49 *Willamette Law Review* 165.

After briefly introducing the origin and the formulations of DRE, as well as the controversies surrounding it, this chapter will focus on recharacterising DRE according to Keeton's and Dworkin's perceptions of the distinction between legal principles and legal doctrines. Insurance law decisions that treated DRE or PREC in one way or another in each US state jurisdiction are examined for this purpose. Based on this, and particularly on Keeton's characterisation system, which he reiterated[4] six years after proposing DRE,[5] it is argued in this chapter that DRE in the American version should and can be more appropriately recharacterised as a principle, rather than as the doctrine often referred to in US insurance law academia and by the judiciary. The most notable exception to this tendency of doctrination is Kenneth Abraham's stand-alone argument that in insurance law the reasonable expectations 'principle' underlying the 'minor doctrine' that policyholder's reasonable expectations are to be honoured in spite of clear policy language to the contrary, 'is of major significance'.[6]

The recharacterisation has fundamental implications for the controversy over the American DRE/PREC. As a whole, this chapter paves the way for discussing and possibly embracing PREC in English insurance law in Chapter 6.

I. The Doctrine of Reasonable Expectations in the US: A Brief Overview

A. What is its Origin?

In the US, the notion that policyholder's reasonable expectations of coverage should be honoured can be traced back to Karl Llewellyn as early as 1925, to Fredrich Kessler in 1943 and to Spencer Kimball (one of the first insurance law scholars in the US) in 1960. Llewellyn argued moderately for giving 'the insured … the protection he might decently believe he was buying, without too much close regard to the exceptions in the policy'.[7] In his seminal discussion of contracts of adhesion, Kessler used insurance contract as a prototype to expound the impact of adhesive contracts on freedom of contract. He argued that 'In dealing with standard contracts courts have to determine what the weaker contracting party could legitimately expect … and to what extent the stronger party disappointed reasonable expectations based on typical life situation.'[8] Kimball identified 'policyholder's

[4] R Keeton, 'Reasonable Expectations in the Second Decade' (1976) 12 *Forum* 275, 276.

[5] R Keeton, 'Insurance Law Rights at Variance with Policy Provisions, Part One' (1970) 83 *Harvard Law Review* 961.

[6] KS Abraham, 'The Expectations Principle as a Regulative Ideal' (1998) 5 *Connecticut Insurance Law Journal* 60, 61.

[7] K Llewellyn, 'The Effect of Legal Institutions upon Economics' (1925) 15 *American Economic Review* 665, 673.

[8] F Kessler, 'Contract of Adhesion—Some Thoughts about Freedom of Contract' (1943) 43 *Columbia Law Review* 629, 637.

reasonable expectations' as a principle that could qualify insurers' efforts to draft policy forms that would expressly negate coverage'.[9]

However, it was only after Professor (and subsequently Judge) Robert Keeton's seminal *Harvard Law Review* article, in two instalments,[10] in 1970 that DRE rose to prominence in the US. Keeton found, amongst other things, that 'The objectively reasonable expectations of [insurance] applicants and intended beneficiaries regarding the terms of insurance contracts will be honoured even though painstaking study of the policy provisions would have negated those expectations.'[11]

The case law commonly recognised for articulating DRE was *Kievit v Loral Protection Life Insurance Co*[12] in New Jersey, preceding Keeton's seminal article referred to above.[13] In *Kievit*, the insured purchased an accident policy providing coverage for loss 'resulting directly and independently of all other causes from accidental bodily injuries', but excluding loss 'resulting from or contributed to by any disease or ailment'. The insured's disability was caused in part by Parkinson's disease, which developed at the same time that the covered accident happened. It was held that the insured's disability was covered in spite of the policy's rather plain language; the judge said: 'When members of the public purchase policies of insurance they are entitled to the broad measure of protection necessary to fulfil their reasonable expectations.'[14]

After the *Kievit* decision, many courts supported the premise that insurance policies should be enforced according to the policyholder's reasonable expectations.[15] It was from those many early court decisions that Keeton found and formulated[16] what has generally been known as the doctrine of reasonable expectations (DRE) in insurance law, although he classed it as a principle. It is noteworthy that DRE is applied, if at all, mostly in cases in which the policyholder is a consumer. In this regard, 'the reasonable expectations doctrine is used by courts to protect consumers, not to adjust a commercial relationship between parties with roughly equal bargaining power'.[17]

[9] S Kimball, *Insurance and Public Policy: A Study in the Legal Implementation of Social and Economic Public Policy, Based on Wisconsin Record 1835–1959* (Madison, Wis, University of Wisconsin Press, 1960) 210–11, 224.

[10] R Keeton, 'Insurance Law Rights at Variance with Policy Provisions, Part One' (1970) 83 *Harvard Law Review* 961; R Keeton, 'Insurance Law Rights at Variance with Policy Provisions, Part Two' (1970) 83 *Harvard Law Review* 1281.

[11] R Keeton, 'Insurance Law Rights at Variance with Policy Provisions, Part One', above n 10, 967.

[12] *Kievit v Loral Protection Life Ins Co* 170 A 2d 22 (NJ 1961).

[13] But also note *Lacks v Fidelity & Casualty Co* 306 NY 357, 118 NE 2d 555 (1954) preceding *Kievt*. See KS Abraham, 'Judge-Made Law and Judge-Made Insurance: Honouring the Reasonable Expectations of the Insured' (1981) 67 *Virginia Law Review* 1151, 1155–56.

[14] *Kievit v Loral Protection Life Ins. Co* 170 A 2d 22 (NJ 1961).

[15] Jerry and Richmond, above n 1, 144.

[16] Abraham, above n 13, 1153.

[17] Jerry and Richmond, above n 1, 146–47.

B. Controversies over the Doctrine of Reasonable Expectations

There is no consensus on what DRE really is, or how it actually works. Part of the difficulty is that DRE 'represents not a single concept but a bundle of related ideas ... [which] range from close adherence to traditional policy interpretation techniques to sharp departure from them'.[18] From its employment by the courts, commentators have deduced several—ranging from only two[19] to as many as seven[20]—different versions of DRE. These versions, as described by different commentators, overlap. To sum up briefly, with minimal overlapping, those relatively frequently employed are as follows:

1. *The Keeton version.* Also known as the 'strong version'[21] of DRE, this is apparently and uncontroversially the most faithful to Keeton's formulation, under which the courts apply DRE to unambiguous insurance policy language.
2. *The ambiguity-based version*, under which courts use DRE as a rule of construction analogous to the *contra proferentem* rule. This is also known as the 'weak version'[22] of DRE, whereby it is the policyholder's reasonable expectations of coverage that is controlling if there is ambiguity or inconsistency in the meaning of the language used in the insurance policy.
3. *The unconscionability or unfairness version*, under which '*fairly often*, courts employ reasonable expectations analysis to adjust contract terms that would otherwise have an effect that is unfair or unconscionable to the insured'.[23]
4. *The fine-print or prominence-based version*, under which courts will invalidate a clear policy provision if it is hidden or not prominent in the policy.[24]

Other relatively insignificant versions of or approaches to the DRE are the purpose/insurability approach, which was 'very rarely' and 'very seldom'[25] used, and the

[18] M Rahdert, 'Reasonable Expectations Revisited' (1998) 5 *Connecticut Insurance Law Journal* 107, 111.

[19] J Fischer, 'The Doctrine of Reasonable Expectations is Indispensable, if We Only Know What For?' (1998) 5 *Connecticut Insurance Law Journal* 151, 155.

[20] JW Stempel, 'Unmet Expectations: Undue Restriction of the Reasonable Expectations Approach and the Misleading Mythology of Judicial Role' (1998) 5 *Connecticut Insurance Law Journal* 181, 192–93; Fischer, above n 19, 156.

[21] Fischer, above n 19, 155.

[22] Ibid.

[23] Rahdert, above n 18, 112–14 (also Part I), further commenting that this approach, more broadly in contract law, is 'one of the great legacies of the realist jurisprudence that swept contract law in the middle decades of this [20th] century [in the USA].'

[24] SM Popick and CD Quockenbos, 'Reasonable Expectations after Thirty Years: A Failed Doctrine' (1998) 5 *Connecticut Insurance Law Journal* 425, 442.

[25] Rahdert, above n 18, 136, referring at 137 to *Wood v American Family Mutual Insurance Co* 436 NW 2d 594 (Wis 1989) as the only close example. Courts use DRE to avoid enforcing policy language that would defeat what courts believe are the essential objectives or the essential value of the insurance policy for most insured who typically buy the particular kind of insurance product in question.

public policy or 'compensability' approach used 'in very rare instances (so rare that they approach zero)'.[26]

Apparently, given the variety of approaches or versions, DRE has largely lost its original formulation as propounded by Keeton. The variety of DRE approaches also 'has led to a number of confusing interpretive conclusions in trying to ascertain exactly which reasonable expectations doctrine has been adopted—or has not been adopted—in various jurisdictions'.[27] The variety makes it generally unimportant,[28] not to mention almost impossible, to generalise reliably how many American state jurisdictions have adopted DRE. For this purpose, however, it suffices to make three general points. First, in the wake of Keeton's seminal article, DRE rose to prominence in the 1970s in the US in its different versions and variations. Secondly, DRE's prominence in the 1970s was followed by continued growth in its application until the mid-1980s in some jurisdictions, though with obvious judicial retreat from it in others. Thirdly, the 1990s saw a steady retreat from DRE, traceable to the mid-1980s.

Another controversy is whether DRE is 'dead' in the US. It has been argued that at least the 'strong version' of DRE (see above) is 'dead and discarded', and that it 'does not play an important role in the landscape of contemporary American insurance law'.[29] On the other hand, it is also argued that 'In the main the doctrine remains very much alive.'[30] However, as will be shown in section II. below, even merely concerning whether DRE is premised on ambiguity in insurance policy terms, it is impossible to put forward a ready generalisation.

Both controversies might be connected with another question: Is there really a *doctrine* of reasonable expectations (of the insureds/policyholders) in American insurance law? As regards this, there is even a meta-question: Does 'doctrine' here mean narrowly a legal rule, as opposed to a legal principle? Or is it just a *general reference* to a legal norm, with no need to distinguish a legal doctrine from a legal principle in this context? As Dworkin famously pointed out,

> The difference between legal principles and legal rules [or doctrines] is a logical distinction. Both sets of standards point to particular decisions about legal obligation in particular circumstances, but they differ in the character of the direction they give.[31]

[26] Rahdert, above n 18, 113, referring at 141 to *Keen Corp v Insurance Co of North America* 667 F 2d 1034, 1041 (DC Cir 1981) as the only example. Courts would avoid policy limitations that would contravene important overriding public policies regarding assured compensation. Courts use the reasonable expectations doctrine to protect the interests of persons other than the insured. This is so with insurance involving injuries arising from exposure to asbestos.

[27] P Swisher, 'A Realistic Consensus Approach to the Insurance Law Doctrine of Reasonable Expectations' (2000) 35 *Tort and Insurance Law Journal* 729, 763.

[28] Fischer, above n 19, 155. Fischer says: 'The jurisdiction body count is not important.'

[29] Swisher, above n 27, 763.

[30] Rahdert, above n 18, 111.

[31] R Dworkin, 'The Mode of Rules' (1967) 35 *University of Chicago Law Review* 14, 25. See also R Dworkin, *Taking Rights Seriously* (London, Duckworth 1978) 26.

Further discussion along these lines will follow later. Here it is necessary and more important to note that the distinction between legal principles and legal doctrines is actually relevant in Keeton's discussion of PREC. In his seminal article in 1970, Keeton referred to PREC as a principle first and foremost, rather than a doctrine; he referred to waiver, estoppel in its various forms, election, reformation, rescission and so forth specifically as doctrines, but to PREC as a principle, maintaining an underlying distinction between them. Additionally, and more importantly, a few years later, when revisiting PREC in American insurance law, Keeton specifically discussed the distinction between doctrines/rules and principles in law. This is discussed further in section II. below.

II. Recharacterising the Doctrine of Reasonable Expectations: From 'Doctrine' to 'Principle'

A. Keeton's 'Characterisation System'

Although American insurance lawyers discuss the *doctrine* of reasonable expectations, it seems that characterising the concept of protecting a policyholder's reasonable expectations as a doctrine and taking that for granted has deviated from what Keeton intended. In his seminal article, Keeton presented honouring reasonable expectations as one of the 'two broad *principles*'[32] (emphasis added) in insurance law—the other being disallowing unconscionable advantage—along with the principle of granting redress for detrimental reliance. Drawing on the operative effects of a number of contract law doctrines, these principles

> cut across a number of doctrinal theories frequently invoked in recognizing rights at variance with policy provisions. These doctrines include waiver, estoppel in its various forms, election, reformation, rescission, the defense of breach by the other party of a contractual or non-contractual duty, modification of rights under the policy by subsequent agreement (either before or after a claim arises), and a considerable range of agency law.[33]

More specifically regarding protection of a policyholder's reasonable expectations, Keeton argued that several contract law doctrines served judicial regulation of insurance as contracts of adhesion, and that

> [u]nderlying [these] congeries of *doctrines*, however, one can discern *a principle* broader than the separate bodies of doctrine it has sustained. With a focus limited to insurance

[32] Keeton, 'Insurance Law Rights at Variance with Policy Provisions, Part One', above n 10, 961.

[33] Ibid 962.

cases (though surely it applies in other contexts as well), this principle may be stated in the following way:

> The objectively reasonable expectations of applicants and intended beneficiaries regarding the terms of insurance contracts will be honored even though painstaking study of the policy provisions would have negated those expectations.[34] (emphasis added)

Clearly, Keeton classed honouring a policyholder's reasonable expectations of coverage as a principle. In the meantime he saw that a legal principle was different from a legal doctrine, although he did not expressly state so in 1970, nor point out the differences. Nevertheless, by saying that 'one can discern *a principle broader than the separate bodies of doctrine* it has sustained',[35] Keeton would have certainly agreed that a legal principle is broader than a doctrine, and that a legal principle could be supported by a number of doctrines, or that out of a number of particular doctrines one could synthesise a legal principle. However, lawyers do not always distinguish principles from doctrines,[36] nor do they always appreciate the relevance of the distinction between them. That is perhaps partly why insurance lawyers more often discuss the doctrine, rather than the principle, of PREC.

Nevertheless, six years later when briefly revisiting the concept of protecting a policyholder's reasonable expectations, Keeton expressly highlighted the distinction between legal principles and legal doctrines or rules. He observed that protection of a policyholder's reasonable expectations evolved from a presumably vague principle into an express doctrine, and that then, in the 1970s, it boomeranged into being a more influential principle:

> As an aid to understanding this development in insurance law, it may be useful to observe a distinction between what we might call a 'principle' and a 'doctrine' of honoring reasonable expectations. What has happened in the 1960s and 1970s is explicit judicial endorsement of a new ground of decision—a development connoted by the term 'doctrine.' The influence of the principle was apparent even earlier, and its influence during the 1960s and 1970s was considerably more pervasive than the applications of the doctrine.[37]

Keeton proceeded to point out:[38]

> Because we depend on language to express substantive distinctions, we are always in danger of mistaking semantics for deeper substance. Nevertheless, the distinction between a 'principle' and a 'doctrine' of reasonable expectations is one of deeper substance, however imprecisely it may be expressed by our linguistic usages.

34 Ibid 967.

35 Ibid.

36 For example, in insurance law, until recently, the principle of utmost good faith was largely equated with the doctrine of pre-contractual disclosure.

37 Keeton, above n 4, 276.

38 Ibid 276–77.

> Principles collide in a sense beyond doctrinal conflict. Doctrines are sets of explicit rules of decision—the outcomes of accommodation among competing principles. Conflicts among doctrines are imperfections yet to be worked out as the operational rules of the legal system evolve. The collision of principles, on the other hand, is a phenomenon that does not signal imperfection of the legal system but rather signals the underlying conflict of interests with which the legal system must grapple.
>
> A principle is a generalization so broad that it does not express all the qualifications and limitations that must be expressed in an accurate statement of a rule, or a set of rules of decision that constitute at least the framework, though not the full body, of a doctrine. The qualifications and limitations arise because of the collision of underlying principles.

Although it seems that Keeton regarded honouring reasonable expectations as both a 'new doctrine'[39] and a 'principle',[40] there is no contradiction in doing so. That is because a legal doctrine could derive from a broad and general legal principle that could be the forerunner of the legal doctrine. In this regard, for example, Abraham argued in 1981 that it was time for the expectations principle to mature into a body of doctrine.[41] At an intermediate stage, a doctrine and a principle can be both overlapping and distinguished. In this respect, again, Abraham saw in 1998 the limited scope of the reasonable expectations *doctrine*, which by then was 'static' and 'going nowhere';[42] meanwhile a reasonable expectations *principle* lying behind the doctrine had huge influences in the rise of managed health care, the explosion of commercial general liability coverage litigation, the large verdicts for insurer bad faith and the controversies over insurance rate.[43]

Keeton treated a decision as applying a *doctrine* of honouring reasonable expectations 'only if, first, it explicitly does so, and, second, it appears explicitly to adopt not merely the term "reasonable expectations" but also an explanatory theory of decision that goes beyond resolving ambiguities against the party responsible for them'.[44] By that standard, decisions reasoned on the ground of resolving ambiguities against the insurer are not adoptions of a reasonable expectations doctrine, although such decisions point in that direction. It also seems that the answer to 'the question as to whether the principle has developed into a full-fledged doctrine'[45] is negative. That is because, at least before 1998, 'most references to the "reasonable expectations of the insured" still come in the context of judicial inquiry into and resolution of insurance policy ambiguity'.[46] This has remained so since 1998, with only a few exceptions. The year 1998 is used here as a watershed only for

[39] Ibid 279–80.
[40] Ibid 280.
[41] Abraham, above n 13, 1197.
[42] Abraham, above n 6, 63.
[43] Ibid 64–67.
[44] Keeton, above n 4, 279.
[45] RC Henderson, 'The Doctrine of Reasonable Expectations in Insurance Law after Two Decades' (1990) 51 *Ohio State Law Journal* 823, 824.
[46] Rahdert, above n 18, 112.

convenience in examining or rediscovering the DRE law. It is seen as convenient because the input of leading American insurance lawyers at the unprecedented and intensive DRE symposium[47] held in January 1998 at the Insurance Law Centre, University of Connecticut Law School, could be safely be assumed to be the scholarly important (albeit judicially otherwise)[48] fruit of those lawyers' detailed research of the positive law as it was then. That means that, for the purpose of this research, it is necessary first to survey the law from 1998 onwards, and to comb through relevant court decisions in different American state jurisdictions.

On re-examination, the issue of whether DRE should be predicated on ambiguity in insurance policy terms still persists. Given Keeton's characterisation quoted above, this relationship determines whether the concept of protecting a policyholder's reasonable expectations of coverage has been used in specific American state jurisdictions as a doctrine or as a principle. Measured by the judicial approaches to DRE/PREC in relation particularly to the relationship between DRE/PREC and ambiguity in insurance policies, the US state jurisdictions in this regard and for this purpose can be grouped into the following types:

— *Type 0—Rejection.* This is where DRE/PREC has been expressly rejected.
— *Type 1.0—Ambiguity as* the *prerequisite.* This is where DRE/PREC has been applied, but ambiguity in insurance policy terms is the prerequisite for such application.
— *Type 1.5—Ambiguity, or other rationales, as* a *prerequisite.* This is in between Type 1.0and Type 2.0. It is where DRE/PREC is applied, but ambiguity in policy terms is only one possible prerequisite or rationale for the application, and there are other judicially recognised alternative rationales.
— *Type 2.0—Ambiguity* not *as a prerequisite at all (just other rationales).* This is where PREC is applied, but ambiguity in policy terms is not the prerequisite or rationale for such application. Instead courts have other rationales for applying PREC. Consistent with Keeton's classification system, this is the only instance when DRE/PREC can be properly characterised as a legal 'doctrine'.
— *Type 3.0—Adopted conceptually, but without clear rationale.* This is where DRE/PREC was applied, but its relationship with ambiguity is not clear, or no rationales for its adoption were (clearly) stated. In the case of the latter, courts have often simply mentioned or referred to a policyholder's 'reasonable expectations' in the reasoning, without discussing what the concept was or its rationales. Though this judicial approach is not unimportant, it seems that only a concept or an idea of DRE/PREC was adopted. It is suggested[49] that this is how DRE/PREC is used as an interpretative principle. But it could be open to discussion whether a judge's brief mention of or reference to a

[47] See the collection of papers in (1998) 5 *Connecticut Insurance Law Journal* 1–473.

[48] Professor Daniel Schwarcz helpfully pointed this out to me.

[49] Professor Daniel Schwarcz in his kind and helpful comments on aspects of the draft of this chapter.

'semi-controversial'[50] point in law means that he or she uses that point as an interpretative principle; and even if the judge does so, it still remains to be asked how strong or weak the principle is judicially intended to be.

— *Type 4.0—Totally unclear.* This is where it is not clear, for a number of reasons, whether PREC is adopted or rejected. As will be seen in section 5.II.C. below, a few state jurisdictions are to be found in this group/type before 1998.

Sections 5.II.B. and 5.II.C. below will show how certain state jurisdictions have fallen into one or other of the types since 1998 and before 1998 respectively. In section 5.II.B, we look at state jurisdictions that considered or discussed DRE/PREC both before 1998 and after 1998. This makes it unnecessary to look at the old pre-1998 DRE/PREC law in these same state jurisdictions, because the new law from or after 1998 supersedes the pre-1998 law. However, as regards those state jurisdictions that have not considered or discussed DRE/PREC since 1998, and of which the law is therefore assumed to remain as it was before 1998, it is necessary to look into their pre-1998 DRE/PREC law, the subject of section 5.II.C.

B. Cases from 1998 to Date

From 1998 to the time of writing (18 November 2015), the supreme courts of 24 American states have considered DRE/PREC in at least 65 cases, as have the US Courts of Appeals for a number of circuits in around 47 cases. In light of their approaches to the subject, they are of the types described below. There are no Type 4.0 cases.

Type 0—Rejection of DRE/PREC

Given the controversy over DRE, it is not surprising that some state jurisdictions expressly reject it: this is so with South Dakota and Michigan. In South Dakota, 'Although the doctrine [of "policyholder's reasonable expectations"] governs interpretation of insurance contracts in other states, it is not the declared law in South Dakota.'[51] More noteworthy is Michigan, where DRE/PREC has been expressly rejected on the ground that it is thought to be functionally the same as *contra proferentem*. The Supreme Court of Michigan stated:

> In sum, the rule of reasonable expectations clearly has no application when interpreting an unambiguous contract because a policyholder cannot be said to have reasonably expected something different from the clear language of the contract. Further, it is already well established that ambiguous language should be construed against the drafter, ie, the insurer. Therefore, stating that ambiguous language should be interpreted

[50] JW Stempel, PN Swisher and ES Knutsen, *Principles of Insurance Law*, 4th edn (Albany, NY., LexisNexis, 2012) 123.

[51] *American Family Mutual Insurance Group v Kostaneski*, 688 NW 2d 410, 414 (SD 2004).

> in favor of the policyholder's reasonable expectations adds nothing to the way in which Michigan courts construe contracts, and thus the rule of reasonable expectations should be abolished. … [W]e hold that the rule of reasonable expectations has no application in Michigan, and those cases that recognized this doctrine are to that extent overruled.[52]

Justice Cavanagh dissented that the reasonable expectations doctrine, when correctly applied, 'is not limited to those circumstances in which a document is clearly ambiguous on its face. Rather, the doctrine may assist a court in making the ambiguity determination'.[53] Even this dissenting argument, however, led to circular reasoning: on one hand, Justice Cavanagh viewed ambiguity in policy terms as a prerequisite for applying DRE/PREC; but on the other hand, he suggested using DRE/PREC to determine whether there was ambiguity in policy terms.

Type 1.0—Ambiguity is the *prerequisite for applying DRE/PREC*

A few jurisdictions—Alabama, Kansas, Kentucky, Vermont, Montana, Wisconsin, Wyoming and West Virginia—clearly view ambiguity in insurance policy language as a prerequisite for PREC. The Supreme Court of Alabama ruled in 1999 that 'For the rule of reasonable expectations to apply, there [must] be, as a predicate, doubts as to the real intent of the policy.'[54] More recently, it was stressed by the Supreme Court of Alabama that

> expectations that contradict a clear exclusion are not 'objectively reasonable'. Such a limit on the doctrine is necessary. Otherwise, this Court will be faced with the strong temptation to substitute its notion of equity for the unambiguous terms of a contract and the doctrine could be used to invalidate every policy exclusion.[55]

Likewise, the Supreme Court of Kansas is unequivocal: 'Before applying the doctrine of reasonable expectations there must be a finding that the written instrument being interpreted is ambiguous.'[56] In Kentucky, the doctrine of reasonable expectations 'applies only to policies with ambiguous terms, eg, when a policy is susceptible to two or more reasonable interpretations'.[57] In Vermont, 'apart from circumstances where an agent of the insurance carrier promises specific coverage', the Supreme Court of Vermont has 'not held that the expectations of an insured

[52] *Wilkie v Auto-Owners Insurance Company*, 664 NW 2d 776, 788 (Mich 2003).

[53] Ibid 789.

[54] *State Farm Fire & Casualty Co v Slade*, 747 So 2d 293, 312 (Ala 1999). It is also qualified: the doctrine 'is not so expansive that any ambiguity in a policy will automatically justify disregarding an unambiguous exclusion in the policy' (citing *American Resources Insurance Company v H & H Stephens Construction Inc*, 939 So 2d 868, 880 (Ala 2006)).

[55] *Federated Mutual Insurance Company v Abston Petroleum Inc*, 967 So 2d 705, 713–15 (Ala 2007).

[56] *Liggatt v Employers Mutual Casualty Company*, 273 Kan 915, (Kan 2002), relying on *Penalosa Co-op Exchange v Farmland Mut Ins Co*, 789 P 2d 1196; 14 Kan App 2d 321, 323 (Kan 1990).

[57] *True v Raines* 99 SW 3d 439, 443 (Ky 2003), citing *Consolidated American Ins Co v Anderson*, Ky App, 964 SW 2d 811, 44 14 Ky L Summary 5 (1997), and *St Paul Fire & Marine Ins Co v Powell-Walton-Milward, Inc*, Ky, 870 SW 2d 223, 227 (1994).

can control over unambiguous policy language'.[58] In Wisconsin, 'if the language in an insurance policy is ambiguous', courts 'interpret that language by trying to determine "what a reasonable person in the position of the insured would have understood the words of the policy to mean"'.[59] In Wyoming,

> in order to state a claim under the 'reasonable expectations' doctrine, the plaintiff must show the subject contract is ambiguous as to the provision in dispute. The doctrine will not be applied where the insurance contract is plain and unambiguous.[60]

In Montana,

> The question of whether a provision is sufficiently 'clear' to render the reasonable expectations doctrine inapplicable is a different question than whether a provision is ambiguous. If the reasonable expectations doctrine only applied when a provision was ambiguous, there would be no need for the doctrine, as Montana law independently construes ambiguous provisions against the insurer and in favor of coverage. [Internal citations and quotations omitted.] However, a finding that a provision 'unambiguously precludes coverage' is a factor to be considered in determining whether it violates reasonable expectations. … '[T]he reasonable expectations doctrine is inapplicable where the terms of the policy at issue clearly demonstrate an intent to exclude coverage.' 'The reason, of course, is that "expectations which are contrary to a clear exclusion from coverage are not 'objectively reasonable.'"'[61]

Although, referring to a Supreme Court of Colorado case,[62] the Supreme Court of Montana intimated that the doctrine might apply where there was no ambiguity,[63] this might be misleading. That is because the Supreme Court of Colorado in fact stressed that 'the doctrine of reasonable expectations applies when policy coverage-provisions may not be ambiguous in a technical sense … *but are ambiguous from the perspective of an ordinary reader*'.[64] (emphasis added) This means that in Colorado, DRE/PREC applies where there is ambiguity in policy language. Hence it seems that Montana has incorrectly drawn a reference point from Colorado.

[58] *Vermont Mutual Insurance Company v Parsons Hill Partnership et al*, 1 A 3d 1016, 1025 (VT 2010), referred to approvingly in *Bradford Oil Company, Inc v Stonington Insurance Company and State of Vermont Agency of Natural Resources*, 54 A 3d 983, 988 (VT 2011), where it was summarised that 'reasonable expectations of insured cannot control over unambiguous policy language'.

[59] *Taylor v Greatway Ins Co*, 628 NW 2d 916, 920 (Wisc 2001), citing *Dowhower v West Bend Mut Ins Co*, 2000 WI 73, P35, 236 Wis 2d 113, 613 NW 2d 557.

[60] *Harper v Fidelity and Guaranty Life Ins Co*, 234 P 3d 1211, 1222 (WY 2010), citing *Ahrenholtz v Time Ins Co*, 968 P 2d 946 (WY 1998) and *WN McMurry Constr Co v Community First Ins, Inc*, 160 P 3d 71, 78 (WY 2007).

[61] *Fisher v State Farm Mutual Automobile Insurance Company*, 305 P 3d 861, 867 (Mont 2013), quoting *Wellcome v Home Ins Co*, 849 P 2d 190, 194 (Mont 1993). See also *American Family Mutual Insurance Company v Livengood*, 970 P 2d 1054, 1059 (Mont 1998); *Miller v Title Insurance Company of Minnesota*, 987 P 2d 1151 (Mont 1999); *Giocomelli v Scottsdale Insurance Company*, 221 P 3d 666, 674 (Mont 2009).

[62] *Bailey v Lincoln Gen Ins Co*, 255 P 3d 1039, 1050 (Colo 2011).

[63] *Fisher v State Farm Mutual Automobile Insurance Company*, 305 P 3d 861, 866–67 (Mont 2013).

[64] *Bailey v Lincoln Gen Ins Co*, 255 P 3d 1039, 1050 (Colo 2011).

Regarding the relationship between ambiguity and the applicability of PREC, particularly noteworthy is the Supreme Court of West Virginia, which stated that

> generally in West Virginia, the doctrine of reasonable expectations is limited to those instances … in which the policy language is ambiguous. The doctrine is essentially a rule of construction, and unambiguous contracts do not require construction by the courts.[65]

One year earlier, however, citing *Romano v New England Mutual Life Insurance Co*[66] and *Keller v First Nat'l Bank*,[67] the Supreme Court of West Virginia also recognised that 'in limited circumstances, the doctrine may be applied even in cases where the policy is clear and unambiguous'.[68] But *Romano* and *Keller* were very special, in that the insureds in both cases never received an insurance policy or a certificate of insurance at all. In light of the particularly unusual facts, Justice Ketchum more recently, in *New Hampshire Insurance Company v RRK*,[69] strongly and persuasively questioned the application of DRE to a situation where the policy is received but its language is clear and unambiguous.

In 1998, the Supreme Court of Wisconsin agreed with a policyholder's argument

> to the extent that 'the law of contracts attempts the realization of reasonable expectations' of the parties at the time they entered into the insurance policy. If possible, however, this reasonable expectation should be inferred 'solely from the language of the contract itself.'[70]

The opinion that PREC should be inferred 'solely' from the language of the insurance contract means firstly there is no other basis except the insurance policy language for PREC and secondly in order for PREC to be honoured there should be ambiguity in the language of the insurance contract. Other than that, there can be no consideration or protection of PREC.

Type 1.5—Ambiguity is a prerequisite (with other rationales)

State jurisdictions falling into this type are Colorado, Minnesota and Oklahoma. For the Supreme Court of Colorado, there are two main ways in which the

[65] *Jenkins v State Farm Mutual Automobile Insurance Company*, 632 SE 2d 346, 352 (W Va 2006), citing *National Mut Ins Co v.McMahon & Sons, Inc*, 177 W Va 734, 742, 356 SE 2d 488, 496 (1987). See also *Luikart v Valley Brook Concrete & Supply Inc*, 613 SE 2d 896, 903 (W Va 2005).

[66] *Romano v New England Mutual Life Insurance Co*, 178 W Va 523, 362 SE 2d 334 (1987).

[67] *Keller v First Nat'l Bank*, 184 W Va 681, 403 SE 2d 424 (1991).

[68] *Luikart v Valley Brook Concrete & Supply Inc*, 613 SE 2d 896, 903 (W Va 2005), citing *Romano v New England Mutual Life Insurance Co*, 178 W Va 523, 362 SE 2d 334 (1987) and *Keller v First Nat'l Bank*, 184 W Va 681, 403 SE 2d 424 (1991).

[69] *New Hampshire Insurance Company v RRK*, 736 SE 2d 52, 60–61 (W Va 2012).

[70] *Weimer v Country Mutual Insurance Company*, 216 Wis 2d 705, 720; 575 NW 2d 466, 472 (Wis 1998), quoting JH Mathias Jr et al, *Insurance Coverage Disputes* (New York, NY., Law Journal Press, 1997) § 7.01 at 7-3.

reasonable expectations approach has manifested itself while ensuring that insurers have conveyed coverage limitations to insureds 'fully and fairly':

> The first is where an ordinary, objectively reasonable person would, based on the language of the policy, fail to understand that he or she is not entitled to the coverage at issue. … The second manifestation of the doctrine is where, because of circumstances attributable to an insurer, an ordinary, objectively reasonable person would be deceived into believing that he or she is entitled to coverage, while the insurer would maintain otherwise.[71]

It can be seen from these two manifestations that ambiguity is *not always* necessary for application of PREC. Although the first manifestation effectively occurs where there *is* ambiguity in the language of the insurance policy, the second manifestation does not require it. Regarding the second manifestation, 'in order for reasonable expectations to prevail over exclusionary policy language, an "insured must demonstrate through extrinsic evidence that its expectation[s] of coverage [are] based on specific facts which make these expectations reasonable"'.[72] The evidentiary requirement of 'extrinsic evidence' means that it is not quite an issue of ambiguity in the policy language; rather it refers to scenarios where a policyholder's reasonable expectations are induced by specific facts attributable to an insurer.

In Minnesota, it is not sufficiently clear whether ambiguity is the premise for applying DRE. The Supreme Court of Minnesota

> limited the use of the reasonable expectations doctrine to 'resolving ambiguity' in policy terms 'and for correcting extreme situations,' such as 'where a party's coverage is significantly different from what the party reasonably believes it has paid for and where the only notice the party has of that difference is in an obscure and unexpected provision.'[73]

That being said, one year earlier the Supreme Court of Minnesota 'rejected ambiguity as a rigid requirement',[74] but had it as 'a factor in determining the reasonable expectations of the insured'[75] along with other factors. However, in no other cases since *Atwater Creamery Co v Western National Mutual Insurance Co*[76] has the Supreme Court of Minnesota used the doctrine to find coverage in contravention of unambiguous policy terms. Moreover, criticisms of and confusions over the doctrine have given the Supreme Court of Minnesota 'pause'[77] in applying it.

[71] *Bailey v Lincoln Gen Ins Co*, 255 P 3d 1039, 1055 (Colo 2011).

[72] Ibid, citing *O'Neill Investigations, Inc v Ill Emp Ins of Wausau*, 636 P 2d 1170, 1177 (Alaska 1981).

[73] *West Bend Mut Ins Co v Allstate Ins Co*, 776 NW 2d 693, 701 (Minn 2009), citing *Carlson v Allstate Ins Co*, 749 NW 2d 41, 49 (Minn 2008).

[74] *Carlson v Allstate Ins Co*, 749 NW 2d 41, 48 (Minn 2008).

[75] *Atwater Creamery Co v Western Nat'l Mutual Ins Co*, 366 NW 2d 271, 277–78 (Minn 1985).

[76] Ibid.

[77] *Carlson v Allstate Ins Co*, 749 NW 2d 41, 49 (Minn 2008).

In Oklahoma, the relationship between ambiguity in insurance policy terms and PREC is also opaque, if not confusing. Here, ambiguity in insurance policy language is *a* premise, but not *the* premise, for protecting PREC. Ambiguity is just one of the circumstances in which the doctrine can be applied. The Supreme Court of Oklahoma has ruled that DRE may be applied 'only when (1) the challenged policy language is ambiguous, or (2) an exclusion within the policy is (a) masked by technical or obscure language, or (b) hidden in a policy's provisions'.[78] Given the alternative circumstances, ambiguity is not always essential for protecting a policyholder's reasonable expectations. Where ambiguity actually happens to be essential and relevant, 'the test for ambiguity is whether the language "is susceptible to two interpretations on its face ... from the standpoint of a reasonable prudent layperson, not from that of a lawyer"'.[79] This test for ambiguity, however, seems to have further obscured rather than clarified the normative relationship, as prescribed by Keeton, between ambiguity in insurance policy language and the PREC conception. In Oklahoma, it seems that the conception of PREC was used instead to identify ambiguity, or partly became the prerequisite for ambiguity, rather than the other way round. If ambiguity could be identified by way of PREC, the insurance policy would then be interpreted to the effect of honouring the policyholder's reasonable expectations. This, however, is obviously circular reasoning.

Type 2.0—Ambiguity is not a prerequisite at all

A group of state jurisdictions—Alaska, Arizona, Iowa, Ohio, South Carolina, and New Mexico—have given judicial support to DRE/PREC regardless of the absence of ambiguity in insurance policy terms. Without resorting to ambiguity, PREC in these jurisdictions could be properly be characterised as a doctrine under Keeton's classification system. This is obviously so in Alaska and Arizona. The Supreme Court of Alaska stated:

> Alaska has adopted the doctrine of reasonable expectations. ... But because insurance policies are contracts of adhesion, they are construed according to the principle of 'reasonable expectations.' Under the reasonable expectations doctrine, 'the objectively reasonable expectations of applicants ... regarding the terms of insurance contracts will be honored even though painstaking study of the policy provisions would have negated those expectations.' ... The court need *not* find the policy ambiguous, however, to construe it under the reasonable expectations doctrine.[80]

[78] *American Economy Ins Co v Bogdahn*, 89 P3d 1051, 1054 (OK 2004), citing *Max True Plastering Co v USF&G*, P24, 912 P 2d 861, 870 (OK 1996).

[79] *American Economy Ins Co v Bogdahn*, 89 P 3d 1051, 1054 (OK 2004), citing *Cranfill v Aetna Life Ins Co*, 49 P 3d 703, 706 (OK 2002)), *Spears v Shelter Mutual Ins Co*, 73 P 3d 865 (OK 2003).

[80] *West v Umialik Insurance Company*, 8 P 3d 1135, 1138 (Alas 2000) (internal citation omitted].

This strictly and plainly follows Keeton's formulation of PREC. The Supreme Court of Alaska stated more specifically and more resolutely:

> To determine the parties' reasonable expectations, the court examines (1) the language of the disputed policy provisions; (2) the language of other provisions in the same policy; (3) extrinsic evidence; and (4) case law interpreting similar provisions.[81]

It also stressed:

> We have held that, although we will not ignore or rewrite provisions in an insurance contract, even unambiguous language in an insurance contract will be interpreted to comport with the reasonable expectations of a layperson.[82]

It is similar for the Supreme Court of Arizona, where the protection of reasonable expectations

> applies to a limited number of cases in which the boilerplate contract clauses are unambiguous but still operate oppressively. Specifically, those situations are:
>
> (1) Where the contract terms, although not ambiguous to the court, cannot be understood by the reasonably intelligent consumer who might check on his or her rights, the court will interpret them in light of the objective, reasonable expectations of the average insured;
> (2) Where the insured did not receive full and adequate notice of the term in question, and the provision is either unusual or unexpected, or one that emasculates apparent coverage;
> (3) Where some activity which can be reasonably attributed to the insurer would create an objective impression of coverage in the mind of a reasonable insured;
> (4) Where some activity reasonably attributable to the insurer has induced a particular insured reasonably to believe that he has coverage, although such coverage is expressly and unambiguously denied by the policy.[83]

Clearly, Alaska and Arizona take a doctrinal approach to PREC, an approach similar to what Keeton described in 1976 in his short article.[84] Both jurisdictions expressly do not resort to ambiguities in policy terms as the premise for applying PREC, and each has a separate 'explanatory theory' as stressed by Keeton for applying PREC as a 'doctrine'. In Alaska, the theory is contract of adhesion, as insurance contracts often are. In Arizona, the theory is regulation of oppressive or unconscionable clauses in a contract. This approach in both jurisdictions is consistent with Keeton's characterisation of an insurance law 'doctrine' of a policyholder's reasonable expectations under his classification system.

[81] Ibid.

[82] *Allstate Insurance Company v Watts*, 100 P 3d 2, 6 (Alas 2005), citing *Farquhar v Alaska Nat'l Ins Co*, 20 P 3d 577, 579 (Alas 2001); see also *Bering Strait School District v RLI Insurance Company*, 873 P 2d 1292, 1295 (Alas 1994) ('Construction of an insurance policy under the principle of reasonable expectations does not depend on a prior determination of policy ambiguity.').

[83] *Philadelphia Indemnity Ins Co v Barerra* 21 P 3d 395, 403 (Ariz 2001), citing *Gordinier v Aetna Casualty & Surety Co*, 742 P 2d 277; 154 Ariz 266, 272–73 (Ariz.1987).

[84] Keeton, above n 4, 279.

Accepting PREC as a doctrine without regard to ambiguity in insurance policy terms, Iowa and Ohio have their own similar approach. In the Supreme Court of Iowa, DRE 'is carefully circumscribed ...The doctrine is only invoked when an exclusion (1) is bizarre or oppressive, (2) eviscerates terms explicitly agreed to, or (3) eliminates the dominant purpose of the transaction.'[85] However, after citing Keeton's famous statement in his seminal *Harvard Law Review* article, the Supreme Court of Iowa stated:

> Evidence of reasonable expectations comes from the underlying negotiations or the inferences arising from the circumstances of when the parties entered the policy. Only representations made by the insurer at the time of policy negotiation and issuance are relevant. (citation omitted here) For the doctrine to apply, a prerequisite must first be satisfied. The insured must prove circumstances attributable to the insurer that fostered coverage expectations or show that the policy is such that an ordinary layperson would misunderstand its coverage.[86]

This all aligns with the approach in Ohio. In *Anderson v Highland House Company*,[87] the only post-1998 case dealing with PREC in that state, the majority in the Supreme Court of Ohio admittedly made 'no determination on the merits of the reasonable-expectations doctrine'. But they found the rationale of the doctrine of reasonable expectations to be *The Restatement of the Law 2d, Contracts (1981)*, Section 211, Comment *f*, as follows:

> **Terms excluded**
>
> Although customers typically adhere to standardized agreements and are bound by them without even appearing to know the standard terms in detail, they are not bound to unknown terms which are beyond the range of reasonable expectation. Similarly, a party who adheres to the other party's standard terms does not assent to a term if the other party has reason to believe that the adhering party would not have accepted the agreement if he had known that the agreement contained the particular term. Reason to believe may be inferred from the fact that the term is bizarre or oppressive, from the

[85] *Boelman v Grinnell Mutual Reinsurance Company*, 826 NW 2d 494, 506 (Iowa 2013), citing *Clark-Peterson Co v Indep Ins Assocs Ltd* 492 NW 2d 675, 679 (Iowa 1992). See also *Benavides v JC Penney Life Ins Co*, 539 NW 2d 352, 356–57 (Iowa 1995); *Monroe County v Int'l Ins Co*, 609 NW 2d 522, 526 (Iowa 2000); *LeMars Mut Ins Co v Joffer*, 574 NW 2d 303, 311 (Iowa 1998); *Farm Bureau Mut Ins Co v Sandbulte*, 302 NW 2d 104, 112 (Iowa 1981); *C & J Fertilizer, Inc v Allied Mut Ins Co*, 227 NW 2d 169, 176 (Iowa 1975). See also *Farm Bureau Life Ins Co v Chubb Custom Ins Co*, 780 NW 2d 735, 743 (Iowa 2010); *Nationwide Agri-Business Ins Co v Goodwin*, 782 NW 2d 465, 473 (Iowa 2010); *Bituminous Cas Corp v Sand Livestock Sys*, 728 NW 2d 216, 221 (Iowa 2007); *Vos and Anderson v Farm Bureau Life Insurance Company*, 667 NW 2d 36, 50 (Iowa 2003); *Westfield Insurance Companies v Economy Fire & Casualty Company*, 623 NW 2d 871, 881–82 (Iowa 2001); *Iowa Comprehensive Petroleum Underground Storage Tank Fund Bd v Federated Mut Ins Co*, 596 NW 2d 546, 551 (Iowa 1999); *Zaragoza v West Bend Mut Ins Co*, 549 NW 2d 510, 515 (Iowa 1996).

[86] *Boelman v Grinnell Mutual Reinsurance Company*, 826 NW 2d 494, 506 (Iowa 2013), citing *Vos and Anderson v Farm Bureau Life Insurance Company* 667 NW 2d 36, 50 (Iowa 2003) and *Nationwide Agri-Business Ins Co v Goodwin*, 782 NW 2d 465, 473 (Iowa 2010). See also *American Family Mutual Ins Co v Corrigan*, 697 NW 2d 108, 118 (Iowa 2005).

[87] *Anderson v Highland House Company*, 757 NE 2d 329, 338 (Ohio 2001).

fact that it eviscerates the non-standard terms explicitly agreed to, or from the fact that it eliminates the dominant purpose of the transaction.

The rationale was applied to the case. This rationale, however, has little to do with ambiguity in the terms of an agreement. Instead it concerns 'unknown terms' and a contract term that is not ambiguous but 'bizarre or oppressive', or that 'eviscerates the non-standard terms explicitly agreed to' or 'eliminates the dominant purpose of the transaction'. These are the explanatory theories other than ambiguity.

It is similar in New Mexico, where the rationale for PREC is not identical to that in Ohio and Iowa, but neither is it based on ambiguity. To date, the Supreme Court of New Mexico has ruled in only one post-1998 PREC case, in which it was stated that 'The purpose of the "reasonable expectations" doctrine is ... rather to protect the insured from disclaimers based on information that is hyper-technical, obscure, or hidden.'[88] Here the rationale for applying PREC is not that the insurance policy term at issue is ambiguous, but that it is too technical or just too difficult for a policyholder to understand, or it is contained in fine-print hidden from the policyholder.

Type 3.0—Adopted conceptually, but without clear rationale

A number of state jurisdictions have adopted, or at least referred to, a general concept of PREC/DRE, but have not made clear the relationship between PREC/DRE and ambiguity in policy language. These states are: California, New York, New Hampshire, Nevada and Hawaii, and South Carolina

In the State of New York, the only case in this regard since 1998 was litigated in the Court of Appeals of New York, where it was stated, 'Insurance contracts must be interpreted according to common speech and consistent with the reasonable expectation of the average insured.'[89] In so holding, the Court only referred to the concept of PREC, without discussing what it was and how it was applied, let alone discussing the relevance or otherwise of ambiguity to PREC. The Supreme Court of California referred to ambiguity as a circumstance in which PREC was to be considered, holding that 'Any ambiguous terms are resolved in the insureds' favor, consistent with the insureds' reasonable expectations.'[90] However, this failed to clarify whether the Court viewed ambiguity as the (only) prerequisite for considering PREC, or as an alternative prerequisite for or as a complement to rationales of PREC.

[88] *United Nuclear Corporation v Allstate Insurance Company*, 285 P 3d 644, 655 (New Mexico 2012), referring particularly to *Atwater Creamery Co v Western Nat'l Mutual Ins. Co*, 366 NW 2d 271, 278 (Minn 1985); *Whole Enchilada, Inc v Travelers Prop Cas Co of Am*, 581 F Supp 2d 677, 690 (WD Pa 2008).

[89] *Dean v Tower Insurance Company of New York*, 979 NE 2d 1143, 1145 (New York 2012), citing *Cragg v Allstate Indem Corp*, 17 NY 3d 118; 950 NE 2d 500 (New York 2011).

[90] *Safeco Insurance Company of America v Robert et al*, 28 P 3d 889, 893 (California 2001), citing *Kazi v State Farm Fire & Casualty Co* (2001) 24 Cal 4th 871, 879; 103 Cal Rptr 2d 1; 15 P 3d 223.

The relationship between ambiguity and a concept of PREC is not clear in New Hampshire either. It can only be inferred that in New Hampshire, if there is ambiguity, it will be construed in favour of PREC. The Supreme Court of New Hampshire stated that 'When we interpret insurance policies, the general rule is that [we] will honor the reasonable expectations of the policyholder.'[91] It is also recognised that 'An insurance company is free to limit its liability through clear and unambiguous policy language. Such language must be so clear, however, as to create no ambiguity that might affect the insured's reasonable expectations.'[92] This is indicative of a rightly-held judicial assumption that ambiguity might run counter to PREC. Nevertheless, it is equally unclear in New Hampshire whether ambiguity is or should be the predicate for honouring PREC.

Similarly, in Nevada, 'if an insurance policy has any ambiguous terms, this court will interpret the policy to effectuate the insured's reasonable expectations'.[93] It is not clear, however, whether ambiguity is or should be the prerequisite for applying PREC. Also noteworthy is that in the Supreme Court of Nevada, the perception is that 'The question of whether an insurance policy is ambiguous turns on whether it creates reasonable expectations of coverage as drafted.'[94] More recently the same Court stated, 'An insurance policy is considered ambiguous if it creates [multiple] reasonable expectations of coverage as drafted. A seemingly clear policy can be rendered ambiguous when applying the policy to the facts leads to multiple reasonable interpretations.'[95] Using the conception of reasonable expectations to identify ambiguity, this is circular reasoning, as in the Supreme Court of Oklahoma discussed above.

In the Supreme Court of Hawaii, judges refuse to 'apply a mechanistic reading of insurance contracts'.[96] Although the terms of the policy should be interpreted according to their plain, ordinary and accepted sense in common speech, if it appears from the policy that a meaning different from the plain ordinary meaning is intended, the policy will be construed in favour of that intended different meaning.[97] It has been made clear in the Supreme Court of Hawaii that insurance policy terms have been construed 'liberally, in favour of the insured, and in accord with the reasonable expectations of a layperson'.[98] Further, 'the objectively reasonable expectations … will be honored even though painstaking study of the

[91] *Contoocook Valley School District v Graphic Arts Mutual Insurance Company*, 788 A 2d 259, 261 (NH 2001), citing *Funai v. Metropolitan Prop & Cas Co*, 145 NH 642, 644, 765 A 2d 689 (2000).

[92] Ibid, citing *Weeks v St Paul Fire & Marine Ins Co*, 140 NH 641, 643, 673 A 2d 772 (1996) and *Gelinas v Metropolitan Prop & Liability Ins Co*, 131 NH 154, 170–71, 551 A 2d 962 (1988).

[93] *Century Surety Company Casino West, Inc*, 329 P 3d 614, 617 (Nev 2014), referring to *Rubin v State Farm Mut Auto Ins Co*, 43 P 3d 1018, 1021 (Nev 2002); *Farmers Ins Exch v Young*, 832 P 2d 376, 377 (Nev1992).

[94] *Powell v Liberty Mut Fire Ins Co*, 252 P 3d 668, 672 (Nev 2011), citing *United Nat'l Ins Co v Frontier Ins Co*, 120 Nev 678, 684; 99 P 3d 1153, 1157 (Nev 2004).

[95] *Century Surety Company Casino West, Inc*, 329 P 3d 614, 617 (Nev 2014), referring to *Rubin v State Farm Mut Auto Ins Co*, 43 P 3d 1018, 1021 (Nev 2002); *Farmers Ins Exch v Young*, 832 P 2d 376, 377 (Nev1992).

[96] *Guajardo v AIG Haw Ins Co*, 118 Haw 196; 187 P 3d 580, 587 (Haw 2008).

[97] *Dairy Rd Partners v Island Ins Co*, 992 P 2d 93, 106 (Haw 2000).

[98] *Park v Government Employers Insurance Company et al*, 974 P 2d 34, 38 (Haw 1999).

policy provisions would have negated those expectations',[99] and 'policies are to be construed in accord with the reasonable expectations of a layperson'.[100] However, although obviously a faithful and ardent proponent of Keeton's original idea in 1970, the Supreme Court of Hawaii does not make it clear to what extent ambiguity in insurance policy terms is relevant for applying Keeton's original concept of a policyholder's reasonable expectations.

In South Carolina, the reasonable expectations of parties entering an insurance contract will be honoured within the confines of its interpretive rules and fairness principles.[101] However, the rationale, especially on the relationship with ambiguity in insurance policy terms, does not seem clear. This is because in 2014 in the same case[102] the Supreme Court of South Carolina on the one hand cited as persuasive authority a case in 1982 in the Supreme Court of Delaware; it was stated in the Delaware case:

> ... the [Delaware] Court will look to the reasonable expectations of the insured at the time when he entered into the contract if the terms thereof are ambiguous or conflicting, or if the policy contains a hidden trap or pitfall, or if the fine print takes away that which has been given by the large print. But the doctrine is not a rule granting substantive rights to an insured when there is no doubt as to the meaning of policy language.[103]

It seems that in Delaware ambiguity was only one of the several alternative prerequisites for applying DRE. That being said, on the other hand, in looking for persuasive authority, the Supreme Court of South Carolina also referred to Iowa cases[104] which however did not have ambiguity as a prerequisite at all. Then, the Supreme Court of South Carolina confirms that 'This approach [of Delaware and Iowa] is supported by South Carolina law.'[105] However, the Delaware approach and the Iowa approach are very different from each other.

C. Cases before 1998

Having the year 1998 as a watershed, and to reveal how DRE/PREC has been applied or otherwise in the US state jurisdictions up to today, it is naturally

[99] Del Monte Fresh Produce (Hawaii), Inc v Fireman's Fund Ins Co, 117 Haw 357, 183 P 3d 734, 745 (Haw 2007) (quoting Keeton).

[100] *Guajardo v AIG Haw Ins Co*, 118 Haw 196; 187 P 3d 580, 587 (Haw 2008) (internal quotation marks omitted). See also *Apana v Tig Insurance Company*, 574 F 3d 679, 683–84 (9th Circuit, 2009).

[101] *Bell v Progressive Direct Insurance Company*, 407 SC 565, 581; 757 SE 2D 399, 406 (SC 2014), referring to *SC Farm Bureau Mutual Ins Co v Kennedy*, 398 SC 604, 615, 730 SE 2d 862, 867 (SC 2012).

[102] *Bell v Progressive Direct Insurance Company*, 407 SC 565, 581; 757 SE 2D 399 (SC 2014).

[103] *Hallowell v State Farm Mut Auto Ins Co*, 443 A 2d 925, 927 (Del 1982) (citations of Delaware and Iowa cases omitted).

[104] *Clark-Peterson Co v Indep Ins Assocs Ltd* 492 NW 2d 675, 677 (Iowa 1992); *Aid (Mut) Ins v Steffen*, 423 NW 2d 189, 192 (Iowa 1988); *Farm Bureau Mut Ins Co v Sandbulte*, 302 NW 2d 104, 112 (Iowa 1981). They essentially had *The Restatement of the Law 2d, Contracts (1981), Section 211, Comment f*, quoted above, as the rationale for honouring PREC as did the Supreme Court of Ohio. The Iowa cases and the Ohio cases are discussed in Section II.B. (for Type 2.0) of this Chapter.

[105] *Bell v Progressive Direct Insurance Company*, 407 SC 565, 581; 757 SE 2d 399, 407 (SC 2014).

necessary to look into whether and how it was applied before 1998. From 1998 onward, 26 state jurisdictions *did not* consider or discuss DRE/PREC cases. This certainly does not mean that they did not accept or adopt DRE/PREC. Rather, their laws in this regard could be assumed to remain as they were *before* 1998. These 26 states and their laws on DRE/PREC also fall into one of the six types discussed above.

Type 0—Rejection of DRE/PREC

More state jurisdictions rejected DRE/PREC before 1998 than after that year, either expressly or because they could be assumed to have rejected it by not considering it over the decades. Those states were Florida, Idaho, Utah, and perhaps Washington as well. By July 1996, Florida had failed to adopt PREC, and so it has remained. The Court of Appeal of Florida, Fourth District, noted 'the new doctrine of reasonable expectations' in insurance law in other jurisdictions. Having concluded that the trial court erred by effectually applying this new doctrine, it stated that there was an error for two reasons: 'The first and foremost is ... that the Florida Supreme Court has not adopted the doctrine of reasonable expectations; instead the rule here is that ambiguities result in coverage.'[106] There are no cases indicating that Florida adopted the doctrine afterwards.

Idaho rejected PREC in the 1980s and has not changed its stance since then. In 1985 it was restated in the Supreme Court of Idaho that 'the doctrine of reasonable expectations has not been adopted as the law in Idaho'.[107] Idaho's early rejection of PREC actually occurred in 1979 in *Casey v Highlands*,[108] where DRE was expressly rejected in favour of traditional contract rules of construction.

The Supreme Court of Utah may be understood more clearly to have rejected PREC. Justice Zimmerman, with whom Chief Justice Hall and Associate Chief Justice Howe were in agreement, declared: '[i]n sum, we reject the various versions of the reasonable expectations doctrine';[109] '[w]e also recognize that the reasonable expectations doctrine was developed in part because established equitable doctrines were found to be inadequate theoretically';[110] 'Our existing equitable doctrines have not been shown to be inadequate to the task of protecting insureds from over-reaching insurers.'[111] Although Justice Stewart concurred with this and Justice Durham dissented from it, when the issue of PREC arose again within one year in the same court, it was no longer disputed that 'This court, however, has never adopted any version of the doctrine.'[112]

[106] *State Farm Fire & Casualty Insurance Co v Deni Associates of Florida, Inc*, 678 So 2d 397, 402 (Flor 1996)

[107] *Meckert v Transamerica Insurance Company*, 108 Idaho 597, 601; 701 P 2d 217, 221 (Ido 1985), citing *Foremost Ins Co v Putzier*, 102 Idaho 138; 627 P 2d 317 (1981).

[108] *Casey v Highlands*, 100 Idaho 505, 600 P 2d 1387 (Ido 1979)

[109] *Allen v Prudential Property and Casualty Insurance Company*, 839 P 2d 798, 807 (Utah 1992).

[110] Ibid 806.

[111] Ibid 807.

[112] *Nielsen v O'Reilly, French, and Metropolitan Property & Liability Insurance C* o, 848 P 2d 664, 667 (Utah 1992). Justice Stewart concurred, but did not raise issues about DRE itself.

Washington State accepted at most a very general concept of 'policyholder's reasonable expectations' over which the insurance policy language prevailed. It was stated that courts

> will not, under the guise of public policy, rewrite a clear contract between the parties. The efficient proximate cause rule should be applied to enforce the reasonable expectations of the parties based on the language of the insurance contract ...[113]

In the meantime, the same Court more clearly rejected a *doctrine* of policyholder's reasonable expectations:

> The contention that exclusions from coverage in all-risk insurance policies generally violate public policy is not supported by Washington law. The 'reasonable expectation' doctrine has never been adopted in Washington, and there is no reasonable expectation that no exemptions to coverage exist.[114]

Type 1.0—Ambiguity is the *prerequisite for applying DRE/PREC*

Pre-1998 state jurisdictions of Type 1.0 were Texas and Missouri. In the Supreme Court of Texas, although it was stated in a strongly persuasive dissenting opinion (by Justice Cornyn, joined by Chief Justice Phillips and Justices Cook and Hecht) in *Forbau v Aetna Life Insurance Company*[115] that DRE was not the law of Texas, it was soon confirmed in the US District Court for the Northern District of Texas that courts in Texas had recognised DRE, subject to the qualification that it 'is premised upon the presence of an ambiguity in the contract in question; it is not available in the face of an unambiguous contract'.[116]

Although the Supreme Court of Missouri stated that it 'has not determined the viability of the objective reasonable expectations doctrine in Missouri',[117] it did not reject it categorically. Instead it set out two conditions for its application. It recalled in 1991:

> In *Robin v Blue Cross Hospital Service, Inc*, 637 SW 2d 695, 697 (Mo banc 1982), this Court described the objective reasonable expectations doctrine as a 'rule providing the objective reasonable expectations of adherents and beneficiaries to insurance contracts will be honored even though a thorough study of the policy provisions would have negated these expectations.' In that case, however, this Court found no need to consider the merits of the doctrine, determining that the insurance contract in question there

[113] *Findlay v United Pacific Insurance Company*, 129 Wn 2d 368, 380 (Wash 1996); see also at 377, 'this Court emphasized that "the purpose of the efficient proximate cause rule is to provide a 'workable rule of coverage that provides a fair result within the reasonable expectations of both the insured and the insurer"' (citing *Kish v Insurance Co of N Am*, 125 Wn 2d 164, 172(1994), and quoting *Garvey v State Farm Fire & Casualty Co*, 48 Cal 3d 395, 404; 770 P 2d 704; 257 Cal Rptr 292 (1989)).

[114] *Findlay v United Pacific Insurance Company*, 129 Wn 2d 368, 378 (Wash 1996), citing *State Farm Gen Ins Co v Emerson*, 102 Wn 2d 477, 485 and 480 (Wash 1984).

[115] *Forbau v Aetna Life Insurance Company*, 36 Tex Sup Ct J 140.

[116] *Bartley v National Union Fire Ins Co*, 824 F Supp 624, 636 (ND Tex 1992).

[117] *Rodriguez v General Accident Insurance Company of America*, 808 SW 2d 379, 382 (Mo 1991).

> was not a contract of adhesion. Without a contract of adhesion, the objective reasonable expectations doctrine does not apply.[118]

The 1982 description is essentially a verbatim rendition of Keeton's formulation (see section II.A. above). The necessary condition then set for its application was that the insurance contract at issue should be a contract of adhesion. This is not sufficient, however. Another condition was indicated in 1991, being that there must be ambiguity in the language of the policy. It was held in the Supreme Court of Missouri that a policyholder's 'argument for the application of the objective reasonable expectation doctrine depends on the presence of an ambiguity in the contract language'.[119] The insurance clause in question in the instant case was found to be 'neither ambiguous nor misleading. There is no basis for application of an objective reasonable expectation doctrine to this contract.'[120]

Type 1.5—Ambiguity is a prerequisite (with other rationales)

Delaware, Rhode Island, North Dakota before 1998 were in this group. North In the heyday of DRE, the Supreme Court of Delaware stated it would consider DRE in a number of scenarios:

> … the [Delaware] Court will look to the reasonable expectations of the insured at the time when he entered into the contract if the terms thereof are ambiguous or conflicting, or if the policy contains a hidden trap or pitfall, or if the fine print takes away that which has been given by the large print. But the doctrine is not a rule granting substantive rights to an insured when there is no doubt as to the meaning of policy language.[121]

The first sentence of the opinion has ambibutuity in the language of insurance policy in question as one of the prerequisites, alongside another two, for courts to consider DRE. However, it would not go as far as Keeton had proposed: the DRE considerations were qualified anyway by the clear meaning of the insurance policy terms.

In Rhode Island, the relationship between ambiguity in insurance policy provisions and DRE/PREC is not so clear, but it is still detectable in a number of cases. In this jurisdiction, ambiguity is *a* premise for applying PREC, but it is not *the* premise: other circumstances might allow for the application of DRE/PREC. Recalling that Justice Douglas[122] had emphasised, while dissenting, the 'reasonable expectation' of the policyholder on the ground of an ambiguity in the policy, judges in the Rhode Island Supreme Court admitted they 'were

[118] Ibid 381–82.

[119] Ibid 382.

[120] Ibid 383.

[121] *Hallowell v State Farm Mut Auto Ins Co*, 443 A 2d 925, 927 (Del 1982) (citations of Delaware and Iowa cases omitted).

[122] *Grimes v Concord General Mutual Insurance Co*, 120 NH 718; 422 A 2d 1312 (New Hamp 1980).

persuaded [in *Taft v Cerwonka*][123] to a significant degree by a dissenting opinion by Justice Douglas'.[124] Along those lines, in their opinion, the language limiting the insurer's liability was 'completely free of ambiguity', hence 'would preclude any reasonable expectation on the part of the policyholder that he or she would be entitled to intra-policy stacking'.[125] Thus, 'in light of the unambiguous limitation of liability, no reasonable expectation on the part of the plaintiffs is violated'.[126] These opinions consistently viewed ambiguity as the prerequisite for PREC. The story did not end there, however. Ten years later, in 1995, judges in the Rhode Island Supreme Court were '"convinced that reasonable expectations of coverage raised by the declaration page cannot be contradicted by the policy's boilerplate unless the declaration page itself clearly so warns the insured"'.[127] This conversely meant that, in addition to ambiguity in an insurance policy, limitations hidden from or not brought to the policyholder's notice could also lead to the application of PREC.

The Supreme Court of North Dakota confirmed that 'at least in principle', the 'Doctrine of Reasonable Expectations' was accepted.[128] For the Court, the invocation of the doctrine 'may not always be appropriate but is [appropriate] when, as here, ambiguity is created by confusingly dissimilar exclusionary language buried in the bodies of two policies … What the one hand bestows, the other imperceptibly takes away.'[129] It further gave examples of other circumstances in which applying PREC was appropriate:

> This kind of legerdemain by draftsmanship, the lack of notice to the buyer of the policy exclusions, the inconspicuous placement of the exclusionary clauses in the contracts, their obscure relationship to each other, and the reasonable belief of the insured that he was securing general liability coverage … all foster coverage expectations which must be fulfilled in this instance.[130]

This, apart from ambiguity in insurance policy provisions, enhances the doctrine with *additional (or alternative)* rationales, such as the insurer's failure to bring the unusualness of the clauses to the policyholder's attention, and/or their inconspicuousness or fine-print.[131]

[123] *Taft v Cerwonka* 433 A 2d 215, 219 (RI 1981).

[124] *Constant v Amica Mutual Insurance Co*, 497 A 2d 343, 345 (RI 1985).

[125] Ibid.

[126] Ibid 346.

[127] *Mallane v Holyoke Mutual Insurance Company in Salem*, 658 A 2d 18, 21 (RI 1995), quoting *Lehrhoff v Aetna Casualty and Surety Co*, 271 NJ Super 340, 347; 638 A 2d 889, 892 (1994).

[128] *Mills v Agrichemical Aviation, Inc*, 250 NW 2d 663, 672 (ND 1977), relying on *Kooker v Benefit Association of Railway Employees*, 246 NW 2d (ND 1976).

[129] Ibid 672

[130] Ibid.

[131] It must be noted that the case in 1998 in the Supreme Court of North Dakota ie *Close v Ebertz*, 583 N.W.2d 794 (ND 1998) only mentioned or briefly restated DRE twice as the rejected opinion of the minority-view courts in the jurisdiction, and did not in any sense affirm or negate DRE in North Dakota. In other words, hardly any DRE law can be deduced from this case in 1998.

Type 2.0—Ambiguity is not a prerequisite at all

State jurisdictions of Type 2.0 were Alabama, North Carolina and Pennsylvania. The Supreme Court of Alabama was sure, in *Smith v Auto-Owners Insurance Company*,[132] that

> the language of the policy's underinsured motorist provisions is perfectly clear and, when applied to the instant facts, provides no coverage. ... The problem with the literal interpretation and application of this provision lies not in the ambiguity of its language but in the product of its result [that the policyholder could recover nothing under any other set of facts].

Regardless of the clear policy language, the Court held that surely the doctrine of reasonable expectations could be applied.[133] In so holding, the Supreme Court of Alabama cited its own judgment in 1976 in *Lambert v Liberty Mutual Insurance Co*,[134] which itself cited and directly applied Keeton's formulation.

The Supreme Court of North Carolina, in *Great American Insurance Company v CG Tate Construction Company*,[135] a dispute over a notice clause in an insurance contract, was faced with the issue of whether to continue to apply traditional contract interpretation principles, or to embrace the modern view that an insurance clause should be construed in accordance with its purpose and with the reasonable expectations of the parties. Agreeing with the Supreme Court of Pennsylvania,[136] the majority in the Supreme Court of North Carolina rejected the traditional approach and adopted the PREC. It stated:

> Rejection of the strict contractual approach means that the interpretation of the notice provision will be guided more by its purpose—the reason for its inclusion in the insurance contract—than by its seemingly conclusive terms. Additionally, adoption of the modern rule of reasonable expectations promotes the social function of insurance coverage: providing compensation for injuries sustained by innocent members of the public. The rule we adopt today has the advantages of promoting social policy and fulfilling the reasonable expectations of the purchaser while fully protecting the ability of the insurer to protect its own interests. While under the new reasonable expectation rule the number of claims insurers will be obligated to defend may rise, this is no justification for continued application of the [traditional] rule we now reject.[137]

Clearly, in North Carolina, ambiguity is not *the* prerequisite for PREC. The rationale for adopting the PREC is the purpose of insurance generally or public policy in relation to insurance, rather than ambiguity in insurance contract terms.

[132] *Smith v Auto-Owners Insurance Company*, 500 So 2d 1042, 1044 (Ala 1986).

[133] Ibid.

[134] *Lambert v Liberty Mutual Insurance Co*, 331 So 2d 260 (Ala 1976).

[135] *Great American Insurance Company v CG Tate Construction Company*, 303 NC 387 (1981).

[136] *Brakeman v Potomac Insurance Company*, 472 Pa 66, 72; 371 A 2d 193, 196 (1975).

[137] *Great American Insurance Company v CG Tate Construction Company*, 303 NC 387, 395–96 (NC 1981).

In Pennsylvania, PREC can be applied whether there is ambiguity in the insurance contract or not. There have been strong public policy considerations for applying PREC in this jurisdiction. The Supreme Court of Pennsylvania stated in *Collister v Nationwide Life Insurance Co*:[138]

> The reasonable expectation of the insured is the focal point of the insurance transaction involved here. *Eg, Beckham v Travelers Ins Co*, 424 Pa 107, 117–18, 225 A 2d 532, 537 (1967). Courts should be concerned with assuring that the insurance purchasing public's reasonable expectations are fulfilled. Thus, regardless of the ambiguity, or lack thereof, inherent in a given set of insurance documents (whether they be applications, conditional receipts, riders, policies, or whatever), the public has a right to expect that they will receive something of comparable value in return for the premium paid. Courts should also keep alert to the fact that the expectations of the insured are in large measure created by the insurance industry itself. Through the use of lengthy, complex, and cumbersomely written applications, conditional receipts, riders, and policies, to name just a few, the insurance industry forces the insurance consumer to rely upon the oral representations of the insurance agent. Such representations may or may not accurately reflect the contents of the written document and therefore the insurer is often in a position to reap the benefit of the insured's lack of understanding of the transaction. As stated by the New Jersey Supreme Court in *Allen v Metropolitan Life Ins Co, supra*, 44 NJ 294, 302, 208 A 2d 638, 642 (1965):
>
> > 'Much of the difficulty may be laid at the doorstep of the life insurance industry itself for, despite repeated cautions from the courts, it has persisted in using language which is obscure to the layman and in tolerating agency practices which are calculated to lead the layman to believe that he has coverage beyond that which may be called for by a literal reading. The reports are replete with instances where company agents, as here, obtained payment of the full annual premium in advance on the broad representation that there would be interim coverage pending the company's investigation of the application and its action thereon.'
>
> Courts must examine the dynamics of the insurance transaction to ascertain what the reasonable expectations of the consumer are. *See, eg, Rempel v Nationwide Ins Co*, 471 Pa 404, 370 A 2d 366 (1977). Courts must also keep in mind the obvious advantages gained by the insurer when the premium is paid at the time of application. An insurer should not be permitted to enjoy such benefits without giving comparable benefit in return to the insured.

This was affirmed, and quoted in verbatim, in 1987 in the lead opinion in the same court.[139]

[138] *Collister v Nationwide Life Insurance Co*, 479 Pa 579, 594–95 (Pa 1978).

[139] *Tonkovic v State Farm Mutual Automobile Insurance Company*, 513 Pa 445, 456–57 (Pa 1987).

Type 3.0—Adopted conceptually, but without clear rationale

In 1989, Arkansas recognised DRE/PREC as a principle for interpreting insurance policy terms, but it remains unclear whether ambiguity is *the* prerequisite for applying PREC, or whether there are other rationales for applying it. Judges in the Supreme Court of Arkansas reiterated that in interpreting insurance policy terms they were 'guided by well-established principles' as follows:

> [1] When any provision of an insurance policy is subject to more than one reasonable interpretation, the interpretation favoring the insured is adopted. [2] Ambiguity in an insurance policy must be construed against the insurance company preparing the contract, and the policy will be construed so as to provide coverage, unless it is patently unreasonable to do so. [3] Words used in insurance policies are to be taken and understood in their plain, ordinary and usual sense. [4] Courts are to resolve ambiguities in insurance policies in accordance with the reasonable expectations of the insured.[140]

Except for the third principle, these principles are very similar to one another in effect. For the first three, the common theme is how judges interpret ambiguous provisions in an insurance policy. For the fourth, ie the principle of reasonable expectations of the insured, ambiguity is necessary, but it is not clear whether ambiguity is the *only* circumstance in which the principle can be invoked and applied.

This is also similarly unclear in Connecticut. The Appellate Court of Connecticut had held:

> It is a basic principle of insurance law that policy language will be construed as laymen would understand it and not according to the interpretation of sophisticated underwriters, and that ambiguities in contract documents are resolved against the party responsible for its [*sic*] drafting; the policyholder's expectations should be protected as long as they are objectively reasonable from the layman's point of view.[141]

The Supreme Court of Connecticut cited this verbatim, though in a footnote.[142] This restated literal or non-technical interpretation as a default principle, complemented by *contra proferentem*, and also by DRE/PREC. But neither court clarified the relationship between ambiguities and the application of DRE/PREC. Nor did they clarify the more specific circumstances, if any, in which the principle of 'policyholder's reasonable expectations' was to be applied. It seemed that both

[140] *Toney v Shelter Mutual Insurance Company*, (not designed for publication) 1989 Ark App LEXIS 384, 6–7, citing respectively *Aetna Casualty & Surety Co v Stover*, 327 F 2d 288 (8th Cir 1964); *MFA Mutual Ins Co v State Farm Mutual Auto Ins Co*, 268 Ark 746, 595 SW 2d 706 (Ark App 1980); *State Farm Ins Cos v Gilbert*, 3 Ark App 52, 621 SW 2d 880 (1981); *Enterprise Tools, Inc v Export-Import Bank of the United States*, 799 F 2d 437 (8th Cir 1986), *cert denied* 107 S Ct 1569 (1987).

[141] *Ryiz v Federal Insurance Company*, (1985) 5 Conn App 179, 183; 497 A 2d 1001, 1004, citing *Cody v Remington Electric Shavers*, 179 Conn 494, 497, 427 A 2d 810 (1980).

[142] *Pacific Indemnity Insurance Company v Aetna Casualty and Surety Company*, 240 Conn 26, 33; 688 A 2d 319, 323 (Conn 1997) fn 8.

courts simply accepted the concept of a principle of 'policyholder's reasonable expectations', without further considering the specific approach to judicially implementing that principle.

The Supreme Court of Georgia stated in 1995 that 'A contract of insurance should be strictly construed against the insurer and read in favor of coverage in accordance with the reasonable expectations of the insured.'[143] Three years later, it reiterated:

> Under Georgia law, contracts of insurance are interpreted by ordinary rules of contract construction. Three well known rules apply. Any ambiguities in the contract are strictly construed against the insurer as drafter of the document; any exclusion from coverage sought to be invoked by the insurer is likewise strictly construed; and insurance contracts are to be read in accordance with the reasonable expectations of the insured where possible.[144]

As in Connecticut, in Georgia it was not clear whether ambiguity is *the* prerequisite, or just one of a number of circumstances in which PREC could be applied.

The Supreme Court of Illinois affirmed that 'in determining when coverage is appropriate, this court can also consider a policyholder's reasonable expectations and the coverage intended by the insurance policy'.[145] It seems that Illinois accepted the conception or principle of PREC, but not a doctrine thereof, because there was no further discussion of a separate explanatory rationale for it. Even if such a doctrine had been taken for granted, hence without discussion, its relationship with ambiguity is opaque.

The situation is similar in Indiana. According to the Supreme Court of Indiana, 'the courts should strive to give effect to the reasonable expectations of the insured';[146] '[c]ourts should strive to give effect to the reasonable expectation of the insured; an ambiguous policy should be construed to further its basic purpose of indemnifying the insured for his loss';[147] 'In construing an insurance contract, we ultimately must give effect to the intent and reasonable expectations of the parties as expressed in the contract.'[148] There were no further discussions of a doctrine of 'policyholder's reasonable expectations': it was accepted and perhaps

[143] *Frances Roland v Georgia Farm Bureau Mutual Insurance Company*, 265 Ga 776, 778; 462 SE 2d 623, 625 (Geo 1995), citing *Cincinnati Insurance Company v Davis*, 153 Ga App 291 (265 SE 2d 102) (1980).

[144] *Boardman Petroleum (d/b/a Red & Jack Oil Company) v Federated Mutual Insurance Company*, 269 Ga 326, 328; 498 SE 2d 492, 494 (Geo 1998), citing *Richards v Hanover Ins Co*, 250 Ga 613, 615; 299 SE 2d 561 (1983).

[145] *Cummins v Country Mutual Insurance Company*, 178 Ill 2d 474, 485; 687 NE 2d 1021, 1027 (Ill 1997), referring to *Hoglund v State Farm Mutual Automobile Insurance Co*, 148 Ill 2d 272, 279, 170 Ill Dec 351, 592 NE 2d 1031 (1992).

[146] *Eli Lilly v Home Ins Co*, 482 NE 2d 467, 471 (Ind 1985).

[147] *Meridian Mutual Insurance Company v Richie*, 540 NE 2d 27, 30 (Ind 1989), relying on *Eli Lilly v Home Ins Co*, 482 NE 2d 467, 471 (Ind 1985).

[148] *Colonial Penn Insurance Company v Guzorek*, 690 NE 2d 664, 669 (Ind 1997); referring to *Marshall v Universal Underwriters Ins Co*, 673 NE 2d 513, 517 (Ind Ct App 1996).

taken for granted as a broad concept or principle that rebalances the insurance relationship in favour of policyholders. This can be confirmed in a statement of the law in the Court of Appeals of Indiana:

> No Indiana decision has considered this 'doctrine' in depth, and it is not necessary to do so in this case. Indiana courts have addressed the reasonable expectations *concept* in only two insurance contexts: (1) where the policy at issue is ambiguous and (2) where the coverage at issue would be illusory if the policy were enforced.[149]

The Supreme Court of Louisiana stated:

> The court should construe the policy 'to fulfill the reasonable expectations of the parties in the light of the customs and usages of the industry.' … In insurance parlance, this is labelled the reasonable expectations doctrine.[150]

In the Court of Appeals of Louisiana, this was cited approvingly and verbatim in *Morbely v State Farm Mutual Automobile Insurance Company*,[151] and was also referred to affirmatively: the reasonable expectations doctrine 'is to be used to determine the "reasonable expectations of the parties" when there is an ambiguity.'[152]

The relationship between ambiguity and DRE/PREC is not clear in Maine either. The Supreme Court of Maine stated:

> A contract is ambiguous only if it is reasonably susceptible to two or more interpretations. *Fitzgerald v. Gamester*, 658 A.2d 1065, 1069 (Me. 1995). If the contract *is* ambiguous, it will be construed against the insurer so as to comply with the objectively reasonable expectations of the insured.[153]

Although ambiguities are to be construed to give effect to PREC, it is not clear whether ambiguity is *the* prerequisite for or the *only* circumstance in which PREC is to be effectuated. Rather, it seems that the Supreme Court of Maine viewed PREC as the reason or rational for *contra proferentem* in the context of insurance, rather than the other way round.

The Supreme Court of Mississippi accepted the idea or concept of PREC as early as 1973, when, concerning title insurance, it stated, in *Pruett v Mississippi*

[149] *Hastings Mutual Insurance Company v.Webb*, 659 NE 2d 1049, 1054 (Ind Ct App 1995). Internal citations are omitted.

[150] *Louisiana Insurance Guaranty Association v Interstate Fire & Casualty Company*, 630 So 2d 759, 764 (Loui 1994). The internal citation omitted is *Trinity Industries, Inc v Ins Co of North America*, 916 F 2d 269 (5th Cir 1990). The quotation above was footnoted by the Supreme Court of Louisiana with quotations from Keeton (and Widiss). The footnote reads: 'The reasonable expectations doctrine can be capsulized as follows: "courts will protect the [insured's] reasonable expectations … regarding the coverage afforded by insurance contracts even though a careful examination of the policy provisions indicates that such expectations are contrary to the expressed intention of the insurer." R Keeton and A Widiss, *Insurance Law* § 6.13 (1988).'

[151] *Morbely v State Farm Mutual Automobile Insurance Company*, 674 So 2d 1117, 1120–21 (La App 2 Cir 1998).

[152] *Louisiana in Boudreaux v Siarc, Inc*, 714 So 2d 49, 54 (La App 5 Cir 1998).

[153] *Colford v Chubb Life Insurance Company of America*, 687 A 2d 609, 614 (Me 1996), referring to *Peerless Ins Co v Brennon*, 564 A 2d 383, 386–87 (Me 1989).

Valley Title Insurance Company,[154] 'one of the reasonable expectations of a policyholder who purchases title insurance is to be protected against defects in his title that appear of record'. It has been recognised in *Delta Pride Catfish, Inc v Home Insurance Company*[155] that 'the apparent majority rule ... best articulates the insured's objectively reasonable expectations about the scope of coverage. This conclusion is partly a matter of interpretation and partly a matter of common sense.' It is unclear, however, whether ambiguity in insurance policy terms is *the* prerequisite or *a* prerequisite for applying PREC in Mississippi.

Nebraska adopted only a general concept or idea of PREC. The Supreme Court of Nebraska stated that 'Insurance contracts will be interpreted in accordance with the reasonable expectations of the insured at the time of the contract, and a reasonable construction should be given so as to effectuate the purpose for which it was made.'[156] And '"Thus, the party's reasonable expectation of coverage is to be measured not by premiums paid but by the clear terms of the insurance policy as understood by the reasonable, ordinary man."'[157]

In Tennessee, PREC is more a concept that carries some weight than a doctrine that delineates itself from ambiguity in an insurance policy. In settling a dispute over a credit life insurance policy, the Supreme Court of Tennessee stated that it should join the growing number of jurisdictions in abandoning the distinction between 'accidental means' and 'accidental results', 'because the distinction is contrary to the understanding and reasonable expectations of the average insurance policy-holder and contrary to the plain meaning of the terms of the insurance contract'.[158] In 1978, quoting a federal court opinion that the insurer's duty of good faith and fair dealing 'is based on the reasonable expectations of the insured and the unequal bargaining positions of the contractants',[159] and that '[a]fter all, the insured is the one who pays the premiums for the uninsured motorist protection and the "reasonable expectation" that he will be dealt with fairly and in good faith by his insurer is still present',[160] the Supreme Court of Tennessee held that the position taken by the federal court 'more nearly conforms with an insured's expectations'.[161] That being said, there has been no further discussion of DRE/PREC in Tennessee.

The relationships of clear policy language, ambiguity and possible application of DRE/PREC were opaque in New Jersey too. The Supreme Court of New Jersey in the 1960s recognised

[154] *Pruett v Mississippi Valley Title Insurance Company*, 271 So 2d 920, 922 (Miss 1973).

[155] *Delta Pride Catfish, Inc v Home Insurance Company*, 697 So 2d 400, 404 (Miss 1999).

[156] *Central Waste Systems, Inc v Granite State Insurance Company*, 231 Neb 640, 642 (Neb 1989), relying on *Dale Electronics, Inc v Federal Ins Co*, 205 Neb 115, 119–20 (1979).

[157] *Polenz v Farm Bureau Insurance Company of Nebraska*, 227 Neb 703, 711 (Neb 1988), quoting *Kracl v Aetna Cas. & Surety Co*, 220 Neb 869, 874–75.

[158] *Harrell v Minnesota Mutual Life Insurance Company*, 937 SW 2d 809, 810 and 814 (Tenn 1996).

[159] *Craft v Economy Fire and Casualty Co*, 572 F 2d 565, 569 (7th Cir 1978).

[160] Ibid.

[161] *MFA Mutual Insurance Company v Flint*, 574 SW 2d 718, 722 (1978).

> that the terms of an insurance policy are not talked out or bargained for as in the case of contracts generally, that the insured is chargeable with its terms because of a business utility rather than because he read or understood them, and hence an insurance contract should be read to accord with the reasonable expectations of the purchaser *so far as its language will permit.*[162] (emphasis added)

In the 1990s it continued along the same lines: judges stressed that they would 'adhere to the principle that an insurance policy should generally be interpreted "according to its plain and ordinary meaning," ... so as not to disregard the "clear import and intent" of a policy exclusion'.[163] Meanwhile, however, judges also stated:

> We also have held that ambiguities in policy language will be resolved in favor of the insured in order to give effect to the insured's reasonable expectations. Under certain circumstances, even the plain meaning of policy language may be overcome if it conflicts with the reasonable expectations of the insured.[164]

This confounded the relationships between clear policy language, ambiguity and possible application of PREC. In the 1960s, PREC was held to be restrained by insurance policy language. In the 1990s, however, it was held that although clear language controlled, ambiguities in language would be interpreted to honour PREC, *and meanwhile* that PREC could trump clear language '[u]nder certain circumstances'. It is difficult to see how the three positions could very well co-exist. Nonetheless, the New Jersey law has remained muddled in this regard.

Wisconsin adopted the conception of DRE/PREC consistently in a number of cases before 1998. In 1984, the Supreme Court of Wisconsin had its first case in which it accepted PREC more as a concept than as a doctrine:

> The objective in interpreting and construing a contract is to ascertain and carry out the true intention of the parties. The words of an insurance contract are to be construed in accordance with the principle that the test is not what the insurer intends the words to mean but what a reasonable person in the position of the insured would understand the words to mean. The reasonable expectations of coverage of the insured should be furthered by the interpretation given.[165]

[162] *Cooper v Government Employees Insurance Co*, 51 NJ 86, 93–94; 237 A 2d 870, 873–74 (1968), with the Court citing *Allen v Metropolitan Life Ins Co*, 44 NJ 294, 305 (1965); *Merchants Indemnity Corp v Eggleston*, 37 NJ 114, 121 (1962); *Mazzilli v Accident & Casualty Ins Co of Winterthur*, 35 NJ 1, 7–8 (1961); *Kievit v Loral Protection Life Ins Co* 170 A 2d 22 (NJ 1961).

[163] *American Motorists Insurance Company v L-C-A Sales Company*, 155 NJ 29, 41 (NJ 1998), quoting *Voorhees v Preferred Mut Ins Co*, 128 NJ 165, 175; 607 A 2d 1255 (1992) (citing *Longobardi v Chubb Ins Co*, 121 NJ 530, 537; 582 A 2d 1257 (1990)).

[164] *American Motorists Insurance Company v L-C-A Sales Company*, 155 NJ 29, 41 (NJ 1998), citing *Voorhees v Preferred Mut Ins Co*, 128 NJ 165, 175, 607 A 2d 1255 (1992); *DiOrio v New Jersey Mfrs Ins Co*, 79 NJ 257, 269; 398 A 2d 1274 (1979); and *Werner Indus, Inc v First State Ins Co*, 112 NJ 30, 35–36, 548 A 2d 188 (1988).

[165] *Kremers-Urban Company v American Employers Insurance Co*, 119 Wis 2d 722, 735; 351 NW 2d 156, 163 (Wis 1984).

This was cited approvingly verbatim in the same Court in 1994 in *City of Edgerton and Edgerton Sand & Gravel, Inc v General Casualty Company of Wisconsin.*[166] Also in 1984, it was held that 'When construing language covering an obligation such as the insurer's duty to defend the insured, courts must look to the reasonable expectations of the insured.'[167] The same Court stated in 1991:

> The mere fact that a word has more than one dictionary meaning, or the parties disagree about the meaning, does not necessarily make the word ambiguous if the court concludes that only one meaning applies in the context and comports with the parties' objectively reasonable expectations.[168]

Concerning UIM (underinsured motorist) coverage, the Supreme Court of Wisconsin held that 'UIM [insurance] contracts must be construed according to the reasonable expectations of the insured'.[169] However, the rationale of adopting the DRE concept is not clear.

Type 4.0—Unclear whether DRE/PREC was accepted or rejected

It still remains unclear whether Oregon, Massachusetts and Maryland have adopted or rejected PREC. In the Supreme Court of Oregon, after arguing strongly for it in his dissenting opinion, Justice Unis stated:

> This court has not explicitly adopted the doctrine of 'reasonable expectation', at least by name, in any of its forms. Neither has this court explicitly rejected it. … At some point, this court will have to address this series of conflicting precedents in our cases which today's majority opinion simply ignores.[170]

This point, however, has not arrived.

The judicial position of Massachusetts on DRE/PREC was no less difficult to fathom. Although the Supreme Judicial Court of Massachusetts admitted it had 'not yet explicitly adopted such an approach to the interpretation of an insurance policy',[171] it was not disinclined to adopt PREC:

> In any analysis of the scope of the coverage of an insurance policy, it may be appropriate to consider what a policy-holder reasonably should expect his coverage to be in the circumstances. See R Keeton, *Insurance Law* 351 (1971); *Restatement (Second) of Contracts* § 211 comment e (1980) ('Apart from government regulation, courts in construing and applying a standardized contract seek to effectuate the reasonable expectations of the average member of the public who accepts it'). Such an approach may be a better way

[166] *City of Edgerton and Edgerton Sand & Gravel, Inc v General Casualty Company of Wisconsin*, 184 Wis 2d 750, 780; 517 NW 2d 463, 476–77 (Wis 1994).

[167] *Gross v Lloyds of London Insurance Company*, 121 Wis 2d 78, 87; 358 NW 2d 266, 271 (Wis 1984).

[168] *Sprangers v Greatway Insurance Company*, 182 Wis 2d 521, 537; 514 NW 2d 1, 17 (Wis 1994), citing *United States Fire Ins Co v Ace Baking Co*, 164 Wis 2d 499, 503–04, 476 NW 2d 280 (Ct App 1991).

[169] *Matthiesen v. Continental Casualty Company*, 193 Wis 2d 192, 204; 532 NW 2d 729, 733 (Wis 1995).

[170] *Collins v Farmers Insurance Company of Oregon*, 312 Ore 337, 365 (1991).

[171] *Bond Bros, Inc v Odell Robinson*, 393 Mass 546, 551 (Mas 1984).

> of considering claims of policy ambiguity than a clinical study of the policy language, a process that tends to lead to a dispositive, abstract conclusion that the policy either is or is not ambiguous.[172]

The majority in this case found in favour of the insurer, not because they rejected PREC in the first place, but because they conceded that the insured would not be benefited even if they were to consider reasonable expectations of coverage in deciding this case.[173] However, Justice Abraham strongly dissented (joined by Justice Liacos):

> In such circumstances, I would apply the doctrine of reasonable expectations, see *Markline Co v Travelers Ins Co*, 384 Mass 139, 146–147 (1981) (Liacos, J, dissenting), and permit the plaintiff to recover. There is no justification in this case for any departure from our long-standing rule that it is the insurer's responsibility to provide exclusionary clauses 'free from any ambiguity and in such simple language so as to be readily understood by a person not versed in legal technicalities or nuances of phraseology.' *MacArthur v Massachusetts Hosp Serv, Inc*, 343 Mass 670, 672 (1962). Conflicting and confusing clauses should be construed against the insurer. *Vappi & Co v Aetna Casualty & Sur Co*, 348 Mass 427, 431 (1965). …
>
>> '[I]nsurers ought not to be allowed to use qualifications and exceptions from coverage that are inconsistent with the reasonable expectations of a policyholder having an ordinary degree of familiarity with the type of coverage involved. This ought not to be allowed even though the insurer's form is very explicit and unambiguous, because insurers know that ordinarily policyholders will not in fact read their policies. …' R Keeton, Insurance Law 351–352 (1971).[174]

In addition, three years earlier, Justice Liacos also delivered a dissenting opinion in favour of application of PREC, stating, inter alia, 'the general principle that the intent and reasonable expectations of the parties govern the construction of insurance contracts'.[175] He continued, 'The Restatement informs us that "courts in construing and applying a standardized contract seek to effectuate the reasonable expectations of the average member of the public who accepts it."'[176]

It is not clear whether Maryland accepted or rejected DRE/PREC. It seems that neither the state's higher courts (the Court of Appeals of Maryland, and the Court of Special Appeals of Maryland) nor its lower courts have had cases or opportunities before them to discuss DRE/PREC.

[172] Ibid.

[173] Ibid: 'There is nothing about the general nature or purpose of a comprehensive general liability insurance policy that would lead an insured reasonably to expect that the policy covered a loss of the type involved here, caused by his breach of contract and poor workmanship.'

[174] Ibid 553–54.

[175] *Markline Co v Travelers Ins Co*, 384 Mass 139, 147 (Mass 1981), citing *Ayres v Prudential Ins Co of America*, 602 F 2d 1309 (9th Cir 1979).

[176] *Markline Co v Travelers Ins Co*, 384 Mass 139, 147 (Mass 1981), quoting *Restatement (Second) of Contracts* § 237, Comment e, at 54 (Tent Draft Nos 1–7 1973).

D. Rethinking the Doctrine of Reasonable Expectations under Keeton's 'Characterisation System'

The investigation above classifies the US state jurisdictions into six types according to their approaches to DRE/PREC. Tables 5.1 and 5.2 below summarise the approaches in the different jurisdictions. Table 5.1 shows overall how many state jurisdictions fall into each type described above. Table 5.2 shows more specifically which type each individual state jurisdiction falls into. In respect of Table 5.2, where DRE/PREC was discussed in relation to a state jurisdiction both before 1998 and in or after 1998, the judicial opinion in the latter period supersedes that in the former. This is the case with Alabama, and Wisconsin, whose pre-1998 judicial opinions regarding DRE/PREC were superseded by those handed down in or after 1998, hence the pre-1998 opinions were not taken into account for the purposes of Table 5.1. The simple but telling statistics in Table 5.1 are set out accordingly, so that there is no double counting of any of the six types. In Table 5.2, each left-facing arrow for a particular state jurisdiction from 1998 means there has been no judicial consideration of PREC from 1998 up to the time of writing, hence the status (specifically the type) of PREC in that jurisdiction refers back to what it was before 1998.

It can be seen from the two tables that a 'doctrine' of PREC, as in Type 2.0, is applied in only eight American state jurisdictions. Altogether, very broadly 30 state jurisdictions, ie those under Type 1.5, Type 2.0 and Type 3.0 together, have applied or adopted PREC in one way or another. If *contra proferentem* in insurance law could be equated with PREC, then another 10 states, ie for Type 1.0, could be added to this list, totalling 40 at most.

Table 5.1: PREC generally in all state jurisdictions from 1998 onwards

Type	*Numerical Signifier*	*Number of Jurisdictions*
Rejection of PREC	*0*	7
Adopted, having ambiguity as *the* prerequisite	*1.0*	10
Adopted, having ambiguity as *a* prerequisite	*1.5*	6
Adopted, ambiguity *not* as a prerequisite	*2.0*	7
Adopted conceptually, without clear rationale	*3.0*	17
Totally unclear if it is adopted or rejected	*4.0*	3

Table 5.2: PREC in each individual state jurisdiction

State Jurisdictions	*before 1998*	*from 1998*
Alabama	*2.0*	*1.0*
Alaska		*2.0*
Arizona		*2.0*
Arkansas	*3.0*	← *(3.0)*
California		*3.0*
Colorado		*1.5*
Connecticut	*3.0*	← *(3.0)*
Delaware	*1.5*	← *(1.5)*
Florida	*0*	← *(0)*
Georgia	*3.0*	← *(3.0)*
Hawaii		*3.0*
Idaho	*0*	← *(0)*
Illinois	*3.0*	← *(3.0)*
Indiana	*3.0*	← *(3.0)*
Iowa		*2.0*
Kansas		*1.0*
Kentucky		*1.0*
Louisiana	*3.0*	← *(3.0)*
Maine	*3.0*	← *(3.0)*
Maryland	*4.0*	← *(4.0)*
Massachusetts	*4.0*	← *(4.0)*
Michigan		*0*
Minnesota		*1.5*
Mississippi	*3.0*	← *(3.0)*
Missouri	*1.0*	← *(1.0)*
Montana		*1.0*
Nebraska	*3.0*	← *(3.0)*
Nevada		*3.0*
New Hampshire		*3.0*
New Jersey	*3.0*	← *(3.0)*
New Mexico		*2.0*
New York		*3.0*
North Carolina	*2.0*	← *(2.0)*

(*Continued*)

Table 5.2: *(Continued)*

State Jurisdictions	***before 1998***	***from 1998***
North Dakota	*1.5*	← *(1.5)*
Ohio		*2.0*
Oklahoma		*1.5*
Oregon	*4.0*	← *(4.0)*
Pennsylvania	*2.0*	← *(2.0)*
Rhode Island	*1.5*	← *(1.5)*
South Carolina		*3.0*
South Dakota		*0*
Tennessee	*3.0*	← *(3.0)*
Texas	*1.0*	← *(1.0)*
Utah	*0*	← *(0)*
Vermont		*1.0*
Virginia	*0*	← *(0)*
Washington	*0*	← *(0)*
West Virginia		*1.0*
Wisconsin	*3.0*	*1.0*
Wyoming		*1.0*

Type 1.0 and Type 1.5—potentially Type 3.0 as well—are those states where PREC was adopted on a variety of rationales and/or circumstances apart from ambiguity in insurance policy terms. Such variety is one of the features of the application of a legal principle. Due to its relative broadness, a legal principle is often applied on the ground of multi rationales, or in seemingly different scenarios which, however, can justify a common need for the principle. An example of this, also in insurance, is the principle of indemnity, 'the governing principle'[177] which is held to be so 'fundamental' that '[e]very rule of insurance law is adopted in order to carry [it] out', and 'if ever any proposition is brought forward, the effect of which is opposed [thereto], it will be found to be wrong'.[178] The indemnity principle in insurance law operates in a number of scenarios, including but not limited to reinstatement, contribution in 'other insurance' or double insurance, subrogation, capping in over-insurance, proportionality in (non-valued)

[177] J Lowry, P Rawlings and R Merkin, *Insurance Law: Doctrines and Principles*, 3rd edn (Oxford, Hart Publishing 2011) 323.

[178] *Castellain v Preston* [1881–1885] All ER 493, 495 (Brett LJ).

underinsurance, coverage and payment of medical costs in personal insurance, and the requirement of an insurable interest in property insurance. Such a multiplicity of scenarios is consistent with the overarching relevance of indemnity in insurance law, and it also renders it unsound to characterise indemnity in insurance as a legal doctrine/rule—indeed it is seldom referred to other than as a principle in insurance law.

E. Dworkin and Abraham's Perspectives

Dworkin's classic distinction between legal rules/doctrines and principles is helpful for the purpose of characterising and recharacterising DRE/PREC. Dworkin famously pointed out:

> The difference between legal principles and legal rules [or doctrines] is a logical distinction. Both sets of standards point to particular decisions about legal obligation in particular circumstances, but they differ in the character of the direction they give. Rules are applicable in an all-or-nothing fashion. If the facts a rule stipulates are given, then either the rule is valid, in which case the answer it supplies must be accepted, or it is not, in which case it contributes nothing to the decision. This all-or-nothing [fashion] is seen most plainly if we look at the way rules.[179]

Even a concessionary point of view, which might be aligned with how Dworkin distinguishes legal principles from legal rules/doctrine, can still lend substantial strength to the argument that PREC is more like a principle than a doctrine. To illustrate, Dworkin referred to Sherman Act 1890, section 1 of which reads:

> Every contract … in restraint of trade or commerce among the several States, or with foreign nations, is declared to be illegal.

According to Dworkin, the US Supreme Court rendered the decision that the provision 'should be treated as a rule in its own terms (striking down every contract "which restrains trade," which almost any contract does)' rather than 'as a principle, providing a reason for striking down a contract in the absence of effective contrary policies'.[180] In particular:

> The Court construed the provision as a rule, but treated that rule as containing the word 'unreasonable,' and as prohibiting only 'unreasonable' restraints of trade. This allowed the provision to function *logically as a rule* (whenever a court finds that the restraint is 'unreasonable' it is bound to hold the contract invalid) and *substantially as a principle*

[179] Dworkin, 'The Mode of Rules', above n 31, 25. See also Dworkin, *Taking Rights Seriously*, above n 31, 26.

[180] Dworkin, above n 31, 28.

> (a court must take into account a variety of other principles and policies in determining whether a particular restraint in particular economic circumstances is 'unreasonable').[181]

Dworkin pointed out further:

> Words like 'reasonable,' 'negligent,' 'unjust,' and 'significant' often perform just this function. Each of these terms makes the application of the rule which contains it depend to some extent upon principles or policies lying beyond the rule, and in this way *makes that rule itself more like a principle.*[182]

Given this concession, even if PREC *were* a doctrine/rule, the word 'reasonable' and the need to find whether a policyholder's expectation of coverage in a particular dispute is reasonable or not make the PREC doctrine/rule, if it indeed were such, more like a principle.

If an observation from the jurisprudential perspective as above is somewhat too general or broad to be useful for (re)characterising DRE/PREC, the perception particularly from insurance law and as directly concerns DRE/PREC in American insurance law is certainly more telling. In the early 1980s, Kenneth Abraham, largely approving of a 'principle of reasonable expectations' approach in insurance law, argued that 'powerful reasons suggest that it is time for the expectations principle to mature into a body of doctrine composed of a discrete set of rules'.[183] This is convincing, but in the courts the law has not developed in the way wished. Given that, it is not surprising that Abraham has argued, over nearly 20 years, that the reasonable expectations 'principle' is more significant[184] than the reasonable expectations 'doctrine', which has only limited scope and is of a minor nature.[185] Abraham has observed:

> [T]he expectations principle and its corollary constitute a normative statement about the proper relation between the supply side of the insurance market and the demand side of the market. As a normative statement about this relation, the expectations 'principle' is a regulative ideal that influences legal and policy decision-makers in a variety of ways far more important than does the expectations 'doctrine' proper.[186]

The huge influence of the American PREC principle can be detected in the rise of managed healthcare, the explosion of Commercial General Liability coverage litigation, the large verdicts for insurer bad faith and the controversies over insurance rate.[187]

[181] Ibid.
[182] Ibid.
[183] Abraham, above n 13, 1197.
[184] Abraham, above n 6, 61.
[185] Ibid 61–63.
[186] Ibid 64.
[187] Ibid.

III. Conclusion

In the US, DRE/PREC should be re-characterised as a principle, not as the doctrine it has been taken to be. This is, first, because Keeton proposed it as a principle rather than a doctrine in 1970. Secondly and more importantly, when he revisited[188] DRE/PREC in 1976, he emphasised the distinction between legal doctrines and legal principles, as has been recounted in section II.A. above, without intending DRE/PREC to be purely a doctrine. Instead, Keeton treated a decision as applying a *doctrine* of honouring reasonable expectations 'only if, first, it explicitly does so, and, second, it appears explicitly to adopt not merely the term "reasonable expectations" but also an explanatory theory of decision that goes beyond resolving ambiguities against the party responsible for them'.[189] Other than that, judicial reference in whatever manner to PREC is not an application of it as a legal doctrine. The more varied the ways PREC is referred to judicially, the more it is consistent with the broadness of a legal principle. In this regard, it is noteworthy that the American insurance lawyers, in preparing the *Restatement of the Law of Liability Insurance*, have been more inclined to see PREC as an interpretative principle and to reject Keeton's strong formulation of PREC (as a doctrine).[190] Thirdly and the most importantly, US state supreme courts cases before 1998 and from 1998 onwards show that DRE/PREC is not dead; instead it has been adopted in one way or another in most state jurisdictions. The multiplicity of ways in which it is applied evidences that it is more a broad principle adopted on a number of rationales or in different scenarios than a narrowly-applied doctrine.

The implications of recharacterising DRE or the American version of PREC as a principle are three-fold. First, it can substantially lessen the controversy over the multiplicity of 'formulations' of DRE/PREC. When regarded as a doctrine, it has been constantly criticised for its lack of consistency or uniformity. Once characterised as a principle, it is not unusual that it is applied with a multiplicity of rationales or in a number of formulations. Secondly, it puts an end to the doubt over whether DRE/PREC is dead and/or declining in the US. As a principle, it is certainly not dead—rather it enjoys flatly (and perhaps boringly as well) stable judicial consideration, even in the twenty-first century.[191] The findings are consistent with the observation of Stempel et al that 'Today, the reasonable expectations concept is well-established as (1) an aid to interpreting policy language generally, and (2) a means of resolving ambiguity in policy terms about other indicia of meaning.'[192]

[188] Keeton, above n 4.

[189] Ibid 279.

[190] American Law Institute, *Restatement of the Law of Liability Insurance* (Council Draft No 1, 25 Sept 2015) 26–27.

[191] For example, in the majority of post-1998 cases referred to in section II.B.

[192] Stempel, Swisher and Knutsen, above n 50, 127. See also RJ Maniloff and JW Stempel, *General Liability Insurance Coverage: Key Issues in Every State* (New York, Oxford University Press, 2011) Ch 20.

This corresponds to Types 1.0, 1.5, 2.5 and 3.0, but not to Type 0, where DRE is expressly rejected, nor to Type 4.0, where it is not clear whether DRE is applied or adopted. Even for DRE/PREC as a doctrine in the Keetonian sense stated in 1976, ie as Type 2.0, from 1998 onwards there have been six state jurisdictions still taking the Type 2.0 approach, that is, more than did before 1998. Lastly, but not least importantly, the recharacterisation has the effect of substantially weakening the English argument against PREC. The English objection to PREC essentially hinges on the perception that DRE/PREC has been very controversial and declining in its country of origin, ie the US, so that there is no good reason to import it across the Atlantic into the UK. However, such a perception is largely misconceived. Once DRE/PREC in the US is properly recharacterised as a principle, the controversy is substantially lessened and the decline is counter-factual to the stability found in American judicial consideration of PREC. In light of this, the English pessimism about PREC is fundamentally unsound and largely untenable.

6

Reassessing the Objections to Policyholder's Reasonable Expectations of Coverage in English Insurance Law

Mostly from the perspective of general contract law, all previous chapters have built up to this chapter, which will approach PREC directly from the perspective of English insurance contract law. It first considers PREC in consumer insurance; in this regard it is uncontroversial that insurance law actively protects a consumer policyholder's reasonable expectations. Secondly, the chapter addresses the long-term pessimism about or objections to PREC in English insurance law. These objections are that PREC will cause much uncertainty and inconsistency in insurance law, that other alternative doctrines in English (insurance) contract law will suffice, and that English courts seldom consider, and should not consider, public policy in insurance law as American courts do. It is argued that these objections are overstated and that each of them can be substantially alleviated. Thirdly, after consideration of PREC in consumer insurance and of the general objections thereto, this chapter will consider PREC in business insurance. For this purpose, it uses the theory of relational contracts. Specifically, it connects Ian McNeil's classic theory of relational contracts with Robert Merkin and Jenny Steele's relational perception of insurance contract, as well as Catherine Mitchell's more recent argument for reasonable expectations in commercial contracts, to argue that PREC should be seriously considered in business insurance as well. In doing so, it also argues that it is the *policyholder's* reasonable expectations that should prevail over those of the insurer, not the other way round. This is due to the different nature of the insurer's and policyholder's reasonable expectations in connection with the purpose of insurance contracts.

I. Policyholder's Reasonable Expectations of Coverage: Where Are We?—Consumer Insurance

In English insurance law, up till now PREC has a limited role only in consumer insurance. This can be seen in two judicial approaches. The first is the application of other legal doctrines to the similar effect of PREC. The second is the express and direct use of PREC as part of the judicial reasoning in a particular case, which is rare compared with the first approach.

Regarding the first approach, Malcolm Clarke has observed[1] that there is more than one line of cases in England that might converge on the same point to produce law similar to that in some US cases, where the particular insurer generated an expectation in policyholders by creating a misleading impression in regard to coverage and/or the exclusion of particular risks.[2] These lines of cases are as follows:[3]

1. If the insurer knowingly allows the insured to contract insurance under a mistaken belief about its terms, the contract will be rectified (and enforced) in accord with the belief of the insured.
2. If an agent of the insurer leads the proposer to expect that a document contains term X, when the reality is that it contains term Y, it may be enforced as if it contained X rather than Y.
3. The offeror of contract terms is not allowed to rely on clauses presented misleadingly[4] or inconspicuously[5] by the document itself.
4. The English doctrine of fundamental breach, which occurs, inter alia, when a seller delivers something fundamentally different from what was contracted for, resembled certain expectations in the USA, such as in *Kievet v Loyal Protective Life Ins Co*,[6] a case that has been perceived as one of the early precedents of the American insurance law principle of PREC. The argument remains that 'insurance is sold like any other product and should be subject to the same rules and construction. It will be construed so as to fulfil not defeat the main purpose or expectation of the (reasonable) insured.'[7]

Although this 'product argument' did not receive full judicial support, it was not completely negated in relation to consumer insurance.[8] In considering Clarke's foregoing observation and argument, Mustill LJ opined that 'if traces of such a doctrine [of reasonable expectations of the insured] can be discerned, it is because (in the words of the author) certain sorts of insurance are "sold like any other

[1] M Clarke, 'The Reasonable Expectations of the Insured—in England?' [1989] *JBL* 389. See also M Clarke, *The Law of Insurance Contracts*, 6th edn (London, Informa, 2009) 452–53.

[2] Clarke, *The Law of Insurance Contracts*, above n 1, 449, 452.

[3] M Clarke, *The Law of Insurance Contracts*, 4th edn (London, LLP, 2002) [15-5B2]; see also Clarke, *The Law of Insurance Contracts*, above n 1, 452–53.

[4] In *Ryan v Oceanic SN Co Ltd* [1914] 3 KB 731 (CA), 747–48, Vaughan Williams LJ thought that the defendant could not plead a term printed below the point where the contractual part of the document appeared to end.

[5] *Stephen v International Sleeping-Car Co Ltd* (1903) 19 TLR 621. The defendant was not allowed to plead a clause on a voucher on the same side of the paper as 22 advertisements. See also *Woolfall & Rimmer Ltd v Moyle* [1942] 1 KB 66, 73.

[6] *Kievit v Loral Protection Life Ins Co*, 170 A2d 22 (NJ 1961).

[7] Clarke, 'The Reasonable Expectations of the Insured—in England?', above n 1.

[8] More recently it has been recognised as one of the 'conceptions' of insurance. See K Abraham, 'Four Conceptions of Insurance' (2013) 161 *University of Pennsylvania Law Review* 653.

product and should be subject to the same rules of law"'.[9] Although Mustill LJ declined to apply or transplant the American doctrine of policyholder's reasonable expectations into (English) business insurance cases, he seemed content with its limited and covert role in consumer insurance, meanwhile cautioning that 'If English law is moving in this direction [toward PREC], it plainly has a very long way to go.'[10]

But it turned out to be only a short way, though it is as narrow as it is short. This is the second approach to PREC in English insurance law. Less than a decade after the comment made by Mustill LJ (above), the House of Lords, in deciding for the policyholder of disability insurance in *Cook v Financial Insurance Co Ltd*,[11] expressly emphasised the consumer insured's reasonable expectations of coverage. This amounted to a small step towards PREC in consumer insurance. In this case, Mr Cook took out disability insurance that commenced on 15 October 1992, and he signed a declaration that he had not consulted a doctor other than for minor illnesses. One of the terms included in an insurance certificate was as follows:

> *Exclusions.* No benefit will be payable for disability resulting from: (a) Any sickness, disease, condition or injury for which an insured person received advice, treatment or counselling from any registered medical practitioner during the 12 months preceding the commencement date.

Prior to the inception of the policy, Mr Cook had a condition which his doctor then was unable to diagnose. On 16 October 1992, Cook's condition was rightly diagnosed as angina. In December 1992 he was advised by his doctor to cease work. He therefore made a claim under the policy, but this was rejected by the insurer. It was held for Cook in the House of Lords that he had not received advice, treatment or counselling particularly for angina prior to 15 October, when it was not diagnosed as such, and that the more general term 'condition' in the exclusion could not be taken to include vague symptoms that could relate to anything or nothing, but instead should be read as meaning an identifiable medical condition.

Lord Lloyd opined that the policyholder's insurance certificate 'must be construed in the sense in which it would have been *reasonably understood* by him as the consumer'.[12] (emphasis added) He stated further that:

> In the present case the plaintiff signed a declaration that he had not consulted a doctor other than for minor illnesses. When he came to read the exclusion clause he was entitled to assume that it related only to major illnesses for which he had consulted a doctor. It could not relate to minor illnesses with which, as the insurers had made clear from the form of the declaration, they were not concerned.[13]

In other words, through the declaration signed by the policyholder he was induced by the insurer to believe that it was major illness that was excluded and that minor

[9] *Smit Tak Offshore Services v Youell* [1992] 1 Lloyd's Rep 154 (CA), 159.
[10] Ibid.
[11] *Cook v Financial Insurance Co Ltd* [1998] 1 WLR 1765 (HL), [1998] UKHL 42.
[12] *Cook v Financial Insurance Co Ltd* [1998] 1 WLR 1765 (HL), 1768.
[13] Ibid 1767.

sickness would be covered. In this context his reasonable expectations should have been honoured in spite of the scarcely ambiguous exclusion clause. By stating that the policyholder 'was *entitled to assume* that [the exclusion] related only to major illnesses for which he had consulted a doctor', Lord Lloyd was not far from saying that it was a legitimate or reasonable expectation of the policyholder that minor illness was within the coverage.

Nevertheless, this House of Lords decision was not followed in any subsequent court case. However, this is not because it is not good law. Rather, it is because consumer insurance disputes are seldom taken to court in the UK; instead, most of them are resolved by ombudsman, namely, by the Insurance Ombudsman Bureau from its establishment in 1981 till 2001, after which it was replaced by the Financial Ombudsman Service (FOS). The FOS was established under the Financial Services and Markets Act (FSMA) 2000, which set out the principles and rules for insurance and financial regulation. One of the principles of insurance (and financial) regulation in the UK is that 'A firm must pay due regard to the interests of its customers and treat them fairly.' Commonly known as the 'principle of Treating Customers Fairly' ('TCF Principle'), this was stipulated as Principle 6 of the Financial Services Authority Principles for Businesses, and remains unchanged as Principle 6 of the current Financial Conduct Authority Principles of Business. The TCF Principle and the 'fair and reasonable' approach by the FOS are in line with PREC. All of them must not simply be ignored by courts resolving insurance disputes. At the very least, any judicial construction of policy wordings shall not contravene, though it need not actively enhance, the regulatory principles and rules, unless they are found to be unlawful during judicial review.

Consumer financial, including insurance, disputes that individually involve contested amounts of not more than £100,000 are within the jurisdiction of the FOS. The FOS is obliged under the FSMA 2000 to resolve consumer financial disputes 'by reference to what is, in the opinion of the ombudsman, fair and reasonable in all the circumstances of the case'.[14] Interestingly, the broad 'all the circumstances of the case' is quite close to, and actually goes further than, the 'factual matrix' contextual approach as restated by Lord Hoffmann.[15] When it comes to *construction* of insurance policy wordings, the FOS has even more flexibility: '[T]he FOS does not seem to struggle so hard to rely on the wordings, and will impose whatever meaning it considers fair and reasonable, even if that meaning is contrary to the obvious meaning of the wording.'[16] This is proximate to Keeton's formulation of PREC.

[14] FSMA 2000, s 228(2); *FCA Handbook: Dispute resolution: Complaints*, DISP 3.6.1R and 3.6.2G. For the question 'Why does the ombudsman use "fair and reasonable" as the basis for deciding cases, rather than the strict legal approach?', see the FOS answer at www.financial-ombudsman.org.uk/faq/businesses/answers/decide_cases_a7.html.

[15] See Chapter 3 above, the text in relation to fn 103.

[16] J Summer, *Insurance Law and the Financial Ombudsman Service*, 2nd edn (London, Taylor & Francis, 2013) [5.17].

Moreover, it seems that the 'fair and reasonable' approach by the FOS can be traced back to the Unfair Contract Terms Act (UCTA) 1977. Although insurance contract was exempted from the UCTA 1977, and the exemption had been adverse to consumer policyholders—hence leading to the establishment of the Insurance Ombudsman Bureau as the precursor to the FOS so far as insurance is concerned—the 'fair and reasonable' approach under the FSMA 2000 brought insurance contract under regulatory control. That in many ways makes up for the exemption of insurance from the UCTA 1977, which did mandate, amongst other things, that the non-consumer party to a contract cannot, by reference to any contract term, claim to be entitled to render a contractual performance substantially different from the consumer's reasonable expectations, except in so far as the contract term satisfies 'the requirement of reasonableness'.[17]

The affinity between what is 'fair and reasonable' and the reasonableness of expectations can be seen in the UCTA 1977 definition of 'the requirement of reasonableness', which is that 'the term shall have been a *fair and reasonable* one to be included having regard to the circumstances which were, or ought reasonably to have been, known to or in the contemplation of the parties when the contract was made'.[18] Again, this certainly will remind readers of Lord Hoffmann's restatement about interpretation of contract:

> Interpretation is the ascertainment of the meaning which the document would convey to a reasonable person having all the background knowledge which would reasonably have been available to the parties in the situation in which they were at the time of the contract. ... [The background knowledge] includes absolutely anything which would have affected the way in which the language of the document would have been understood by a reasonable man.[19]

The resemblance is not surprising. After all, Lord Hoffmann was reiterating the principles of interpretation of contract as stated by Lord Wilberforce in *Prenn v Simmonds*[20] and *Reardon Smith Line Ltd v Yngvar Hansen-Tangen*,[21] around 1977 when the statute was enacted. Given that, it would be unimaginable that the concept of 'fair and reasonable' proposed by the Law Commission was not influenced at all by Lord Wilberforce's statement of a contextual approach to interpretation of contract. Its development into the FSMA 2000 further aligned the 'fair and reasonable' approach, to be taken by the FOS, with the contextual approach to contract interpretation. As has been argued in the Chapter 3, section IV., the contextual approach is one that can be useful for protecting reasonable expectations. As a corollary, the FOS 'fair and reasonable' approach has the effect, at least potentially, of protecting contractual parties' reasonable expectations, particularly PREC as far as consumer insurance is concerned.

[17] UCTA 1977, s 3(2).

[18] UCTA 1977, s 11(1).

[19] *Investors Compensation Scheme Ltd v West Bromwich Building Society* [1997] CLC 1243 (HL), 1257–58. See Chapter 3, section IV.A.

[20] *Prenn v Simmonds* [1971] 1 WLR 1381, 1384–86.

[21] *Reardon Smith Line Ltd v Yngvar Hansen-Tangen* [1976] 1 WLR 989 (HL).

With the contextual approach to PREC in English consumer insurance, perhaps there is no strong need for English lawyers to always turn to the American insurance law principle of PREC. Instead, as Clarke has observed,[22] other doctrines in English contract law operate to the same effect as PREC in consumer insurance. As a corollary, the controversy over the doctrine in the US should present no big hurdle to possibly investing PREC with more weight in English insurance law.

Lastly but not least importantly, the Court of Appeal's rejection of PREC in *Smit Tak Offshore Services Ltd v Youell*[23] and *Yorkshire Water Services Ltd v Sun Alliance & London Insurance Ltd*[24] should not be overstated. The rejection was primarily in connection with business insurance. The reason why Mustill LJ declined to apply PREC was that it was a dispute over maritime insurance individually negotiated between and by business parties, who were assumed to be well able to take care of their own interests. Conversely, that leaves room for PREC in consumer insurance. Mustill LJ considered Malcolm Clarke's observation in this regard, and did not seem to have categorically dismissed Clarke's moderate inclination toward PREC. Given that, the English judiciary's unreceptiveness to PREC in *Smit Tak* in business insurance should not be understood to ripple outwards to affect consumer insurance. After all, the current disregard of PREC in English insurance law 'fails to acknowledge the disparity between the parties [to an insurance contract], the significance of insurance in social policy and the nature of the division between commercial and consumer insurance'.[25] In particular, more than 20 years after *Smit Tak Offshore Services Ltd v Youell*,[26] the distinction in law between consumer insurance and business (or non-consumer) insurance has been made clearer and more relevant. The recent insurance contract law reform has expressly distinguished[27] consumer insurance from non-consumer insurance for different legal treatment in matters of the policyholder's pre-contractual duty of information, of warranties and other matters,[28] thus making consumer protection apparently more important than ever in insurance law. This not only makes it unnecessary and untenable to extend the rejection of PREC in business insurance to consumer insurance, but also to some extent justifies an incremental move toward PREC in consumer insurance. In addition, it keeps relevant Clarke's suggestion that 'It may now be time to draw these strands together in England to form a rule of reasonable

[22] Clarke, *The Law of Insurance Contracts*, above n 1, 449–53.

[23] *Smit Tak Offshore Services Ltd v Youell* [1992] 1 Lloyd's Rep 154 (CA).

[24] *Yorkshire Water Services Ltd v Sun Alliance & London Insurance Ltd* [1997] CLC 213 (CA), 221. Stuart-Smith LJ found, inter alia, that PREC, as applied in some jurisdictions in the US, reflected a substantial element of public policy, which was not part of the principles of construction of contracts in English law.

[25] J Lowry, P Rawlings and R Merkin, *Insurance Law: Doctrines and Principles*, 3rd edn (Oxford, Hart Publishing, 2011) 269.

[26] *Smit Tak Offshore Services Ltd v Youell* [1992] 1 Lloyd's Rep 154 (CA).

[27] Consumer Insurance (Disclosure and Representations) Act 2012, s 1.

[28] See generally Law Commission, Insurance Contract Law: Business Disclosure; Warranties; Insurers' Remedies for Fraudulent Claims; and Late Payment (Law Com No 353, 2014) [2.13]–[2.14] and also 303–07.

expectations applied to insurance contracts.'[29] This will bring insurance law into line with the theme that runs through the English law of contract, that the reasonable expectations of honest men must be protected.[30]

Nevertheless, there has been wide pessimism about, if not outright objection to, PREC generally, or to its application in business insurance particularly. Sections II. and III. below will address this pessimism and further discuss why it is necessary to allow PREC to have more relevance in business insurance law, as well as how that may be feasible.

II. Addressing the Objections to Policyholder's Reasonable Expectations of Coverage

The ongoing pessimism about or objections to PREC in English insurance law is based on the belief that it will introduce excessive uncertainty and even inconsistency into insurance law, that other doctrines in English insurance law and contract law can effectively serve to protect a policyholder's reasonable expectations, and that, unlike US courts, English courts are reluctant to take into account issues of public policy that underlie PREC.[31] These arguments are addressed in turn below.

A. Uncertainty and Inconsistency?

A principal criticism of PREC is that its application will introduce inconsistency and uncertainty into insurance law. As far as inconsistency is concerned, the criticism is far less sound in the UK than in the US. One major reason for the inconsistencies among US jurisdictions in this regard is that insurance law in the US is state law rather than federal law, and decisions of courts in one state are not binding on courts in another state. 'In the area of insurance law [in the US], the "wilderness of single instances" is wilder … No proposition about insurance law is uniformly, or even mainly, true throughout the United States.'[32] Hence, even on the same issue, it is difficult for different state jurisdictions to develop a unified judicial approach, and unlikely that they will do so. However, this problem is apparently much less likely to occur in England and Wales, due to the non-federal and more centralised court system in that jurisdiction. It is not surprising that, owing to inconsistency in the decisions of different state courts in the US, American insurance law cases are of limited assistance to the courts in England and Wales in respect of PREC.[33]

[29] Clarke, *The Law of Insurance Contracts*, above n 1, 454.

[30] *First Energy (UK) Ltd v Hungarian International Bank Ltd* [1993] 2 Lloyd's Rep 194 (CA), 196.

[31] Lowry et al, above n 25, 268-69.

[32] M Davies, 'Insurer's Pre-Contractual Disclosure Obligations: The Proposition in the United States of America' (2012) 23 *Insurance Law Journal* 70, 79.

[33] Clarke, *The Law of Insurance Contracts*, above n 1, 416.

But inconsistency might arise from uncertainty itself. The worries about uncertainty arise from the qualifying word 'reasonable', but there is perhaps no need to be over-concerned. Qualifying words such as 'reasonable', 'proper', 'due', 'fair', etc are unavoidable inconveniences, if they are inconvenient at all, in legal reasoning. Principles and/or doctrines such as 'beyond reasonable doubt', 'reasonable care', 'reasonable man/person', 'due process', 'due diligence', 'fair use' are not unfamiliar to lawyers and judges. Though sometimes difficult to grapple with, they have been part and parcel of the corresponding branches of law. In court cases where there is indeed much uncertainty, they are not abstract concepts. Their meanings are always to be understood and ascertained in specific cases and contexts, rather than in a vacuum or in the abstract. When it comes to the issue of uncertainty in the language of the law, Scott Styles vividly and persuasively pointed out:

> Both the English and Scottish courts make much of the need for certainty in the law. But to a large extent, when courts try to find certainty by relying on words alone, they are attempting an impossible task. The problem is one, long discussed by philosophers, of the basic ambiguity of language. All language, even that of meticulously drafted contracts, contains an inherent penumbra of ambiguity. Much of this ambiguity is, however, resolved by the context of the words and also by contact and co-operation between the participating parties. As Pinker has pointed out, 'People work around its (ie, the language's) limitations by tacitly agreeing on how to use it.' The difficulty for legal draftsmen, whether of contracts, statutes, or other documents is that, as Pinker further observes: 'The law requires language to do something for which it is badly designed: to leave nothing to the imagination.' The important point for present purposes is that the meaning of words is always contextual, and cannot be understood apart from the relevant context. Even the classical approach to contract law recognizes that the context of a contract is sometimes essential for its interpretation and, typically, resolves such cases by use of the notion of an implied term. … Just because a word needs to be interpreted in context does not mean it is ambiguous or uncertain. Consider the simple example of the word 'tall'. The actual height described by the word tall will depend on its context. A tall person is a very different height from a tall tree. Indeed, a tall man, say six feet plus, is the same height as a small tree. Nevertheless we understand the meaning of the word, and do not find it too vague to be unworkable. The concept of good faith (and for that matter the concepts of fairness and reasonableness) works in a similar way. Much of the meaning of good faith will necessarily depend on the context of the contract.[34]

Although the above was in the context of discussion of supposed uncertainty in the principle of good faith, the critique stands equally well in relation to the principle of reasonable expectations. This is particularly so, as has been argued in Chapter 4, since good faith is a means to reasonable expectations as an end. Just as the meaning of good faith necessarily depends on the context of the contract, so does PREC: 'This is not a weakness, but a strength, and should alert judges to the need to take into account the intentions of the parties: intentions,

[34] S Styles, 'Good Faith: A Principled Matter' in ADM Forte (ed), *Good Faith in Contract and Property* (Oxford, Hart Publishing. 1999) 169–70.

which, typically, will be heavily context-dependent.'[35] Lord Penrose has said, 'The expression "reasonable expectations" does not lack clarity. It occurs in a variety of contexts.'[36] The supposedly inherent uncertainty in the concept of PREC is manageable because what counts is 'objectively reasonable' expectations rather than subjective ones, and also because a policyholder's 'objectively reasonable expectations' are those of a reasonable person in the shoes of the policyholder at the time of concluding the insurance contract. The 'reasonable person' standard in itself entails an objective test.

Excessive concerns over subjectivity and uncertainty in the test of reasonableness arise to large extent from confusing a reasonable person with a rational person. As Rawls put it,

> reasonable persons [are moved by a desire for] a social world in which they, as free and equal, can cooperate with others on terms all can accept. They insist that reciprocity should hold within that world so that each benefits along with others.[37]

Rawls continued, 'reasonableness takes agents to the world of the others, where they become equals that are ready to propose or accept fair terms of interaction'.[38] In contrast,

> [the rational] applies to a single, unified agent (either an individual or corporate person) with the powers of judgment and deliberation in seeking ends and interests peculiarly its own. The rational applies to how these ends and interests are adopted and affirmed, as well as to how they are given priority.[39]

A rational person is more likely to be one who is intent on pursuing his or her own interest without due regard to those of others, hence rational expectations are likely to be arbitrarily subjective. However,

> in this Rawlsian framework, private law concerns itself with what is appropriate as a standard of behavior for individuals *in interaction with the others* rather than what is fair for individuals considered *on their own*. … Furthermore, law interprets those actions or words in light of a publicly accessible, or (objectively) reasonable, understanding.[40]

So it is interaction with others, that is, with the other party to the contract and with other parties to similar contracts or other parties in the trade, that ensures that reasonable expectations are both reasonable and objective. Therefore, the reasonableness immediately involves more objectivity, and thus less uncertainty.

More generally, although the pursuit of certainty in law is necessary, it should not go to extremes at the expense of other pursuits and values such as justice and reasonableness. In the House of Lords in *Golden Strait Corp v Nippon Yusen*

35 Ibid 170.
36 Lord Penrose, *Report of the Equitable Life Inquiry* (HC290, TSO 2004) 437–38 [47] and [48].
37 J Rawls, *Political Liberalism* (New York, Columbia University Press. 1993) 50.
38 Ibid.
39 Ibid.
40 M Hevia, *Reasonableness and Responsibility: A Theory of Contract Law* (New York, Springer, 2013) 93.

Kubishika Kaisha,[41] while Lord Bingham would have allowed the appeal because 'the existing decision [of the Court of Appeal] undermines the quality of certainty which is a traditional strength and major selling point of English commercial law, and involves an unfortunate departure from principle',[42] this opinion was not shared by other Law Lords hearing the case. Lord Scott, in delivering the majority opinion and the lead speech, said:

> The argued justification for thus offending the compensatory principle is that priority should be given to the so-called principle of certainty. My Lords, there is, in my opinion, no such principle. Certainty is a desideratum and a very important one, particularly in commercial contracts. But it is not a principle and must give way to principle. Otherwise incoherence of principle is the likely result. The achievement of certainty in relation to commercial contracts depends, I would suggest, on firm and settled principles of the law of contract rather than on the tailoring of principle ...[43]

Lord Bingham stressed instead:

> The importance of certainty and predictability in commercial transactions has been a constant theme of English commercial law at any rate since the judgment of Lord Mansfield CJ in *Vallejo v Wheeler* (1774) 1 Cowp 143, 153).[44]

Indeed, Lord Mansfield CJ had said:

> [I]n all mercantile transactions the great object should be certainty: and therefore, it is of more consequence that a rule should be certain, than whether the rule is established one way or the other. Because speculators in trade then know what ground to go upon.[45]

However, according to Macneil,

> the significance of legal uncertainty in commercial law can be said to be quite low so long as an adequate response is available. ... [When legal certainty cannot be achieved], the result may not be as disastrous as is sometimes claimed.[46]

He went on, 'a tolerable limit for legal uncertainty is itself a function of the tools that the law provides to solve uncertainty'.[47]

Nevertheless, that is

> of course not to say that the House of Lords might not be persuaded under the Practice Statement (*Judicial Precedent*) to depart from an earlier decision where that decision has been demonstrated to work unsatisfactorily in the market place and to produce manifestly unjust results.[48]

[41] *Golden Strait Corp v Nippon Yusen Kubishika Kaisha* [2007] UKHL 12.

[42] Ibid [1].

[43] Ibid [38].

[44] Ibid [23].

[45] *Vallejo v Wheeler* (1774) 1 Cowp 143, 153; 98 ER 1012, 1017.

[46] I Macneil, 'Uncertainty in Commercial Law' (2009) 13 *Edinburgh Law Review* 68, 99.

[47] Ibid. In Part F of his article, Macneil uses the laws on company formation, on pre-contractual disclosure in insurance, and on material breach of contract to substantiate his point above.

[48] *Jindal Iron and Steel Co Ltd v Islamic Solidarity Shipping Co Jordan Inc ('The Jordan II')* [2004] UKHL 49 [16] (per Lord Steyn).

Actually, as Lord Steyn noted,[49] Lord Bingham made such a departure in *R v G and Another*.[50] That was a departure from the decision in *R v Caldwell*,[51] which until then had been an established precedent on the meaning of 'recklessness' in the Criminal Damage Act 1971, section 1. One of the reasons stated by Lord Bingham for not following *R v Caldwell* was that it 'is capable of leading to obvious unfairness';[52] and further that the interpretation by the majority in *R v Caldwell*[53] of 'recklessly' in section 1 of the 1971 Act was a misinterpretation that offended principle and gave rise to injustice, and hence there was a compelling need for the judiciary to correct the misinterpretation.[54] The majority interpretation of 'recklessly' had the benefit of ensuring certainty in the law of criminal damage, and it had been affirmed in the House of Lords. Nevertheless, in *R v G and Another* that interpretation had to give way to considerations of fairness and justice.

Undoubtedly there is more need for certainty in criminal law than in private (and commercial) law. However, now that it is not taboo to subordinate certainty in criminal law to fairness and justice, the need for certainty in commercial law is not so formidable either, at least not as much as in Lord Mansfield's era, when commercial activities were much less diverse than they are in the twenty-first century. At least for Clarke, the tendency of some judges to approach matters of construction of commercial contracts in a conservative fashion for fear of lessening 'certainty' was a matter for concern.[55]

The excessive concern with uncertainty in PREC arises from another problem as regards traditional approaches in English contract law. The problem is that courts 'often ignore the actual factual context of a contract and, instead, understand all contracts as being set in the same context: that of 'one-off' deal negotiations in the open market'.[56] When it comes to contract law, in the view of Hugh Collins, the legal rules and decisions frequently undermine the reasonable expectations of contractual parties, which in the commercial context are based 'on considerations of long-term business relation, the customs of the trade, and the success of the deal'.[57] Although an insurance contract is often on a one-year basis, it can be renewed annually, unless one of the parties chooses not to do so. In this manner, insurance increasingly becomes long-term or relational:[58]

> [T]he arguments in England against the introduction of a general principle of good faith, on the ground that it will be productive of uncertainty, sits strangely with the fact that

[49] Ibid.
[50] *R v G and Another* [2003] UKHL 50.
[51] *R v Caldwell* [1982] UKHL 1, [1982] AC 341.
[52] *R v G and Another* [2003] UKHL 50 [33].
[53] *R v Caldwell* [1982] UKHL 1, [1982] AC 341, 354 (per Lord Diplock).
[54] *R v G and Another* [2003] UKHL 50 [35].
[55] M Clarke, 'Trends in the Interpretation of Marine Insurance Contracts' in DR Thomas (ed), *Marine Insurance: The Law in Transition* (London, Informa 2006) 1–13.
[56] Styles, above n 34, 170.
[57] H Collins, *Regulating Contracts* (Oxford, Oxford University Press, 1999) 271.
[58] Note that here it is 'relational' in a more conventional sense, consistent with the theory of relational contracts. It is different from Merkin and Steele's characterisation of insurance contract as

> English law contains that eclectic bundle of principles and doctrines known as equity. To cavil at a general principle of good faith, yet accept the principles of equity, is to strain at a civilian gnat, whilst happily swallow an equitable camel. The breadth of the two maxims of equity is quite breath-taking. … Are these equitable maxims inherently any more certain than [the principle of good faith]?[59]

Hence 'the effectiveness of contract law can no longer be measured by its certainty in promulgating and enforcing a strict body of doctrinal rules, but by its success in supporting and upholding the more elusive "reasonable expectations of the parties"'.[60]

Lastly but not least importantly, 'it is the business of insurers to achieve certainty by pooling what are for insured uncertain events'.[61] If they fail to do so, they have to bear the consequences of uncertainty, which they should have tried to minimalise *ex ante*, rather than the courts seeking to ensure certainty *ex post*. Admittedly, the courts may be concerned that reasonableness or PREC sounds abstract, subjective and prone to more uncertainty; nonetheless, contextualised in insurance disputes, PREC is always specific and often certain. In the medium term, honouring PREC will establish new certainty in insurance law. As recently as May 2015, in the UK Supreme Court, Lord Sumption stated, albeit obiter, that PREC could be considered 'as background to the construction of the policy'.[62] Use of background for construction of commercial contracts has in this regard set 'new parameters'; 'It is submitted that one of the consequences of these new parameters will be an increased certainty in the [insurance] sector as the new approach mirrors the processes undertaken by parties at the negotiation stage.'[63]

B. Other Doctrines Will Do?

A second objection to PREC in English insurance law is that

> aspects of English law may well produce the same results as might be achieved by applying Keeton's thesis [of policyholder's reasonable expectations of coverage]: for instance, the presumption in favour of coverage, the *contra proferentem* rule, the requirement [ie Article 7(1)] in the Unfair Terms Regulation that written terms be expressed in plain, intelligible language (article 7(1)).[64]

'relational' in the sense of 'multi-party relations'. See R Merkin and J Steele, *Insurance and Law of Obligations* (Oxford, Oxford University Press, 2013) 19–20.

[59] Styles, above n 34, 174.

[60] C Mitchell, *Interpretation of Contracts* (London, Routledge, 2007) 14.

[61] R Jerry II and D Richmond, *Understanding Insurance Law*, 5th edn (New York, LexisNexis, 2012) 151.

[62] *Zurich Insurance Plc UK Branch v International Energy Group Ltd* [2015] UKSC 33 [164]

[63] B Soyer, 'New Parameters in Construing Insurance Contracts' in R Thomas (ed), *Modern Law of Marine Insurance*, vol 4 (London, Informa, 2016) 64.

[64] Lowry et al, above n 25, 268, referring to Council Directive 93/13/EEC of 5 April 1993 on unfair terms in consumer contracts.

So may the laws of mistake and of misrepresentation, and the operation of the FOS 'fair and reasonable' approach might similarly have the same results as that of the PREC.[65] Upon closer scrutiny, these objections are challengeable, or at least their persuasiveness can be substantially reduced.

Presumption in Favour of Coverage

The presumption in favour of coverage is indeed part of insurance law in Canada and the US. It was held in the Supreme Court of Canada that one of the general principles of interpretation of insurance policies was that 'coverage provisions should be construed broadly and exclusion clauses narrowly'.[66] In the US, 'most jurisdictions today observe that insuring agreements should be interpreted broadly to maximize coverage, that policy exclusions should be interpreted narrowly to limit their effect, that the insurance may not invoke the undisclosed terms to defeat coverage'.[67]

However, the presumption in favour of coverage is not well-accepted as part of English insurance law. The (mis)understanding to the contrary has as authority the decision in *Wayne Tank and Pump Co Ltd v Employer's Liability Assurance Co Ltd*.[68] Nonetheless, this case does not suffice to show that the presumption in favour of coverage is well-established in English insurance law—no such rule or principle can be found in that case. This case involved public liability insurance and concurrent causes of losses. Wayne installed equipment to store and convey liquid wax in a factory. After installation, the factory was destroyed by a fire that followed two acts. The first was the supply of plastic pipe to convey hot wax and of an ineffective thermostat, and the second was the act of the engineers in switching on the equipment and leaving it unattended. The public liability policy's coverage clause stated that the insurers 'will indemnify the Insured against all sums which the Insured shall become legally liable to pay as damages consequent upon … damage to property as a result of accidents as described in the Schedule'. Meanwhile, the policy also had an exception for 'damage caused by the nature or conditions of any goods or the containers thereof sold or supplied by or on behalf of the insured'. The Court of Appeal took the view that 'goods' included the pipe and thermostat, that the proximate cause of the loss was the defective equipment, and therefore that the exclusion clause meant the insurers were not liable. This case did not favour coverage at all.

Neither does the reference to the American case *State Farm Mutual Auto Insurance Co v Partridge*[69] serve that line of analysis. This case also involved concurrent causes, one of which was covered and the other of which was excluded. Nevertheless, it did not involve an interpretation of either the coverage clause or the exclusion clause: what was at issue was not the meaning of the coverage clause or of the

[65] Ibid.

[66] *Reid Crowther & Partners Ltd v Simcoe & Erie General Insurance Co* [1993] I SCR 252, 259.

[67] ER Anderson, JS Stanzler and LS Masters, *Insurance Coverage Litigation, 2012 Supplement* (NewYork, NY, Aspen Publishers, 2012) [2-25]–[2-28].

[68] *Wayne Tank and Pump Co Ltd v Employers' Liability Assurance Co Ltd* [1974] QB 57 (CA).

[69] *State Farm Mutual Auto Insurance Co v Partridge* 10 Cal 3d 102 (1973).

exclusion clause, but the combined conflicting effects thereof in relation to causation; it was a matter of how the court applied the rule of causation in insurance law. In this regard it was held that

> the crucial question presented is whether a liability insurance policy provides coverage for an accident caused jointly by an insured risk (the negligent filing of the trigger mechanism) and by an excluded risk (the negligent driving). Defendants correctly contend that when two such risks constitute concurrent proximate causes of an accident, the insurer is liable so long as one of the causes is covered by the policy.[70]

There was indeed a judicial inclination in favour of coverage, but it was hardly the result of interpreting the *contractual clauses* in question: it was an interpretation of the *legal rule* of causation in insurance law.

Moreover, in the context of English insurance law, 'presumption in favour of coverage' is more a non-legal observation than a legal principle; and even if it *were* recognised in law at all, it certainly would not be enshrined, like other presumptions in law, such as the principle of 'presumption of innocence'. It is at most a weak non-legal presumption that can frequently be rebutted in law. In *Pilkington UK Ltd v CGU Insurance Plc*,[71] the Court of Appeal was referred to two American cases[72] in which the insurance clauses in question were construed in favour of coverage. Potter LJ found them not useful to the instant case, and went on to stress:[73]

> In relation to Pilkington's reliance upon American authority, it seems to me that the comments of Stuart-Smith LJ in *Yorkshire Water Services Ltd v Sun Alliance & London Insurance plc* [1997] 2 Lloyd's Rep 21, 28 should be borne in mind, namely that
>
> > ... the American Courts adopt a much more benign attitude towards the insured; this seems to be based variously on the 'folly' argument in *Leebov* or 'general principles of law and equity' (Slay at page 1368) or that insurance contracts are: 'contracts of adhesion between parties who are not equally situated' giving rise to the principle ... that doubts as to the existence or extent of coverage must generally be resolved in favour of insured ...
>
> ...
>
> As further observed by Stuart-Smith LJ:
>
> > For the most part these notions which reflect a substantial element of public policy are not part of the principles of construction of contracts under English law.

[70] Ibid 109.

[71] *Pilkington UK Ltd v CGU Insurance Plc* [2004] EWCA Civ 23.

[72] *Sturges Manufacturing Company v Utica Mutual Insurance Company* 371 NYS 2d 444 (NY 1975), a decision of the Court of Appeals of New York, and *Maryland Casualty Company v W R Grace & Company* 23 F 3d 617 (CA 2 1993), a decision of the United States Court of Appeals, 2nd circuit. In addition, Potter LJ found that in *Travelers Insurance Company v Eljer Manufacturing Inc* 757 NE 2d 481 (Ill. 2001) the Illinois Supreme Court held that the majority decision in *Eljer v Liberty Mutual* was wrong according to the law of Illinois and that it was not useful for the instant English case either. See *Pilkington UK Ltd v CGU Insurance Plc* [2004] EWCA Civ 23, [42, 40, 44].

[73] *Pilkington UK Ltd v CGU Insurance Plc* [2004] EWCA Civ 23, [46], [47].

Clearly neither Potter LJ nor Stuart-Smith LJ accepted that insurance contract should as a principle be interpreted in favour of coverage. Therefore the 'presumption in favour of coverage' cannot be an effective alternative to PREC in English insurance law: in practice there is no such alternative. Rather, the perceived presumption in favour of coverage is largely the result of *contra proferentem* (see below).

Contra Proferentem

The effect of regulation 7(2) of the Unfair Terms in Consumer Contracts Regulations 1999 (SI 1999/2083) and of the Consumer Rights Act 2015, section 69(1) is application of the *contra proferentem* rule of construction. Often insurers are the offerors of insurance contract terms, hence construction of such terms is more often against insurers and in favour of the insured as regards coverage.

However where the issue is not ambiguity in insurance clauses, *contra proferentem* does not apply. Therefore, it does not always suffice to settle insurance disputes over coverage. This means that although this aspect of English law can produce the same results as PREC, it cannot completely fill any gap that might arise due to the inapplicability of PREC in English insurance law. *Contra proferentem* is only a secondary or subsidiary approach to interpretation of contracts; the primary approach is to ascertain the common intentions of the parties. Over-reliance on the *contra proferentem* rule would move the courts to wishfully and quickly find ambiguities that do not really exist, thus raising the suspicion that this canon of construction of contract is being used to create ambiguity[74] so that its application can be justified. However, as an orthodox rule of construction of ambiguities, *contra proferentem* 'ought only to be applied for the purpose of removing a doubt, not for the purpose of creating a doubt, or magnifying an ambiguity, when the circumstances of the case raise no real difficulty'.[75] For *contra proferentem* to be applied there must be genuine ambiguity in the first place;[76] it should not 'be used to create the ambiguity it is then employed to solve'.[77] Regardless of that, *contra proferentem* does not apply in reinsurance as in primary insurance, nor is it likely to apply where the insurance clause is proposed by a sophisticated policyholder or its brokers. Given all these considerations, *contra proferentem* is no panacea. Moreover,

[74] *Yorkshire Insurance Co Ltd v Campbell* [1917] AC 218 (HL), 223 (per Lord Sumner).

[75] *Cornish v Accident Insurance Co Ltd* (1889) 23 QBD 453, 456 (per Lindley LJ), applied, eg, in *Tektrol v Int Ins Co of Hanover* [2005] EWCA Civ 845 [8] (per Buxton LJ). See also in this sense *McGeown v Direct Travel Insurance* [2003] EWCA Civ 1606 [13] (per Auld LJ, with whom the other members of the Court of Appeal agreed); *Reilly v National Insurance & Guarantee Corporation Ltd* [2008] EWCA Civ 1460 [21] (per Moore-Bick LJ, with whom the other members also agreed.)

[76] *Hayward v Norwich Union* [2001] Lloyd's Rep IR 410 (CA) [17] (per Gibson LJ).

[77] *R v Personal Investment Authority Ombudsman Bureau ex parte Royal & Sun Alliance Life & Pensions Ltd* [2002] Lloyd's Rep IR 41 (QBD Comm), 43 (per Langley J).

> [*contra proferentem*] may also operate against the insured, first, as regards any words of contract for which he is primarily responsible,[78] including statements defining the scope of the risk[79] of the kind found in Lloyd's slip[80] prepared by a Lloyd's broker ...[81]

For the reasons given above, *contra proferentem* cannot be an effective alternative to PREC either.

Mistake

The law of mistake and the law of misrepresentation are useful for resolving disputes over the ambit of the coverage clause and/or the exception clause in an insurance policy *only* where there is a mistake in and/or misrepresentation as to these clauses. Where there is a common mistake by the insurer and the insured, the law of non-disclosure and misrepresentation on the part of the insured will operate to defeat the insured's claim for insurance money. In this scenario, a settlement agreement between the insurer and the insured is void,[82] because underlying it is the fundamental common mistake that the insured has a right to claim insurance money. Where there is a fundamental mutual mistake that makes an essential agreement between the insurer and the insured unascertainable, there is no matching offer and acceptance, hence there is no contract at all. In this regard, Professor Clarke describes the law:

> For example, if a fire contract is 'concluded', the insured intending to insure number 16, Highfield Avenue but the insurer believing that the subject-matter is number 16, Highfield Close, there is no contract, provided that the reasonable observer would be left in genuine doubt about the true subject-matter. If, however, the reasonable observer would have understood Highfield Avenue, there is a contract on 16, Highfield Avenue, ie in the sense (reasonably) understood by the insured. If the reasonable observer would have understood Highfield Close, there is a contract on 16 Highfield Close, as understood by the insurer, albeit a contract which is unenforceable for lack of insurable interest unless, of course, the insured has an interest in both properties. Equally, if the insurer is aiming to sell insurance to the holders of a particular credit card, including holder A, but sends the policy made out to non-holder B who lives at the same address as A, there is a contract of insurance nonetheless but one which can be rectified to name A instead of B, and which is enforceable by A.

[78] *Travellers Casualty v Sun Life of Canada* [2006] EWHC 2716 [29] (per Clarke J).

[79] *Birell v Dryer* (1884) 9 AC 345 (HL), 352 (per Lord Blackburn); *Condogianis v Guardian Assurance Co* [1921] 2 AC 125 (HL), 130–31 (per Lord Shaw).

[80] *American Airlines Inc v Hope* [1973] 1 Lloyd's Rep 233, 250 (per Roskill LJ); *Balfour v Beaumont* [1982] 2 Lloyd's Rep 493, 503 (per Webster J); *Ikerigi CN SA v Palmer* [1991] 1 Lloyd's Rep 400, 416 (per Hobhouse J).

[81] Clarke, *The Law of Insurance Contracts*, above n 1, 455.

[82] In *Magee v Pennine Insurance Co Ltd* [1969] 2 QB 507, Lord Denning MR held, rightly, in line with *Solle v Butcher* [1950] 1 KB 671, that it was common mistake in equity therefore it was voidable, rather than void as at common law. However, the Court of Appeal held in *Great Peace Shipping v Tsavliris* [2003] QB 679 that *Solle v Butcher* was not good law.

The fire insurance scenario is proximate to a scenario where PREC might be applicable. The 'reasonable observer' stands for reasonableness and objectiveness. If the reasonable objective expectation is consistent with that of the insured—or in other words, if the insured has objective reasonable expectations of coverage of his or her intended subject matter (ie 16 Highfield Avenue)—there is an insurance contract on it and the property is covered. If the insured's expectations of coverage of 16 High Avenue as intended is not consistent with the objective reasonable expectation—ie 16 Highfield Close—then there is a contract on 16 Highfield Close, and 16 High Avenue is not covered by the insurance as intended by the insured.

The equitable remedy of rectification can be of use. Where there is a unilateral mistake on the part of the insured about the terms of the insurance contract, and the insurer at the time of conclusion of the contract is aware that the insured is mistaken, there is no contract.[83] However, if there has been agreement on the terms of contract but a mistake, such as misspelling or miscalculation, occurs in the insurance policy or other documents recording the agreement, the document may be rectified and the contract may be enforced as rectified; if the insured has agreed terms with an insurer's agent of apparent authority, but the terms are not those intended by the insurer, there is a contract on the terms agreed with the agent.[84] Nonetheless, the equitable remedy of rectification might be barred in some circumstances,[85] that is: by affirmation of the contract by the party who claims rectification, in a way inconsistent with the subsequent exercise of the right to rectification; by lapse of time; by its being impossible to return the parties to the status quo ante; or by a third party's having acquired rights for value in property which is the subject matter of the contract in question. The multiple bars to rectification will to a large extent make it an insufficient remedy for the insured in the case of his or her unilateral mistake as to terms of the contract.

Insurer's Misrepresentation

The law of misrepresentation for the insurer is the same as it is for the insured (see above). However, compared with the avalanche of lawsuits concerning misrepresentation and/or non-disclosure by the insured, there have been only a few English cases[86] involving misrepresentation by insurers, and not many of them were concerned with disputes over the ambit of coverage; instead they involved the return of premiums[87] and the payment of bonuses[88]—more similar to PREB introduced in Chapter 1 and to be discussed in detail in Chapter 7—under life insurance

[83] *Hartog v Colin & Shields* [1939] 3 All ER 566 (HC).
[84] Clarke, *The Law of Insurance Contracts*, above n 1, 676.
[85] Ibid 412–13.
[86] *Mutual Reserve Life Insurance Co v Foster* (1904) 20 TLR 715 (HL); *Molloy v Mutual Reserve Life Insurance Co* (1906) 22 TLR 525 (CA); *Cross v Mutual Reserve Life Insurance Co* (1904) 21 TLR 15 (HC).
[87] *Pontifex v Bignold* (1841) 3 Man & G 63; 133 ER 1058. *Refuge Assurance Co Ltd v Kettlewell* [1909] AC 243 (HL); *Duffell v Wilson* (1808) 1 Camp 401; 170 ER 999.
[88] *Sun Life Assurance Co of Canada v Jervis* [1943] 2 All ER 425 (CA).

policies. Given the scarcity of misrepresentation precedents concerning disputes over coverage per se, it would be more than difficult for a policyholder whose expectation of coverage is defeated by the terms of the insurance contract to argue effectively for coverage or for insurance money on the ground that the insurer has made misrepresentations about the coverage. That is because a misrepresentation is a positive and untrue statement of fact or of law, whereas generally a promise of any particular coverage is a statement about the future, and therefore not as to a past or present fact; nor can the promise as to coverage be true or untrue at the time it is made. Therefore an insurer's 'misrepresentation' of coverage can hardly be a misrepresentation in the strict sense in law.

Even if the policyholder's claim for misrepresentation could be successful, the remedies available hardly serve insurance purposes. The primary remedy is avoidance of the insurance contract, and the secondary remedy is damages. Avoidance of contract clearly fails the policyholder's purpose of taking out insurance coverage. It is also doubtful whether damages, if readily measurable and awardable at all, can put the policyholder back into the state in which it (or he or she) would have been had the risks at issue been covered. Indeed, there is a broad measure of damages in regard to misrepresentation. In *Royscott Trust Ltd v Rogerson*,[89] the Court of Appeal held that the measure of damages for an innocent misrepresentation giving rise to a cause of action under the Misrepresentation Act 1967, section 2(1) was the tortious measure—as if the misrepresentation were fraudulent—so as to put the representee in the position in which he would have been if he had never entered into the contract, not the contractual measure so as to put the representee in the position in which he would have been if the misrepresentation had been true. Therefore it was also held that the claimant was entitled to damages for all losses flowing from the misrepresentation, provided that they were not too remote.

Nevertheless, even damages to be awarded under such a broad measure, if a claim to that effect could succeed at all, cannot serve to indemnify the policyholder, because it can hardly be argued that the policyholder's losses 'flowed from' the insurer's 'misrepresentation' of coverage. Under the tortious measure of damages confirmed by the Court of Appeal, had the policyholder never entered into the insurance contract, the losses would still have resulted from the occurrence of the risks in dispute.

Discretionary damages in lieu of recession under the Misrepresentation Act 1967, section 2(2) will not satisfy the policyholder's need for indemnity either, because, as is recognised in section 2(3), damages under section 2(2) are possibly or even likely to be less than those under section 2(1). It must also be noted that since an award of damages under section 2(2) is an equitable remedy at the discretion of courts, and it is only secondary, it is less likely that it will be used often. This is particularly so when an insurance contract often lasts only one year, though subject to renewal. When disputes over coverage go to court, more often the contract

[89] *Royscott Trust Ltd v Rogerson* [1991] 3 All ER 294 (CA).

expires or will expire soon. It is not practical for courts to declare the contract still subsisting and to award damages in lieu of rescission.

Insurer's Waiver (or Election) and Estoppel

Waiver (also or better known as 'election',[90] or 'waiver by election')[91] and estoppel (or 'waiver by estoppel',[92] also known as equitable estoppel or promissory estoppel)[93] are two of the several defences that might be available to policyholders as against insurers. There is distinction between them,[94] but the distinction is largely ignored in English law. That is because it owes more to legal history than to functional necessity, and also because, practically, one and the same question in each situation is usually whether the insurer is to be barred from raising a defence to the policyholder's claim.[95] However, it is difficult for policyholders to argue for waiver or estoppel, because 'common to both is the need for communication [by the insurer] to the other party [ie the policyholder] of an unequivocal representation'.[96] For waiver, it would be the representation of the insurer's choice of one of the 'alternative rights inconsistent with one another'.[97] For estoppel, it would be the representation of 'a promise not to rely upon a defence (per Lord Diplock) or a right (per Lord Goff)'[98] available to it. But rarely does an insurer expressly communicate its representations as such. Although the distinction between waiver and estoppel is ignored in practice in English law, what used to be seen as 'waiver of breach of warranty' in insurance is now viewed as promissory estoppel.[99]

Promissory estoppel is perhaps even more difficult for claimants. The doctrine of estoppel is meant to be 'used as a shield not a sword'.[100] The policyholder as a claimant using the doctrine must have had detrimental reliance on the insurer's promissory representations not to rely on a particular defence or right. If the claim is one of a number of similar claims, payment of other such claims does not necessarily estop the insurer from rejecting the claim in question, because the insurer may well be proceeding on a case-by-case basis.[101] The insurer's appraisal or

[90] *Kammins Ballrooms Co Ltd v Zenith Investments (Torquay) Ltd* [1971] AC 850 (HL), 883 (per Lord Diplock).

[91] *Kosmar Villa Holidays Plc v Trustees of Syndicate* 1243 [2008] EWCA Civ 147 [1] (per Rix LJ).

[92] Ibid [1]; also *Argo Systems v Liberty* [2011] EWCA 1572 [39] (per Atkins LJ).

[93] *Motor Oil Hellas v Shipping Corp of India, The Kanchenjunga* [1990] 1 Lloyd's Rep 391(HL), 399 (Lord Goff).

[94] Clarke, *The Law of Insurance Contracts*, above n 1, 886–87.

[95] Ibid 869.

[96] *Kosmar Villa Holidays Plc v Trustees of Syndicate* 1243 [2008] EWCA Civ 147 [1] (per Rix LJ).

[97] *Kammins Ballrooms Co Ltd v Zenith Investments (Torquay) Ltd* [1971] AC 850 (HL), 882 (per Lord Diplock).

[98] *Kosmar Villa Holidays Plc v Trustees of Syndicate* 1243 [2008] EWCA Civ 147 [38] (per Rix LJ).

[99] The nature of what used to be known as 'waiver of breach of warranty' is not waiver but estoppel. See Clarke, 663–64, relying on *Motor Oil Hellas v Shipping Corp of India, The Kanchenjunga* [1990] 1 Lloyd's Rep 391 (HL), 399 (Lord Goff).

[100] *Combe v Combe* [1951] 1 KB 215, 224 (used by the counsel for the defendant, accepted by Birkett LJ).

[101] *Kosmar Villa Holiday* v *The Trustees of Syndicate 1243* [2007] EWHC 458 (Comm). The underwriters' appeal was allowed: [2008] EWCA Civ 147. However, this point was unaffected.

investigation, which may affect the need for formal notice of loss or of particulars of loss, does not estop it from requiring the claimant to provide proof of loss in accordance with the policy terms.[102] The insurer's total silence or inactivity, even when it knows a claim is pending, does not amount to estoppel.[103]

In addition, even if all these other doctrines do always work to protect a policyholder's reasonable expectations, the piecemeal approach is not always better and more efficient than a stand-alone approach, nor does it mean that there cannot or should never be a development toward a stand-alone approach such as PREC. This can be illustrated by the judicial attitude to good faith. For dealing with bad faith practices in contract, English law traditionally favours the piecemeal approach involving the law of mistake, misrepresentation and other vitiating factors, rather than an overarching good faith principle in contract law. But recently there a small step has been made, as in *Yam Seng Pte Ltd (Singapore) v International Trade Corporation Ltd*,[104] toward the principle of good faith in relation to performance of long-term commercial contracts. Since this can be the case with good faith, why not with PREC? An insurance contract is a paradigm of a contract of (utmost) good faith, and it requires the good faith not only of the policyholder in pre-contractual disclosure, but also of the insurer as to contractual performance. From that, it is a corollary that insurers should not unjustifiably reject a policyholder's claim, and instead should honour the policyholder's reasonable expectations of coverage. So should the courts.

C. No Public Policy Considerations?

Another reason for pessimism about the prospect of PREC in English insurance law is that English courts are seldom willing to consider public policy in contract law in the same way that their American counterparts were during the rise of PREC in the US.[105] Nevertheless, only 'in very rare instances'[106] do US courts base their application of PREC on the grounds of public policy. In any event, there can be no inherent difficulty for English courts to consider public policy in insurance disputes like their US counterparts do. That is because, traditionally, English judges are cautious, mainly with what is known as the 'disabling' type of public policy. However, not all public policies are 'disabling'.

[102] Eg, *Maple Leaf Milling Co v Colonial Assurance Co* (1917) 36 DLR 202 (Man CA).

[103] *Accident Insurance Co v Young* (1891) 20 SCR 280, 284, per Taschereau J (PA).

[104] *Yam Seng Pte Ltd (Singapore) v International Trade Corporation Ltd* [2013] EWHC 111 (QB). Admittedly, the Court of Appeal reiterated that there is 'no general doctrine of good faith in English contract law'. See *Compass Group UK and Ireland Ltd v Mid-Essex Hospital Services NHS Trust Ltd* [2012] EWCA Civ 781 [105] (per Jackson LJ).

[105] Lowry et al, above n 25, 269.

[106] M Rahdert, 'Reasonable Expectations Revisited' (1998) 5 *Connecticut Insurance Law Journal* 107, 112–14 (also Part I).

Public Policies: 'Disabling' and 'Enabling'

Public policy, when considered at all in contract law, is mostly 'disabling', as Lord Wright described below:

> I must first attempt to explain what I think to be the modern law in regard to the duty of the Court concerning rules based on public policy. In one sense every rule of law … has been based on considerations of public interest or policy. In that sense Sir George Jessel MR referred to the paramount public policy that people should fulfil their contracts. But public policy in the narrower sense means that there are considerations of public interest which require the Courts to depart from their primary function of enforcing contracts, and exceptionally to refuse to enforce them. Public policy in this sense is disabling. It is important to determine first of all on what principles a judge should exercise this peculiar and exceptional jurisdiction when a question of public policy is raised. What is, I think, now clear is that public policy is not a branch of law to be extended.[107]

A public policy 'in the narrower sense' is disabling in that, by applying it, courts will disable the enforcement of a contract or a term thereof on the ground that it contravenes a particular public policy. It is the judicial application of this type of public policy that was frowned upon by Lord Wright and that has been cautioned against in English courts.

However, not all public policy considerations are disabling. Some are intended, at least by the claimant, to enable the performance of contract as the claimant might reasonably expect. If supported judicially, these public policy considerations are certainly enabling. This is the case with the test for implication of terms in law (as opposed to in fact), 'the essence of the test is a consideration of the nature of contract and of how to maximise the social utility of the relationship'[108] under the type of contract concerned, which underpins policy considerations that courts appear quietly to balance in deciding whether or not to imply a term in law.

Similarly, a public policy orientated toward PREC is often not disabling but *enabling* instead, in that it enables insurance contract performance by way of affirming and providing insurance coverage or protection in relation to the particular risks in question. It does not disable the specific insurance transaction. Therefore, there can perhaps be no strong need for judges to frown upon the PREC principle due to reluctance to be engaged in public policy considerations that are disabling. Indeed it seems so in *Cook v Financial Insurance Co Ltd*,[109] where one can also clearly see the express application of PREC, which is clearly underpinned by the public policy of consumer protection in the context of insurance. If it must be conceded that the public policy of protection of consumer policyholders was not as clear in insurance law before the twenty-first century, that concession can go no further, because the recent insurance contract law reform has clearly drawn

[107] *Fender v Mildmay* [1938] AC 1 (HL), 38.

[108] E Peden, 'Policy Concerns behind Implications of Terms in Law' (2001) 117 *LQR* 459; see also ibid 467–75 on a non-exhaustive list of 12 public policy considerations in judgments.

[109] *Cook v Financial Insurance Co Ltd* [1998] 1 WLR 1765 (HL), [1998] UKHL 42.

the lines between consumer insurance and business insurance, has made substantially different rules for each in respect of pre-contractual duties, and has become more policyholder-friendly in this regard in consumer insurance than in business insurance.

It must also be noted that Lord Wright emphasised that 'Public policy, like any other branch of the common law, is governed by the judicial use of precedents.'[110] Accordingly, there is no outright ban on the invocation of public policy in courts, but only to the effect that public policy considerations deviating from precedents shall not be applied. Once a precedent establishes a public policy in insurance law, or it can be interpreted that a common law case has established or is consistent with a public policy, that public policy can be followed directly or indirectly by other courts.

In the meantime, Lord Wright conceded that

> it is true that it has been observed that certain rules of public policy have to be moulded to suit new conditions of a changing world: but that is true of the principles of common law generally. I find it difficult to conceive that in these days any new head of public policy could be discovered.[111]

Three points can be made about this. In the first place, admittedly to Lord Wright, public policies evolve with societal development, and so do principles of common law. Secondly, common law evolves incrementally on precedents, and so will public policies. Thirdly, this opinion of Lord Wright was delivered in the 1930s; it might indeed be difficult to conceive of the discovery of new heads of public policies, but since the 1950s it has actually not been that difficult. Rather, sometimes it might be necessary, for courts to discover new public policies, because since then the world has undergone vast changes, such as the rise and fall of welfare state in Western Europe, the rise of human rights law, the rapid growth in the use of motor vehicles and hence the concerns over road safety and injuries, European integration, the boom of the consumer society, the pervasiveness of information technology, etc. All these have public policy considerations that ripple outwards to touch contract law and insurance law.

The observation that courts do not consider public policies in insurance cases perhaps does not stand very well, because

> in practice, there are signs that elements of public policy do influence courts' interpretation of the contract. The impact of value judgements offers one explanation of the variety of interpretation courts have put on the exception [clauses in insurance contracts].[112]

Examples of this in English insurance law include at least *Gray v Barr*,[113] where the deterrence of violence and the use of guns was a factor for interpreting the policy wording 'caused by accident' in a manner that denied liability coverage for

[110] *Fender v Mildmay* [1938] AC 1 (HL), 39.
[111] Ibid.
[112] Clarke, *The Law of Insurance Contracts*, above n 1, 608.
[113] *Gray v Barr* [1971] 2 QB 554 (CA).

the gun-user; see also *Lancashire County Council v MMI*,[114] where the Court of Appeal held that insurance of exemplary damages was not per se contrary to public policy in English law; and also *KR v Royal & Sun Alliance*,[115] where the liability insurer was released from indemnifying the insured company, whose the managing director and majority shareholder sexually abused children under its care. A more recent and significant example of public policy consideration in insurance law is the UK Supreme Court case *BAI (Run Off) Ltd v Durham*.[116] There, three courts took into consideration 'the public policy which plainly underlay both the Workmen's Compensation Acts … and the Employers Liability (Compulsory Insurance) Act 1969, namely facilitating … continuity of cover for employers of a given year'.[117] In particular, Lord Clarke briefly but emphatically noted the justifiability of public policy considerations in 'a *Fairchild* type situation',[118] as the instant case was. Given these case, it seems that English courts are not as unwilling as might be believed to consider public policy issues in resolving contract disputes. Actually, considering 'the significance of insurance in social policy',[119] courts in insurance disputes should not hesitate to do so. In addition, the requirement for an insurable interest is one of the fundamental principles in insurance law, and it serves the public policy against wagering and moral hazards. This is where judges have to consider public policy in resolving insurance disputes.

With the Canadian case *Coronation Insurance Co v Taku Air Transport Ltd*[120] as an example, it is thought that 'where there is a public policy or regulatory requirement for the insurance in question, the expectations of the insurer and assured may be different to those which usually entertained in the case of most commercial or consumer insurances'.[121] The Canadian recognition of the relevance of public policy to insurance contract can shed more light on English courts than do American courts, because generally the Canadian judicial tradition is much closer to English law than is the American judicial tradition: after all, the right to appeal from Canada to the Judicial Committee of the Privy Council in the UK was abolished in criminal cases only in 1933, and in civil and other cases as late as 1949. English judges frequently look across the Atlantic more at the judicial reasoning of their Canadian counterparts than that of their US counterparts. For example,

[114] *Lancashire County Council v MMI* [1996] EWCA Civ 1345.

[115] *KR v Royal & Sun Alliance* [2006] EWCA Civ 1454.

[116] *BAI (Run-Off) Ltd v Durham* [2012] UKSC 14.

[117] *BAI (Run-Off) Ltd v Durham* [2008] EWHC 2692 (QBD) [240]. See also *BAI (Run-Off) Ltd v Durham* [2010] EWCA Civ 1096 [186], [324]; *BAI (Run-Off) Ltd v Durham* [2012] UKSC 14 [47] (Lord Clarke).

[118] This is a situation 'when (a) there are two separate potential causes exposing the claimant to the same risk, one involving an act or omission by the defendant, (b) either one of which causes would have been sufficient to give rise to the injury, and (c) one of which did so, but (d) neither of which can as a matter of probability be shown to have done so'. *BAI (Run-Off) Ltd v Durham* [2012] UKSC 14 [56] (per Lord Mance); see also *Fairchild v Glenhaven Funeral Services Ltd* [2002] UKHL 22.

[119] Lowry et al, above n 25, 269.

[120] *Coronation Insurance Co v Taku Air Transport Ltd* [1991] 3 SCR 622.

[121] PM Eggers, P Foss and S Picken, *Good Faith and Insurance Contracts* (London, LLP, 2010) [3.39].

in *Petrofina (UK) Ltd v Magnaload Ltd*,[122] Lloyd J found that *Commonwealth Construction Co Ltd v Imperial Oil Ltd*,[123] heard in the Supreme Court of Canada, was 'indistinguishable from the present case' and 'highly persuasive authority'[124] for his decision. *Constitution Insurance Co of Canada v Kosmopoulos*,[125] another case in the Supreme Court of Canada, was also considered by the Court of Appeal in *Feasey v Sun Life Assurance Co of Canada.*[126]

Insurance and the Decline of the Welfare State

Public policy in the context of insurance must also take into account the rise and the fall of the welfare state. There has been a close connection between insurance and the welfare state. This exists in two ways. First, in the UK, the insurance principle was fundamental in the post-1945 construction of the modern welfare state under the Beveridge plan. The Beveridge Report dealt with private insurance for workers' compensation and sickness insurance, and with industrial life insurance. Secondly, the breadth of state welfarism influences the legal approaches to insurance. This can be seen from the difference between the US and the UK. In the US, courts and state regulators are more willing to take an interventionist approach to insurance contract, whereas courts and regulators in the UK see insurance contract as a private transaction, subject to only minimal and necessary regulatory and judicial intervention. The difference is due in large part to the different welfare philosophy in the two countries.[127] In the US, welfare is seen primarily as a matter for the individual to arrange, usually through private insurance, therefore the interventionist approach is taken to ensure that the insurance industry delivers proper provision of insurance. In the UK, in contrast, there has been, at least until more recent times, much emphasis on delivery of welfare through the State, and insurance has been seen as a matter of private choice. Hence English law traditionally and continually leaves the parties free to choose the content of their insurance contracts and is less sensitive to the potential for insurers to exploit their strength.[128]

In line with the second connection of insurance to the welfare state, as long as the welfare state remained robust in the UK, English insurance law could continue to be non-interventionist. The reality, however, is that the British state welfare has been in decline since the Thatcher era,[129] and that decline 'continued even during the tenure

[122] *Petrofina (UK) Ltd v Magnaload Ltd* [1984] QB 127.

[123] *Commonwealth Construction Co Ltd v Imperial Oil Ltd* [1978] 1 SCR 317.

[124] *Petrofina (UK) Ltd v Magnaload Ltd* [1984] QB 127, 138E (per Lloyd J).

[125] *Constitution Insurance Co of Canada v Kosmopoulos* (1987) 34 DLR (4th) 208.

[126] *Feasey v Sun Life Assurance Co of Canada* [2003] EWCA Civ 885.

[127] R Hassen, 'The Special Nature of the Insurance Contract: A Comparison of American and English Law of Insurance' (1984) 47 *MLR* 505.

[128] Lowry et al, above n 24, 10–11.

[129] J Millar, 'Diminishing Welfare: The Case of the United Kingdom' in GS Goldberg and MG Rosenthal (eds), *Diminishing Welfare: A Cross-Nation Study of Social Provision* (Westport, CT, Auburn House, 2002); J Hills, *Thatcherism, New Labour and the Welfare State* (London, Centre for Analysis of Social Exclusion, LSE, 1998).

of Labour Party governments under Tony Blair and Gordon Brown … [t]hough historically, the Labour Party has been a votary of the welfare state'.[130] Even general public support for the welfare state has been in decline: 'On a range of measures, support for the welfare system has fallen dramatically over the last two decades.'[131] Given this social-economic background, insurance has a bigger role to play, and there will be greater need for alternative private insurance where social welfare or social insurance is inadequate. In relation to healthcare and the National Health Service, which has been fraught with issues, from 1990 to 2003, around 11.5 per cent of the UK population were private medical insurance policyholders each year.[132] In 2010, on average around 15 per cent of the population in different areas of the UK (not including Northern Ireland due to the unavailability of data) took out private medical insurance coverage.[133] As an active response to the market, in September 2011 the Association of British Insurers (ABI) published the ABI Statement of Best Practice for Sales of Individual and Group Private Medical Insurance. More recently in the UK, economic and demographic factors have been creating irresistible pressure for further reform of the UK welfare system. Seeing the failure of the state welfare to provide protection for the 40 per cent of middle-income working-age households that suffer from an unexpected and drastic fall in income due to inability to work as a result of serious illness or injury of the income-earner, in 2014 the ABI put forward a business proposal for income protection insurance.[134] These are typical but not unusual examples of how there is a stronger need for private insurance in the UK as the welfare state continues to wobble toward further decline. This makes it incrementally more necessary for regulators and the judiciary to take an incrementally interventionist approach in insurance business.

Conceptions of Insurance

Although American insurance law has only limited influence on its English counterpart, it is still enlightening to look at how insurance is perceived in the US in this field. Just a couple of years ago Kenneth Abraham observed[135] that there might be four conceptions of insurance, which may shed light on the two fundamental questions that modern insurance law has continually faced. One question is

[130] P Singh and LN Bhusal, 'Austerity, Welfare State and Eco-Socialism: With Special Reference to the United Kingdom' (2014) 39 *Economic and Political Weekly* 111, 115.

[131] 'Attitudes of Different Generations to The Welfare System' (Joseph Rowntree Foundation, 2013) 1, as the summary of the Foundation-funded research by D O'Leary, B Duffy, S Hall, S Pope, *Generation Strains: A Demos and Ipsos MORI Report on Changing Attitudes to Welfare* (York, Joseph Rowntree Foundation, 2013).

[132] T Foubister et al, *Private Medical Insurance in the United Kingdom* (Copenhagen, WHO, on behalf of the European Observatory on Health Systems and Policies, 2006) 55.

[133] Office of Fair Trading, Private Healthcare Market Study: Report on the market study and final decision to make a market investigation reference (London, OFT, 2012) 32.

[134] Association of British Insurers, Welfare Reform for the 21st Century: The Role of Income Protection Insurance (London, ABI, 2014) 4.

[135] Abraham, above n 8.

the extent to which the language or terms of an insurance contract should determine its legal effect. The other is the influence of public law, or public policy more broadly, on the scope of private insurance coverage.

The four concepts of insurance are:[136]

1. *The contract conception.* This understands insurance as a voluntary agreement between an individual policyholder and an insurer, subject to the constraints and rules of construction that are ordinarily placed on such agreements by law of contract. This conception supplies the 'literal' view of insurance with which the other conceptions, understood as metaphors or analogies, contrast themselves.
2. *The public utility-regulated industry conception.* Under this conception, contracts are a mere tool for bringing the regulated relationship into existence. On this view, insurance is a cartelised industry selling a good sufficiently essential that it requires government regulation in the public interest.
3. *The product conception.* This sees insurance as resembling a tangible good more than a promise to perform financial services, and therefore as appropriately subject to rules analogous to those that govern defectively designed products. Tort rather than contract is therefore the core paradigm here.
4. *The governance conception.* This views insurance as a surrogate for government in controlling behaviour and protecting against misfortune, as well as an organisational arrangement among policyholders. These governance relationships create the risk of abuse by the insurer for its own ends, and for the ends of the majority of policyholders at the expense of the minority. Insurance law rules analogous to those that protect the populace against government, and that protect the minority of the populace against overreaching by the majority, are therefore desirable.

The lesson is that 'employing different conceptions of insurance may help us see the entirety of insurance and insurance law more clearly, and may highlight certain normative possibilities that other conceptions hide or underemphasize'.[137] Having different conceptions of insurance may also shed additional light on the two fundamental questions referred to above in insurance law. With the contract conception of insurance, it is challenging to grapple with the highlighted importance of insurance policy language at variance with the policyholder's rights and expectations. The public utility/regulated industry conception, applicable largely to health insurance and liability insurance, and the governance conception merit and necessitate consideration of public policies. The buyer's reasonable expectations provide the foundation for an implied warranty of quality.[138] With the product conception, by analogy, policyholders are entitled to reasonable expectations

[136] Ibid 657.
[137] Ibid 697.
[138] MA Geistfeld, *Principles of Products Liability* (New York, Foundation Press, 2006) 11.

of insurance coverage as part of the quality of the insurance product, just as consumers generally are entitled to reasonable expectations of the quality, particularly of the safety, of products[139] and services.[140]

III. Business Insurance and Policyholder's Reasonable Expectations of Coverage

Mustill LJ was quoted as saying that, except, at most, for consumer insurance, in English insurance law there would be no rule like the American doctrine of 'policyholder's reasonable expectations',[141] particularly not in an insurance policy as 'a one-off contract placed at arm's length'.[142] However, it can be argued that business insurance is more often relational than one-off. For a relational contract, the reasonable expectations of the parties need to be taken seriously. This section first evaluates Catherine Mitchell's argument that commercial contracts are relational, so that reasonable expectations should have a more important role in commercial contract law. Secondly, it discusses the argument by Robert Merkin and Jenny Steele that insurance is relational. Thirdly, it points out a general approach to reasonable expectations without recourse to the American insurance law principle of 'policyholder's reasonable expectations'. Lastly, it considers the expectations of insurers vis-à-vis PREC, and argues that, in principle, PREC should prevail.

A. Reasonable Expectations in Relational Commercial Contracts[143]

Contract parties' commercial expectations, which are usually derived from previous experience, shared norms or social institutions, including commonly accepted practices,[144] are important because they present a more accurate picture of the parties' agreement and accord with what Catherine Mitchell calls, in HLA Hart's term, 'the internal views' of participants in commercial practice; in addition, they are consistent with the perceived values of commercial law, which, according to Roy Goode, are party autonomy, predictability, flexibility, good faith, encouragement of self-help, facilitation of security interest, protection of vested interests

[139] Consumer Protection Act 1987, s 3.

[140] See also D Schwarcz, 'A Product Liability Theory for the Judicial Regulation of Insurance Policies' (2007) 48 *William & Mary Law Review* 1389.

[141] *Smit Tak Offshore Services v Youell* [1992] 1 Lloyd's Rep 154 (CA), 159.

[142] Ibid.

[143] This section draws primarily on C Mitchell, *Contract Law and Contract Practice* (Oxford, Hart Publishing, 2013).

[144] C Mitchell, 'Leading a Life of its Own? The Roles of Reasonable Expectations in Contract Law' (2003) 23 *OJLS* 639.

and the protection of innocent third parties.[145] Mitchell points out[146] that there is a noteworthy anomaly between parties' legal rights under the English law applicable to commercial contracts and commercial expectations. Dissatisfied with the inadequacy of promissory theories and economic analysis of contract law for consideration of commercial expectations, Mitchell turns to the late Professor Ian Macneil's theory of relational contract. Drawing primarily on that theory, Mitchell argues that commercial contract law should become more 'relational'. That means, as Beale comments and recounts, that

> the law should take greater account of the context in which the parties made their agreement, the understandings that they derived from that context, and the difficulties that they may have faced in translating those understandings into contract terms.[147]

Mitchell relates her argument closely to the late Ian Macneil's 'relational theory',[148] initially of contract and later of contract law as well. The upshot[149] of Macneil's theory is that the common contract behavioural patterns and norms constitute a highly effective vehicle for satisfying the core propositions:

> First, every transaction is embedded in complex relations.
>
> Second, understanding of any transaction requires understanding of all essential elements of its enveloping relations.
>
> Third, effective analysis of any transaction requires recognition and consideration of all essential elements of its enveloping relations that might affect the transaction significantly.
>
> Fourth, combined contextual analysis of relations and transactions is more efficient and produces a more complete and sure final analytical product than does commencing with non-contextual analysis of transactions.[150]

There is adequate sufficiency and validity in using Macneil's relational theory. Few could dispute or seriously disagree with the first two propositions.[151] The third might meet some challenges, but

> [r]ecognition and consideration of all the significant relational elements of a transaction does not mean reinventing the wheel every time any given transaction or type of transaction is analysed. Common sense and normal practices of building knowledge on

145 R Goode, *Commercial Law in the Next Millennium* (London, Sweet & Maxwell, 1998) 32–33.

146 Mitchell, above n 143, 101.

147 H Beale, 'Bridging the Gap: A Relational Approach to Contract Theory' (2014) 41 *Journal of Law and Society* 641, 641.

148 Although decades later, in 2000, Macneil renamed his theory of relational contract 'essential contract theory', to distinguish his theory from others' relational contract theories or others' reinterpretation of his own theory, it has nonetheless been known as 'relational contract theory' and, by his definition, it affirms others' theories.

149 I Macneil, 'Relational Contract Theory: Challenges and Queries' (2000) 94 *Northwestern University Law Review* 877, 893.

150 Ibid 881. The fourth proposition is particularly relevant to and helpful for Robert Merkin and Jenny Steele's relational theory of insurance contract, to be discussed in section III.B. below.

151 Ibid 884.

the basis of past experience are as much in order in analysing contracts as in any other human endeavour.[152]

The fourth proposition seems consistent with the contemporary contextual approach to interpretation of contracts under English contract law. Almost four decades after Ian Macneil put forward the relational contract theory, there are fewer controversies over the relational theory of contract. As Scott has accepted, 'We are all relationalists now. In that sense Macneil and Macaulay have swept the field. Contract, we now know, is complex and subjective and synthetic in every sense of those terms.'[153]

Nevertheless, the validity of the theory of relational contract does not necessarily validate a relational contract *law*. Is there, or should there be, a 'relational contract *law*' that Mitchell argues for? It is necessary to answer this question, because Mitchell's argument would be substantially weakened if the answer were to be 'no' either descriptively or prescriptively, or normatively. Macneil has met such a challenge, notably from Scott, Eisenberg and Posner. For them, contract law is not relational, nor should it be. For Scott, the debate over Macneil's theory 'is not over the nature of contract as an institution. We are all relationalists now. ... The debate, rather, is over the proper nature of *contract law*.'[154] (emphasis added) Scott thinks that interpretation of relational contracts is justifiably formalist rather than relational, because the formalist approach offers the best prospect for maximising the value of contractual relationships;[155] and that although contracts are relational, complex and subjective 'contract law, whether we like it or not, is none of those things. Contract law is formal, simple, and (returning to Macneil's terminology) *classical*.'[156] (emphasis added) For Macneil, this does not necessarily prevent heavily relational approaches to the law of relations involving exchange and reciprocity; all it necessarily does is to divide the law of such relations into the part encompassed by narrowly defined contract law and all the rest of the law applicable to relations.[157]

Another challenge is posed by Eisenberg, who thinks that there is no relational contract law. For Eisenberg, fundamentally, the idea that there should be a body of special rules collectively known as 'relational contract law' for relational contracts is based on the incorrect premise that relational contracts are only a special category of contracts as a class. But once a relational contract is properly defined as 'a contract that involves not merely an exchange but also a relationship between the contracting parties',[158] a definition sometimes favoured by Macneil, it can be seen

[152] Ibid 884.
[153] R Scott, 'The Case for Formalism in Relational Contract' (2000) 94 *Northwestern University Law Review* 847, 852.
[154] Ibid 852.
[155] Ibid 875.
[156] Ibid 852.
[157] Macneil, above n 149, 902.
[158] M Eisenberg, 'Why There Is No Law of Relational Contracts' (2000) 94 *Northwestern University Law Review* 805, 816.

that *all* contracts, whether relational or discrete, either create or reflect relationships, so that relational contracts are not a special subcategory, and therefore there should not be and cannot be a relational contract law for them.[159]

Macneil has addressed this definitional problem. He concedes that the use of the root 'relation' to describe two separate things, ie relational contract and discrete contract, does cause confusion, because even the most discrete exchange occurs in relations. But this might not be a serious problem, because the idea of discrete transactions has had a great influence on intellectual endeavours, and 'what we think of as discrete transactions … are the deliberate or habitual treatment within complex relations of certain events *as if* they were discrete transactions'.[160] Hence Macneil's clarified relational/as-if-discrete spectrum of contractual behaviour patterns. More specifically:

> As-if-discrete transactions give rise to an intensification in exchange relations of *two* common contract behaviours—implementation of planning and effectuation of consent—and hence to an intensification of the norms arising out of these behaviours. When so intensified, these transactions may usefully be labelled as following the as-if-discrete norm, and thus as enhancing discreteness and presentation.
>
> Relational contracts, by contrast, give rise to an intensification in exchange relations of *several other* common contract behaviours, and hence to their norms. Primary among these are (1) role integrity, (2) contractual solidarity, and (3) harmonization with the social matrix, especially the internal social matrix.
>
> In addition, relational contexts affect the nature of other common contract norms. For example, flexibility in relations is at least partially an internal, rather than an entirely external norm as it is (in theory) in as-if-discrete transactions. Hence, flexibility comes into partial conflict with the planning and consent norms in ways not occurring in as-if-discrete transactions. Reciprocity also becomes an important internal matter, lest the relation break down. Power is also an important internal matter in relations.[161] (emphasis added)

The implication of Macneil's clarification is that since there is genuine distinction, as described and quoted above, between relational contract and as-if-discrete contract, there is no logical problem with part of contract law being more relational.

A third doubt over relational contract law comes from Eric Posner, who argues that courts are '*radically incompetent*'[162] in meeting the demands placed on them by relational contracts, though they can deter opportunistic behaviour. If the courts are indeed so incompetent, that would certainly render Macneil's argument for relational contract law untenable. In response, Macneil finds that Posner's analysis is limited to repeat trading transactions, which are far from being the

[159] Ibid 817.
[160] Macneil, above n 149, 895.
[161] Ibid 896–97.
[162] E Posner, 'A Theory of Contract Law under Conditions of Radical Judicial Error' (2000) 94 *Northwestern University Law Review* 749, 754.

paradigms of relational contracts; that Posner's proposal for a system of massive and highly speculative litigation penalties for breakdown of relations irrespective of fault is limited to cases where the parties purportedly intend such penalties to be imposed in the event of breakdown; that Posner's argument is limited to the legal consequences of complete breakdown of living contract relations, which transforms contracts in discrete ways; that complete breakdowns are far from the only, or even the most important, arena for disputes in contract law; that Posner's paper is limited to a narrow part of the legal system: courts of general jurisdiction with their non-specialist judges and juries; and, lastly, that Posner's observation of judicial incompetence applies only to that small part of contract law relating to dispute resolution, and such limitation results in omission of the socio-economic matrix in which contracts always occur.[163] Given these limitations, Posner effectively fails to weaken Macneil's proposition for relational contract law.

But the term 'relational contract law' is not to be understood literally, at least not by Macneil. It is not, as Einsenberg viewed it, a systematic body of rules of law applicable to relational contracts. For Macneil, relational contract law is instead what he called the 'relational approach' to relational contracts. He identifies three steps in this approach:

> (1) acquiring an overall grasp of the essential relations of which the transactions are an integral part; (2) working through the interaction of the pertinent transactions with the remainder of the relations until the limitations of transactional analysis are firmly established, and (3) engaging in whatever detailed discrete analysis is desired, subject to whatever constraints the first steps suggest.[164]

Macneil has no ambition of developing a system of relational contract law that would overwhelm the discretist orthodox law of contract. As he recognises, detailed 'discrete analysis' in terms of evaluating and applying or disapplying orthodox contract law is still part of the approach to contract law. What is essential to the relational approach, however, is that the orthodox discrete analysis must be subject to the relational characteristics of the contract in question and the transactions concerned. As mentioned above, for Macneil, the doubts of Scott and of Einsenberg do not necessarily hamper heavily relational approaches to the law of contracts involving exchange and reciprocity.[165] Mitchell also rightly does not push Macneil's relational theory to a far and wide sphere for the purpose of her argument. She recognises that

> Macneil's relevance lies not in yielding concrete proposals for the reform of contract law, but in bringing to the fore, and making us confront directly, the elements of contractual behaviour that may remain resolutely obscured through the application of legal doctrine.[166]

[163] Macneil, above n 149, 904–06.
[164] Ibid 888.
[165] Ibid 902.
[166] Mitchell, above n 143, 199.

Not surprisingly, due to its cooperative and even paternalistic philosophy, the theory of relational contract seems irreconcilable with the individualistic philosophy and doctrines of classic English contract law. 'But this certainly was not Macneil's intention, and the relational theory can readily be restated in such a way as to give competition a central place in it.'[167] According to David Campbell,[168] the classic contract law conceives of real contractual exchanges only as having an individualistic basis. Such a basis is thought to be essential for the free market, and is to be analysed by neo-economics and classic contract law. Classic contract law itself turns on *caveat emptor*, meanwhile conceiving of other paternalism-based exchanges as endogenous material which it has to incorporate. This incorporation has led to enormous difficulties and policy limitations that overwhelm a falsified classic contract law. However, once this falsification is recognised, the relational theory can be of superior explanatory power.[169] This reconciliation, coupled with *Yam Seng*[170] and cases following it, is likely to pave the way for more judicial recognition and application of the conception of relational contract that embraces good faith as a doctrine, if not as a general principle.

'Pragmatism, context and flexibility are the hallmarks of a relational approach to contractual agreements.'[171] But only the contextualist hallmark can be pinned down to a principle in positive law, namely, that contract is to be interpreted contextually. As has been argued in Chapter 3, a contextual interpretation of contract takes into consideration commercial purposes and expectations. This is consistent with Lord Hoffmann's opinion that the context against which a contract is interpreted includes 'absolutely anything ["relevant"[172]] which would have affected the way in which the language of the document would have been understood by a reasonable man'.[173] However, if contextual interpretation is to provide a means to give effect to the purpose of a contract and reasonable expectations, 'it must be grasped that the subject matter for interpretation is the entire commercial relationship, of which the text may be an important but not exclusive and conclusive part'.[174] With keen observation, Mitchell sees *Transfield Shipping Inc v Mercator Shipping Inc ('The Achilleas')*[175] as a precedent where, for Lord Hoffmann, assessment of

[167] D Campbell, 'Good Faith and the Ubiquity of the "Relational" Contract' (2014) 77 *MLR* 460, 483. See also D Campbell, 'The Relational Constitution of Remedy: Co-operation as the Implicit Second Principle of Remedies for Breach of Contract' (2005) 11 *Texas Wesleyan Law Review* 455.

[168] D Campbell, 'The Relational Constitution of the Discrete Contract' in D Campbell and P Vincent-Jones (eds), *Contract and Economic Organisation* (Aldershot, Dartmouth Publishing, 1996) 61.

[169] See Campbell, 'The Relational Constitution of Remedy: Co-operation as the Implicit Second Principle of Remedies for Breach of Contract', above n 168; and also D Campbell, 'A Relational Critique of the Restatement (Third) of Restitution § 39' (2011) 68 *Washington and Lee Law Review* 1063.

[170] *Yam Seng Pte Ltd v International Trade Corporation Ltd* [2013] EWHC 111.

[171] Mitchell, above n 143, 266.

[172] *Bank of Credit and Commerce International v Ali* [2001] UKHL 8 [39] (per Lord Hoffmann).

[173] *Investors Compensation Scheme Ltd v West Bromwich Building Society* [1997] CLC 1243 (HL), 1257–58.

[174] Mitchell, above n 143, 248.

[175] *Transfield Shipping Inc v Mercator Shipping Inc ('The Achilleas')* [2008] UKHL 48.

liability was not to determined by *Hadley v Baxendale*[176] but was dependent on the tacit industry understanding, which was part of the context of the agreement, that the charterer's liability was limited to the difference between the market rate and the charter rate for the period of delay. It is further observed that *The Achilleas* is 'a far-reaching but inevitable consequence of [Lord Hoffmann's] contextual interpretative approach to contractual relationships'.[177] Other case examples observed by Mitchell as being similar to *The Achilleas* in respect of their contextual interpretation are *RTS Flexible Systems Limited v Molkerei Alois Müller GmbH,*[178] *Total Gas Marketing v Arco British*[179] and *Valley Airport Ltd v BMIBaby Ltd.*[180]

There will be costs involved in developing a relational approach to contract law, but the institutional costs of not doing so are likely to be greater, particularly in terms of our confidence in contract law's capacity to facilitate commercial dealing and commercial expectations in all their forms.[181] A contextual and relational approach to contractual disputes could in addition be articulated in the language of reasonable expectations and good faith.[182] As has been argued in Chapter 4, protection of reasonable expectations is an end for which good faith is the means.

B. Business Insurance as Relational

Mitchell's application of relational contract theory to commercial contracts is relevant to business insurance too, because, as Feinman initially saw, insurance contract, along with landlord-tenant relationships and product liability, evidences the power of the relational contract theory and an independent relational context.[183] More recently, Feinman has argued in more detail that an insurance relationship is relational. As Feinman sees it, the relationship between an insurance company and its consumer policyholder is perhaps the best example of a relational contract of dependence and inequality, and business insurance bears some of the same characteristics as consumer insurance.[184] Such an exemplary relational contract relationship is due to the fact that an insurance relationship is often *de facto* long-term as the result of frequent renewal of the policies, that cooperation is required from both parties once the insurer's aleatory obligation of payment materialises as

[176] *Hadley v Baxendale* (1854) 9 Ex 341, [1854] EWHC J70.

[177] Mitchell, above n 143, 249.

[178] *RTS Flexible Systems Limited v Molkerei Alois Müller GmbH* [2010] UKSC 14.

[179] *Total Gas Marketing v Arco British* [1998] 2 Lloyd's Law Rep 209 (HL).

[180] *Valley Airport Ltd v BMIBaby Ltd* [2010] EWCA Civ 485.

[181] Mitchell, above n 143, 266.

[182] H Collins, *Regulating Contracts* (Oxford, Oxford University Press, 1999) 146–48.

[183] J Feinman, 'Relational Contract Theory in Context' (2000) 94 *Northwestern University Law Review* 737, 744–46.

[184] J Feinman, 'The Insurance Relationship as Relational Contract and the "Fairly Debatable" Rule for First-Party Bad Faith' (2009) 46 *San Diego Law Review* 553, 556 and fn14.

a response to the consequences of the risks it underwrites, and that an insurance relation

> is situated in a context of social relationships; the single insurance contract is an instance of a system of insurance on which policyholders, dependents, tort victims, and society at large depend to provide security in the event of harm.[185]

Further:

> From the company's perspective, the policy plans in detail the terms of the relationship, specifying the risks covered and excluded and the duties of the company and the insured in the event of loss. The policy, in the jargon of relational contract theory, 'presentiates' the relationship at the moment of formation by projecting all elements of performance and risk from the future into the present and at that moment defining the performance and risk terms that govern the relationship. From the insured's perspective, the policy is at best a modest exercise in planning, specifying a few important items such as policy limits. This conflict of perceptions suggests that the company views the policy as having more discrete elements because the norms of implementation of planning and effectuation of consent are intensified. The insured is likely to have a different perspective. The details of the insurance policy become important to the insured only at the point of loss.[186]

More noteworthy:

> The typical insured understands the insurance relationship to be one in which the company promises security and protection, rather than a detailed and obscure set of specifications and exclusions of coverage. This understanding is fostered by the presentation of the relationship by insurance companies themselves through extensive advertising. Many of the iconic slogans of American marketing portray insurance as a place of security and refuge from the dangers of the world: 'Like a good neighbour, State Farm is there' and 'You're in good hands with Allstate.' More recently, Liberty Mutual's slogan: 'Responsibility. What's your policy?'[187]

Feinman is not alone in seeing insurance as relational. More recently, in 2013 Merkin and Steele put forward what they call 'the relational model or vision of insurance' as parallel to the actuarial model of insurance. They use the term 'relational' and the theory of relational contract to emphasise the affinity between insurance and private law:

> The key feature of a 'relational' model of insurance is that it focuses on relationships between parties, considering insurance in terms of the party relations of which it is an inherent part. The relationship in issue in a given case may be between insurer and assured, and further relationships may also enter the frame. These include relationships with other insurers or potential indemnifiers; with reinsurers; or with other contracting parties or potential tort claimants. Private law as a whole is concerned with the relationships between parties, and the relational model has direct affinities with the structure of private law.[188]

[185] Ibid 557.

[186] Ibid 558.

[187] Ibid 559.

[188] R Merkin and J Steele, *Insurance and the Law of Obligations* (Oxford, Oxford University Press, 2013) 20.

Their use of the term 'relational' is intended to focus not only on issues of risk transfer, but also on multi-party relations,[189] which particularly underlie liability insurance, reinsurance, domestic or international sales under which it is agreed that one of the parties will take out insurance of the goods for the other party, and many other insurances (such as construction insurance) taken out in a complicated commercial context. That considered:

> [P]urchase of insurance, and bargaining around both duties to insure and the location of risk more generally, underpin and help to facilitate commercial relationships of every sort. 'Insurance' in a relational view is to be understood as primarily an arrangement through which the incidence of risk is identified and, where appropriate, allocated. Seen in this light, insurance is a key factor in party relations as they are addressed by private law, particularly through the law of contract and related sources of obligation and remedy, as well as the macro-level state regulation which is an emanation of the actuarial model.[190]

The actuarial model or perception of insurance 'by its nature views insurance at a macro level'.[191] On the one hand, the actuarial model of insurance certainly explains the actuarial-technical nature of insurance operation. On the other hand, actuarial pricing is only one of the varieties of techniques used by insurers to bear the risks they underwrite. 'Diversification; investment; time; and the capacity to use reinsurance capacity and financial markets to meet losses ex post are all additional techniques available to insurers, beyond the form of pooling or spreading inherent in actuarial pricing.'[192] Apart from that, actuarial technique itself invariably involves risk classification, which, however, is parallel to hierarchical status grouping[193] that disadvantages both individuals and groups. In fact, what is essential to the actuarial model is that

> [i]nsurance companies do not view any insured as a whole person. Rather, every insured is compartmentalized. He is the sum of the many roles he plays as a result of being a member of many status groups. … Although the multiplicity of roles may cause the individual to suffer normative conflict and uncertainty, role or status inconsistency does not impede insurers.[194]

As a result, the representations produced by actuarial practices 'place us in a cultural space even more alienating and disempowering than the disciplinary bureaucratic practices we have occupied for most of the last century'.[195] In addition, under the actuarial model of insurance, insurers do not look beyond the particular group a policyholder belongs to: they disregard the multi-party relationships underlying the insurance and beyond the particular risk pool.

[189] Ibid 20–21.
[190] Ibid 21.
[191] Ibid 19.
[192] Ibid 30.
[193] R Austin, 'The Insurance Classification Controversy' (1983) 131 *University of Pennsylvania Law Review* 517, 535.
[194] Ibid 547.
[195] J Simon, 'The Ideological Effects of Actuarial Practices' (1988) 22 *Law and Society Review* 771, 787.

Merkin and Steele's relational perception of insurance is closer to Macneil's relational contract theory than they think. Although the increasingly rich relational literature is an incentive for them to use the term 'relational', they cautiously keep a controlled distance from Ian Macneil's relational theory, which they think has more specific connotations than their use of the term. They stress that they do not imply that insurance relationships are not necessarily long-term and cooperative or characteristic of some features that are typically associated with a debated 'category' of relational contracts. That is true indeed as far as insurance is concerned. Nevertheless, although the phrase 'long-term contracts' has been taken as virtually a synonym for relational contracts, 'temporal extension *per se* is not the defining characteristic'[196] of relational contracts. A relational contract need not be a long-term contract, although it usually would be.[197] An insurance is cooperative to a large extent between the insurer and the policyholder as regards pre-contractual disclosure and in claims-handling, and is certainly so in an insurance-related relationship, which involves not only the insurer and the policyholder but also other underlying parties such as the third-party victim in liability insurance, the mortgagee in a mortgage insurance and other third-party beneficiaries—in a general sense—for example a creditor for whose benefit the debtor takes out insurance on the debtor per se.

According to Merkin and Steele, the relational model or vision of insurance is more expressive than the actuarial model of the essence or true nature of insurance. The actuarial model may be identified with the calculated spreading of risk by distributing losses within a risk pool, whereas the relational model is identified with risk transfer generally within a contractual framework. The risk-spreading perspective, consistent with the actuarial model, looks from the point of view of the achievement of insurance across a group, the techniques applied and what both mean for society. In contrast, the risk-transfer perspective consistent with the relational model of insurance focuses on and prioritises the object or purpose of individual relationships by and for which insurance is provided. From the point of view of risk transfer:

> [T]he defining feature of insurance lies in reduction of uncertainty for the assured—and, we would add, for those doing business, or otherwise entering relationships with the assured—by transferring a defined risk to another party, in return for a premium. The nature of insurance is thus to accomplish the transfer of 'risks'. 'Risk', in insurance terms, has a positive connotation, because it is what insurers seek: it is a positive feature of an insurance market that it is joined by 'new risks', for example. This second definition emphasizes the economic character of insurance and its role in market activity and in the economic planning of individuals and households.[198]

[196] C Goetz and R Scott, 'Principles of Relational Contracts' (1981) 67 *Virginia Law Review* 1089, 1091. See also Eisenberg, above n 159, 814.

[197] M Haviid, 'Long-Term Contracts and Relational Contracts' in B Bouckaert and G De Geest (eds), *Encyclopaedia of Law and Economics*, vol III: *The Regulation of Contracts* (London, Edward Elgar, 2000) 46.

[198] Merkin and Steele, above n 189, 27.

Interestingly for Merkin and Steele, they find that the general definitions[199] of 'insurance' appear to focus primarily on the risk-transfer element of insurance, and are therefore more consistent with the relational model of version of insurance as they perceive it.

In summary, given the planning function of insurance as Feinman sees it, and more importantly Merkin and Steele's innovative relational perception of insurance and the drawbacks of the conventional actuarial perception, it is sound that insurance be understood as a kind of relational contract and as consistent with Macneil's relational contract theory, from which Merkin and Steele do not have to keep a controlled distance.

C. A General Approach to Policyholder's Reasonable Expectations of Coverage in Business Insurance

As has been argued by Mitchell, relational contracts and the theory thereof require a relational, contextual approach that would take contractual parties' expectations more into account in judicial reasoning. Now that insurance contract is also relational, the corollary is that the reasonable expectations of the parties to an insurance contract should also be taken more seriously by adjudicators.

Royal and Sun Alliance Insurance Plc v Dornoch Ltd[200] (hereafter '*Dornoch*'), a reinsurance case, seems consistent with this approach. The case is further noteworthy because it seems at least like a departure from Mustill LJ's opinion[201] that reasonable expectations have no place in English insurance law, particularly in a business insurance contract placed at arm's length by an insurance broker with an insurer. Without looking at a PREC approach generally, or the American approach to PREC, the High Court took the contextualist approach to the interpretation of

[199] Examples given by Merkin and Steele are that Oxford Dictionaries (online) define 'insurance' as 'an arrangement by which a company or the state undertakes to provide a guarantee of compensation for specified loss, damage, illness, or death in return for payment of a specified premium', and that likewise BusinessDictionary.com defines 'insurance' as follows: 'Risk-transfer mechanism that ensures full or partial financial compensation for the loss or damage caused by event(s) beyond the control of the insured party. Under an insurance contract, a party (the insurer) indemnifies the other party (the insured) against a specified amount of loss, occurring from specified eventualities within a specified period, provided a fee called premium is paid. In general insurance, compensation is normally proportionate to the loss incurred, whereas in life insurance usually a fixed sum is paid.' The Lloyd's Glossary definition of 'insurance' is also given by Merkin and Steele as an example: Insurance is 'A contract whereby an insurer promises to pay the insured a sum of money or some other benefit upon the happening of one or more uncertain events in exchange for the payment of a premium. There must be uncertainty as to whether the relevant event(s) may happen at all or, if they will occur (eg death) as to their timing.' It seems that a Lloyd's definition is more professional and specialised though it is only 'intended for general guidance'. These online dictionary definitions are respectively at www.oxforddictionaries.com/definition/english/insurance; www.businessdictionary.com/definition/insurance.html; www.lloyds.com/common/help/glossary?Letter=I&Term=insurance.

[200] *Royal and Sun Alliance Insurance Plc v Dornoch Ltd* [2004] EWHC 803 (QBD Comm), [2005] EWCA Civ 238.

[201] *Smit Tak Offshore Services Ltd v Youell* [1992] 1 Lloyd's Rep 154 (CA), 159.

wording in a reinsurance contract, and in doing so took into account the honouring of commercial parties' reasonable expectations.

Royal and Sun Alliance Insurance Plc (RSA), the reinsured, sought a declaration that the defendant reinsurers were obliged to indemnify RSA under two contracts of reinsurance. The original or primary insurance underlying the reinsurance claims was liability insurance for and in relation to Coco Cola. Under a Master Subscription Policy (MSP), and among other insurers led by Allianz, RSA underwrote liability risks for some Coca Cola group companies for the period April 1997 to April 2002. Section V of the MSP covered 'Directors' and Officers' Liability' on a 'claims made' basis, and it insured losses to Coca Cola that arose from claims against the company itself, or from claims against directors and officers whom the company had indemnified. 'Loss' was defined differently in Clause VE and Clause XIE of Section V. Clause VE (in the first part of Section V) provided:

> Loss means any amount the Named Insured shall have paid with respect to any Securities Claim and any amount the Named Insured shall have paid to a Director or Officer as indemnity for a Claim arising out of those matters set forth in Item II. Insuring Agreement above (whether actual or asserted) and subject to the provisions of this Coverage Section.

Clause XIE (in the second part of Section V) provided that 'Loss(es) means any amount which the Insureds are legally obligated to pay for Claim for Wrongful Acts.' The definitions were different because in Clause VE, the cover provided was against losses of Coca Cola companies, who were 'the Named Insured', and also against the losses of directors and officers of Coca Cola who had been indemnified by the company, whereas in Clause XIE, the cover was for losses of the directors and officers when they had not been indemnified by the company.

Royal and Sun Alliance Insurance Plc reinsured 100 per cent of its participation on section V of the MSP, by way of two Lloyd's slip policies that represented two layers of reinsurance. The cover as subsequently extended was from 1997 to 2002. The reinsurance slip policies were in the same terms and contained a Full Reinsurance Clause (FRC) and a Claims Control Clause (CCC), as follows:

> FULL REINSURANCE CLAUSE
>
> Being a Reinsurance of and warranted same gross rate, terms and conditions as the Original Policy, so far as they may be applicable hereto and shall pay as may be paid thereon, but subject nevertheless to the terms, clauses and conditions of the Reinsurance.
>
> CLAIMS CONTROL CLAUSE
>
> Notwithstanding anything herein contained to the contrary, it is a condition precedent to any liability under this policy that:
>
> (a) the Reassured shall upon knowledge of any loss or losses which may give rise to claim under this policy, advise the Underwriters thereof by cable within 72 hours,
> (b) the Reassured shall furnish the Underwriters with all information available respecting such loss or losses and the Underwriters shall have the right to appoint adjusters, assessors and/or surveyors and to control all negotiations, adjustments and settlements in connection with such loss or losses.

As it happened, two class actions were brought in Georgia against Coca Cola the company and three of its directors and officers on 27 October 2000 (referred to as the 'Carpenters action' in the judgment) and on 13 November 2000 (the 'Lavalla action'). The complainants in the Carpenters action had purchased Coco Cola stock shares between 21 October 1999 and 6 March 2000, and alleged that Coca Cola the company and some of its directors and officers intentionally and knowingly made false statements and participated in a fraudulent scheme to inflate the value of the company's stock, so that the complainants had purchased the stock shares at artificially inflated prices. The allegations in the Lavalla action were much the same. The brokers in relation to the Carpenter action notified Allianz of the complaint by letter dated 1 November 2000, and the brokers in relation to the Lavalla action notified Allianz of the complaint between 20 and 29 November 2000. Both notifications were given with a copy of the respective complaint. The brokers notified RSA of the claims by fax on 30 December 2000. On 4 January 2000 RSA faxed the brokers, asking them to confirm that the reinsurers had been notified. The reinsurers were finally notified on 19 January 2001.

The reinsurers rejected RSA's claim for indemnity. But both sides agreed that the FRC meant that the subject matter of these reinsurance contracts was the same as that of the original insurance and that, due particularly to the phrase 'warranted same … terms and conditions as the Original Policy, as far as they may be applicable thereto' in the FRC, the MSP terms and conditions were incorporated into the reinsurance to the extent that they were appropriate thereto and not supplanted by the express terms of the reinsurance itself. In addition, both also agreed that the definitions in Section V were not incorporated in the reinsurance for the purpose of defining words used in the express terms, particularly the CCC, of the reinsurance contracts.

There were two issues before the trial court. The first was whether the word 'loss' in the CCC referred to the loss of third-party complainants against Coca Cola, or the loss suffered by Coca Cola. The reinsurers argued that the loss was that of third-party complainants, and that it was this loss that had to be notified within 72 hours of two class actions being brought. Royal and Sun Alliance Insurance Plc argued that 'loss' in the CCC referred to that of Coca Cola, and that the company could only suffer a loss once its liability had been ascertained either by judgment or settlement of the complaints. Accordingly, there was no obligation on RSA to inform the reinsurers until the class actions had either been settled or the Georgia court had adjudicated on them. The second issue was whether, if the reinsurers were right on the meaning of 'loss' in the CCC, RSA was only required to notify once it had knowledge of actual losses and not simply alleged losses.

Aikens J held that the words 'loss or losses' in the CCC referred to the loss or losses of third-party claimants against the original insured,[202] and that on or

[202] *Royal and Sun Alliance Insurance Plc v Dornoch Ltd* [2004] EWHC 803 (QBD Comm) [86], affirmed by Longmore LJ obiter. See further below.

before 11 January 2011 RSA did not have actual knowledge of actual losses of third-party claims against Coco Cola, and therefore RSA was not in breach of the condition precedent (of giving notice of losses) to the reinsurer's liability under the reinsurance contracts.[203] Given these rulings, as long as the third-party claimants' losses proved to be actual, RSA the reinsured was entitled to indemnity by and from the reinsurer.

What is more noteworthy in this reinsurance dispute is how Aikens J followed Lord Hoffmann's principles[204] to interpret the wording 'loss or losses' in the CCC. Having cited Lord Hoffmann's statement, the judge said:

> I have not found particularly persuasive any of the arguments adduced by each side as to the possible practical and commercial consequences of one construction or the other. In the end I have to decide what the words of the CCC mean using the basic rules of construction or interpretation of contractual documents. Those principles are not in issue. They were authoritatively stated by Lord Hoffmann in his speech in *ICS Ltd v West Bromwich BS*. ...[The famous speech is omitted here for brevity.[205]]
>
> The 'background' to the interpretation of the CCC includes the following relevant facts: (1) Coca Cola and its Directors and officers are insured against legal liability under Section V of the MSP. (2) The type of 'loss' of Coca Cola, its Directors and officers that is insured by Section V of the MSP is financial loss suffered as a result of claims made against one, two or all three by third party claimants. The claims by third party claimants will be for money compensation for financial loss that the third party claimants assert they have suffered as a result of the acts, defaults or omissions of Coca Cola, its Directors or Officers. (3) The terms of Section V of the MSP, including the definition of 'loss', were known to the Reinsurers when the reinsurance contracts were concluded. (4) The reinsurance is on the same terms and conditions as the original policy, so far as applicable. Moreover, the subject matter of the reinsurance is the same as that of the original insurance in Section V of the MSP: viz the liability of Coca Cola and its Directors and officers to third party claimants for acts, defaults or omissions of Coca Cola, its Directors and officers. (5) The original insurance is a 'claims made' policy. Therefore, in order to be entitled to indemnity under the MSP, claims by third party claimants must first be made against Coca Cola or its Directors and officers during the policy period (or any agreed extensions). (6) Under Clauses VII B(2) and XIII B(2) of Section V of the MSP, it is a condition precedent to the liability of the Consortium that it receives written notice 'as soon as is practicable' from Coca Cola or its Directors and officers, of any 'Claim' that is made against them. (7) There are provisions in Section V of the MSP which stipulate that the insurers under the MSP will not pay for any 'losses' by the original Insured where a settlement has been agreed with third party claimants, unless the insurers have consented to the settlement.[206]

[203] Ibid [96]. This is because at that time the third-party complainant's allegation of loss had yet to be proved to be actual.

[204] *Investor Compensation Scheme v West Bromwich Building Society* [1997] UKHL 28, [1997] CLC 1243, 1257–58.

[205] What is omitted here is Lord Hoffmann's point (1) and point (4) in his famous speech, as quoted in full in Chapter 3 section IV. A.

[206] *Royal and Sun Alliance Insurance Plc v Dornoch Ltd* [2004] EWHC 803 (QBD Comm) [83], [84].

The learned judge gave nine reasons more specific to and relevant to the original MSP and the reinsurance contract in question. He summarised in the ninth reason:

> (9) I think that, for the reasons I have given, *this interpretation accords with the expectations of reasonable commercial men who know the background facts.* I accept that my conclusion means that 'loss or losses' in the CCC does not have the same meaning as the definition in clauses VE and XIE of section V of the MSP. But, given all the other factors involved, I have concluded that the parties to the reinsurance contracts did not intend that the words should have the same meaning or effect [as clauses VE and XIE].[207] (emphasis added)

Although this apparently is not an invocation of the American version of PREC, 'the expectations of reasonable commercial men' approach is consistent with Lord Steyn's decades of advocacy to the effect that contract law should protect the reasonable expectations of honest men, consumers or businesses, and that 'commercially-minded judges would regard the commercial purpose of the contract as more important than niceties of language. And, in the event of doubt, the working assumption will be that a fair construction best matches the reasonable expectations of the parties.'[208] Also noteworthy in *Dornoch* is that the reasonable expectations of the commercial parties ascertained from the commercial background are given more weight than the express language of definitions in Clause VE and Clause XIE.

Ostensibly, the Court of Appeal in this case seemed to have rejected the contextual approach to construction of contracts when Longmore LJ dismissed the reinsurer's reliance on Lord Hoffmann's famous restatement[209] of the principles of construction of contracts and also on Lord Steyn's similar statement[210] in an insurance dispute. It seemed more so, considering that Longmore LJ indicated it would be more dangerous to construe part of a disputed clause in accordance with business common sense.[211]

Nonetheless, it will be both misleading and misled to read the judicial reasoning in the Court of Appeal to that effect. Rather, in this case Longmore LJ wholeheartedly embraced the contextual and business common sense approach. This is because firstly he thought it was more dangerous 'if it is *only one part* of

[207] Ibid [86].

[208] J Steyn, 'Contract Law: Fulfilling the Reasonable Expectations of Honest Men' (1997) 113 *LQR* 433, 441.

[209] *Investors Compensation Scheme Ltd v West Bromwich Building Society* [1997] CLC 1243 (HL), 1257–58, quoted in Chapter 3 section IV. A.

[210] *Sirius General Insurance v FAI General Insurance* [2004] UKHL 54 [18]: 'The aim of the inquiry is not to probe the real intentions of the parties but to ascertain the contextual meaning of the relevant contractual language. The inquiry is objective: the question is what a reasonable person, circumstanced as the actual parties were, would have understood the parties to have meant by the use of specific language. The answer to that question is to be gathered from the text under consideration and its relevant contextual sense.'

[211] *Royal and Sun Alliance Insurance Plc v Dornoch Ltd* [2005] EWCA Civ 238 [16].

such a clause which is to be construed in accordance with "business common sense".[212] (emphasis added) Regarding part (a) and part (b) of the contested CCC, Longmore LJ thought that the notification-within-72-hours requirement under part (b) was draconian as a condition precedent to a reinsurer's liability though it might be sound for direct insurers of cargo insurance. Therefore, he would not

> give a purposive or business common sense construction to one part of a clause [ie part (a) of the CCC] in favour of one party [ie the reinsurer] and thus enable that party [ie the insurer] to seek to take advantage of another part of the clause [ie part (b) of the CCC] which has draconian consequences for the other party [ie RSA, the reinsured].[213]

The judicial intention to avoid the 'draconian consequences' for the policyholder (of reinsurance) was essentially result-orientated. This is consistent with even the orthodoxy of the functionalist principle of reasonable expectations in American insurance law. Secondly, regarding Aiken J's decision on the meaning of 'loss or losses', although Longmore LJ ruled that the question of 'whose losses' was not material to the outcome of the appeal,[214] in passing he also stated that if the question of 'whose losses' had been material, he would have come to the same conclusion on this question as Aikens J.[215] In other words, Longmore LJ was ready to interpret 'loss or losses' as Aikens J did to the contrary of the express definition thereof in the contract of primary insurance. Thirdly, and in connection with the second point, there is an oddity or surprise that reflects how far both courts have gone in this case for sake of honouring the policyholder's expectation of coverage. The oddity or surprise is that, despite the current English reinsurance law, Aikens J interpreted 'loss or losses' in reinsurance contract as contrary to the express definition in primary insurance, and Longmore LJ indirectly accepted this interpretation. Should they not be the same under the current law? After all, under English reinsurance law, it has been entrenched that the risk covered under reinsurance is the same as that covered under primary insurance.[216] Given this, it seems counterintuitive that on one hand reinsurance covers the same risk as primary insurance, yet on the other hand the meaning of 'loss' under reinsurance is interpreted differently from that under the underlying primary insurance. In spite of this oddity, the Court of Appeal was indirectly agreed with the High Court in this regard. In summary, given the fact of this case and Longmore LJ's readiness to interpret 'loss or losses' contrary to the express contractual definition, the decision of the Court of Appeal was obviously and strongly result-orientated. Of the Court of Appeal decision in this reinsurance dispute, it can be said that, contrary to the

[212] Ibid.

[213] Ibid [18].

[214] This was because RSA, the policyholder of the reinsurance, did not know of the loss in whichever sense or of whomever it was; and therefore without knowledge of the loss, RSA was not obliged to notify the reinsurer within 72 hours.

[215] *Royal and Sun Alliance Insurance Plc v Dornoch Ltd* [2005] EWCA Civ 238 [28].

[216] *Charter Reinsurance Co Ltd v Fagan* [1997] AC 313 (HL), 392; *British Dominions General Insurance Co Ltd v Duder* [1915] 2 KB 394 (CA), 400.

long-held view, judicial considerations of a policyholder's reasonable expectations of coverage sometimes are actually given considerable weight, albeit inconspicuously, in business insurance cases.

In summary, given the fact of this case and Longmore LJ's readiness to interpret 'loss or losses' contrary to the express contractual definition, the decision of the Court of Appeal was obviously and strongly result-orientated. Of the Court of Appeal in this reinsurance dispute, it can be said that, contrary to the long-held view, judicial considerations of a policyholder's reasonable expectations of coverage sometimes are actually given considerable weight, albeit inconspicuously, in business insurance cases.

Particularly more noteworthy are a few insurance cases from the highest courts in Canada—if not any court in the US—and in the UK. The Supreme Court of Canada held in *Reid Crowther & Partners Ltd v Simcoe & Erie General Insurance Co*:[217]

> Without pronouncing on the reach of this doctrine, it is settled that where the policy is ambiguous, the courts should consider the reasonable expectations of the parties: ... The insured's reasonable expectation is, at a minimum, that the insurance plan will provide coverage for legitimate claims on an ongoing basis. The presumption must be that the intention of the parties is to provide and obtain coverage for all legitimate claims on an ongoing basis, whether through renewal with the same insurer or through securing new insurance with a different insurer. This presumption is consistent with the discovery principle discussed earlier in these reasons, in that the insurer is able to secure a means of certainty in calculating its risk without unfairly creating gaps in coverage. Yet the construction of the policy which the insurer urges upon us may well not achieve that goal.

Three years previously, the Supreme Court of Canada had heard a slightly unusual insurance case: *National Bank of Greece (Canada) v Katsikonouris*.[218] Katsikonouris was a debtor who secured loans from the National Bank of Greece (Canada) (NBGC). Ancillary to the loan, Katsikonouris mortgaged his properties to NBGC. In the meantime, Katsikonouris took out fire insurance on the mortgaged properties through a standard mortgage clause, the effect of which in relation to the insurance, inter alia, was that there were two fire insurance contracts: one between Katsikonouris (the mortgagor) and the insurer, and the other between NBGC (the mortgagee) and the same insurer. The mortgaged properties were destroyed by arson. The Bank sought an indemnity from the insurer, but this was rejected for nullity *ab initio* of the insurance contract between Katsikonouris and the insurer due to his broker's pre-contractual material misrepresentation, which also nullified NBGC's insurance. Nullity was found despite part of the standard mortgage clause reading:

[217] *Reid Crowther & Partners Ltd v Simcoe & Erie General Insurance Co* [1993] SCR 252, 271.
[218] *National Bank of Greece (Canada) v Katsikonouris* [1990] 2 SCR 1029.

IT IS HEREBY PROVIDED AND AGREED THAT:

(1) This insurance and every documented renewal thereof—AS TO THE INTEREST OF THE MORTGAGEE ONLY THEREIN—is and shall be in force notwithstanding any act, neglect, omission or misrepresentation attributable to the mortgagor, owner or occupant of the property insured, including transfer of interest, any vacancy or non-occupancy, or the occupation of the property for purposes more hazardous than specified in the description of the risk.

It was held that by virtue of the foregoing clause, the insurer represented to the mortgagee that a separate and distinct contract existed between them, and its validity depended solely on the course of action between the mortgagee and the insurer.[219] Considering the nature of the full standard mortgage clause and the advantages to all parties in insuring through the medium of the clause, Justice La Forest further held that mortgagees using this medium

> can only be doing so on the reasonable expectation that their interests will be protected in the same way as if they had entered into an independent contract evidenced by a separate piece of paper. … I have already drawn attention to the fact that insurers cannot rely on anything short of the clearest language when offering coverage on terms that would go to frustrating the legitimate expectations as to coverage of those purchasing the policy. … Any other interpretation would, in my view, fail to concord with the reasonable expectations of the parties as to the coverage offered by the standard mortgage clause, and, indeed … would strike at the very *raison d'être* of the standard mortgage clause.[220]

It was reaffirmed that 'in the construction of a contract of insurance a court must seek the interpretation which most fairly reflects what can reasonably be supposed to have been the intention of the parties when entering into the contract'.[221] As recently as May 2015 in the UK Supreme Court, to some degree Lord Sumption implied that PREC could be considered 'as background to the construction of the policy'.[222] This effectively lends force to and confirms the contextual approach to insurance dispute resolution in relation to PREC.

D. Whose Expectations Should Prevail in Business Insurance?

Meanwhile, in the context of insurance, the generic approach to reasonable expectations in contract law cannot be taken at face value, because the seemingly inherent hard question of 'which party's reasonable expectations should prevail?' is not as difficult as it first seems. It can be argued that in principle the reasonable expectations of the policyholder should prevail over those of the insurer. This is due to

[219] Ibid 1046 (per Justice La Forest).

[220] Ibid 1057–58 (per Justice La Forest).

[221] Ibid 1056 (per Justice La Forest); see also *Consolidated-Bathurst Export Ltd v Mutual Boiler and Machinery Insurance Co* [1980] 1 SCR 888 and *Scott v Wawanesa Mutual Insurance Co* [1989] 1 SCR 1445, 1454–55.

[222] *Zurich Insurance Plc UK Branch v International Energy Group Ltd* [2015] UKSC 33 [164].

the different nature of their respective expectations and an insurance dispute's different nature for each party, and also due to the normative business purpose of any insurance contract.

Insurer's Expectations

An insurer's expectation is that of receipt of premiums and/or of non-liability for particular risks. In insurance disputes, for an insurer to claim or expect payment of premiums is not unheard of, but it is uncommon: that a policyholder under a valid insurance contract is obliged to pay premiums is hardly controversial, and whether a particular premium has been paid is a question of fact that is much easier to resolve than is a dispute over coverage. On the part of insurers, most insurance disputes concern the insurer's claim of non-liability for particular risks. An insurer could allege non-liability on such grounds as the exception/exclusion clause in the insurance contract, the policyholder's non-disclosure and/or misrepresentation, breach of warranty, lack of insurable interest, the absence of a proximate causal link between the risk and the loss, or that the risk occurred outside the period of coverage, etc. Whether a risk is covered or not depends on risk classification, and more often on how the exception/exclusion clauses and/or the coverage clauses are interpreted.

Some alleged grounds for an insurer's non-liability are not so much concerned with questions of interpretation of the insurance contract. An insurer's rejection of liability on the ground of the policyholder's non-disclosure and/or misrepresentation does not involve much interpretation of the *insurance contract* in question, although it does involve interpretation of the *common law* of non-disclosure and/or misrepresentation, particularly in the context of insurance. Whether a fact or circumstance is 'material', so that the policyholder must truthfully disclose it or represent it to the insurer, is essentially a question of fact, not of interpretation of the text in an insurance contract. Whether the policyholder has breached a warranty is largely a matter of fact too, though whether the insurance clause in question is a warranty may be a matter of interpretation of law. Under the current English insurance law, whether the policyholder has insurable interest in the subject matter of the insurance is a question of fact and of the underlying law, for example property law and tort law, by which insurable interest can be identified or otherwise. Under the rule of causation, the issue of whether the risk or occurrence of risk in question is the proximate cause of the loss is also essentially a question of fact.[223] So is the question of whether the risks in question occurred outside the period of coverage. All these largely factual questions mean that the question of an insurer's expectation of non-liability for particular risks is addressed less as a matter of interpretation of policy terms than as a matter of fact.

[223] *Leyland Shipping Co v Norwich Union Fire Insurance Society* [1918] AC 350 (HL), 358 (per Lord Findlay), 359 (per Viscount Hardane), 362 (per Lord Dunedin). See also *Brownsville Holdings v Adamjee Insurance* [2000] 2 All ER (QBD Comm) 803 [20] (Aikens J); J Birds, *Birds' Modern Insurance Law*, 8th edn (London, Sweet & Maxwell, 2010) 263–64.

That, however, does not mean that the contextual approach to interpretation is irrelevant. Rather, due to the factual nature of those questions, the contextual approach is no less relevant to the finding of facts than it is to the interpretation of contract. In this regard, the contextual approach, as far as its result is concerned, already seems to take a policyholder's expectations of coverage into consideration more than an insurer's expectations of non-liability for particular risks. This can be seen in several aspects of insurance law, as described below.

Concerning pre-contractual non-disclosure and misrepresentation, the Insurance Act 2015 has discarded the much-criticised draconian 'all-or-nothing' approach to an insurer's liability. In the past, the insurer might elect either to accept liability, which however was unlikely, or to reject liability by avoiding the insurance contract, and thereby refuse the policyholder's insurance claims in full. This certainly frustrated the reasonable expectations of coverage of policyholders who might have only carelessly breached the duty of disclosure. Under the Insurance Act 2015, the consequence of a policyholder's non-disclosure and misrepresentation hinges on what the insurer would have done if the policyholder had complied with the duty. Only if the policyholder's non-disclosure or misrepresentation is deliberate or reckless may the insurer avoid the contract and refuse all claims. In the absence of deliberate or reckless breach, if the insurer would not have entered into the contract on any terms, the insurer may avoid the contract and refuse all claims, but must in that event return the premiums paid. If the insurer would have entered into the contract, but on different terms (other than terms relating to the premium), the contract is to be treated as if it had been entered into on those different terms if the insurer so requires. In addition, if the insurer would have entered into the contract (whether the terms relating to matters other than the premium would have been the same or different), but would have charged a higher premium, the insurer may reduce proportionately the amount to be paid on a claim. To 'reduce proportionately' means that the insurer need pay only *x* per cent of what it would otherwise have been under an obligation to pay on the claim under the terms of the contract (or, if applicable, as mentioned above, under the different terms).[224] As far as policyholders are concerned who have made innocent (that is, neither deliberate nor reckless) non-disclosure and/or misrepresentation, the new approach to remedy surely is intended at least to *partly* protect a policyholder's expectations of coverage. The departure from the draconian old law has in part let an innocent policyholder's expectations of coverage prevail over the insurer's expectation of non-liability for the risks it has intended to underwrite.

In respect of warranty in insurance, even though whether a policyholder has breached an insurance warranty is a question of fact, whether a particular clause in the insurance contract is a warranty or not depends on the interpretation or characterisation of the clause in question. In this regard, English insurance law takes a restrictive approach, in that an insurance contract clause should not be

[224] Insurance Act 2015, sch 1. The remedies are similar for consumer insurance in Consumer Insurance (Disclosure and Representations) Act 2012, sch 1.

construed as a warranty, 'except on very clear indications that it was the intention of the contracting parties that it should have that effect'.[225] Before an insurance contract clause is held to have the effect of a warranty,

> it is necessary to see that the language is such as to shew that the assured as well as the insurer meant it, and … the language in the policy being that of the insurers, if there is any ambiguity, it must be construed most strongly against them.[226]

The law refrains from readily characterising a clause in an insurance contract as a warranty, partly because the consequence of a policyholder's breach of warranty is that, by orthodox rules, the insurer may terminate the contract even though the breach is material neither to the risk nor to the loss. Apparently an active or a broad characterisation of insurance warranties would make it more likely to frustrate the policyholder's expectations of coverage. As a corollary, a restrictive approach toward identifying warranties in insurance leans toward subordinating an insurer's expectation of non-liability for risks to moderate protection of PREC *ex ante*. Also noteworthy is that the 2015 Act prohibits a policyholder's representations from being converted into a warranty,[227] and in addition it has abolished any rule of law that breach of a warranty (express or implied) in a contract of insurance results in the discharge of the insurer's liability under the contract.[228] Again, in respect of warranties in insurance, the law now leans more towards the possible protection of a policyholder's reasonable expectations than meeting the insurer's expectation of non-liability for risks.

The combination of a restrictive judicial attitude and industry self-refrainment in regard to the requirement of an insurable interest means that the insurer's expectation of non-liability is subordinated again to PREC. Although insurers can use a policyholder's non-compliance with the requirement or lack of insurable interest as a technical defence for rejecting the policyholder's claim, in this respect the courts nevertheless recognisably favour finding an insurable interest in commercial transactions,[229] so that the defence is not readily available to insurers and so that PREC can be protected. Moreover, insurers themselves are reluctant to raise that defence, out of concern that the use of such a technical defence would damage the image of the insurance industry.[230]

Similar but more balanced subordination of an insurer's expectations of non-liability to PREC also exists in relation to the rule of causation in insurance law.

[225] *Wheelton v Hardisty* (1857) 8 EI & BI 232, 300 (per Bramwell B); *Union Insurance Society of Canton Ltd v George Wills & Co* [1916] 1 AC 281(HL), 287 (per Lord Parmoor); *Joel v Law Union & Crown Insurance Co Ltd* [1908] 2 KB 863 (CA) (per Moulton LJ); *Re Bradley and Essex and Suffolk Accident Indemnity Society* [1912] 1 KB 415 (CA), 430–33 (per Farwell LJ).

[226] *Thomson v Weens* (1884) 9 App Cas 671, 682 (per Lord Blackburn). See also *CTN Cash & Carry Ltd v General Accident Fire and Life Assurance Corporation plc* [1989] 1 Lloyd's Rep 299 (QBD Comm).

[227] Insurance Act 2015, s 9.

[228] Insurance Act 2015, s 10.

[229] *Feasy v Sun Life Assurance Co of Canada* [2003] EWCA Civ 885 [97] (Waller LJ), [121] (Dyson LJ), [145] (Ward LJ). See also *Stock v Inglis* (1844) 12 QBD 564, 571.

[230] Clarke, *The Law of Insurance Contracts*, above n 1, 137.

On one hand the rule is that insurers have liability for the particular risks only if the risks are *the proximate* cause, not just *a* cause, of the losses to the policyholder. This restrictive requirement might make it more difficult for PREC to be honoured. On the other hand, where there are multiple effective or proximate causes involving exception or exclusion clauses, it is not clear or consistent that the law leans in favour of only one party: 'If one of these causes is insured against under the policy and none of the others is expressly excluded from the policy, the assured will be entitled to recover.'[231] However, 'if the loss is caused by two causes effectively operating at the same time and one is wholly expressly excluded from the policy, the policy does not pay'.[232] It seems that the *consideration of exclusion* carries more weight, so that where no causes are excluded the policyholder's expectations of coverage would be protected, but where one of the concurrent causes is excluded the insurer's expectation of non-liability would be met. This more balanced result is more due to the effect accorded to exceptions and/or exclusions in insurance contract than the causation rule itself.

The difficulty posed by causation coupled with exceptions and/or exclusions in insurance contract is not surprising. After all, the effect of exceptions and/or exclusions and of the coverage clause is perhaps that over which insurance disputes arise most frequently and most demandingly: as regards these type of clauses a policyholder's claim for insurance money is an expectation of coverage of the risks in question, and the insurer's rejection of the policyholder's claim is an expectation of non-liability in relation to the same risks. In principle, whose expectations should prevail? When technical rules cannot yield a principled answer to this question, there should be broader considerations concerning the institution of insurance itself.

PREC, Risk Pool Solvency and the Purpose of Insurance

Arguably, PREC should in principle prevail over the insurer's expectations of non-liability if there is dispute over whether the particular risk in question is covered, or excepted/excluded or subject to a limitation clause. This is certainly not to say that PREC should always prevail, but simply that, assuming there are no other issues as considered above, such as non-disclosure, breach of warranty, lack of insurable interest or causal link, etc, PREC ought to prevail unless there are strong reasons to the contrary. Apart from those realistically strong anti-PREC reasons discussed in section II. above, perhaps another strong reason against PREC prevailing over insurers' expectations is that a policyholder gets coverage and insurance payment for the amount of premium it pays. In other words, the insurance payment or the extent of coverage is actuarially proportionate to the amount of the premium; if

[231] *Halsbury's Laws of England*, vol 25, 4th edn, (London, Butterworth, 1980) [181], quoted by *Slade LJ in JJ Lloyd Instruments Ltd v Northern Star Insurance Co Ltd* (The 'Miss Jay Jay') [1987] 1 Lloyd's Rep 32 (CA) to the same effect.

[232] *Wayne Tank and Pump Co Ltd v Employers' Liability Assurance Co Ltd* [1974] QB 57 (CA), 75.

insurers pay insurance claims above the particular actuarial proportionality, it will be prejudicial to solvency in relation to the particular risk pool into which the risk or loss in question falls.

Such an argument seems broadly consistent with the conventional actuarial model of insurance, but meanwhile it is vulnerable to scrutiny on two points. First, although it would not be unimaginable that, in setting premium rates and the corresponding insurance payment proportionate thereto, insurers or their actuaries take into consideration that the coverage clauses or exception/exclusion/limitation clauses are prone to ambiguity and hence to dispute, the practice of considering the clauses in this manner presupposes that insurers, in the in-house actuarial calculation and long before insurance disputes arise, have already had knowledge of, or at least predicted, the ambiguities from which insurance disputes arise. This, however, is paradoxical. If an insurer in its policy clauses drafting practice already has knowledge about or specific predictions of uncertainties and ambiguities, it must avoid the uncertainties or ambiguities in the first place, rather than leaving such clauses untouched or unamended to become the seeds of dispute. After all, 'it is the business of insurers to achieve certainty by pooling what are for insured uncertain events'.[233] If an insurer fails to do so, it must bear the consequence. That being said, genuine ambiguities in an insurance contract tend not to come to the attention of the insurer until an insurance dispute arises. Instead, the normal practice is that an insurer's drafting or product design department will endeavour to make sure that insurance contract clauses are free from uncertainties and ambiguities, unless they do otherwise for the strategic purpose of taking advantage of policyholders at the claims stage—but such strategic behaviour may backfire, so prudent insurers and optimal drafting practice will try to avoid this. Even so, actuaries will have to assume that the insurance clauses that they must seriously take into consideration in actuarial practice, in connection with the particular insurance product and the particular risk pool, are generally free from uncertainties and ambiguities.

In addition, for solvency purposes, insurers must have financial provision or reserves to cope with liabilities or insurance claims that arise outside their actuarial speculation. An insurer's reserve of this nature is intended for insurance payments in relation to disputed insurance claims. In this sense, and to the extent of the capacity of an insurer's financial reserve for contingencies, insurers are already, and are required to be, prepared to meet a policyholder's reasonable expectations. Therefore, it follows that it is not so legitimate for insurers to make every effort to reject insurance claims and to make their expectations of non-liability prevail over PREC and hence payment.

The second point against the actuarially-based argument is that an insurer keeps itself solvent as a whole or in relation to particular risk pools by multiple approaches, of which measuring payment against premiums income is only one of

[233] Jerry and Richmond, above n 60, 151.

them. Insurers endeavor to remain solvent not only just according to the actuarial rule of large numbers alone, but also by way of other complementary mechanisms: they impose deductibles, exercise subrogation and seek contribution from other insurers in the event of double insurance or 'other insurance'. Insurers themselves transfer their potential liability risks to reinsurers too. Even if the need to maintain the funds of the particular risk pool always prevails, the need can be met by way of *ex post* approaches, that is, by deducting from the insurance payment the increased amount of premium that correlates thereto and that could have been charged; alternatively, the insurer could at least make a proportionate and partial payment that correlates to the lower premium charged, as prescribed in the Insurance Act 2015 and the Consumer Insurance (Disclosure and Representations) Act 2012. Admittedly, although the two statutes apply to a policyholder's breach of the pre-contractual informational duty, proportionate payment as a remedy that has similarly broad actuarial considerations should also be useful for the purpose of insurance payment in line with PREC. It can also be noted that where and if the monetary value of PREC does not exceed the balance of the agreed maximum payment less the undisputed amount of payment under the insurance contract, the PREC does not necessarily prejudice the solvency of the risk pool in relation to the insurance contract in question. In summary, while insurers certainly need to be financially prudent and to be solvent in connection with the risk pool in which the risk in question belongs, PREC under a particular insurance contract does not necessarily prejudice the solvency. Given that insurers have other complementary means for maintaining solvency, their financial prudence is not to be bolstered at the expense of PREC.

The third objection to the actuarially-based argument is that, despite actuarial calculations for solvency purposes, insurers might have been over-investing into non-underwriting business for a long time, rather than paying policyholders generously. Insurers, especially life insurers, use premiums also to make investments—often into non-insurance business—and it seems that they over-invest and under-pay. Certainly insurers must have actuarial considerations for the premiums collected for particular risk pools. Although investment-related actuarial considerations are necessary as long as investment is not excessive, *investment-oriented* actuarial calculations are not essential for insurance. This is because the essential function and purpose of insurance is *not* to make investments. By 2000, however, British life insurers alone were already 'responsible for a large part of the UK's savings and investment markets', with 'over 20 per cent of all UK equities on behalf of individual investors and pension schemes.'[234] Today, the UK insurance and long term savings provider industry is the largest in Europe, and third largest in the world, managing investments of £1.9trn (equivalent to 25 per cent of the UK's total net worth).[235] Now that insurers have been making

[234] P Myners, Institutional Investment in the United Kingdom: A Review (London, 2001) [9.1].
[235] Association of British Insurers website: www.abi.org.uk/Insurance-and-savings/Industry-data.

enormous investments, should they invest a little less so that they can pay more to policyholders whose reasonable expectations should be honoured? After all, 'the insurance industry is about risk-taking and pooling, thus providing risk coverage to the interested parties, and not about financial operation aimed at producing some return.'[236]

The purposes of insurance and of business insurance contract, as well as the latter's business context, must always be taken into account where an interpretation of insurance clauses is disputed. This is because, as has been argued by Merkin and Steele, insurance contract is relational—it is particularly so for business insurance, which often is collateral to another legal relation or transaction. Risk-allocation arrangements in general should be considered in the light of their context, which may include a broad network of relations that involve insurance and insuring obligations and relationships.[237] Given that, insurance is a context for a non-insurance risk-allocation arrangement, and vice versa. Just as it is necessary to take insurance into consideration in non-insurance arrangements,[238] so is it necessary to take non-insurance contexts into consideration in insurance issues.

For this purpose, some leading business insurance cases concerning the insurable interest are good examples of the contextual approach to PREC. That is because the courts, in determining whether the requirement of an insurable interest was met, would have to look at both the law relevant to the underlying business or commercial relationship and the law of insurable interest. When faced with an insurance claim, insurers might reject it on the ground that the policyholder has no insurable interest in the subject matter of the insurance. The orthodox test for an insurable interest, established by Lord Eldon[239] and codified into the Marine Insurance Act 1906, section 5(2), is that the insured has a legal or an equitable relation to the subject matter of the insurance. Meanwhile in the same case, Lawrence J, dissenting, put forward 'the factual expectancy test' for an insurable interest:

> *A man is interested in a thing to whom advantage may arise or prejudice happen from the circumstances which may attend it*; ... interest does not necessarily imply a right to the whole, or a part of a thing, nor necessarily and exclusively that which may be the subject of privation, but the having some relation to, or concern in the subject of the insurance, which relation or concern by the happening of the perils insured against may be so affected as to produce a damage, detriment, or prejudice to the person insuring: and where a man is so circumstanced with respect to matters exposed to certain risks or dangers, as to have a moral certainty of advantage or benefit, but for those risks or dangers he may be said to be interested in the safety of the thing. *To be interested in the preservation*

[236] PM Liedtke and J Monkiewicz, 'The Future of Insurance Regulation and Supervision', in PM Liedtke and Jan Monkiewicz (eds), *The Future of Insurance Regulation after the Financial Crisis* (Palgrave Macmillan 2011) 1.

[237] Merkin and Steele, above n 188, 21.

[238] R Merkin, 'Tort, Ideology and Insurance: Further Thoughts' (2012) 75 *MLR* 301, in relation to contract particularly at 311–16.

[239] *Lucena v Craufurd* (1806) 2 Bos & PNR 269 (HL).

> *of a thing, is to be so circumstanced with respect to it as to have benefit from its existence, prejudice from its destruction.*[240] (emphasis added)

This non-orthodox test gained notable acceptance in *Waters v Monarch Life and Fire Assurance Co*,[241] almost 50 years after it was put forward by Lawrence J in his dissenting opinion. In this case, Waters, the insured, was a warehouseman and wharfinger. He had in his warehouses goods belonging to his customers, which were deposited with him in that capacity and on which he had a lien for the charges for cartage and warehouse rent, but no further interest of his own. Waters took out a policy on his own goods in the warehouse, and also on 'goods in trust or on commission therein' against fire. The customers were not charged fees for the insurance, neither were they informed of the existence of the insurance policy. As it happened, all goods in the warehouse were consumed by fire. The defendant insurer paid the value of Waters' own goods and the amount of his lien on his customers' goods, but refused to pay the value beyond the lien. It was held unanimously that Waters as a bailee had an insurable interest in *all* the goods and property deposited in the warehouse to their *full* value. In delivering the lead judgment, Lord Campbell CJ said:

> What is meant in those policies by the words 'goods in trust'? I think that means goods with which the assured were entrusted; *not goods held in trust in the strict technical sense, so held that there was only equitable obligation on the assured* … but goods with which they were entrusted in the ordinary sense of the word. They were so entrusted with the goods deposited on their wharfs. I cannot doubt the policy was intended to protect such goods …[242] (emphasis added)

By refusing to construe 'in trust' in the technical sense under the law of trust, Lord Campbell CJ distanced himself from the formalist legal interest test and embraced the realist alternative. In doing so, he took into account the business context:

> [I]t would be very inconvenient if wharfingers could not protect such goods by a floating policy … It would be most inconvenient in business if a wharfinger could not, at his own cost, keep up a floating policy for the benefit of all who might become his customers.[243]

Meanwhile, Wightman and Crompton JJ were aware of the fact that the plaintiff as a bailee would benefit from the existence of all the goods deposited with him and would be prejudiced by their destruction. The benefit was in terms of the plaintiff-bailee's lien, which, however, could not become a vested legal right of the bailee unless the debt and/or obligation of the bailor to the bailee was already due,[244] or liability had accrued and a cause of action had arisen.[245] The prejudice

240 Ibid 302.
241 *Waters v Monarch Life and Fire Assurance Co* (1856) 5 EI & BI 870.
242 Ibid 880.
243 Ibid 880-81.
244 G Paton, *Bailment in Common Law* (London, Stevens & Sons Ltd, 1952) 184.
245 *Dyson v Peat* [1917] 1 Ch 99, 103–04 (per Eve J).

was in terms of the plaintiff-bailee's 'being accountable'[246] and having 'responsibility'[247] to the bailor, but 'responsibility is here used in a different sense from legal liability'.[248] Simply put, the benefit and the prejudice were not necessarily legal rights or interests, but they would still suffice as an insurable interest in this case. This is close to the 'factual expectancy' test put forward by Lawrence J in *Lucena v Craufurd*,[249] although Lord Campbell CJ did not actually refer to that test. Similarly, 110 years later, affirming the judgment of Lord Campbell CJ, the House of Lords in *Tomlinson (Hauliers) Ltd v Hepburn*[250]—also concerning insurance in the context of bailment (consignor and consignee in particular)—opined that 'To hold otherwise would be commercially inconvenient and would have no justification in common sense.'[251]

Liability insurance is another example where courts take a contextual or relational approach to interpretation of the coverage clauses. The relationships underlying liability insurance are employment, general public engagement, contracts for the sale of goods, director's and officer's duties, etc. Courts have generally taken a contextual approach to interpreting terms in liability insurance coverage clauses so that the PREC thereunder could be met. For example, in employer's liability insurance, the terms 'labour only sub-contractor' and 'arising out of and in the course of employment' are not narrowly interpreted, having due regard to the employment relationship as a context and also to the purpose of employer's liability insurance. In *Calder v H Kitson Vickers & Sons (Engineers) Ltd*,[252] Calder had worked both as an employee and as a labour only sub-contractor for the defendant company, which took out employer's liability insurance from an insurer. In 1979 Calder was employed by the company as a lorry driver, and then to help to break up a steelworks. In November 1979 he replaced one man in a team that was engaged in breaking up a minesweeper, on the suggestion of a director of the company. The men were paid on a tonnage-recovered basis. The company's yard manager calculated the amount of the tonnage removed by these men, and paid Calder in cash. Calder then shared the receipts with other men in the team. No deduction for tax or for National Insurance Contributions was made. The equipment was provided by the company. Unfortunately, a terrible accident happened due to the faulty equipment, and Calder was seriously injured. The indemnity clause of the employer's liability policy provided that if any employee should, while employed on the business of 'the insured, sustain bodily injury … arising out of and in the

[246] *Waters v Monarch Life and Fire Assurance Co* (1856) 5 El & Bl 870, 881 (per Wightman J).
[247] Ibid 880 (per Crompton J).
[248] *Petrofina (UK) Ltd v Magnaload Ltd* [1984] 1 QB 127 (QBD Comm) 135, per Lloyd J, who said further, 'A bailee might by contract exclude his legal liability for loss of or damage to the goods in particular circumstances, eg by fire. But he would still be "responsible" for the goods in a more general sense, sufficient, at any rate, to entitle him to insure the full value.'
[249] *Lucena v Craufurd* (1806) 2 Bos & Pul (NR) 269 (HL).
[250] *Tomlinson (Hauliers) Ltd v Hepburn* [1966] AC 451 (HL).
[251] Ibid 481.
[252] *Calder v H Kitson Vickers & Sons (Engineers) Ltd* [1988] ICR 232 (CA).

course of employment by the insured the company will … indemnify the insured up to an unlimited amount against liability at law for damages'. An 'employee' was defined in the policy as any person '(1) engaged under a contract of service … with the insured, (2) engaged as a labour only sub-contractor'.

It was undisputed that Calder was not engaged under a contract of service. Meanwhile the insurer denied liability on the ground, inter alia, that Calder was not a 'labour only sub-contractor' either. The Court of Appeal firmly rejected this contention, emphasising that it was a commercial document that was being construed, and that the industry used the term 'sub-contractor' in a wide sense. It approved the High Court judgment, which was said to be rendered

> to include within the cover the activities of persons such as workers in the building industry who were and are known colloquially as 'on the lump,' that is to persons who were, to all intents and purposes, employees but who were regarded as self-employed because they were paid without deductions for tax or National Insurance. The word 'sub-contractor' was a natural one to use because, in the vast majority of cases, there will be a contractor between the building owner and the workmen in question. However, to exclude from the ambit of the extended meaning workmen 'on the lump' who happen to be engaged by a building owner direct seems to me to be entirely restrictive and liable to lead to absurd results. Thus, in the instant case, if the defendants had started breaking the minesweeper as contractors and then had bought the minesweeper and continued to break the vessel as principals, cover that would otherwise avail the workman would cease from the moment the defendants purchased the vessel. I take 'labour-only sub-contractor' in this context to denote one who is paid only for his labour and who is paid without deduction of tax and National Insurance.[253]

The Court of Appeal in addition found support for this view 'from the rules relating to sub-contractors in the construction industry':

> Since 1972 the general effect of the rules has been that when a contractor makes a payment to a sub-contractor under a contract, other than a contract of employment, relating to construction operations the contractor must deduct and pay to the Inland Revenue a percentage of the payment on account of tax. If the sub-contractor has been issued with the sub-contractor's tax certificate the payment may be made without deductions. The status of subcontractor for the rules does not, however, depend upon the person who makes the payment being in strict sense a 'contractor.' He may be a person who carries on a business which includes construction operations, or any local authority or other similar body.[254]

In respect of 'in the course of employment', the Court of Appeal held[255] that the test was not the strict test of whether the employee was at the relevant time performing a duty for his or her employer; an employee might be in the course of employment even when he or she acted casually, negligently or even disobediently,

[253] Ibid 256.
[254] Ibid 256–57.
[255] *R v Industrial Injuries Commissioners, ex parte Almalgamated Engineering Union* (No 2) [1966] 2 QB 31 (CA).

so long as it was something reasonably 'incidental to'[256] the work which he or she was employed to do. Though the course of employment may be interrupted, this principled contextual approach helps to meet a policyholder's reasonable expectations, and that will in turn help to make optimal, *ex post*, the relations underlying the liability insurance concerned.

Also concerned with employer's liability insurance, the UK Supreme Court rendered a flexible interpretation of diseases 'sustained' in relation to asbestos. While the word 'sustained' may initially appear to refer to the manifestation of an injury, the nature and underlying purpose of the employer's liability insurance look to the initiation or causation of the accident or disease that injured the employee. Accordingly, a disease may properly be said to have been 'sustained' by an employee in the period when it was caused or initiated, even though it only developed or manifested itself later. This is 'the only approach, consistent with the nature and underlying purpose of these insurances both before and after the [Employer's Liabilities (Compulsory Insurance) Act 1969]'.[257] Once it had been held, in *Fairchild v Glenhaven Funeral Services Ltd*[258] and *Barker v Corus UK Ltd*,[259] that employers are liable to employees for exposing those employees to asbestos, it would be remarkable not to hold the insurers liable under the employers' liability policies.[260] Here the human element is powerful, and it is part of the context that influences the decisions.[261]

However, the picture is not always rosy; sometimes it is patchy. A common law case where PREC could have been honoured is *New World Harbourview Hotel Co Ltd v ACE Insurance Ltd*[262] in the Hong Kong Court of Final Appeal. There, the hotel and policyholder was insured by the insurer under business interruption insurance from July 2002 to July 2003. In question was clause 14.5 of the policy:

> This Policy is extended to insure actual loss sustained by the Insured, resulting from a Reduction in Revenue and increase in Cost of Working as a result of …, infectious or contagious disease, … all occurring on the Premises of the Insured or of notifiable human infectious or contagious disease occurring within 25 miles of the Premises.

It was 'notifiable human infectious or contagious disease' that was at issue. Meanwhile, it was undisputed that the 25-mile condition would be satisfied once such a disease occurred anywhere in Hong Kong. The infectious or contagious disease was the deadly Serious Acute Respiratory Syndrome (SARS), which spread to Hong Kong in February 2003 from the neighbouring Guangdong Province in

[256] *Charles R Davidson & Co v M'Robb* [1918] AC 304 (HL), 314; note also (per Lord Finlay) that 'The word "employment" must mean the same thing when in apposition with "in the course of" as it means when in apposition with "out of"'.

[257] *BAI (Run-Off) Ltd v Durham* [2012] UKSC 14 [50].

[258] *Fairchild v Glenhaven Funeral Services Ltd* [2002] UKHL 22.

[259] *Barker v Corus UK Ltd* [2006] UKHL 20.

[260] *BAI (Run-Off) Ltd v Durham* [2012] UKSC 14 [88].

[261] This keen observation was kindly suggested by Professor Malcolm Clarke when he commented on this chapter.

[262] *New World Harbourview Hotel Co Ltd v ACE Insurance Ltd* (2012) 15 HKCFAR 120.

mainland China. The hospitality industry as a whole inevitably suffered loss from this saga. The hotel claimed indemnity for losses, the earliest dating from 9 March 2003. The insurer rejected the claim on the ground that losses occurring before 27 March was not as a result of a 'notifiable' human infectious disease, because the word 'notifiable' connoted a mandatory obligation under law to notify, whereas the Hong Kong executive government did not make it mandatory to notify the authority of the disease until 27 March.

The Court of Final Appeal and the lower courts did consider the relevant factual context in terms of the SARS saga in Hong Kong. On 11 February 2003m the World Health Organisation (WHO) announced that it had received reports from Chinese authorities of an epidemic of acute respiratory syndrome, with 300 cases and five deaths in Guangdong Province neighbouring Hong Kong. On 12 February, the Hong Kong Hospital Authority set out procedures for requesting public hospitals to notify the Department of Health of any case of severe community-acquired pneumonia. On 13 February the same request for notification was made to private hospitals. On 22 February, a Mr Dr Liu, who had arrived in Hong Kong the previous day from the neighboring Guangdong Province and had recently treated SARS patients in that area, was admitted to hospital in Hong Kong. He died in the hospital on 4 March. He was later confirmed as the first SARS patient in Hong Kong, and was the source of the disease's spread into Hong Kong. On 12 March, the WHO issued a global alert notice about cases of the endemic disease in Hong Kong, in Guangdong Province in mainland China and in Vietnam. On 15 March, the WHO issued an emergency travel advisory statement, identifying the disease as SARS for the first time. On 22 March, scientists discovered the cause of SARS. On 27 March, the Hong Kong government added SARS to the list of infectious diseases under the First Schedule to the Quarantine and Prevention of Diseases Ordinance (QPDO, repealed in July 2008), making it mandatory for SARS cases to be notified to the Hong Kong government.

In interpreting the wording 'notifiable', the Court referred first to dictionary meanings. Generally, one prong of the word's meaning connotes that a disease is notifiable it if must or shall be notified to the authorities.[263] The other connotes that a disease is notifiable if it 'warrants (or legally requires)'[264] notification to the authorities, appearing 'to contemplate that there may be some cases where the seriousness of a disease is enough to make it notifiable, even though there is no mandatory obligation to do so'.[265] This was what the policyholder maintained to be the meaning of 'notifiable', but it was not accepted in the courts. In rejecting the policyholder's submission, the Court of Final Appeal further consulted medical dictionaries and found that a disease was notifiable if it would be required by law to be notified to an authority. It also considered the context of clause 14.5, and

[263] Ibid [36], citing The Cambridge Advanced Learner's Dictionary and The Oxford English Dictionary (per Chief Justice Ma).

[264] Ibid [37], citing The Oxford English Dictionary Online and The Shorter Oxford Dictionary (per Chief Justice Ma).

[265] Ibid (per Chief Justice Ma).

found it natural, in connection with the first part of the clause, to have a stringent interpretation of 'notifiable' in the second part. In addition, the QPDO was considered relevant in the context of interpretation.

Nevertheless, it was not unreasonable for the policyholder to have expectations of SARS coverage, even though it was a new risk. Insurers might contend that they would not cover new risks devoid of actuarial history and experience, but it could not be so in this case. That is because, after all, clause 4.15 in its first half had meant to provide coverage for losses resulting from *any* (unqualified in the clause) 'infectious or contagious disease', inter alia, 'all occurring on the Premises of the Insured'. Supposing an incidence of SARS occurred on the policyholder's premises, it would be within the policy, and the insurers would be obliged to provide coverage and indemnity for the policyholder, as long as all other insurance payment conditions could be met, regardless of the lack of actuarial history and experience with SARS.

Given that, the Court's approach perhaps ought to be re-thought. First, the resort to medical dictionaries might be too technical. For a business interruption insurance, where diseases are only one among many other kinds of risks, it might be doubted that the understanding of 'notifiable' in relation to diseases by commercial persons and by the medical community would coincide or overlap. Although an overlapping understanding might be necessary in strongly medically-relevant health and/or accident insurance, the instant case involved a business insurance concerning the hospitality and hotelier industry. Secondly, although it was indeed necessary to consider the first part of clause 14.5 as a context for the wording 'notifiable' in the second part thereof, and hence to find that the second part should be more stringent concerning risks occurring within 25 miles of the premises, in contrast to unqualified risks in the first part, interpreting 'notifiable' as warranting notification would also serve a similar purpose. In other words, the second part of clause 14.5 could justifiably be rendered more stringent, but it did not have to be rendered *so* stringent by a narrow interpretation that the policyholder's reasonable expectations of coverage of SARS would be frustrated. Thirdly, whilst having the QPDO as a context was necessary, the Court was nevertheless formalistic in approaching the QPDO because the judges focused narrowly on texts without due regard to the legislative intention and the factual context in which Hong Kong responded to SARS. Indeed, a disease did not become 'notifiable' under the QPDO unless it was added to the list in the First Schedule, which required the disease to be reported or notified to the Director of Health. The QPDO and its subsidiary legislation

> provide a legislative framework for the prevention of communicable diseases of public health importance. Regulation 4 of the Regulations requires medical practitioners to notify the Director if they have reason to suspect the existence of any of the infectious diseases specified in the First Schedule to the Ordinance in a form as prescribed in the Schedule to the Regulations.[266]

[266] HKSAR Health, Welfare and Food Bureau: Legislative Council Brief: Quarantine and Prevention of Disease Ordinance (Chapter 141) Quarantine and Prevention of Disease Ordinance (Amendment

The QPDO 'empowers the Director of Health to amend the First Schedule to the Ordinance and any form prescribed under section 8 of the Ordinance'.[267] Therefore the purpose, particularly of notification of infectious disease, is, first, to ensure that the Director of Health has knowledge of the severity of the infectiousness of the disease concerned. Secondly, it is also for ensuring that the Department of Health and its Director of Health can use such knowledge and data for effective 'surveillance, control and prevention of outbreak of infectious diseases'.[268] These purposes can be referred to for defining whether a disease is notifiable, but it is not to be taken as constitutive or determinative of the identifiable attribute of the disease concerned. For an effective response to infectious diseases, it is perhaps better to recognise or to *regard or deem* the disease concerned as notifiable. This, however, is fact-specific, hinging on the context. In the scenario of SARS in Hong Kong, it seems that SARS could be deemed to have become 'identifiable' from 12 February 2002, because on that day the Hospital Authority, which routinely reported to the Department of Health, set out procedures for requesting notification by public hospitals to the Department of Health of any case of severe community-acquired pneumonia (CAP, which was later to be termed by the WHO by description as SARS), and the same request was sent to private hospitals on 13 February. This would ensure that the Department of Health and its Director would have knowledge of the infectious condition, and undoubtedly was part of their early efforts regarding surveillance, control and the prevention thereof. Given that, it is excessively formalistic and legalistic to hinge notification, or the meaning of 'notifiable', on SARS being listed in First Schedule to the QPDO. Doing so runs counter to the very purpose of business interruption insurance, which is to indemnify business policyholders for losses that arise from the occurrence of unexpected events, including contagious diseases, old or new.[269]

of First Schedule) Order 2003, Prevention of the Spread of Infectious Diseases Regulations (Amendment Of Form) Order 2003 (File Reference: HWF/H/21/4 Pt 3(96)) [2].

[267] KSAR Health and Welfare Bureau: Legislative Council Brief: Quarantine and Prevention of Disease Ordinance (Chapter 141) Quarantine and Prevention of Disease Ordinance (Amendment of First Schedule) Order 1998, Prevention of the Spread of Infectious Diseases Regulations (Amendment of Form) Order 1998 (File Reference: HWB/M/21/4 Pt 2) [2].

[268] HKSAR Health, Welfare and Food Bureau, above n 267, [2].

[269] An outbreak of the Middle East Respiratory Syndrome (MERS) in South Korea was reported in late May 2015. At the time of writing early drafts of this chapter on 9 June 2015, seven people infected with the MERS had died in South Korea and 2,500 people remain in quarantine. In a prepared speech to be given at a luncheon, the South Korean Finance Minister, Choi Kyung-hwan, said he was 'concerned over the negative influence the recent MERS outbreak could have on the local economy, including private consumption and investment sentiment'. See www.reuters.com/article/health-mers-southkorea-economy-idUSL3N0YU1CH20150608.

How insurers in South Korea will respond to business interruption insurance claims in relation to policyholders' losses arising from the MERS outbreak is particularly noteworthy. According to WHO, by 1 July 2015, in South Korea, a total of 182 MERS cases, including 33 deaths, were reported., Globally, from September 2012 to 17 May 2016, 27 countries have reported cases of MERS-CoV, and WHO has been notified of 1,733 laboratory-confirmed cases of infection with MERS, including 628 MERS-related deaths. (Source at www.who.int/mediacentre/news/mers/briefing-notes/update-1-july-2015/en/ and www.who.int/emergencies/mers-cov/en/.) Although this is perhaps a relatively mild example, it should not be taken lightly, and certainly it is relevant to insurance.

E. The Lingering General Concern

In spite of the arguments set out above, there might still be lingering concern and doubts about the reasonable expectations approach in commercial/business contract, including business insurance contract. In this regard, however, the UNIDROIT Principles of International Commercial Contracts 2010 ('the UNIDROIT Principles 2010') are enlightening for doubters. They embrace the reasonable expectations approach in connection with two aspects of paramount importance. One aspect is illegality of contract. Under Article 3.3.1(2), where a contract infringes a mandatory rule that does not expressly prescribe the effects of such an infringement, the parties have the right to exercise such remedies under the contract as are reasonable in the circumstances; and in determining what is reasonable, regard is to be had in particular, inter alia, to the reasonable expectations of the parties.[270] The other aspect, which is more pertinent to the discussion here, is interpretation of standard terms in contracts. Under the UNIDROIT Principles 2010, a contract shall be interpreted according to the common intention of the parties. Nevertheless, if such an intention cannot be established, the contract 'shall be interpreted according to the meaning that reasonable persons of the same kind as the parties would give to it in the same circumstances'.[271] For the interpretation of standard terms, it is noted in particular:

> Indeed, given their special nature and purpose, standard terms should be interpreted primarily in accordance with the reasonable expectations of their average users irrespective of the actual understanding which either of the parties to the contract concerned, or the reasonable persons of the same kind as the parties, might have had.[272]

Although the UNIDROIT Principles 2010 could be applicable to international business insurance only if the parties choose them as the applicable law, the point is that it is not taboo to give parties' reasonable expectations a role in commercial/ business or non-consumer contract law, nor should it be taboo in business insurance. In the context of insurance, however, the real questions are: What are the reasonable expectations of the insurer and of the policyholder? And whose reasonable expectations should prevail? Answers have been given to these questions in section III.D. above.

IV. Conclusion

It is understandable that English insurance law treats PREC differently in consumer insurance than it does in business insurance. After all, as a matter of legal

[270] UNIDROIT Principles of International Commercial Contracts 2010, Art 3.3.1(3)(g).
[271] UNIDROIT Principles 2010, Art 4.1(2).
[272] UNIDROIT Principles 2010, Art 4.1, Comment 4.

policy and as the result of 'consumer-welfarist'[273] interventionism, contract law has taken a pro-consumer approach. Unsurprisingly, the pro-consumer approach tilts toward consumer policyholders. That is also the very purpose of the American insurance law principle of PREC, a principle applied primarily to consumer insurance. Although English insurance law has not really embraced PREC, it has, as Malcolm Clarke observed, used operative contract law doctrines that turn out to have effects similar to that of PREC in the US. *Cook v Financial Insurance Co Ltd*[274] could have been accepted as a starting point for a principle of PREC in English consumer insurance law. However, it has been eclipsed by the pervasive use of alternative dispute resolution at the FOS, which has in itself been obliged under the FSMA 2000 to take a 'fair and reasonable' approach that is essentially contextualist and protective of consumer policyholders' interests. It must be stressed that the rarity of consumer insurance disputes that go through court proceedings does not mean that PREC has no part in English consumer insurance law. Instead, where an appropriate insurance dispute next happens to arise before the courts, they should perhaps look back at *Cook v Financial Insurance Co Ltd*[275] and apply PREC without hesitation.

In contrast, commercial contract law has remained 'market-individualist'[276] for both contractual parties, which are business entities. This is not normative, however. As Catherine Mitchell has effectively argued, commercial contracts are usually relational, and commercial expectations should have more of a role in commercial law because they are more consistent with the nature and the purpose of the commercial relationships underlying the commercial contract.

In the meantime, insurance can be also viewed as relational, and this is particularly so as regards business insurance, which usually backs some commercial relationships or undertakings. In resolving business insurance coverage disputes, courts should likewise take the business policyholder's reasonable expectations of coverage more into consideration, with reference to the context of the particular insurance and the business purpose of the line of insurance concerned. Such a relational approach to PREC is consistent with the contextualist principle, famously restated by Lord Hoffmann,[277] for interpretation of commercial contracts, and also with the homogeneous purposive approach to construction of contract terms. Also noticeable is the closeness to and usefulness of a contextualist interpretation of contract to PREC. Such closeness and usefulness can be found for the law of consumer insurance, as reiterated above, and more markedly for business insurance too, thanks to Lord Hoffmann's restatement of the principles of interpretation of contract.

The implication following from all the above is that for English insurance law to take policyholder's reasonable expectations seriously, there is perhaps

[273] J Adams and R Brownsword, 'The Ideologies of Contract' (1987) 7 *LS* 205, 206.
[274] *Cook v Financial Insurance Co Ltd* [1998] 1 WLR 1765 (HL), [1998] UKHL 42.
[275] Ibid.
[276] Adams and Brownsword, above n 273, 206.
[277] *Investors Compensation Scheme Ltd v West Bromwich Building Society* [1997] CLC 1243 (HL), 1257–58.

no indispensable need to follow, or to be restricted by, the American PREC 'doctrine', which has been fraught with controversy. There is certainly no need to follow it in an 'either-or' manner, ie to choose just one of the several different versions of the American 'doctrine'. With its 'fair and reasonable' approach, the FOS will continue to resolve most consumer insurance disputes over coverage in the UK. Where one such dispute results in litigation, for the purpose of PREC, the House of Lords case *Cook v Financial Insurance Co Ltd*[278] is likely to suffice. For business insurance, a contextual approach to interpretation of the insurance contract, with a view to the reasonable expectations of the *parties*, has been adopted in *Royal and Sun Alliance Insurance Plc v Dornoch Ltd*[279] in a generic manner without looking specifically to PREC. However, this generic manner may be a good starting point for moving towards PREC in business insurance, because once consideration is given to the reasonable expectations of the parties to insurance contracts, the balance should usually tilt in favour of the *policyholder's* reasonable expectations of coverage rather than the insurer's expectations of non-liability. This is essentially because insurance can be viewed as relational, as a result of which an insurer has a variety of mechanisms—such as risk-spreading based on risk classification, subrogation, proportionate payment and insurance—to make sure that it is usually able to remain solvent in relation to particular risk pools to which the insurance contract in question is related. Regarding the contextual approach in insurance law, particularly more noteworthy is that as recently as May 2015 in the UK Supreme Court, Lord Sumption stated that PREC could be considered 'as background to the construction of the policy'.[280] This effectively lends force to and confirms the contextual approach to resolving insurance disputes over PREC.

[278] *Cook v Financial Insurance Co Ltd* [1998] 1 WLR 1765 (HL), [1998] UKHL 42.

[279] *Royal and Sun Alliance Insurance Plc v Dornoch Ltd* [2004] EWHC 803 (QBD Comm), [2005] EWCA Civ 238.

[280] *Zurich Insurance Plc UK Branch v International Energy Group Ltd* [2015] 1 Lloyd's Rep IR 598, 642 [164]; [2015] UKSC 33 [164].

7

Policyholder's Reasonable Expectations of Bonuses in With-Profits Life Insurance

This chapter discusses the policyholder's reasonable expectations of bonuses (PREB), which was introduced very briefly in Chapter 1 as one of the two prongs of the meaning of 'policyholder's reasonable expectations'. It will be shown in this chapter that, specific to investment-type life insurance, PREB has a particular actuary-related meaning that has been incorporated into insurance regulation. A knowledge gap has persisted between the actuarial profession (hence also the life insurance industry) and insurance lawyers, except for the select few who represented or sat in the celebrated case *Equitable Life Assurance Society v Hyman*[1] ('*Equitable Life*'), a huge investment-type insurance dispute that was finally resolved in the House of Lords. Still there is hardly any in-depth *insurance law* literature regarding PREB.[2] As a result, PREB is liable to be confused with the better-known PREC, and in practice it does seem that there has been such confusion.[3] A discussion of PREB will help to clarify and highlight its unique meaning, and its practical implications for policyholders in with-profits or investment-type life insurance.

The discussion starts with revisiting *Equitable Life*. In contemporary English law, perhaps few civil lawsuits have had such UK-wide lasting financial consequences as *Equitable Life* has had not only for *both* parties, but also for the UK Government. Having lost the case in the House of Lords in 2000, Equitable Life Assurance Society, the oldest mutual life insurer in the world and the pioneer of modern life insurance, was faced with enormous payment obligations to hundreds of thousands of its policyholders. Consequently, struggling to stay solvent, it had to close its new businesses, and in the end it only just managed to survive a near

[1] *Equitable Life Assurance Society v Hyman* [2000] 3 All ER 961, [2000] UKHL 39, [2002] 1 AC 408.

[2] But see J Smethurst et al, 'Conduct of business Regulation: a survey of the UK regime and a comparison with the US, German and Hong Kong approach' in J Burling and K Lazarus (eds), *Research Handbook on International Insurance Law and Regulation* (London, Edward Elgar, 2012) 355, 378–79. The two pages briefly describe with-profits insurance regulation under the FCA Handbook COBS 20.2 and 20.3.

[3] M Clarke, *The Law of Insurance Contracts*, 6th edn (London, Informa, 2009) 454.

collapse. Meanwhile, more than one million policyholders like Mr Hyman suffered large cuts to the value of their prospective and/or current pensions. A number of investigations were launched and reports were published.[4] The Government pledged in January 2009 to compensate the Society's entitled policyholders for the regulatory failure. One year later, the Equitable Life (Payments) Act 2010 was enacted, 'to provide finance for payments in cases where persons have been adversely affected by maladministration in the regulation'.[5] 'Set up by HM Government to make fair and transparent payments'[6] to eligible policyholders, by 30 September 2015 the Scheme had issued payments of nearly £1.08 billion to 915,453 policyholders. This meant that the Scheme had paid 88 per cent of eligible policyholders, and 92.9 per cent of the money due.[7] Despite the Scheme's having made major efforts to trace non-claiming eligible policyholders, however, there remained approximately 125,000 policyholders whom the Scheme had been unable to pay by that time.[8] As the Chancellor announced in the Summer Budget on 8 July 2015, on the last day of the year the Scheme was to be closed to new claims.

In this chapter, it is revealed that PREB has been an actuarial principle with its origins in and recognition by the British actuarial profession, and also with incorporation into insurance regulation in the UK. These findings have huge practical implications for with-profits life policies. Admittedly, the *Equitable Life* saga has brought with-profits insurance products into disrepute and decline in the UK. However, in Asia—for example in Hong Kong,[9] Singapore[10] and China[11]—the market for with-profits insurance (also known as 'participating insurance' or 'par business') still remains big, and the demand for it remains strong (though less so in India).[12] Another implication is that, although all the previous chapters of this book have built up to the argument that English insurance law should take PREC more seriously, *Equitable Life* should not be taken as an authority for that purpose—that is because it was PREB, rather than PREC, that was at issue in *Equitable Life*. Instead, as has been shown in Chapters 3 to 6, the rationale and the authorities for protecting PREC are sought from the broader perspective of general contract law.

[4] The Equitable Life Assurance Society: Joint Opinion of Ian Glick QC and Richard Snowden for the Financial Services Authority (May 2001); Report of the Corley Committee of Inquiry Regarding the Equitable Life Assurance Society (Sept 2001); Report of the Financial Services Authority on the Review of the Regulation of the Equitable Life Assurance Society (Oct 2001); Lord Penrose, Report of the Equitable Life Inquiry (March 2004); European Parliament, Report on the crisis of the Equitable Life Assurance Society (May 2007); Parliamentary and Health Service Ombudsman, Equitable Life: A decade of Regulatory Failure (July 2008); House of Commons Public Relations Select Committee, Justice delayed: The Ombudsman's Report on Equitable Life (Dec 2008); The Office of Sir John Chadwick, Advice to Government in relation to the proposed Equitable Life payment scheme (July 2010).

[5] Equitable Life (Payments) Act 2010, the long title.

[6] See www.gov.uk/equitable-life-payment-scheme.

[7] HM Treasury, Equitable Life Payment Scheme: November 2015 Progress Report.

[8] Ibid.

[9] WY Lee and A Bryant, *Participating Business in Asia* (Singapore, Milliman, 2014) [3.19].

[10] Ibid [4.26].

[11] Ibid [6.12].

[12] Ibid [5.26].

I. Discovering Policyholder's Reasonable Expectations of Bonuses: Revisiting *Equitable Life*

A. Salient Facts and Issues

Equitable Life was a class action. Mr Hyman was a policyholder and a representative of the interests of approximately 90,000 policyholders who held about 116,000 pre-1988 policies with the Equitable Life Assurance Society ('the Society'). These policies were issued by the Society with provision for guaranteed annuity rates (GARs).[13] Hence they were what had been known as 'with-profits (life) policies'. In those pre-1988 years, the current annuity rates (CAR) were high in the market, and GARs were fixed at a level well below CARs. The policies were marketed on the footing that the GAR would provide a minimum level of bonuses and that the annuity obtained by the policyholder would not fall below that minimum level. There was no special charge for including GAR provisions in the policies. Hyman's policies were issued between 1972 and 1983 with GAR provisions. The policies provided for two options for the policyholder to take benefits. The first option was to take an annuity from an insurer other than the Society. The second option was to take an annuity from the Society at its CAR.

However, from October 1993, CAR in the market fell below GAR, or in other words, contrary to the Society's practice of fixing GAR well below CAR, GAR rose above CAR. This was still the case when the litigation started in 1999, by which time the Society had about 300,000 with-profit policies without GAR provisions. Given the fluctuation of CAR vis-à-vis GAR, upon maturity of the policies concerned the Society allocated final bonuses to GAR policyholders but at a rate lower than that for non-GAR policyholders who had opted to take an annuity from the Society at its CAR. Policyholders with GARs were not happy with this, hence the dispute. The Society filed the lawsuit, seeking a court declaration of whether it was entitled to allocate the bonuses in that manner. The High Court held that under Article 65 of the Society's articles of association, it had the discretion to do that. The Court of Appeal found for Hyman and the policyholders concerned. So the Society appealed to the House of Lords, which affirmed the decision of the Court of Appeal 'to give effect to the reasonable expectations of the parties'[14]

[13] GAR is calculated on the combined value of the minimum level of benefits specified in the policy plus the annual bonuses (aka 'reversionary bonuses') and whatever the appropriate final bonus is (aka 'terminal bonus'), if any. The annual bonus is an amount added to the sum assured of a with-profits policy and must be declared out of the surplus profits of the insurance company; once declared, the value of the bonus is guaranteed. Final bonus is a bonus paid to policyholders in the year in which their policy matures; it is a means by which insurance companies seek to ensure that each with-profits policyholder receives a due share of the investment returns achieved by the company. See *Equitable Life Assurance Society v Hyman* [2002] 1 AC 408, 411–12 [2] and [3] (per Lord Woolf MR).

[14] *Equitable Life Assurance Society v Hyman* [2002] 1 AC 408, 460G–H.

on the ground that the insurer's discretion should not frustrate the policyholder's reasonable expectations. As has been briefly described above, this final decision has had overwhelming consequences.

To anyone with some general knowledge of American insurance law, it appears that the House of Lords indeed had recourse to what *seems* like the American insurance law 'doctrine' of reasonable expectations. After all, in delivering the majority opinion, which implied a term that would preclude the Society from exercising its discretion in the way it had been, Lord Steyn stressed that 'The implication is essential to give effect to the reasonable expectations of the parties.'[15] Lord Cooke, concurring, also briefly referred to policyholders' reasonable expectations elsewhere[16] in the majority opinion.

It was Article 65(3) of the Society's articles of association into which Lord Steyn implied a term to honour the policyholder's reasonable expectations of bonuses under the with-profits life policies. Article 65(3) read:

> **Art. 65(3).** The amount of any *bonus* which may be declared or paid pursuant to paragraph (1) or paragraph (2)[17] of this regulation and the amount (if any) to which any participating policyholder may become entitled under any mode of payment or application of any such bonus, shall be matters *within the absolute discretion of the directors*, whose decision thereon shall be final and conclusive. (emphasis added)

Hyman contended that the Society's approach to allocating bonuses was both a breach of contract and an improper exercise of its discretionary power. In the House of Lords the dispute prima facie was summarised by Lord Steyn as:

1. whether, on the construction of the Society's GAR policies, the Society breached the insurance policy or contract in allotting different amounts of bonuses;
2. whether the directors of the Society in allotting the bonuses had improperly exercised the discretion vested in them under Article 65 of its articles of association.[18]

[15] Ibid 460H.

[16] Ibid 460G (per Lord Steyn), 461H–462A (per Lord Cooke).

[17] Under Art 65: '(**1**) The directors shall, at such intervals as they may deem expedient, but at least once in every three years, cause an investigation to be made into the financial condition of the Society, including a valuation of its assets and liabilities, by the actuary. Provided that in the valuation of the assets the values thereof be not estimated beyond the market prices (if any) of the same, unless for reasons to be set out in the directors' report to the members upon the results of the valuation. After making such provision as they may think sufficient for such liabilities, and any special or other reserve they may think fit, the directors shall, at a special board meeting, declare what amount of the surplus (if any) shown by such valuation may, in their opinion, be divided by way of bonus, and they shall apportion the amount of such declared surplus by way of bonus among the holders of the participating policies on such principles, and by such methods, as they may from time to time determine. The directors may pay or apply the bonus so apportioned to each participating policyholder, either by way of reversionary bonus (that is to say, by way of addition to the sum assured when it shall become a claim), cash payment, reduction of premium for the whole of life or any less period, or in any other way they and any participating policyholder may agree. (**2**) The directors (after obtaining such report or reports from the actuary as they may in their discretion consider to be necessary or desirable in the circumstances) may, in cases where participating policies become claims in the interval between two valuations, pay such interim or additional or special bonuses as they shall think fit.'

[18] *Equitable Life Assurance Society v Hyman* [2002] 1 AC 408, 457A–C (Lord Steyn).

However, because with-profits policyholders were also members of the mutual Society, their policies had to be be read in conjunction with the powers and decisions of the directors in respect of the declaration and payment of final bonuses. Therefore, 'it follows that there are not two separate principal issues but only one';[19] 'the real issue is, namely whether the Society is entitled to declare a differential final bonus because the CAR have fallen below the GAR'.[20]

B. Policyholder's Reasonable Expectations of Bonuses in the House of Lords

In resolving the issue, Lord Steyn considered whether it was necessary to imply into Article 65 of the articles of association a term that would preclude the Society from exercising its discretion in the way it had been. In this regard Lord Steyn stated:

> [Final bonuses] are a significant part of the consideration for the premiums paid. And the directors' discretions as to the amount and distribution *of* bonuses are conferred for the benefit of policyholders. In this context the self-evident commercial object of the inclusion of guaranteed rates in the policy is to protect the policyholder against a fall in market annuity rates by ensuring that if the fall occurs he will be better off than he would have been with market rates. The choice is given to the GAR policyholders and not to the Society. It cannot be seriously doubted that the provision for guaranteed annuity rates was a good selling point in the marketing by the Society of the GAR policies. It is also obvious that it would have been a significant attraction for purchasers of GAR policies. The Society points out that no special charge was made for the inclusion in the policy of GAR provisions. So be it. This factor *does not alter the reasonable expectations of the parties.* The supposition of the parties must be presumed to have been that the directors would not exercise their discretion in conflict with contractual rights. These are the circumstances in which the directors of the Society resolved upon a differential policy which was designed to deprive the relevant guarantees of any substantial value. In my judgment an implication precluding the use of the directors' discretion in this way is strictly necessary. *The implication is essential to give effect to the reasonable expectations of the parties.*[21] (emphasis added)

Similarly, Lord Cooke opined:

> Although discretionary and uncertain, *bonuses are a very significant part of the benefits which policyholders expect*. The attractions of a GAR policy would be much diminished if it were explained that adverse discrimination in bonuses might be involved. A reasonable reader in the shoes of the policyholder would not understand this unless it had been clearly specified in the policy. In my opinion the general discretion in article 65(1) is inadequate to justify such an adjustment of policy benefits.[22] (emphasis added)

19 Ibid 458F (Lord Steyn).
20 Ibid 458A (Lord Steyn).
21 Ibid 460G–H.
22 Ibid 461H–462A.

Given that, it was held that the Society and its directors, though not in breach of the many insurance contracts with policyholders, had exercised the discretion improperly and therefore had frustrated the policyholders' reasonable expectations of bonuses or profits, and that the Society must pay these bonuses to GAR policyholders.

However, the 'reasonable expectations' of policyholders as expressly referred to in *Equitable Life* is not the same as the usual and conventional meaning, ie policyholder's reasonable expectations of coverage (PREC), which has been well known to insurance lawyers. It must also be noted that in the previous two instances of *Equitable Life*, the courts employed 'policyholders' reasonable expectations' as a distinctive terminology in connection with the actuarial profession. This use and analysis of the terminology was not overturned but sustained, though much less intensively, in the House of Lords. Therefore, to fully understand 'policyholders' reasonable expectations', it is necessary to revisit the decisions in the High Court and in the Court of Appeal.

C. Policyholder's Reasonable Expectations of Bonuses in the Lower Courts

At trial, Sir Richard Scott V-C in the Chancery Division found that the representations made by the Society to GAR policyholders regarding the final bonuses were 'relevant to policyholders' reasonable expectations (PRE)',[23] and that PRE was a matter that he must take into account in considering the manner in which the directors of the Society exercised their discretionary powers in respect of final bonuses. Sir Richard further found:

> PRE has been the subject of debate in the actuarial profession but has no statutory definition. The expression was first used in a statutory context in the Insurance Companies Amendment Act 1973 which gave powers to the Secretary of State to intervene in the affairs of an assurance company on various grounds. One ground was that the company might be unable to meet its liabilities or 'the reasonable expectations of policyholders …' (See sections 12 and 21 of the 1973 Act.) The statutory successors to these provisions are section 37 and 45 of the Insurance Companies Act 1982. These provisions recognise that policyholders may have a reasonable expectation of benefits over and above their contractually guaranteed benefits.[24]

In addition, a working report of the actuarial profession was quoted by the Vice-Chancellor as stating that 'in the normal day-to-day actuarial management of a life policy, PRE is synonymous with equity and the almost universal method for measuring it is asset share calculation'.[25] Following from the knowledge about PRE

[23] *Equitable Life Assurance Society v Hyman* [1999] PLR 297 [83].
[24] Ibid [84]–[86].
[25] Ibid [87]. See also M Shelley, M Arnold and P Needleman, 'A Review of Policyholders' Reasonable Expectations' (2002) 8 *British Actuarial Journal* 705, 710.

and in connection with the instant case, the Vice-Chancellor delicately applied the conception of PRE to the case and ruled for the insurer. Specifically, in relation to PRE and the Society's discretion, the trial judge's opinions can be summarised as follows:

1. The Society's communications to GAR policyholders and the Society's practice regarding final bonuses *did* produce in them a reasonable expectation that the final bonus declared for all policyholders would be allocated to them.
2. But when it came specifically to policyholders who had opted to take CAR annuities, the communications and previous practices of the Society could *not* be believed to have provided the basis for any reasonable expectation that such policyholders would be entitled to CAR annuities equal to GAR annuities.
3. Policyholders could not have reasonable expectations that the same rate of final bonuses would be applied to all policyholders, because a variable final bonus had for some time been used to cater for variations in premium investment profits.[26]
4. A reasonable expectation could not become a contractual right, because this was only one of the factors to be considered by the Directors, and its effective weight in the balance would also depend on those other factors, and the balance was always for the Directors, not for courts, to strike.[27] On the Society's specific business practices, the Vice-Chancellor found that he was 'not satisfied that the Society failed, when exercising its discretion regarding final bonus over the period since 1994, to take into account PRE'.[28]

The trial analysis of PRE in the instant case was most delicate, and it was a correct and necessary start. Therefore it is not surprising that, although the trial judgment was overturned, both the Court of Appeal and subsequently the House of Lords did not overrule the trial judge's reasoning on the first three points set out above; the point of departure was only as to the fourth. On the first and the third points the trial judge found for PRE generally in the case, but on the second point he found against it on a narrower finding of facts. On the fourth point the trial judge found that PRE was *not contractually* binding on the Society, and therefore the Society could exercise its discretion. In the end, he found that the Society, in exercising its discretion, had taken PRE into consideration, and therefore the Society's discretion was proper.

Although the Court of Appeal reversed the Chancery Division's decision, Sir Richard Scott's reference to PRE was not disregarded as irrelevant or incorrect.

[26] *Equitable Life Assurance Society v Hyman* [1999] PLR 297 [102].
[27] Ibid [103].
[28] Ibid [105].

Instead, in closer connection to the case in hand, Lord Woolf MR stated in the Court of Appeal:

> The declarations of final bonus which are in issue in this case therefore involved an impermissible exercise of discretion. It was an exercise of discretion reducing *the policyholder's reasonable expectation that he would receive his asset share irrespective of how he exercised his rights under the policy*. The purposes for which the powers contained in article 65 are conferred on the Society do not include treating a policyholder differently depending on the manner in which he seeks to exercise his rights under the policy which he has been granted by the Society in return for his premium.[29]

In the foregoing statement, which is consistent with what the Vice-Chancellor found in the High Court, Lord Woolf MR attached the 'asset share' measurement to the policyholder's reasonable expectations of bonuses. This is a technique widely used in the British actuarial profession.[30] Similarly, Lord Steyn in the House of Lords also confirmed the relevance of 'asset share':

> The Society's bonus philosophy … is to deliver, as far as possible, to each with-profits policyholder his asset share. 'Asset share' is an actuarial concept widely used amongst life offices. It is the share of the with-profits fund notionally attributable to a particular policy and represents the premiums (net of initial charges) paid under such policy together with the smoothed investment return generated by the Society on such premiums over the period of time for which they have been invested with the Society.[31]

From the consistent relevance of the concept of PRE at all three instances, one can see clearly that PRE, as applied in *Equitable Life* in the House of Lords, did not refer to the policyholder's reasonable expectations of coverage (PREC) of particular risks. Instead it meant the policyholder'sreasonable expectation of bonuses (PREB), which might be allocated by the insurer to with-profits policyholders in life insurance.

II. Policyholder's Reasonable Expectations of Bonuses in the Actuarial Profession

A. The Origin of the Concept in the Actuarial Profession

It has seldom been publicly noted in the legal profession that it was PREB, a technical and actuarial concept, that was relevant in *Equitable Life*. Given this, it is necessary and helpful to examine the meaning and the brief history of PREB.

[29] *Equitable Life Assurance Society v Hyman* [2002] 1 AC 408, 425 [54].

[30] PD Needleman and PA Toff, 'Asset Shares and Their Use in the Management of With-profits Fund' (1995) 1 *British Actuarial Journal* 603, 606 [2.1.1].

[31] *Equitable Life Assurance Society v Hyman* [2002] 1 AC 408, 453G.

For the actuarial profession in the UK, PREB is known simply as 'the PRE principle'. It originated in the 1960s from the profession's consideration of the solvency standard of life insurers. The expression 'policyholders' reasonable expectations' was first used by Ronald Skerman in his paper 'A Solvency Standard for Life Assurance Business',[32] published in 1966. In that paper, Skerman identified three problems in valuing a life insurer's liabilities, the third of which was:

> *Participation in profits.* Holders of with-profit policies have taken them out in the expectation that they will benefit from a share of profits from time to time. Although an office is not under a contractual obligation which can be quantified in relation to the benefits which its policyholders will derive from future profits, it would be unsatisfactory not to take some account of the *policyholders' reasonable expectations* when determining the value of the liabilities.[33] (emphasis added)

Before discussing problems associated with liability valuation, Skerman set out certain fundamentals of life insurance business:

> The essence of the financial operations of a life office is that it receives premiums, interest and other items of income and undertakes liabilities to pay claims, expenses and other items of outgo. There is no means of ensuring with absolute certainty that it will be able to meet its liabilities; it is inevitably vulnerable to extremely adverse mortality experience and financial conditions. All that can be hoped for is a solvency standard which will ensure that it has every reasonable prospect of fulfilling its obligations.[34]

Skerman thought that, in selecting the method to be used for determining the value of liabilities, the valuing actuary should have regard to the reasonable expectations as to policyholders' participation in future bonuses or profits. With that notion in his mind, during subsequent years in his capacity as an officer of the Life Offices Association and of the British Insurers Association, Skerman was involved in the discussions in 1972 with government officials about the proposed changes in legislation on insurance regulation. Much of the departmental discussion focused on the actuarial or bonuses aspect of PRE, ie PREB.

The actuary-related PRE principle, ie PREB, mainly concerns with-profits life policies. Under with-profit policies, 'policyholders pay premiums greater, and sometimes materially greater, than are required to provide the sums assured on death or maturity'.[35] The insurer uses the premium collected to make investment, and part of the profits derived from the premium investment will be payable to eligible policyholders. Two types of bonuses can be yielded under with-profit policies. One is 'guaranteed bonus', the amount of which is pre-set in the policies and, due to its contractual nature, can seldom be varied. The other, and the more significant part of the bonuses provided under with-profits policies, is the profit

[32] R Skerman, 'A Solvency Standard for Life Assurance Business' (1966) 92 *Journal of the Institute of Actuaries* 74.

[33] Ibid 77.

[34] Ibid 76.

[35] Ibid 78.

made by the insurer's investment of the long-term premium; it hinges on the insurer's investment performance, and therefore is at the discretion of the insurer. It is understood in the British actuarial profession that 'PRE [ie PREB in this context] is only a relevant concept for contracts where the [insurance] company exercises discretion which impacts the benefits received by the policyholder'.[36] This was precisely how PREB naturally emerged and featured in *Equitable Life*. The British actuarial profession, in a working party's report in 1990, recognised, regarding policies with a discretionary element, that 'The [policy] holders may reasonably expect that life offices will behave fairly and responsibly in exercising the discretion which is available to them. They may also expect a reasonable degree of continuity in an office's approach to determining variable charges or benefits.'[37]

Regarding the specific actuarial techniques employed for this purpose, the working party recognised that 'in the normal day-to-day actuarial management of a life policy, PRE [ie PREB] is synonymous with equity and the almost universal method for measuring it is asset share calculation'.[38] Although 'no standard definition exists of what an asset share is or what goes into one',[39] in less technical terms, 'asset share' can 'be defined as the premiums paid, less deductions, plus the allocations of miscellaneous profits, all accumulated at a suitable rate of investment return'.[40]

> The level of allocations and deductions and the rates of investment return will normally reflect an office's past operating experience and its asset share philosophy.
>
> Allocations of miscellaneous profits may include some or all of the following items: surrender profits on with-profits businesses; profits from non-profit business; allocations from the estate; and windfall profits such as unexpected tax gains.
>
> ...
>
> Deductions normally include all of the following items: commissions and expenses, net of taxes if appropriate; the cost of providing life cover and any other benefits and options; tax on income, taxable realised and unrealised gains, and profits if appropriate; and shareholders' transfers. There may also be a charge deducted from the asset share in respect of the cost of providing the guarantees and smoothing under contract.
>
> ...
>
> There is no universal approach to defining the rate of investment return. ... Approaches used by offices responding to the asset share survey included: notional returns on calculated using a notional asset mix and returns on indices; the overall return on the non-linked assets in the fund; and the return on assets notionally allocated to with-profits businesses or to specific product lines within the with-profits portfolio.[41]

[36] Shelley et al, above n 25, 714.
[37] Ibid 710.
[38] Ibid 710.
[39] Needleman and Toff, above n 30, 606 [2.1.1].
[40] Ibid 607 [2.1.1].
[41] Ibid [2.1.1], [2.1.2], [2.1.4] and [2.1.6].

B. Policyholder's Reasonable Expectations of Bonuses under the Guidance Note of the Actuarial Profession

From 1975, it was stated in the British actuarial profession's Guidance Note 1 (GN1) that 'It is incumbent on all appointed actuaries to ensure, so far as is within their authority, that long-term business is operated on sound financial lines.'[42] As guidance to actuaries, it was stated:

> The possibility of insolvency, or intervention by the Secretary of State on the grounds of the company's being unable to fulfil the reasonable expectations of its policyholders, may arise from factors, some of which are within the control of the company and some not. To the extent that they are under the control of the company, it is the appointed actuary's duty to assess the limits within which the company must act and to advise the company of the necessity for these limits. For that purpose, it is the appointed actuary's duty to assess the limits within which the company must act and to advise the company of the necessity for these limits.[43]

This remained as paragraph 7.2 of subsequent GN1 versions[44] until December 2001, by which time PRE had been reinforced in GN1 through various statements. This reinforcement started in 1988, followed by more marked enhancement from 1992 onwards.

In addition to the statement quoted above, GN1 Version 2.0 required that PRE should be interpreted by reference to an appointed actuary's appraisal of the relevant experience, his or her understanding of the life insurer's financial and business objectives, as well as his or her assessment of the life insurer's continuing ability to meet its statutory solvency requirement. In addition, the appointed actuary should assume that the conditions for the fulfilment of those expectations were:

1. that groups of participating policies were appropriately and equitably distinguished having regard, inter alia, to the terms of the policies, their duration and their relevant pooled experience;
2. that the company conducted its affairs, including its new business and investment strategies, with due regard for its financial resources.[45]

These requirements remained in paragraph [8.3.4] of subsequent versions of GN1.[46]

[42] Boards of Actuarial Standards, GN1 Version 1.0 (1975), [1.0].

[43] Ibid [7.1].

[44] Namely GN1 Version 1.1 (1978–1979), Version 1.2 (1979–1980), Version 1.3 (1983–1984), Version 1.5 (1985–1986); Version 1.6 (1987), Version 2.0 (1988), Version 2.1 (1990), Version 3.0 (1992), Version 4.0 (1994), Version 5.0 (1996), Version 5.1 (1998).

[45] GN 1 Version 2.0 (1988) [8.3.4].

[46] See paragraph [8.3.4] of GN1 Version 2.1 (1990), Version 3.0 (1992), Version 4.0 (1994), Version 5.0 (1996), Version 5.1 (1998), also paragraph [7.4] of GN1 Version 6.0 (2001), Version 6.1 (2003), Version 6.2 (2004).

The British actuarial profession made PRE more express in GN1 after 1992. The most recent GN1 Version 6.2 stressed that 'It is incumbent on all Appointed Actuaries to ensure, so far as is within their authority, that the long-term business of the company is operated on sound financial lines and *with regard to its policyholders' reasonable expectations*.'[47]

It was part of the appointed actuary's continuing responsibility to advise the life insurance company of his or her interpretation of its policyholders' reasonable expectations; when a significant change was likely to take place, the appointed actuary should take all reasonable steps to ensure that the life insurance company appreciated the implications for the reasonable expectations of its policyholders.[48] When assessing the liabilities of a life company, the appointed actuary also had to have regard to policyholders' reasonable expectations.[49] More specifically it was recognised that

> Some companies may include in their policy contracts a requirement that terms be determined by the Appointed Actuary, ... In determining such terms, or in providing advice to the company in this area, the Appointed Actuary should have regard to policyholders' reasonable expectations and to existing legislation, including that covering unfair contract terms, where relevant.[50]

> For unit linked business, unit pricing, fund charges, and deductions in respect of taxation are key elements of policyholders' reasonable expectations, to the extent that the company has discretion in applying its policy conditions. The Appointed Actuary must be satisfied that all discretionary elements of unit pricing and fund charges are applied consistently with policyholders' reasonable expectations. In particular, the Appointed Actuary must be satisfied that the procedures for determining: (a) the prices at which units are allocated to or de-allocated from policies; (b) the prices at which units are created or cancelled; and (c) compensation where errors or inequities of a material size in unit pricing have occurred are equitable to any policyholders affected both directly and indirectly. For these purposes the Appointed Actuary should have regard to the value of the assets of the unit fund, the tax position of the unit fund, the materiality of amounts involved and any other matters considered relevant.[51]

[47] GN1 Version 6.2 (2004) [3.6]. Also para. [1.1] of GN1 Version 3.0 (1992), Version 4.0 (1994), Version 5.0 (1996), Version 5.1 (1998), and para [3.6] of GN1 Version 6.0 (2001), Version 6.1 (2003).

[48] GN1 Version 6.2 (2004), [3.6]. Also para. [3.3] of GN1 Version 3.0 (1992), Version 4.0 (1994), Version 5.0 (1996), Version 5.1 (1998), and para [5.2] of GN1 Version 6.0 (2001), Version 6.1 (2003).

[49] GN1 Version 6.2 (2004) [5.2]. Also para [6.3] of GN1 Version 3.0 (1992), Version 4.0 (1994), Version 5.0 (1996), Version 5.1 (1998), and para [5.2] of GN1 Version 6.0 (2001), Version 6.1 (2003).

[50] GN1 Version 6.2 (2004) [4.9]. Also para [5.7] of GN1 Version 5.0 (1996), Version 5.1 (1998), and para [4.9] of GN1 Version 6.0 (2001), Version 6.1 (2003).

[51] GN Version 6.2 (2004) [5.8]. Also para [5.8] of GN1 Version 5.0 (1996), Version 5.1 (1998), and para [4.10] of GN1 Version 6.0 (2001), Version 6.1 (2003).

C. Policyholder's Reasonable Expectations of Bonuses and the Insurance Technical Actuarial Standard

Guidance Note 1, together with other Guidance Notes, became inoperative from 1 November 2011 due to implementation of the Insurance Technical Actuarial Standard ('Insurance TAS') issued by the Board for Actuarial Standards of the Financial Reporting Council (hereafter 'the BAS'). Although the Insurance TAS does not itself make any reference to PRE, it does *not* follow that PRE is no longer relevant to actuarial practice. In contrast to GN1's being applicable only to life or long-term insurance, the Insurance TAS is applicable to both general insurance and long-term insurance. The BAS chose to propose a single TAS for insurance, 'because the commonalities [between general insurance and long-term insurance] were bigger than the differences, and because other regulatory developments are heading in this direction'.[52] In relation to a single TAS for insurance, the BAS was aware that some areas of actuarial work are specific to either long-term or general insurance, but it believed that 'the TAS can be structured so that those principles that apply only to particular areas of work are clearly indicated'.[53]

For that purpose, Part E of the Insurance TAS contains those principles specific to actuarial responsibilities concerning the exercise of discretion by long-term insurers—as was the case in *Equitable Life*. In this regard, there was a draft statement in Part E: 'Aggregate reports shall describe the rationale for any change in the assumptions about the way discretion is exercised in any stressed scenarios considered.'[54] The final version of clause E.2.1 substantially amplified the draft clause, stating that an actuary's

> [a]ggregate reports for work which requires projecting cash flows under alternative scenarios shall describe how any changes in the assumption about the way discretion is exercised in the alternative scenarios considered are consistent with the *fair treatment of the policyholders* affected.[55] (emphasis added)

The enhanced clause E.2.1, with the added reference to 'fair treatment of the policyholders', is apparently connected to the principle of 'treating customers fairly' ('the TCF Principle'), a regulatory principle closely related to PRE in the actuarial profession, as will be shown in section III. below. From the Insurance TAS reference to the closely-related TCF Principle, it can be gathered that despite GN1's becoming inoperative after 1 November 2011, the actuarial profession continues to regard PRE as relevant. This is consistent with insurance regulation in the UK.

[52] BAS, *Insurance: Consultation* (2009) 1, 'Preface'. Also BAS, *Exposure Draft: Insurance* (2010) 5–6, [2.1]–[2.7].

[53] BAS, Exposure Draft: Insurance (2010) 5, [2.6].

[54] Ibid 48, draft cl E.2.1.

[55] BAS, *Insurance TAS* (2010) 17.

III. Policyholder's Reasonable Expectations of Bonuses in Insurance Regulation

A. Policyholder's Reasonable Expectations of Bonuses and the Insurance Companies Acts

As was mentioned in section II.A. above, Skerman proposed the concept of PRE in life insurance, and with that concept in mind he played a major part in the government departmental discussions in 1972 about the proposed changes in insurance legislation. Much of the departmental discussion focused on the actuarial or bonuses aspect of PRE, ie PREB. As a result of Skerman's contribution, PRE (or PREB actually) was initially required in the Insurance Companies Amendment Act 1973, section 12(1)(a) and section 21. The two sections read as follows (emphasis added):

> 12.(1) Any power conferred on the Secretary of State by sections 13 to 21 below shall be exercisable in relation to any insurance company to which the Act of 1958 applies and shall be exercisable on any of the following grounds—
>
> (a) that the Secretary of State considers the exercise of the power to be desirable for protecting policy holders or potential policy holders of the company against the risk that the company may be unable to meet its liabilities or, in the case of long term business, to *fulfil the reasonable expectations* of *policy holders* or potential policy holders;
>
> ...
>
> 21. The Secretary of State may require a company to take such action as appears to him to be appropriate for the purpose of protecting policy holders or potential policy holders of the company against the risk that the company may be unable to meet its liabilities or, in the case of long term business, *to fulfil the reasonable expectations of policy holders* or potential policy holders.

During the three decades that followed, the statutory provisions quoted above had continued existence as the Insurance Companies Act 1982, sections 37(2)(a) and 45(1), which remained effective under the Financial Services Act 1986.[56] 'These provisions recognise that policyholders may have a reasonable expectation of benefits *over and above their contractually guaranteed benefits*.'[57] (emphasis added) The statutory PRE regulatory provisions in the Insurance Companies Acts were translated into the British actuarial profession's guidance described in section II. above.

[56] Financial Services Act 1986, Sch 10, para 6(4). This Act was repealed, and superseded by the Financial Services and Markets Act 2000.

[57] *Equitable Life Assurance Society v Hyman* [1999] PLR 297 [86].

B. From Policyholders' Reasonable Expectations of Bonuses to the 'Treating Customers Fairly' Principle under the 2000 Act

Through the Financial Services and Markets Act (FSMA) 2000, under which consumer financial disputes are supposed to be resolved 'by reference to what is, in the opinion of the ombudsman, fair and reasonable in all the circumstances of the case',[58] the kernel of the provisions discussed above found new life in 2001 as Principle 6 of the Financial Services Authority (now the Financial Conduct Authority and the Prudential Regulation Authority, hereafter the FSA, the FCA and the PRA respectively) Principles for Businesses. Principle 6 is also commonly known as the principle of 'treating customers fairly', or the TCF Principle. Particularly noteworthy is that the FSA 'see[s] Principle 6 … as being the foundation for the substantive materials within the Handbook on the insurance concept of policyholders' reasonable expectations'.[59] The concept refers to the actuarial and regulatory PRE (or PREB essentially) principle. This can be evidenced by a report of the customers' interest working party within the actuarial profession in response to the FSA Principle of Business concerning the TCF Principle. The terms of reference of the working party were basically 'to consider the [FSA's] proposal to replace the concept of "policyholders' reasonable expectations" (PRE) as set out in the Insurance Companies Act by that of "customers' interests" as defined by FSA Principle 6'.[60] Apart from that, the homogeneity between PRE (or PREB) and TCF can also be substantiated from the FCA Handbook COBS 20.2, 'Treating Customers Fairly' (effective as of 1 November 2007), which states, inter alia:

> With-profits policyholders have an interest in the whole and in every part of the with-profits fund into which their policies are written and from which the amounts payable in connection with their policies are to be paid. Those amounts include those required to satisfy their contractual rights and such other amounts as the firm is required to pay in order *to treat them fairly (including but not limited to the amounts required to satisfy their reasonable expectations)*.[61] (emphasis added)

Nonetheless, although closely related to PRE (or PREB), TCF is not identical to it;[62] it is actually believed to be broader.[63] Dr Hare, Fellow of the Faculty of Actuaries, found that

> treating customers fairly is far bigger than PRE. Broadly speaking, PRE involves doing what you hinted that you would do at the time of writing the policy, or in the literature

[58] FSMA 2000, s 228(2); DISP 3.6.1R and 3.6.2G. See also at www.financial-ombudsman.org.uk/faq/businesses/answers/decide_cases_a7.html.

[59] FSA, The FSA Principles for Business: Response on Consultation Paper 13 (October 1999) [33].

[60] Research Committee of the Life Board, *Report of the Customers' Interests Working Party* (November 2002) 1.

[61] Financial Conduct Authority, *FCA Handbook COBS* 20.2.1(2); Available at www.handbook.fca.org.uk/handbook/COBS/20/2.html.

[62] Shelley et al, above n 25, 706.

[63] Association of British Insurers: *A Guide of Good Practice for Unit Linked Funds*, 2nd edn (London, ABI, 2012) [1.1.3].

going forward; whereas treating customers fairly is to do what, with the benefit of hindsight, policyholders think was in the spirit of the agreement that they entered into with you.[64]

That TCF is broader than PRE can also be seen from, and is consistent with, the FSA (now FCA/PRA) Handbook definition of an insurer's 'liability to a policyholder', which more precisely, includes

any liability or obligation of that firm to, or in respect of, a policyholder, including any liability or obligation arising: (a) from the requirement to treat customers fairly under Principle 6, including with respect to policyholders' reasonable expectations;[65]

At least two implications can be drawn from the understanding that TCF is broader than PRE (or PREB). In the first place, TCF 'is a much bigger concept … that would certainly resolve some of the issues with PRE that we have raised already'.[66] Secondly, PRE has consistently remained relevant not only to insurance actuary but also to insurance regulation in the UK. This is because, as shown in section II. above, PRE was emphasised in all versions of GN1 after 1975 by the actuarial profession for facilitating insurance regulation. This is also because, closely related to PRE, TCF has been reintroduced into the Insurance TAS more recently in relation to the insurer's exercise of discretion in long-term insurance business. More than that, the International Actuary Association recognises that 'the responsible actuary can, *as part of the regulatory requirements*, monitor the reasonable expectations of policyholders and how they are treated as the insurer exercises the contractual discretion in the policy'.[67] (emphasis added)

Due largely to the dire consequences of *Equitable Life*, the Financial Services Act 2012 paid more attention than the FSMA 2000 to with-profits insurance business. By the Financial Services Act 2012, section 6, adding a new section 3F into the FSMA 2000, the PRA and the FCA were to have a Memorandum of Understanding on their regulation of with-profits insurance. The PRA-FCA Memorandum reached in 2013 recognises, inter alia:

[The exercise of discretion by with-profits insurers] gives rise to questions of fairness—as between policyholders and shareholders of the insurer, for example, and also between different groups of policyholders—and that is a matter for the FCA. The PRA on the other hand has responsibility under the Act for measures designed to contribute to the securing of an appropriate degree of protection for current and future policyholders. The PRA will therefore be concerned about the impact on the safety and soundness of insurers, and in particular their solvency, of any Relevant Actions taken or proposed by the

[64] DJP Hare, in M Shelley, M Arnold and P Needleman, 'A Review of Policyholder's Reasonable Expectations' (Abstract of the Discussion) (2002) 8 *British Actuarial Journal* 905, 911.

[65] Financial Conduct Authority, *FCA Handbook Glossary;* available at www.handbook.fca.org.uk/handbook/glossary.

[66] Hare, above n 64, 911.

[67] International Actuarial Association, *The Function of the Actuary in Prudential Supervision* (Ottawa, IAA, 2002) 6.

> insurer. It will be the FCA's responsibility to satisfy itself that firms are behaving fairly in relation to those Relevant Actions: the PRA's concern will be to ensure that discretionary increases in liabilities do not adversely affect the insurer's ability to meet, and continue to meet, the PRA's standards for safety and soundness (and in particular its ability to meet the Threshold Conditions). In so doing, the PRA will contribute to the securing of an appropriate degree of protection for current and future with-profits policyholders.[68]

In line with this and the Directive 2009/138/EC of the European Parliament and of the Council (Solvency II), the new PRA Rulebook effective as of 1 January 2016 has separate Parts[69] on with-profits business, but not applicable to what is known as 'Holloway sickness policy'.[70] Likewise, the new FCA Handbook's substantial Code of Business Sourcebook (COBS), applicable to designated investment business and long-term insurance business in relation to life policies, as well as to activities connected with them, devotes the whole of Chapter 20 (effective as of 1 November 2007) to with-profits life policies.[71] At great length, the with-profits policies chapter defines 'with-profits fund' in COBS 20.1A (effective as of 1 January 2016), prescribes measures 'treating with-profits policyholders fairly' in COBS 20.2 (effective as of 1 November 2007), states in COBS 20.3 (effective as of 1 November 2007) the 'principles and practice of financial management' according to which a with-profits insurer conducts this line of business, decrees in COBS 20.4 (effective as of 1 November 2007) how the business firm must make 'communications with with-profits policyholders', and advises in COBS 20.5 (effective as of 1 April 2012) how an insurer in this line of business must implement 'with-profits governance' in relation thereto.

The place of PRE (or essentially PREB) as rediscovered and stressed in insurance regulation in the wake of *Equitable Life* has an important implication for protection of PREB. Admittedly, as a general rule, public law does not create directly enforceable private rights. Therefore the public law of insurance regulation does not create private rights for policyholder's vis-à-vis insurers. Public law, however, 'has indirect persuasive authority to determining [*sic*] private law relations because the public law creates the general framework for private law interactions'.[72]

[68] Prudential Regulation Authority (PRA) and Financial Conduct Authority (FCA), *With-Profits, Memorandum of Understanding* (London, Bank of England, 2013) [4], available at www.bankofengland.co.uk.

[69] Prudential Regulation Authority, *PRA Rulebook: Solvency II Firms: With-Profits* (London, Bank of England, 2016); *PRA Rulebook: Non-Solvency II Firms: With-Profits* (London, Bank of England, 2016).

[70] According to the PRA Rulebook Glossary, 'Holloway sickness policy' means a contract of long-term insurance offered or effected by a friendly society under the Holloway system, providing permanent health benefits and, in addition, investment benefits, where the investment benefits: (1) are derived from surpluses accrued by the friendly society and apportioned to policyholders; and (2) are payable to policyholders at maturity, on retirement, on death, or as otherwise specified by contractual provisions or individual society rules.'

[71] Financial Conduct Authority, '*Chapter 20 With-Profits*' in *FCA Handbook, Conduct of Business Sourcebook,* (London, FCA, 2016), available at www.handbook.fca.org.uk/handbook/COBS/20.pdf.

[72] EA Engle, 'Tort Law and Human Rights' in M Bousani and AJ Sebok (eds), *Comparative Tort Law: Global Perspectives* (Cheltenham, Edward Elgar Publishing, 2015) 73.

All public law is ultimately for the effective protection of private rights. In particular, insurance regulation has the protection of policyholders as a core objective. Hence, although insurance regulation does not in itself create policyholders' rights or a cause of action for policyholder rights, it has 'indirect persuasive authority or interpretative value'[73] for protecting the substantive rights of policyholders.

IV. Reflections on *Equitable Life* in the House of Lords

A. Contract Law Realism versus Formalism

As a case with overwhelming consequences, *Equitable Life* in the House of Lords inevitably draws much attention from practising and academic lawyers. It seems that the discussion has been mainly from a company law perspective.[74] After all, though originally established in 1762, and for more than a century existing as a mutual, the Equitable Life Assurance Society ('the Society') had been incorporated under the Companies Acts since 1892 as an unlimited company without share capital. When the litigation arose, it had already been a company under the Companies Act 1985, section 735. Policyholders were also members, like shareholders, of this mutual company. This means that company law was relevant to this special company in a challenging way, particularly in respect of the law applicable to articles of association and the company board's discretionary powers.

However, a contract law perspective on this case is particularly necessary, because two types of contract were relevant in it: one was the insurance contracts between the policyholders and the insurer; the other was the contract, in terms of the articles of association, between the Society and all its members/policyholders. There could be a potential conflict between PREB under the contracts of insurance, and the discretion under the articles of association by which the insurer could allocate bonuses. In this case, the potential conflict turned out to be all too real. To resolve it, the House of Lords implied a term into Article 65 of the Society's articles of association. Some commentators touched upon the dual legal nature of the judicial approaches to the discretion under the said Article 65 of the insurer's articles of association.[75] Others focused on how life insurers, in relation to the type of policies concerned, should be constrained in exercising their

[73] Ibid.

[74] A Berg, '*Equitable Life Assurance Society v Hyman*—The Extrinsic Facts Issue' [2002] *JBL* 570.

[75] T Daintith, 'Contractual discretion and administrative discretion: a unified analysis, (2005) 68 *MLR* 554, 573. See also M Conaglen, 'Public-Private Intersection: Comparing Fiduciary Conflict Doctrine and Bias' [2008] *Public Law* 58, 58–59; L Sealy '"Legitimate Expectations" in Company Law and Public Law' [2000] *LMCLQ* 308.

discretion.[76] Some saw *Equitable Life* as 'a turning point in relation to the law on implied terms',[77] whereas others perceived Lord Steyn's opinion as framed in the conventional necessity test of implication of terms.[78] Whichever view is correct, in *Equitable Life* Lord Steyn consistently reinforced his strong perception that 'a theme that runs through our law of contract is that the reasonable expectations of honest men must be protected'.[79]

All those perspectives and comments are insightful and helpful for understanding of and reflection upon *Equitable Life*. Meanwhile, one can also see that there is in *Equitable Life* an underlying conflict between contract law realism, in terms of consumer-welfarism, and contract law formalism.[80] Under a formalist approach, judges could have simply and literally given effect to Article 65(3) (see section I.A. above), which granted the insurer 'absolute discretion' in declaring bonuses. Under a realist approach, which is result-orientated, the interests of consumer policyholders must adequately be taken into account and be protected. The House of Lords, did not take the formalist approach; instead it implied a term into the said Article 65, by which the insurer's discretion was substantially qualified so that PREB could be protected. In this regard it has rightly been observed that in *Equitable Life* there'is the underlying judicial philosophy that, whether in public law or private law, broad discretions may not be utilized to undermine legitimate expectations. Construction is simply the technical device deployed to give effect to that foundational principle.'[81]

B. The Necessity Test for Implication of the Term in *Equitable Life*

As far as implication of terms is concerned, *Equitable Life* does not seem to be sufficiently persuasive. With the benefit of hindsight, one might suspect that the 'necessity' argument of Lord Steyn in *Equitable Life* could have been stronger. It seems that his Lordship did not adequately explain why it was necessary to imply a term that would preclude the Society from exercising its discretion in the way it had been (see section I.B. above). After all, as the Society contended, the GAR clauses were included in the insurance policies without charges: there was no consideration for GAR. Besides, PRE or PREB was not strictly a contract-based right under the terms of the insurance policies in question. In addition, under its articles of association, the insurer did have the discretion to lower the GAR. These

[76] C O'Brien, 'Constraints on discretion: Distributing surplus in with-profits life insurance' (2004) 12 *Journal of Financial Regulation and Compliance* 118.

[77] J McCaughran, 'Implied Terms: The Journey of the Man on the Clapham Omnibus' (2011) 70 *CLJ* 607, 612.

[78] M Hemsworth, 'United Kingdom Insurance Decisions 2000' [2001] LMCLQ 504, 506.

[79] *First Energy (UK) Ltd v Hungarian International Bank Ltd* [1993] 2 Lloyd's Rep 194, 196.

[80] J Adams and R Brownsword, *Understanding Contract Law*, 5th edn (London, Sweet & Maxwell, 2007) 3, 38–39.

[81] G McMeel, 'Interpreting With-Profits Life Insurance Contracts' [2001] *LMCLQ* 179, 185.

points considered, there seems to be some residual leeway for not implying the term to bar the insurer's discretion.

In *Equitable Life*, the approach to implying the term seems opaque. The conventional approach to or test for the necessity of implying a term into a contract is the business efficacy test, or the officious bystander test. However, before it was briefly revisited in *Attorney General of Belize v Belize Telecom*[82] ('*Belize*'), it was not crystal clear which of the tests was applied in *Equitable Life*. It only *seemed* that it was the business efficacy test that was applied, because in his reasoning towards implying the term to give effect to the reasonable expectations of the policyholders, Lord Steyn went into the details of the commercial objective of GAR provision, of how GAR policies were marketed, how GAR provisions were attractive to potential policyholders and how they generated reasonable expectations in actual policyholders, as well as how the reasonable expectations were not altered by the free provision of GAR bonuses.[83] Nevertheless, he did not really explain 'for what [purpose]'[84] it was 'strictly necessary'[85] or essential to imply the term to the effect of precluding the insurer's discretion in the matter at issue. From Lord Steyn's statement, the apparent answer to this question is that the term was implied to give effect to reasonable expectations (of the GAR policyholders). But recourse to a general concept of reasonable expectations might be too broad to be sufficiently explanatory. Even regardless of such a doubt, it could not be deemed that Lord Steyn established a new test, ie 'reasonable expectations of the parties', for implied terms. It was not so regarded then, and it certainly cannot be so regarded now that *Mark & Spencer v BNP Paribas Securities Services Trust Co Ltd*[86] has confirmed that the traditional test of necessity for implying a term remains unchanged.

It is interesting that in *Belize*, Lord Hoffmann, who also sat in *Equitable Life* and agreed with Lord Steyn there, clarified Lord Steyn's approach. For Lord Hoffmann, when it came to implying a term into a provision,

> the [only] question for the court is whether such a provision would spell out in express words what the instrument, read against the relevant background, would reasonably be understood to mean. … [T]his question can be reformulated in various ways which a court may find helpful in providing an answer—the implied term must 'go without saying', it must be 'necessary to give business efficacy to the contract' and so on—but these are not … to be treated as different or additional tests.[87]

[82] *Attorney General of Belize v Belize Telecom* [2009] UKPC 10.

[83] *Equitable Life Assurance Society v Hyman* [2002] 1 AC 408, 460G–H.

[84] McCaughran, above n 77, 612.

[85] *Equitable Life Assurance Society v Hyman* [2002] 1 AC 408, 460G–H. Lord Steyn stated, '[A]n implication precluding the use of the directors' discretion in this way is strictly necessary. The implication is essential to give effect to the reasonable expectations of the parties.'

[86] *Mark & Spencer v BNP Paribas Securities Services Trust Co Ltd* [2015] UKSC 72.

[87] *Attorney General of Belize v Belize Telecom* [2009] UKPC 10 [21].

Regarding the formulation of 'necessary to give business efficacy', Lord Hoffmann proceeded to say:

> That formulation serves to underline two important points. The first, conveyed by the use of the word 'business', is that in considering what the instrument would have meant to a reasonable person who had knowledge of the relevant background, one assumes the notional reader will take into account the practical consequences of deciding that it means one thing or the other. In the case of an instrument such as a commercial contract, he will consider whether a different construction would frustrate the apparent business purpose of the parties. That was the basis upon which *Equitable Life Assurance Society v Hyman* [2002] 1 AC 408 was decided. The second, conveyed by the use of the word 'necessary', is that it is not enough for a court to consider that the implied term expresses what it would have been reasonable for the parties to agree to. It must be satisfied that it is what the contract actually means.[88]

This made it clear that it was the business efficacy test that was used for implying a term in *Equitable Life*, particularly given that Lord Steyn gave serious consideration and much weight to the commercial background and purpose of the GAR provision in the policies concerned.

However, it does not seem that the qualifying term implied by Lord Steyn is what Article 65 'actually means', unless it could be thought that the insurer or its directors had actually intended to impose some restrictions on their own discretion in allocating bonuses. This was certainly not the case, otherwise the dispute would not have arisen. However, if 'what the contract or instrument actually means' is to be taken as meaning 'what the instrument, read against the relevant background, would reasonably be understood to mean'—both are fairly objective standards—it will not seem problematic to align Lord Steyn's approach in *Equitable Life* with Lord Hoffmann's second point about the business efficacy test for implication of terms. This, however, smacks of wishfully explaining away the difficulties in the approach to implying the term in *Equitable Life*.

C. The Relevance of Background to Implication of Terms

That being said above, regarding *Equitable Life*, if one could disregard the specific business efficacy test and return to the general approach of reading the instrument against 'the relevant background' to see what it reasonably means, that might also work effectively. This is not really a deviation from the mainstream tests for implied terms. That is because the question of the necessity for implying a term 'can be reformulated *in various ways* which a court may find helpful in providing an answer',[89] hence a sufficiently strong background alone could sometimes suffice in providing the necessity for implied terms. After all, in *Equitable Life*, Lord Steyn

[88] Ibid.
[89] Ibid.

himself also stressed the relevance of a commercial setting to the implication of terms: 'If a term is to be implied, it could only be a term implied from the language of [the instrument] read in its commercial setting.'[90]

This background-based approach would have made it less challenging to deal with *Equitable Life* at the time. The relevant background is the actuarial principle of PRE (ie PREB), the actuarial practice in relation thereto and the regulatory requirements, in particular the TCF principle, all of which have been described in the preceding sections of this chapter. This background can be used to enhance the use of the necessity test for implying the term. The actuarial principle and practice of PRE or PREB can more directly explain why it is necessary to imply the term: bound by actuarial practices and insurance regulation, life insurers have already taken PREB into account in their business; and this also renders it necessary for them to actually do so when it comes to their dealings with policyholders. In other words, it at least breaches business integrity,[91] and goes against the life insurance industry's internal practice, when on the one hand an insurer is required by an actuary and regulation to actively consider PREB, but on the other hand, based on its discretion, it tries to deny PREB. Since both the insurance regulator and the actuarial profession have substantially taken PREB into account in life insurance, or have been required by law and by professional standards to consider PREB, it is naturally more necessary for insurers themselves to take PREB more seriously, and it is equally necessary for courts to protect those expectations. All this makes it necessary to imply a term as appropriate to qualify the insurer's discretion which would prejudice PREB. Admittedly, this does not mean that on each and every occasion an insurer engaged in with-profits or investment-linked life insurance business shall allocate bonuses to the full expectation and content of its policyholders, but differentiated treatment, as in *Equitable Life*, will be more likely to be held inappropriate, unjustifiable and frustrating for PREB.

Use of the actuarial background in a scenario like *Equitable Life* would not be surprising or unimaginable. Professor Malcolm Clarke had a glimpse of the relevance of the actuarial and regulatory background more than two decades ago. In the early 1990s he understood that the Insurance Companies Act 1982, section 37(2)(a), which empowered the Secretary of State to take measures on long-term insurance businesses so that they could fulfil a policyholder's reasonable expectations, seemed to be 'a dilute version'[92] of the American insurance law 'doctrine' of PREC. Although the identification is prone to doubt, understanding a policyholder's reasonable expectations from a regulatory perspective is always helpful. This is particularly so, given that the core aim of insurance regulation is to protect the legitimate interests of policyholders.

[90] *Equitable Life Assurance Society v Hyman* [2002] 1 AC 408, 459.
[91] I owe this truism to the keen observation of my colleague Mr Florian Gamper.
[92] M Clarke, 'Reasonable Expectations—Unreasonable Cost?' (1990) 16 *Managerial Finance* 25, 25.

V. Conclusion

Equitable Life is worth revisiting, not just because over recent years it has been referred to in significant cases concerning the implication of terms, but more importantly because it concerned an important but hardly-noticed aspect of reasonable expectations in a very special line of insurance, that is, policyholder's reasonable expectations of bonuses ('PREB') in with-profits or investment-linked life insurance. That is very different from PREC, because, unlike PREC, PREB does not centre on a particular risk or the coverage of insurable risks. Rather, PREB has a fairly technical actuarial underpinnings; it is relevant only in with-profits (life) insurance. In contrast, PREC applies to most lines of insurance, including all property and casualty insurance, and all non-investment life insurance.

The uniqueness of PREB and its distinction from PREC have implications. In *Equitable Life*, PREB was protected by way of an implied term that precluded the insurer's prejudicial discretion in allocating bonuses. The 'business efficacy' test for implication of terms was applied in this infamous case, but the application of this approach was not sufficiently persuasive or clear: it failed to explain more specifically why it was necessary to imply a term—it was not enough to say generally that it was necessary for giving effect to policyholder's reasonable expectations.

The weakness can only be overcome by reference to the newly-discovered actuarial-related meaning, ie PREB, of policyholder's reasonable expectations in this context, as well as its relevance to insurance regulation. The huge implication of this new discovery is that, considering the actuarial underpinnings of PREB, its wide recognition by the British actuarial profession and its relevance to insurance regulation in the UK, courts should and can support with-profits policyholders' claims for bonuses more effectively in resolving disputes similar to that in *Equitable Life* in the future. This can be achieved by having the actuarial principle and practice of PREB, as well as its regulatory relevance, as the strong background for implying a term that would preclude with-profits life insurers from exercising discretions detrimental to PREB. This background-based approach is still consistent with the overarching principle for implication of terms, which is that the necessity of implying a term in an instrument is determined by reading the instrument against the relevant background to find out what it would be reasonably understood to mean. It has been pointed out in *Belize* that this principle can be reformulated 'in various ways' not limited to 'necessary business efficacy' test and the 'officious bystander' test.

The other implication, though moderate, of the new discovery of PREB, is that given the marked difference between PREB and PREC, one cannot effectively argue for PREC on the misperceived doctrinal ground that PREC was applied in the House of Lords in *Equitable Life*. Lawyers should beware of the differences between them in dealing with relevant cases. It is necessary to distinguish the two so that each can be applied in its proper scenarios in the future. An example in this regard is the American case *Vos and Anderson v Farm Bureau Life Insurance Company*,[93] concerning a dispute over the sale of whole-life and universal-life policies. Vos and Anderson contended that their claim regarding the insurer's breach of contract was based solely on whether the insurer knowingly created reasonable expectations in connection with the policies. The court found that the issue in this case concerned not whether insurance coverage existed under the policy, but rather the premium and dividend provisions under the policy. Considering that, the court rightly refused to expand the doctrine of the insured's reasonable expectations (of coverage) to a situation where coverage under the policy was not at issue. Likewise, insurance lawyers shall be acutely aware of the differences between PREB and PREC when appropriate insurance disputes arise before them, and have arguments fit for either in specific scenarios.

[93] *Vos and Anderson v Farm Bureau Life Insurance Company*, 667 NW 2d 36, 50 (Iowa 2003).

8

Conclusion

The stark difference in English judicial attitudes to the notion of reasonable expectations in the context of general contract law and of insurance (contract) law is not justifiable. On one hand, prominent senior judges have consistently called for protection of parties' reasonable expectations in contract law, and this is hardly contested. On the other hand, the English judiciary generally has remained clearly unreceptive to the idea of policyholder's reasonable expectations in insurance law, even though the House of Lords expressly made use of the notion of reasonable expectations in insurance law cases.[1] Even only considering generally the homogeneity between general contract law and insurance (contract) law, the judiciary and contract lawyers perhaps should in the long run be ready to align English insurance law with general contract law in this regard.

Thus parties' reasonable expectations ought to count, though not necessarily control, when resolving insurance disputes. That being said, in the context of insurance, it is the policyholder's, rather than the insurer's, reasonable expectations that are *practically* more important. This is because the very function of insurance is to spread risks for policyholders by providing conditional coverage for them, and also because in practice, much more often it is policyholders who claim indemnity or payment by insurers, and for this purpose they initiate court proceedings or alternative proceedings more often than insurers if insurance disputes arise. The policyholder's reasonable expectations broadly fall into two categories: the policyholder's reasonable expectations of coverage (PREC) of risks; and the policyholder's reasonable expectations of bonus (PREB). Disputes over PREC might occur in any line of insurance, as they do in most insurance law cases. Disputes over PREB occur only as regards with-profits life insurance products, and mainly in consumer insurance, due to PREB's business nature as a consumer financial product. This is so, for example, in the (in)famous case *Equitable Life Assurance Society v Hyman*.[2]

More specifically, there can be an interpretative principle of 'policyholder's reasonable expectations' in English insurance law. The latter should be aligned

[1] *Cook v Financial Insurance Co Ltd* [1998] UKHL 42, [1998] 1 WLR 1765; *Equitable Life Assurance Society v Hyman* [2000] 3 All ER 961, [2000] UKHL 39, [2002] 1 AC 408.

[2] *Equitable Life Assurance Society v Hyman* [2000] 3 All ER 961, [2000] UKHL 39, [2002] 1 AC 408.

with general contract law in protecting parties' reasonable expectations, in particular a policyholder's reasonable expectations. This is in the first place because insurance (contract) law and general contract law are homogeneous—as has been stressed by Malcolm Clarke and in Chapter 2, insurance law is not, nor should it be thought to be, fundamentally different from general contract law. Whilst insurance does have an economic mechanism that is distinctive from that of non-insurance transactions the prototype of which is sales, general contract law to a very large extent governs both insurance and non-insurance transactions. From the perspective of private law, both are homogeneously subject to the same legal framework of contract law in respect of the formation and the performance of contract, and of the remedies for breach of contract; and more importantly, the principles for interpretation of contract terms are homogeneous too. The perceived particular difference in the pre-contractual duty of disclosure entrenched in insurance law more than two centuries ago has been significantly diluted as a result of more recent insurance law reform; the claimed difference in the meanings of 'conditions' and 'warranties' in insurance law and in contract law is mainly formalistic due to nominally different legal terminologies. Given the homogeneity between general contract law and insurance contract law, where general contract law recognisably protects parties' reasonable expectations, it is unjustifiable that courts and judges in the context of insurance refuse to take seriously parties' reasonable expectations, particularly the policyholder's reasonable expectations, whose relative greater importance has been discussed in Chapter 6, section III.D. and reiterated above.

Apart from that, the second major reason for aligning English insurance law with contract law in protecting reasonable expectations is that the proper function of insurance is for insurers to provide coverage of particular (types of) risks and/or benefits to policyholders, to the extent that the particular insurer is financially able to underwrite and bear the risks. An insurer might legitimately and reasonably expect that it has no liability or payment obligations in relation to a particular risk or risks. Nevertheless, given insurance's function and purpose of providing coverage of particular risks, in principle the policyholder's reasonable expectations should prevail over the insurer's reasonable expectations of non-liability or non-payment, unless the risk in question is *expressly and clearly* excluded from coverage.

In this respect, there is greater social need for protection of a consumer policyholder's reasonable expectations of coverage. The ongoing decline of the welfare state in the UK inevitably means that there will be a shift from social insurance to consumer private/commercial insurance for personal risks such as accidents, costs of longevity and health issues. See, for example, *Cook v Financial Insurance Co Ltd*,[3] where the policyholder's reasonable expectations of coverage of the medical condition in question were expressly given more weight in the House of Lords than in the insurance policy language. In this regard, to the undoubted relief of readers, it will not be challenging for consumer insurance

[3] *Cook v Financial Insurance Co Ltd* [1998] UKHL 42, [1998] 1 WLR 1765.

law to protect policyholder's reasonable expectations, largely because the long-held notion of a 'fair and reasonable' approach in consumer law has already been accepted in consumer insurance dispute resolution by English courts and in alternative consumer dispute resolution schemes in the insurance industry, such as (formerly) the Insurance Ombudsman Bureau and (currently) the Financial Ombudsman Service. In particular, the 'fair and reasonable' approach has been consolidated in the Consumer Rights Act 2015 and is applicable to consumer insurance where it is needed, though most consumer insurance disputes can be and actually are resolved through and by the Financial Ombudsman Service.

Although taking the policyholder's reasonable expectations seriously *is* more challenging in business insurance, it should not be. This is because, as Catherine Mitchell has effectively argued, commercial or business contracts are usually relational and commercial expectations should have more of a role in commercial law due to their greater consistency with the nature and the purpose of the commercial relationships underlying the commercial contract. Business insurance can be also viewed as relational, not necessarily because these are long-term contracts, but because they are usually integrated into some other commercial relationships or undertakings. In resolving disputes over business insurance coverage, courts should likewise take into consideration the business policyholder's reasonable expectations of coverage, with reference to the context of the particular insurance and the business purpose of the line of insurance concerned. Such a relational approach to PREC is consistent with the contextualist principle restated by Lord Hoffmann[4] for interpretation of commercial contracts.

A third justification for English insurance law to take a policyholder's reasonable expectations seriously concerns the American insurance law 'doctrine' of reasonable expectations. The English perception of this 'doctrine' has been a major obstacle to its acceptance in English insurance law. That is because the controversies, concerns and criticisms focusing on the varied formulations, and hence the alleged inconsistencies and uncertainties of this 'doctrine', have already been uncritically imported into English insurance law. However, those controversies, concerns and criticisms are fundamentally misplaced, even in the US; 'fundamentally' in that 'reasonable expectations' has been taken for granted as a 'doctrine', but not characterised as a 'principle' as it was intended[5] to be by Robert Keeton, its acclaimed author. Keeton treated an insurance law decision as applying a *doctrine* of honouring reasonable expectations 'only if, first, it explicitly does so, and, second, it appears explicitly to adopt not merely the term "reasonable expectations" but also an explanatory theory of decision that goes beyond resolving ambiguities against the party responsible for them'.[6] Nevertheless, this has been almost ignored: somehow this expectedly broad principle has mostly been understood and described as a doctrine, a concept which is usually supposed to be narrow and clear-cut.

[4] *Investor Compensation Scheme v West Bromwich Building Society* [1997] UKHL 28, [1997] CLC 1243, 1257–58.

[5] See particularly R Keeton, 'Reasonable Expectations in the Second Decade' (1976) 12 *Forum* 275, 276.

[6] Ibid 279.

Combing through American state court cases that have made reference to the policyholder's reasonable expectations in one way or another shows that this American insurance law 'doctrine' has actually been applied more like a rather broad and perhaps even vague principle, with several formulations or versions, certainly less like the clear-cut narrow doctrine it is usually thought to be. Hence, as a 'doctrine' it has been subject to controversies, criticisms and concerns, though actually it was intended as a principle and has operated more like a principle. In short, the American version of PREC has been mis-characterised as a doctrine.

Once this American insurance law 'doctrine' is properly recharacterised as a principle, the controversies, concerns and criticisms referred to above can no longer stand well. As a principle, it naturally has more than one formulation as regards its application. In this regard, similarly and without fundamental controversy, the insurance law principle of indemnity operates likewise in connection with various scenarios, including but not limited to reinstatement, contribution in 'other insurance' or double insurance, subrogation, capping in over-insurance, proportionality in (non-valued) under-insurance, coverage and payment of medical costs in personal insurance, and the requirement of an insurable interest in property insurance. Such a multiplicity of scenarios is consistent with the overarching relevance of indemnity in insurance law, and renders it difficult to characterise it as a legal doctrine/rule. It is also natural and unsurprising that PREC, when viewed as an overarching principle, carries with it some room for variation, and prima facie some uncertainty in the abstract—but once applied in a specific context, it becomes specific with certainty.

Besides, the uncritically imported English concerns fail to appreciate a special contributing factor that accounts for the apparent further inconsistencies and uncertainties in the US. This special and undoubtedly contributory factor is that insurance law in the US is state law rather than federal law, and that therefore, naturally, the law of one state in this regard is not followed in another state, hence giving rise to what seem like pervasive inconsistencies and uncertainties too. However, this is not the case in England and Wales, and therefore the English concerns in this regard are seriously misplaced. Rather, an incremental acceptance of an interpretative principle of 'policyholder's reasonable expectations' will lead to certainty in English insurance law, ie the relative certainty of favouring coverage and of making sure that insurance does fulfill its essential or definitive function.

A fourth reason for English insurance law to take a policyholder's reasonable expectations seriously concerns perceptions of the application of some English contract law doctrines to insurance contracts. Sceptics have pointed out that without the PREC principle, other English contract law doctrines, such as *contra proferentem*, mistake, insurer's misrepresentation, and presumption in favour of coverage, can also work to protect PREC. It can be revealed, though, that these doctrines, though useful, cannot work *to the full* to achieve PREC. A presumption in favour of coverage, though well-established in the US, is actually not a part of English insurance law. It has also been pointed out that English contract law does not consider public policies in the same way as American courts do in their application of the PREC 'doctrine'. That is perhaps not surprising, given that many public policies are 'disabling' of performance and/or the enforcement of contracts. But the PREC principle, if it does consider public policies at all, is not disabling but enabling: it enables performance and/or the enforcement of the insurance contract on the insurer's part. Therefore there is nothing taboo in courts or judges taking into account public policy considerations possibly underlying the PREC.

In this regard, as pointed out in more detail in Chapter 6, English courts, for example in *Gray v Barr*,[7] *Lancashire County Council v MMI*,[8] *KR v Royal & Sun Alliance*[9] and more recently the UK Supreme Court in *BAI (Run Off) Ltd v Durham*,[10] have considered questions of public policy in relation to insurance. Also along these lines, there is the enlightening perception of Kenneth Abraham that there are at least four conceptions of insurance: insurance as contract, insurance as a public utility/regulated industry, insurance as a product and insurance as governance.[11] Different conceptions of insurance may shed additional light on understanding insurance and the law of insurance. With the contract conception of insurance, it is challenging to grapple with the highlighted importance of insurance policy language at variance with the policyholder's rights and expectations. Both the public utility/regulated industry conception, applicable largely to health insurance and liability insurance, and the governance conception merit and necessitate considerations of public policies. The buyer's reasonable expectations provide the foundation for an implied warranty of quality.[12] With the product conception, by analogy, policyholders are entitled to reasonable expectations of insurance coverage as part of the quality of the insurance product, just as consumers generally are entitled to have reasonable expectations of the quality, particularly of the safety, of products[13] and services. These broad and philosophical observations mean that insurance is more than just a contract to be dealt with only through narrow contract law rules or doctrines; instead, it is sometimes desirable or necessary to approach it with, but not exclusively with, broad principles such as the PREC principle.

A fifth reason for becoming receptive to a principle of 'policyholder's reasonable expectations' concerns the place of (reasonable) expectations in contract law. This is not actually a deviation from general contract law but instead an alignment with it. This is because, first, as shown in Chapter 3, expectations in general and reasonable expectations in particular actually are more relevant, though not controlling, in contract law than are generally believed. Only with expectations—necessary though not sufficient—will an offeree communicate

[7] *Gray v Barr* [1971] 2 QB 554.
[8] *Lancashire County Council v MMI* [1996] EWCA Civ 1345.
[9] *KR v Royal & Sun Alliance* [2006] EWCA Civ 1454, [2007] Lloyd's Rep IR 368.
[10] *BAI (Run Off) Ltd v Durham* [2012] UKSC 14.
[11] K Abraham, 'Four Conceptions of Insurance' (2013) 161 *University of Pennsylvania Law Review* 653.
[12] MA Geistfeld, *Principles of Products Liability* (New York, Foundation Press 2006) 11.
[13] Consumer Protection Act 1987, s 3.

an acceptance to the offeror. Without an expectation or the assurance of the perhaps strong likelihood that the offeror will perform its promise, the offeree will simply not accept the offer; nor will it do so without an expectation or assurance of the likelihood that it will benefit from the offeror's performance. Considering this, it is not surprising that, as is shown in Chapter 3, section I.B., Adam Smith, John Austin, Anson, Pollock, Corbin, Arthur Goodhart, Roscoe Pound and more recently Hugh Collins have all thought of (reasonable) expectations as the source of the binding force of contractual promises and/or as the foundation of performance in contract. In addition, the concept of 'expectation damages', or the perception that damages for breach of contract are awarded for loss or frustration of expectations, has remained orthodox[14] and dominant, despite the parallel concepts of 'reliance damages' and 'restitution damages' having been proposed and in existence for decades.[15]

Besides, good faith in contract law serves a utilitarian and practical purpose, that is, the protection and realisation of the reasonable expectations of the parties. This can be seen from very recent judicial recognition of a qualified but growing doctrine of good faith in the performance of contract in England and in Canada. In the High Court (of England and Wales), 'recognising an implied duty of good faith in the performance of contracts ... is consonant with the theme identified by Lord Steyn as running through our law of contract that reasonable expectations must be protected'.[16] In the Supreme Court of Canada, it has been pointed out that lack of a generalised and independent doctrine of good faith 'produces results that are not consistent with the reasonable expectations of commercial parties',[17] and that recognising an 'organizing principle of good faith' plus 'a common law duty to act honestly in the performance of contractual obligations' will 'put in place a duty that is just, that accords with the reasonable expectations of commercial parties'.[18] Such a development of contract-law good faith has implications: courts have started to take parties' reasonable expectations more seriously, though still indirectly. For insurance contract, the implication is greater. This is because insurance contract prototypically requires mutual good faith. In contrast to conventionally emphasising the policyholder's duty of good faith in terms of disclosure and non-misrepresentation of material information, highlighting insurers' good faith duty, as is done in Chapter 4, section II., shows that insurance contract law has had a principled but indirect and insufficient mechanism to make sure that a policyholder's reasonable expectations are likely to be honoured. As far as this

[14] WD Slawson, 'Why Expectation Damages for Breach of Contract Must Be the Norm: A Refutation of the Fuller and Perdue "Three Interests" Thesis' (2003) 81 *Nebraska Law Review* 839, 842.

[15] LL Fuller and WR Perdue Jr , 'The Reliance Interest in Contract Damages' (Parts 1 & 2) (1936) 46 *Yale Law Journal* 52 and 373.

[16] *Yam Seng Pte Ltd v International Trade Corporation Ltd* [2013] EWHC 111 (QB) [145] (per Leggat J).

[17] *Bhasin v Hrynew* 2014 SCC 71 [32] (per Justice Cromwell).

[18] Ibid [33], [34] (per Justice Cromwell).

is concerned, the notion of a policyholder's reasonable expectations is not, and should not be, alarming at all, or be prone to pessimism and even objection.

Parallel to PREC, PREB ie policyholder's reasonable expectations of bonuses in with-profits life insurance should also be protected, but with an enhanced approach. A policyholder's reasonable expectations of bonuses is often subject to a life insurer's contractual discretion in allocating the bonuses, and exercise of the discretion might be prejudicial to PREB. There is always a contract law approach to protection of PREB, as in *Equitable Life Assurance Society v Hyman*,[19] by way of implication of terms that could impose restrictions on the discretion. In the meantime, as pointed out in Chapter 7, in *Equitable Life* more consideration should have been given to the actuarial meaning and practice of PREB in the life insurance industry, and to the regulatory principle of 'treating customers fairly'. The actuarial aspect and the regulatory aspect of PREB can be thought of as the background for the necessity to imply a term to preclude a with-profit life insurer from exercising its discretion to the detriment of PREB.

From the above and from the preceding chapters, it can be gathered that English judges and lawyers should accept, incrementally, an interpretative principle of 'policyholder's reasonable expectations', without being uncritically accepting of the largely misleading controversies and concerns over the mischaracterised 'doctrine' of reasonable expectations in American insurance law; instead, the 'doctrine' should more appropriately be recharacterized as a principle. As an interpretative principle with a role in English insurance law, it is not a cause of action. Therefore policyholders could not file for claims solely on the ground that they have reasonable expectations of coverage or of bonuses. Instead, they would still file claims as they normally do.

An incremental receptiveness to the interpretative principle of 'policyholder's reasonable expectations' in English insurance law is feasible, and it fits well with current English insurance law. This is of course, first, because it is recognised that an aim of English contract law, and perhaps of contract law in any jurisdiction, is to protect or honour the reasonable expectations of the parties. Secondly, for both PREC and PREB, the common (though not necessarily identical) path to protection of either is contract law approaches that are consistent with the principle of protection of a policyholder's reasonable expectations. The typical approach is the contextualist approach to interpretation of insurance contract or to the necessity test for implication of terms into contract. Thirdly, this interpretative approach has been adopted recently in a number of insurance cases, with judicial reference to the notion of reasonable expectations. In *Cook v Financial Insurance Co Ltd*,[20] consideration of the policyholder's reasonable expectations of coverage of the particular health risk (a medical condition) was decisive to the ruling of the House

[19] *Equitable Life Assurance Society v Hyman* [2000] 3 All ER 961, [2000] UKHL 39, [2002] 1 AC 408.
[20] *Cook v Financial Insurance Co Ltd* [1998] 1 WLR 1765 (HL), [1998] UKHL 42.

of Lords. In *Equitable Life Assurance Society v Hyman*,[21] though it seemed that the approach to implying the terms for protection of PREB was not sufficiently clear, yet with hindsight from *Attorney General of Belize v Belize Telecom*,[22] it can be seen that in considering the business nature and marketing practices of with-profits GAR life insurance products, Lord Steyn also used a contextual approach to applying the 'necessity in business efficacy' test for implied terms in fact. For business insurance, a contextual approach to interpretation of insurance contracts with a view to the reasonable expectations of the *parties* has been adopted in *Royal and Sun Alliance Insurance Plc v Dornoch Ltd*,[23] though in a generic manner without looking specifically to PREC.

However, this generic manner and the contextualist approach can be a good starting point for moving toward PREC in business insurance. This is because once more consideration is given to the reasonable expectations of the parties to insurance contracts, the balance should, as argued in Chapter 6 and reiterated above, usually tilt toward a *policyholder's* reasonable expectations of coverage rather than the insurer's expectations of non-liability. In this regard, particularly more noteworthy is that as recently as May 2015, in the UK Supreme Court, Lord Sumption stated, though obiter, that policyholder's reasonable expectations could be considered 'as background to the construction of the policy'.[24] This effectively lends force to, and confirms, the contextual approach to the PREC principle in insurance dispute resolution. Given these slow but consistent references to reasonable expectations in insurance cases, it can be hoped and envisaged that a principle of protection of a policyholder's reasonable expectations should and can be incrementally and steadily developed in English insurance law in the not too distant future.

[21] *Equitable Life Assurance Society v Hyman* [2000] 3 All ER 961, [2000] UKHL 39, [2002] 1 AC 408.

[22] *Attorney General of Belize v Belize Telecom* [2009] UKPC 10.

[23] *Royal and Sun Alliance Insurance Plc v Dornoch Ltd* [2004] EWHC 803 (QBD Comm), [2005] EWCA Civ 238.

[24] *Zurich Insurance Plc UK Branch v International Energy Group Ltd* [2015] UKSC 33 [164].

BIBLIOGRAPHY

Abraham, K, 'Judge-Made Law and Judge-Made Insurance: Honouring the Reasonable Expectations of the Insured' (1981) 67 *Virginia Law Review* 1151

Abraham, K, 'The Expectations Principle as a Regulative Ideal' (1998) 5 *Connecticut Insurance Law Journal* 60

Abraham, K, 'Four Conceptions of Insurance' (2013) 161 *University of Pennsylvania Law Review* 653

Adams, J, and Brownsword, R, 'The Ideologies of Contract' (1987) 7 *LS* 205

Adams, J, and Brownsword, R, *Key Issues in Contract* (London, Butterworths, 1995)

Adams, J, and Brownsword, R, *Understanding Contract Law*, 5th edn (London, Sweet & Maxwell, 2007)

ALI, *Restatement of the Law Second: Contracts* 2d, vol 2 (St Paul, Minn ALI Publishers, 1981)

ALI, *Restatement of the Law of Liability Insurance* (Council Draft No 1, 25 Sept 2015)

Ashton, R, 'Keeping the Faith—Good Faith in Insurance and the Emergence of General Contractual Good Faith' (2011) 22 *Insurance Law Journal* 81

Association of British Insurers: *A Guide of Good Practice for Unit Linked Funds*, 2nd edn (London, ABI, 2012)

Association of British Insurers, *Welfare Reform for the 21st Century: The Role of Income Protection Insurance* (London, ABI, 2014)

Alvisi, C, 'The Reasonable Consumer under European and Italian Regulations on Unfair Businessto-Consumer Commercial Practices' in Bongiovanni, G, et al (eds), *Reasonableness and Law* (New York, Springer, 2009)

Anderson, ER, JS Stanzler JS, and LS Masters, LS *Insurance Coverage Litigation, 2012 Supplement* (New York, NY, Aspen Publishers, 2012)

Anson, WR, *Principles of the English Law of Contract and of Agency in its Relation to Contract*, 2nd edn (Oxford, Clarendon Press 1882); 6th edn (Oxford, Clarendon Press, 1891)

Anson, WR, *Principles of the English Law of Contract*, ML Guyer (ed), Oxford, Clarendon, 1923)

Arden, Lady Justice, 'Coming to Terms with Good Faith' (2013) 30 *Journal of Contract Law* 199

Atiyah, PS, 'Contracts, Promises and the Law of Obligations' (1978) 94 *LQR* 193

Atiyah, PS, *The Rise and Fall of Freedom of Contract* (Oxford, Oxford University Press, 1979)

Austin, J, *Lectures on Jurisprudence*, 3rd edn (London, John Murray, 1869)

Austin, R, 'The Insurance Classification Controversy' (1983) 131 *University of Pennsylvania Law Review* 517

Ajzen, I, 'The Theory of Planned Behavior' (1991) 50 *Organizational Behavior and Human Decision Processes* 179

Baker, JH, 'From Sanctity of Contract to Reasonable Expectation?' (1979) 32 *Current Legal Problems* 17

Bar, C von, and Clive, E, (eds), *Principles, Definitions and Model Rules of European Private Law, Draft Common Frame of Reference (DFCF)* (Oxford, Oxford University Press, 2010)

Beale, H, (ed), *Chitty on Contracts*, vol I, 31st edn (London, Sweet & Maxwell, 2012)

Beale, H, 'Bridging the Gap: A Relational Approach to Contract Theory' (2014) 41 *Journal of Law and Society* 641

Beatson, J, et al (eds), *Anson's Law of Contract*, 29th edn (Oxford, Oxford University Press, 2010)

Berg, A, '*Equitable Life Assurance Society v Hyman*—the Extrinsic Facts Issue' [2002] *JBL* 570

Birds, J, *Birds' Modern Insurance Law*, 2nd edn (London, Sweet & Maxwell, 1988)

Birds, J, *Birds' Modern Insurance Law*, 9th edn (London, Sweet & Maxwell, 2013)

Birds, J, 'The Measure of Indemnity in Property Insurance' (1980) 43 *M LR* 456.

Birds, J, B Lynch and S Milnes (eds), *MacGillivray on Insurance Law*, 12th edn (London, Sweet and Maxwell, 2012)

Bower, S, *The Law Relating to Actionable Non-Disclosure*, 2nd edn (Turner, A and Sutton, R, (eds), Butterworths, 1990)

Bratman, M, *Intentions, Plans and Practical Reason* (Cambridge, MA, Harvard University Press, 1987)

Bridge, M, 'Does Anglo-Canadian Law Need A Doctrine of Good Faith?' (1984) 9 *Canadian Business Law Journal* 385

Brownsword, R, Hird, N, and Howells, G, 'Good Faith in Contract: Concept and Context' in Brownsword, R, Hird, N, and Howells, G, (eds), *Good Faith in Contract* (Aldershot, Ashgate, 1999)

Burton, SJ, 'Good Faith Performance of a Contract within Article 2 of the Uniform Commercial Code' (1981) 67 *Iowa Law Review* 1

Campbell, D, 'The Relational Constitution of the Discrete Contract' in Campbell, D, and Vincent-Jones, P, (eds), *Contract and Economic Organisation* (A ldershot, Dartmouth Publishing, 1996)

Campbell, D, 'The Relational Constitution of Remedy: Co-operation as the Implicit Second Principle of Remedies for Breach of Contract' (2005) 11 *Texas Wesleyan Law Review* 455

Campbell, D, 'A Relational Critique of the Restatement (Third) of Restitution § 39' (2011) 68 *Washington and Lee Law Review* 1063

Campbell, D, 'Good Faith and the Ubiquity of the "Relational" Contract' (2014) 77 *MLR* 460

Carter, JW, *The Construction of Commercial Contracts* (Oxford, Hart Publishing, 2013)

Clarke, M, *Policies and Perceptions of Insurance Law in the Twenty-First Century* (Oxford, Oxford University Press, 2005)

Clarke, M, 'The reasonable expectations of the insured—in England?' [1989] *Journal of Business Law* 389

Clarke, M, 'Reasonable Expectations—Unreasonable Cost?' (1990) 16 *Managerial Finance* 25

Clarke, M, 'Trends in the Interpretation of Marine Insurance Contracts' in Thomas, DR, (ed), *Marine Insurance: The Law in Transition* (London, Informa 2006)

Clarke, M, Burling, J, and Purves, R, *The Law of Insurance Contracts*, 6th edn (London, Informa, 2009)

Cohen, PR, and Levesque, HJ, 'Persistent, Intention, and Commitment', in Cohen, PR, et al (eds), *Intentions in Communication* (Cambridge, MA, MIT Press, 1990)

Cohen, PR, and Levesque, HJ, 'Intention is Choice with Commitment' (1990) 4 2 *Artificial Intelligence* 213

Collins, H, *Regulating Contracts* (Oxford, Oxford University Press, 1999)
Collins, H, *The Law of Contract*, 4th edn (London, LexisNexis UK, 2003)
Collins, H, 'Implied Terms: The Foundation in Good Faith and Fair Dealing' (2014) 67 *Current Legal Problems* 297
European Commission, *A Common European Sales Law to Facilitate Cross-Border Transactions in the Single Market* (Communication) COM (2011) 636 final
Law Commission and Scottish Law Commission, *Insurance Contract Law: Post*-Contract *Duties and Other Issues* (2nd Consultation Paper, LCCP 201/SLCDP 152, 2011)
Conaglen, M, 'Public-Private Intersection: Comparing Fiduciary Conflict Doctrine and Bias' [2008] *Public Law* 58
Coote, B, 'The Essence of Contract: Part I' (1988) 9 *Journal of Contract Law* 91
Corbin, A, *Law of Contracts*, vol 1 (St Paul, Minn, West & Co, 1950)
Corley Committee, The, *Report of the Corley Committee of Inquiry Regarding the Equitable Life Assurance Society* (Sept 2001)
Courtney, W, *Contractual Indemnities* (Oxford, Hart Publishing 2014)
Craswell, R, 'Against Fuller and Perdue' (2000) 67 *University of Chicago Law Review* 99
Creel, J, *Intention is Commitment with Expectation—An Amendment to the Cohen-Levesque Theory of Intention* (Saarbrücken, VDM Publishing, 2007)
Creel, J, Menzer, C and Ioerger, T, ' Intention Is Commitment with Expectation' in Wilson, DC, and Sutcliffe, GCJ, (eds), *Proceedings of the Twentieth International Florida Artificial Intelligence Research Society Conference* (Palo Alto, California, The American Association for Artificial Intelligence Press, 2007)
Daintith, TC, and Willoughby, GDM, (eds), *Manual of United Kingdom Oil and Gas Law* (London, Sweet & Maxwell, 1984)
Daintith, T, 'Contractual discretion and administrative discretion: a unified analysis', (2005) 68 *MLR* 554
Davies, M, 'Insurer's Pre-contractual Disclosure Obligations: The Position in the United States' (2012) 23 *Insurance Law Journal* 70
Dworkin, D, 'The Mode of Rules' (1967) 35 *University of Chicago Law Review* 14
Dworkin, D, *Taking Rights Seriously* (London, Duckworth 1978)
Edelman, C, and Burns, A, *The Law of Reinsurance*, 2nd edn (Oxford, Oxford University Press, 2005)
Eggers, PM, Foss, P, and Picken, S, *Good Faith and Insurance Contracts*, 3rd edn (London, LLP, 2010)
Einsenberg, M, 'The Principle of *Hadley v Baxendale*' (1992) 80 *California Law Review* 563
Einsenberg, M, 'Why There Is No Law of Relational Contracts' (2000) 94 *Northwestern University Law Review* 805
Einsenberg, M, 'The Theory of Contracts' in P Benson (ed), *The Theory of Contract Law: New Essays* (Cambridge, Cambridge University Press, 2001) 246
Engle, EA, 'Tort Law and Human Rights' in Bousani, M, and Sebok, AJ, (eds), *Comparative Tort Law: Global Perspectives* (Cheltenham, Edward Elgar Publishing, 2015)
European Parliament, *Report on the crisis of the Equitable Life Assurance Society* (May 2007)
Farnsworth, A, 'The Concept of Good Faith in American Law', a lecture in 1993 in Italy, available at www.cisg.law.pace.edu/cisg/biblio/farnsworth3.html.
Feinman, J, 'Relational Contract Theory in Context' (2000) 94 *Northwestern University Law Review* 737
Feinman, J, 'The Insurance Relationship as Relational Contract and the "Fairly Debatable" Rule for First-Party Bad Faith' (2009) 46 *San Diego Law Review* 553

Finn, P, and Smith, KJ, 'The Citizen, the Government and 'Reasonable Expectations'' (1992) 66 *ALJ* 139

Financial Conduct Authority, '*Chapter 20 With-Profits*' in *FCA Handbook, Conduct of Business Sourcebook*, (London, FCA, 2016)

Financial Services Authority, *The FSA Principles for Business: Response on Consultation Paper 13* (October 1999)

Financial Services Authority, *Report of the Financial Services Authority on the Review of the Regulation of the Equitable Life Assurance Society* (Oct 2001)

Fischer, J, 'The Doctrine of Reasonable Expectations is Indispensable, if We Only Know What For?' (1998) 5 *Connecticut Insurance Law Journal* 151

Forte, ADM, 'Good Faith and Utmost Good Faith: Insurance and Cautionary Obligations in Scots Law' in Forte, ADM, (ed), *Good Faith in Contract and Property* (Oxford, Hart Publishing, 1999)

Foubister, T, et al, *Private Medical Insurance in the United Kingdom* (Copenhagen, WHO, on behalf of the European Observatory on Health Systems and Policies, 2006)

Fried, C, *Contract as Promise* (Cambridge, MA, Harvard University Press, 1981)

Fuller, LL, and Perdue Jr, WR, 'The Reliance Interest in Contract Damages' (Parts 1 & 2) (1936) 46 *Yale Law Journal* 52 and 373

Geistfeld, MA, *Principles of Products Liability* (New York, Foundation Press, 2006)

Glick QC, I, and Richard Snowden, R, *The Equitable Life Assurance Society: Joint Opinion of Ian Glick QC and Richard Snowden for the Financial Services Authority* (May 2001)

Goetz C, and Scott, R, 'Principles of Relational Contracts' (1981) 67 *Virginia Law Review* 1089

Goodhart, A, *English Law and the Moral Law* (London, Sweet & Maxwell, 1953)

Goode, R, *Commercial Law in the Next Millennium* (London, Sweet & Maxwell, 1998)

Gordon, G, 'Risk Allocation in Oil and Gas Contracts' in G Gordon et al (eds), *Oil and Gas Law: Current Practice and Emerging Trends*, 2nd edn (Dundee, Dundee University Press 2011)

Harrison, R, *Good Faith in Sales* (London, Sweet & Maxwell, 1997)

Hasson, R, 'The Doctrine of *Uberrima Fides* in Insurance Law—A critical Evaluation' (1969) 3 2 *M LR* 615

Hasson, R, 'The Special Nature of the Insurance Contract: A Comparison of the American and English Law of Insurance' (1984) 47 *M LR* 505

Haviid, M, 'Long-Term Contracts and Relational Contracts' in Bouckaert, B, and Geest, GD, (eds), *Encyclopaedia of Law and Economics*, vol III: *The Regulation of Contracts* (London, Edward Elgar, 2000)

Hemsworth, M, 'United Kingdom Insurance Decisions 2000' [2001] LMCLQ 504

Henderson, RC, 'The Doctrine of Reasonable Expectations in Insurance Law after Two Decades' (1990) 51 *Ohio State Law Journal* 823

Hertzell, D, 'UK [Report]' in H Heiss (ed), *Insurance Contract Law between Business Law and Consumer Protection* (Zurich, Dike, 2012)

Hesslelink, MW, 'The Concept of Good Faith' in Hartkamp, AS, et al (eds), *Toward a European Civil Code* (Leiden, Kluwer Law International, 2004)

Hevia, M, *Reasonableness and Responsibility: A Theory of Contract Law* (New York, Springer, 2013)

Hills, J, *Thatcherism, New Labour and the Welfare State* (London, Centre for Analysis of Social Exclusion, LSE, 1998)

HM Treasury, *Equitable Life Payment Scheme: November 2015 Progress Report*.
Penrose, Lord, *Report of the Equitable Life Inquiry* (March 2004)
Hoffmann, Lord, '*The Achilleas*: Custom and Practice or Foreseeability?' (2010) 14 *Edinburgh Law Review* 47
Holmes, E, 'A Contextual Study of Good Faith: Good-faith Disclosure in Contract Formation' (1978) 39 *Pittsburgh Law Review* 381
Hooley, R, 'Controlling Contractual Discretion' (2013) 72 *CLJ* 65
House of Commons Public Relations Select Committee, *Justice delayed: The Ombudsman's Report on Equitable Life* (Dec 2008)
International Actuarial Association, *The Function of the Actuary in Prudential Supervision* (Ottawa, IAA, 2002)
Jerry II, R, and Richmond, D, *Understanding Insurance Law*, 5th edn (New York, LexisNexis, 2012)
Jess, D, *The Insurance of Commercial Risks: Law and Practice* (London, Sweet & Maxwell, 2011)
Joseph Rowntree Foundation, *Attitudes of Different Generations to the Welfare System* (2013)
Keeton, R, 'Insurance Law Rights at Variance with Policy Provisions, Part One' (1970) 83 *Harvard Law Review* 961
Keeton, R, 'Insurance Law Rights at Variance with Policy Provisions, Part Two' (1970) 83 *Harvard Law Review* 1281
Keeton, R, 'Reasonable Expectations in the Second Decade' (1976) 12 *Forum* 275
Kuklin, BH, 'The Plausibility of Legally Protecting Reasonable Expectations' (1997) 32 *Valparaiso Law Review* 19
Kessler, F, 'Contract of Adhesion—Some Thoughts about Freedom of Contract' (1943) 43 *Columbia Law Review* 629
Kimball, S, *Insurance and Public Policy: A Study in the Legal Implementation of Social and Economic Public Policy, Based on Wisconsin Record 1835–1959* (Madison, Wis, University of Wisconsin Press, 1960)
Law Commission and Scottish Law Commission, *Insurance Contract Law: Business Disclosure; Warranties; Insurers' Remedies for Fraudulent Claims; and Late Payment* (Cm 8898; SG/2014/131) (Law Com No. 353/ ScotLaw Com No. 238)
Lee, WY and Bryant, A, *Participating Business in Asia* (Singapore, Milliman, 2014)
Lewis, C, 'A Fundamental Principle of Insurance Law' [1979] *LMCLQ* 275
Liedtke, PM, and Monkiewicz, J, 'The Future of Insurance Regulation and Supervision', in Liedtke, PM, and Monkiewicz, J, (eds), *The Future of Insurance Regulation after the Financial Crisis* (Palgrave Macmillan 2011)
Llewellyn, K, 'The Effect of Legal Institutions upon Economics' (1925) 15 *American Economic Review* 665
Lowry, J, Rawlings, P, and Merkin, R, *Insurance Law: Doctrines and Principles*, 3rd edn (Oxford, Hart Publishing, 2011)
Lücke, HK, 'Good Faith and Contractual Performance' in Finn, P, (ed), *Essays on Contract* (Sydney, Law Book Co., 1987)
MacQueen, H, 'Good Faith in Scottish Law of Contract: An Undisclosed Principle?' in Forte, ADM, (ed), *Good Faith in Contract and Property Law* (Oxford, Hart Publishing, 1999)
Macneil, I, 'Relational Contract Theory: Challenges and Queries' (2000) 94 *Northwestern University Law Review* 877
Macneil, I, 'Uncertainty in Commercial Law' (2009) 13 *Edinburgh Law Review* 68

Malle, BF, and Knotbe, J, 'The Distinction between Desire and Intention: A Folk Conception Analysis' in Malle, BF, et al (eds), *Intention and Intentionality* (Cambridge, MA, MIT Press, 2001)

Marshall, J, *Intention in Law and Society* (New York, Funk & Wagnalls, 1968)

McCaughran, J, 'Implied Terms: The Journey of the Man on the Clapham Omnibus' (2011) 70 *CLJ* 607

McMeel, G, 'Interpreting With-Profits Life Insurance Contracts' [2001] *L MCLQ* 179

Meek, RL, Raphael, DD, and Stein, PG, (eds), *The Glasgow Edition of the Works and Correspondence of Adam Smith*, vol 5: *Lectures on Jurisprudence* (Oxford, Oxford University Press, 1978)

Merkin, R, 'Reforming Insurance Law: Is There a Case for Reverse Transportation?' *Report for the English and Scottish Law Commissions* (London and Edinburgh, The Law Commission and Scottish Law Commission, 2008)

Merkin, R, 'Tort, Ideology and Insurance: Further Thoughts' (2012) 75 *MLR* 301

Merkin, R, and Steele, J, *Insurance and Law of Obligations* (Oxford, Oxford University Press, 2013)

Millar, J, 'Diminishing Welfare: The Case of the United Kingdom' in Goldberg, GS, and Rosenthal, MG, (eds), *Diminishing Welfare: A Cross-Nation Study of Social Provision* (Westport, CT, Auburn House, 2002)

Mitchell, C, 'Leading a Life of its Own? The Roles of Reasonable Expectations in Contract Law' (2003) 23 *OJLS* 639.

Mitchell, C, *Interpretation of Contracts* (London, Routledge Cavendish, 2007)

Myners, P, *Institutional Investment in the United Kingdom: A Review* (London, 2001)

Naidoo, A, and Oughton, D, 'The confused post-formation duty of good faith in insurance law: from refinement to fragmentation to elimination' [2005] Journal of Business Law 346

Needleman, PD, and Toff, PA, 'Asset Shares and Their Use in the Management of With-profits Fund' (1995) 1 *British Actuarial Journal* 603

O'Brien, C, 'Constraints on discretion: Distributing surplus in with-profits life insurance' (2004) 12 *Journal of Financial Regulation and Compliance* 118

O'Donovan, J, *Lender Liability* (London, Sweet & Maxwell, 2005) 61

Office of Fair Trading, *Private Healthcare Market Study: Report on the market study and final decision to make a market investigation reference* (London, OFT, 2012) 32

Office of Sir John Chadwick, The, *Advice to Government in relation to the proposed Equitable Life payment scheme* (July 2010).

O'Gorman, DP, 'Expectation Damages, the Objective Theory of Contracts, and the "Hairy Hand" Case' (2011) 99 *Kentucky Law Journal* 327

O'Leary, D, Duffy, B, Hall, S, and Pope, S, *Generation Strains: A Demos and Ipsos MORI Report on Changing Attitudes to Welfare* (York, Joseph Rowntree Foundation, 2013)

European Parliament, *Policy Options for Progress towards a European Contract Law for Consumers and Businesses, Resolution of 8 June 2011*, 2011/2013(INI)

Park, AJ, 'What to Reasonably Expect in the Coming Years from the Reasonable Expectations of the Insured Doctrine' (2012) 49 *Willamette Law Review* 165

Parkington, M, et al (eds), *MacGivallry and Parkington on Insurance Law*, 8th edn (London, Sweet & Maxwell, 1988)

Parliamentary and Health Service Ombudsman, *Equitable Life: A decade of Regulatory Failure* (July 2008)

Paton, G, *Bailment in Common Law* (London, Stevens & Sons Ltd, 1952)

Peden, E, 'Policy Concerns behind Implications of Terms in Law' (2001) 117 *LQR* 459
Penrose, Lord, *Report of the Equitable Life Inquiry* (HC290, TSO 2004)
Perillo, JM, 'The Origins of the Objective Theory of Contract Formation and Interpretation' (2000) 69 *Fordham Law Review* 427
Perugini, M, and Bagozzi, RP, 'The Distinction between Desires and Intentions' (2004) *European Journal of Social Psychology* 69
Plotkin, T, 'Case Note: A Congregation of Vapours: *Clendenin Brothers, Inc. v. United States Fire Insurance Company*, Welding Rod Litigation, the Total Pollution Exclusion, the Futility of the Judicial Search for Ambiguity in Commercial General Liability Insurance Contracts, and the Reasonable Expectations of the Insured' (2007) 13 *Connecticut Insurance Law Journal* 364
Pollock, F, *Principles of Contracts*, 4th edn (London, Stevens & Sons, 1885) viii; also 5th edn (1889); 6th edn (1894); 7th edn (1902); 8th edn (1911); 9th edn (1921); 13th edn (1950)
Popick, SM, and Quockenbos, CD, 'Reasonable Expectations after Thirty Years: A Failed Doctrine' (1998) 5 *Connecticut Insurance Law Journal* 425
Posner, E, 'A Theory of Contract Law under Conditions of Radical Judicial Error' (2000) 94 *Northwestern University Law Review* 749
Powell, R, 'Good Faith in Contracts' (1956) 9 *Current Legal Problems* 16
Pound, R, *Social Control through Law* (New Haven, Ct, Yale University Press, 1942)
Pound, R, 'Considerations in Equity' in JH Wigmore (ed), *Celebration Legal Essays: By Various Authors to Mark the Twenty-Fifth Year of Service of John H. Wigmore, As a Professor of Law in Northwestern University* (Chicago, Ill, Northwestern University Press, 1919)
Prudential Regulation Authority (PRA) and Financial Conduct Authority (FCA), *With-Profits, Memorandum of Understanding* (London, Bank of England, 2013)
Prudential Regulation Authority, *PRA Rulebook: Solvency II Firms: With-Profits* (London, Bank of England, 2016)
Prudential Regulation Authority, *PRA Rulebook: Non Solvency II Firms: With-Profits* (London, Bank of England, 2016)
Rahdert, M, 'Reasonable Expectations Revisited' (1998) 5 *Connecticut Insurance Law Journal* 107
Randall, S, 'Freedom of Contract in Insurance' (2008) 14 *Connecticut Insurance Law Journal* 107
Rawls, J, *Political Liberalism* (New York, Columbia University Press, 1993)
Research Committee of the Life Board, *Report of the Customers' Interests Working Party* (November 2002)
Ripstein, A, 'Reasonable Persons in Private Law' in G Bongiovanni et al (eds), *Reasonableness and Law* (New York, Springer, 2009)
Schoenbaun, T, 'The Duty of Utmost Good Faith in Marine Insurance Law: A Comparative Analysis of American and English Law' (1998) 29 *Journal of Maritime Law and Commerce* 1
Schwarcz, D, 'A Products Liability Theory for the Judicial Regulation of Insurance Policies' (2007) 48 *William & Mary Law Review* 1389
Schultz, F, 'The Special Nature of Insurance Contract: A Few Suggestions for Further Study' (1950) 15 *Law and Contemporary Problems* 376
Scott, R, 'The Case for Formalism in Relational Contract' (2000) 94 *Northwestern University Law Review* 847

Sealy, L, '"Legitimate Expectations" in Company Law and Public Law' [2000] *L MCLQ* 308

Seno, DJ, 'The Doctrine of Reasonable Expectations in Insurance Law: What to Expect in Wisconsin' (2002) 85 *Marquette Law Review* 859

Shelley, M, Arnold M, and Needleman, P, 'A Review of Policyholders' Reasonable Expectations' (2002) 8 *British Actuarial Journal* 705

SICC Committee, The, *Report of the Singapore International Commercial Court Committee* (Nov 2013)

Simon, J, 'The Ideological Effects of Actuarial Practices' (1988) 22 *Law and Society Review* 771

Singh, P and Bhusal, LN, 'Austerity, Welfare State and Eco-Socialism: With Special Reference to the United Kingdom' (2014) 39 *Economic and Political Weekly* 111

Slawson, WD, *Binding Promises* (Princeton, NJ, Princeton University Press, 1996) 52

Slawson, WD, 'Why Expectation Damages for Breach of Contract Must Be the Norm: A Refutation of the Fuller and Perdue "Three Interests" Thesis' (2003) 81 *Nebraska Law Review* 839

Smith, S, '"The Reasonable Expectations of the Parties": An Unhelpful Concept' (2009) 48 *Canadian Business Law Journal* 366

Smith, ML, and Kane, SA, 'The Law of Large Numbers and the Strength of Insurance' in Gustavson, SG, and Harrington, SE (eds), *Insurance, Risk Management, and Public Policy* (Boston, Kluwer, 1994)

Soyer, B, 'New Parameters in Construing Insurance Contracts' in R Thomas (ed), *Modern Law of Marine Insurance*, vol 4 (London, Informa, 2016)

Stempel, JW, 'Unmet Expectations: Undue Restriction of the Reasonable Expectations Approach and the Misleading Mythology of Judicial Role' (1998) 5 *Connecticut Insurance Law Journal* 181

Stempel, JW, *Principles of Insurance Law*, 4th edn (Albany, NY, LexisNexis, 2012)

Steyn, Lord, 'Contract Law: Fulfilling the Reasonable Expectations of Reasonable Men' (1995) 9 *LQR* 433

Steyn, J, 'The Role of Good Faith and Fair Dealing in Contract Law: A Hair-Shirt Philosophy' [1991] *Denning Law Journal* 131

Steyn, Lord, 'The Intractable Problem of the Interpretation of Legal Texts' (2003) 25 *Sydney Law Review* 5

Styles, S, 'Good Faith: A Principled Matter' in Forte, ADM, (ed), *Good Faith in Contract and Property Law* (Oxford, Hart Publishing, 1999)

Swan, J, and Ritter, B, 'Contracts and the Protection of Reasonable Expectations' in Reiter, B, and Swan, J, (eds), *Studies in Contract Law* (Toronto, Butterworths, 1980)

Swisher, PN, 'A Realistic Consensus Approach to the Insurance Law Doctrine of Reasonable Expectations' (2000) 35 *Tort and Insurance Law Journal* 729

Traves, S, 'Utmost Good Faith, Reliance upon and Notification of Terms: The Obligations of Insurers and the Rights of Insureds' (2012) 23 *Insurance Law Journal* 1

Warren AC, M, 'Good Faith: Where We Are at?' [2010] *Melbourne University Law Review* 344

Warshaw, PR, and Davis, FD, 'Disentangling Behavioural Intentions and Behavioural Expectations' (1985) 21 *Journal of Experimental Social Psychology* 213

Whittaker, S, and Zimmermann, R, 'Good Faith in European Contract Law: Surveying the Landscape' in Zimmermann, R, and Whittaker, S, (eds), *Good Faith in European Contract Law* (Cambridge, Cambridge University Press, 2000)

Zeckhauser, R, 'Insurance' in D Henderson (ed), *The Concise Encyclopaedia of Economics*, 2nd edn (Indianapolis, Ind, Liberty Fund Inc, 2008)

INDEX

www.ingramcontent.com/pod-product-compliance
Ingram Content Group UK Ltd.
Pitfield, Milton Keynes, MK11 3LW, UK
UKHW021822170926
15199UKWH00092B/46

9 781509 900763